FOURTH

EDITION

COUNSELING TODAY'S FAMILIES

Herbert Goldenberg

California State University, Los Angeles

Irene Goldenberg

University of California, Los Angeles

BROOKS/COLE

TM

THOMSON LEARNING

Australia • Canada • Mexico • Singapore • Spain • United Kingdom • United States

BROOKS/COLE

™

THOMSON LEARNING

Acquisitions Editor: *Julie Martinez*
Marketing Team: *Caroline Concilla, Megan Hansen*
Editorial Assistant: *Cat Broz*
Assistant Editor: *Shelley Gesicki*
Project Editor: *Kim Svetich-Will*
Production Service: *The Cowans*
Manuscript Editor: *Donald Pharr*

Permissions Editor: *Connie Dowcett*
Interior Design: *The Cowans*
Cover Design: *Lisa Henry*
Art Editor: *Vernon Boes*
Print Buyer: *Nancy Panziera*
Compositor: *The Cowans*
Printing and Binding: *Webcom*

For more information about this or any other Brooks/Cole product, contact:
BROOKS/COLE
511 Forest Lodge Road
Pacific Grove, CA 93950 USA
www.brookscole.com
1-800-423-0563 (Thomson Learning Academic Resource Center)

All products mentioned herein are used for identification purposes only and may be trademarks or registered trademarks of their respective owners.

Printed in Canada

ISBN: 0-534-36711-9

10   9   8   7   6   5   4   3   2   1

Library of Congress Cataloging-in-Publication Data
Goldenberg, Herbert.
    Counseling today's families / Herbert Goldenberg, Irene
Goldenberg.—4th ed.
        p. cm.
    Includes bibliographical references and index.
    ISBN 0-534-36711-9 (pbk.)
    1. Family social work—United States. 2. Family counseling—
United States. 3. Family—United States—Psychological aspects
4. Behavioral assessment—United States.
    I Goldenberg, Irene. II. Title.

HV699.G65 2001
362.82'86'0973—dc21   00-065881

For our grandchildren—
Drew, Emily, Alex, Samantha, Julia, and Adam.
Our blessings abound.

Books of Related Interest

Family Therapy: An Overview, Fifth Edition
Irene Goldenberg and Herbert Goldenberg (2000)
ISBN 0-534-35757-1

Family Explorations: Personal Viewpoints from Multiple Perspectives
Irene Goldenberg and Herbert Goldenberg (2000)
ISBN 0-534-36651-1

Contents

Contents

Preface

With the fourth edition of this text, we once again attempt to bring up-to-date a description of contemporary family living patterns and lifestyles. Since our first edition, over a decade ago, when some of these family forms were still considered nontraditional, we have endeavored with each succeeding edition to elaborate on how each family type has evolved and currently functions. As we have learned more about each type of family structure and as each has gained greater public recognition, we have looked beyond typical problem areas to an examination of family resourcefulness and resiliencies in dealing with those unique sets of problems inherent in their particular family structure. Throughout all four editions, we have tried to help those learning to counsel such families to understand, from a family systems perspective, how best to assess each family form's likely conflict areas and how most effectively to intervene to help families lead more harmonious and contented lives. Increasingly, we have stressed the potential strengths to be found in all families, making the counselor's task more an effort to help them uncover and harness their capabilities as they seek new solutions, and less an effort to identify and repair family pathology.

For every family type, we have attempted to take a broad view of the larger social context in which the family is a part, rather than focus exclusively on narrow family interactive patterns as the source of all dysfunction. Beyond understanding the presenting family relationship problems, today's counselor must also attend to gender roles, cultural background, ethnic heritage, and social class

membership in order to fully assess family functioning and plan effective interventions. For example, when helping a single mother who is having problems
coping with her situation, it is important to comprehend more than her common
day-to-day burdens or parent-child relationship difficulties. To offer effective
help, the counselor must take an integrative view, recognizing the *interactive*
nature of numerous factors, no one of which can be considered alone. Is she
poor, middle class, or wealthy? Does she have a support system of extended family or community resources? Is she native born or an immigrant, perhaps a recent
arrival with few language skills and little know-how about seeking counseling?
What cultural patterns endure in her outlook and child-rearing attitudes, and will
the counselor understand the frame of reference from which she makes assumptions about the world? Being a single mother, in this case, cannot be understood
without reference to her age, her socioeconomic situation, her ethnic background, her educational level, her generation living in this country, her possible
minority status, and much more beyond her presenting problem. The counselor
needs to remain aware that our values, beliefs, and attitudes (clients and counselors alike) are viewed through the prism of our own gender, class position, and
cultural experience.

Similar issues need to be considered for each family type described in this
book. Thus prepared, we believe that the counselor is in a stronger position to be
sensitive to, and work effectively with, new sets of problems (for example, substance abuse and family violence) and other family configurations (such as foster
parents, adoptive families, and immigrant families from new places). Recognizing
that we cannot cover all family forms, we thus offer a template for approaching
family circumstances and entering family systems that we hope the counselor can
apply in helping families find new solutions.

In this edition, along with updating the picture of today's changing demographics and diversity, we have paid attention to new research findings and new
methods for helping families learn to use the flexibility inherent in their structure.
In order to emphasize just how theory is translated into practice, we have added
a new chapter, Chapter 4, in which we first outline six approaches to family counseling and then demonstrate how each might approach the same case. Extending
that discussion, in Chapter 5 we consider the pros and cons of a new movement
in counseling—one based on evidence-supported guidelines—that is research-
based and offers specific directions for what works best for what clients with
which sets of problems.

Each chapter has been rewritten and the sections on counseling guidelines
expanded. New cases have been added that reflect contemporary issues, such as
gay and lesbian parenting, Internet contact and ensuing relationships, and
teenage pregnancy. Other cases have been rewritten, recast in terms of today's
theoretical thinking. We have included up-to-date research, whenever relevant, to
provide a more substantial base for our counseling recommendations.

Thanks are due the following professors who gave us useful suggestions for
how we might improve this current effort:

Dr. Ada Garcia, Andrews University

Dr. Elaine Congress, Fordham University

Dr. Martin Fiebert, CSU Long Beach

David Demetral, Ph.D., LCSW, CSU Sacramento

Dr. Tom Guss, Fort Hays State University

Dr. Elizabeth Sirles, Chair, Dept. of Social Work, University of
   Alaska-Anchorage

Dr. Jean Granger, CSU Long Beach

Jan Wrenn, Assistant Professor of Social Work, Andrews University,
   BSU Program Director

Allison Pinto was helpful in providing the details of a case study. Friends at Brooks/Cole, both old and new, were always available when called upon and, as always, assisted us in making the job that much easier.

Herbert Goldenberg
Irene Goldenberg

PART

ONE

UNDERSTANDING FAMILY RELATIONSHIPS

1

CHAPTER

ONE

Counseling Today's Changing Families

We live in a complex and increasingly diverse society. The family, reflecting other social institutions, is undergoing rapid and dramatic transformations in form, composition, and structure. Americans today are living longer, marrying later (if at all), exiting marriages more rapidly, and opting to live together before marriage, after marriage, between marriages, and as an alternative to marriage (Popenoe & Whitehead, 1999b). As individual life spans have increased, three- and four-generation families have become more common, further expanding family relationships. Today's diversity of family forms increases the probability that individuals are likely to experience more family transitions over their lifetimes than was the case in previous generations (Carlson, Sperry, & Lewis, 1997).

Families once considered exceptional and certainly nontraditional—led by **single parents**[1]—are becoming commonplace. **Stepfamilies** abound, as close to half of all new marriages today involve the remarriage of one partner, and one in four the remarriage of both. **Cohabitation** has replaced marriage as the first significant experience of living together for an increasing number of young adults, and **gay** and **lesbian** couples are a less closeted phenomenon than in the past. Less and less the American norm is the traditional **nuclear family,** in which the man is sole breadwinner; the woman is full-time homemaker, wife, and mother; each has separate, nonoverlapping responsibilities; and the two remain together in an intact marriage until death do them part. A skyrocketing divorce rate (which

---

[1]Terms printed in **boldface** are defined in the glossary at the end of the book.

3

doubled between 1965 and 1985), the surge of women into the labor force, the need to have two or more incomes in order to make ends meet, concerns over proper child care and the need to balance work and family responsibilities for both parents, postponement of marriage, the greater prevalence of remarried families, the large number of children living in poverty, the sharp rise in single people living alone or with a partner of the same or opposite sex, the increased numbers of child-free marriages, the substantial number of intermarriages, the rise in the number of mothers (single teenage or young adult women) with out-of-wedlock children—these are just some of the contemporary realities in what Skolnick (1991) calls an "age of uncertainty" for the North American family.

The marked increase in ethnic and racial diversity in recent years, fueled by immigration, has also added greatly to our society's multiplicity of value systems, languages, types of family structure, and relationships. Changes in U.S. demographics—as we move from a population with predominantly European and Caucasian roots to a broader mix including people with African, Asian/Pacific, and Hispanic roots[2]—have inevitably influenced social mores. These changes have inescapably led to intercultural conflicts over value systems. Unlike the emphasis on individualism in mainstream American culture, Americans whose family origins are in non-Western cultures often emphasize collectivist values—attending to the needs of others, fitting within the community, role relationships, and interpersonal harmony (Sue, 1999).

Ho (1987) offers these examples of value clashes in such a cultural mosaic as ours: Whereas mainstream society is future-oriented, worships youth, and is willing to sacrifice for a "better" tomorrow, ethnic groups may reminisce about the past and take pleasure from experiences in the present. Collective behavior may take higher priority than individual autonomy, again unlike conventional middle-class American ideals. Competitiveness and upward mobility, highly valued in the mainstream U.S. lifestyle, may in some minority subgroups hold considerably less appeal, and American society's traditional emphasis on the nuclear family may in some groups be less understandable than reliance on the extended family. To ignore our increasing *multiculturalism* is to overlook, disregard, or deny that ours is an increasingly pluralistic society. In the last decade of the 20th century, fully one in four Americans was a person of color (Homma-True, Greene, Lopez, & Trimble, 1993).

Not surprisingly, then, today's counselors are being confronted with new sets of clients who present a wide variety of attitudes, experiences, lifestyles—and complexities. Relationship problems have likewise changed. Customary diagnostic categories, designed for individuals, are clearly unsuited for characterizing entire families (Kaslow, 1996). They do not adequately describe a family in which

---

[2]Respondents to the 1990 U.S. census question asking people how they identified themselves reported upwards of 250,000 unique entries other than the 16 conventional categories such as white, black, or Chinese. To cite one example of U.S. population heterogeneity, more than 100 languages are spoken in California's schools (Morrison, 1992).

transactional patterns have broken down or a family that is caught in a period of rapid societal change, unable to adapt old cultural patterns while finding it difficult to develop new adaptive coping techniques. Today's counselor must be prepared to think in terms of couples, extended families, and other combinations of people (including nonbiological, chosen pairings) who think of themselves as family, as well as clients who come individually to seek help for relationship woes or to relieve the discomfort accompanying the search for new life paths.

Today's counselor is likely to confront client difficulties that arise from circumstances that were once far less common, such as helping a same-sex couple work out adoption plans or perhaps an infertile couple struggling with new fertility techniques brought on by their earlier decision to delay having children. To take another current example, the counselor may be called upon to help a client growing up in a home with successive "fathers" or one where **custody** is shared jointly between divorced parents, with one or more children moving from the mother's household to the father's household every three or four days. Problems may also arise from an alternative[3] family life pattern in which two unmarried heterosexual adults share an intimate living arrangement but struggle over differences in their sense of commitment to the future of their relationship. Or perhaps conflict exists between children from two sets of parents joined together in a stepfamily situation, with the concomitant problems in sibling relationships and differing parenting styles. Today's counselor is more likely than at any time in the past to be called upon to help with the extra strain experienced by two-career couples as they work out new role structures in order to balance career, personal, and family demands without benefit of role models from the past.

Counselors need to alert themselves to the general stresses (as well as the resiliencies or recuperative abilities) inherent in each of today's family structures, in addition to grasping the interplay in each specific family situation. We need to become more sensitized to the ethnic, racial, and social class backgrounds of clients, especially if these are different from our own—in order to understand and appreciate differing cultural values, communal ties, and emphases in relationships. Of course, when clients differ from us, we also have an opportunity to examine our own stereotypes and prejudices more objectively. These differences may include client lifestyles such as homosexuality or cohabitation, about which some counselors may have negative prejudices or moral objections. Beyond that, counselors need to become familiar with current clinical assessment and therapeutic strategies for dealing with changes in family life.

In this book, we describe six basic contemporary family structures: families headed by single parents, remarried families, cohabiting heterosexual couples,

---

[3]It might be useful at this point to note the distinction Cazenave (1980) draws between *alternative* and *alternate* families. He considers the former to be ideologically based, representing a choice made by those who have the resources to choose to move beyond traditional patterns to a lifestyle more consistent with their values—for example, living together without being married. Cazenave reserves the latter term for an involuntary arrangement—for example, poor women living as single parents because of the absence of eligible men, welfare system stipulations, or lack of access to abortion.

gay and lesbian couples, dual-career families, and ethnically diverse families.[4] For each family configuration, we develop a format for assessing its common problem areas, discuss typical strategies for surmounting crises and persistent stresses, and then offer suggestions (along with excerpts from sessions) for delivering effective therapeutic interventions.

Today's Families: Some Demographic Notes

Life in North America has changed drastically in the past two or three decades, and that change is reflected in the workplace, in male-female relationships, and, inevitably, in the family. Whether working or going to school, young people today are leaving their parental home earlier than ever before and living on their own longer. Since 1970, the number of single people (including never-married, between marriages, and divorced or widowed individuals who subsequently remain unmarried) has increased by 70% while the number of married persons has increased by only 8% (Saxton, 1996). Lifelong singlehood is on the rise, and between 1960 and 1998, according to U.S. Bureau of the Census (1998) data, the number of unmarried cohabiting couples in the Unites States rose from less than half a million to over four million.

The interrelationship between work and family life has never been stronger—or more complicated—than it is today. Young women, in particular, are increasingly called upon for extended periods of full-time employment and have fewer children than did their counterparts even a decade ago. Changing social attitudes include the prospect that young mothers may work outside the home, even when their children are of preschool age. As noted in Figure 1.1, whereas approximately half of all mothers with school-age children or younger worked for pay in 1980—itself a leap over prior decades—today about 65% do. That increase is especially noteworthy for mothers of preschool children; more than half of today's women with children younger than 3 are working mothers (compared to perhaps one-third in 1980).

Working women, especially single mothers and women among the poor, minority, immigrant, and undereducated population, are hardly a new phenomenon. What is a recent development, however, is the extent to which most families today, regardless of social class membership or whether they are two-parent or single-parent families, depend on a woman's income. Most women, regardless of social class membership or educational level, now work outside the home. Today, over 50% of American women between the ages of 25 and 54 work full-time, year-round (see Figure 1.2). Thirty years earlier, in 1969, women accounted

---

[4]Although we intend to describe these family structures separately, we recognize, of course, that any combination of these categories is possible: an Asian American dual-career couple, a lesbian single parent, a divorced person cohabiting with another not yet finally divorced partner, and so forth. We have followed the present format in order to highlight the main problems and inherent strengths in each type of family.

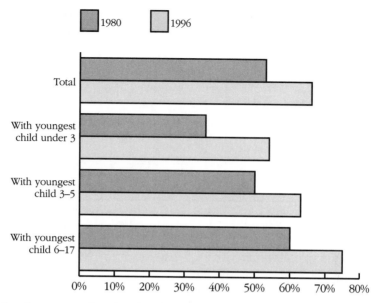

Figure 1.1   Percentages of employed mothers: 1980 and 1996

Source: U.S. Bureau of Labor Statistics, 1999a

for only one-third of those employed away from home. (Men have experienced a slight decrease of full-time work during that period, especially high school graduates.) Along with women's greater participation in the work force[5]—where by and large they still lag behind men in pay—have come efforts to find alternatives to the standard 40-hour, 5-day workweek: part-time work, staggered work hours, temporary employment, and compressed and flexible work schedules for the start and end of the workday. Unconventional schedules and the ability to work at home allow parents with preschoolers, semiretired older workers, middle-aged workers caring for elderly parents, and others to accommodate their personal and family responsibilities. Negotiated within every two-working-parent family is just how best to share home and family obligations in an equitable manner.

Within the professions, the number of women employed now equals the number of men (although many women are still clustered in the female-dominated and lower-salaried professions of teaching and nursing). Dramatically demonstrating this shift in professional opportunity for today's women are these statistics: In 1991, 36% of new physicians, 43% of new lawyers, and 32% of new dentists were women, compared to 1971, when the corresponding figures were only 9%, 7%,

[5]By law, employers may not deny women advancement to upper-level executive positions, although in practice many women may find the way blocked. This **glass ceiling,** typically unacknowledged, often presents an invisible barrier beyond which the company's female employees (or members of many minority groups) may not advance (Morrison & Von Glinow, 1990). Most economic power continues to remain in the hands of men; in 1995 the federal Glass Ceiling Commission reported that women accounted for just 3–5% of senior managers of major corporations.

From 1969 to 1997, the percentage of persons age 25 to 54 working full-time, year-round, increased from 53.0% to 62.6%, with changes varying by sex and educational attainment level.

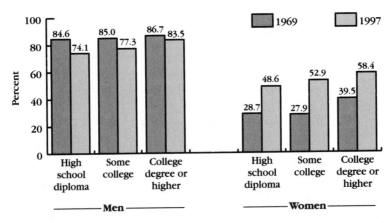

In 1969, a total of 27.5% of women age 25 to 54 worked full-time, year-round; by 1997, that percentage increased to 50.2%. By educational attainment, all groups of women experienced a rise in the percentage working full-time, year-round. However, those women with a college degree or higher reported the smallest increase among the groups shown in the chart, at 18.9 percentage points.

The percentage of men working full-time, year-round, decreased from 80.6% in 1969 to 75.4% in 1997. By educational attainment, all groups of men experienced a decline in the percent working full-time, year-round; the largest decrease among the groups in the chart was for men with a high school diploma, down 10.5 percentage points.

Figure 1.2 Percentage of persons 25–54 working full-time, year-round, by educational attainment and sex, 1969 and 1997

Source: U.S. Bureau of Labor Statistics, 1999b.

and 1%, respectively (Snyder & Hoffman, 1994). Table 1.1 displays the changes over two decades in the percentage of women earning doctoral degrees; in psychology, a particularly striking example, two of every five doctoral-level psychologists today is a woman (Pion et al., 1996). More than 40% of research-based Ph.D.s are awarded to women today (Wyatt, 1999), a far cry from as recently as their mothers' generation, when most women were discouraged by school counselors from entering scientific careers.

Clearly, these statistics reveal significant changes in our attitudes and expectations, and profoundly affect the number and kind of decisions faced by today's woman of marriageable age. She is more likely than ever before to have obtained a higher level of education, and her options can thus be more varied. She must decide what kind of work to do; if, and especially when, to marry; whether to have children and when; the economic feasibility of divorce should a marriage fail; whether to remarry; and so on. Her far greater sexual freedom than her counterpart of three decades ago (balanced in part by greater health dangers than in the past because of such sexually transmitted diseases as AIDS), expanded career

Table 1.1   Percentage of doctoral degrees awarded to women in psychology and other major fields and professions

Major field (degree awarded)	Percentage of women doctorates		
	1971	1981	1991
Psychology (PhD)	24.7	43.9	61.2
Computer sciences (PhD)	16.1	11.2	13.4
Dentistry (DDS or DMD)	1.1	14.0	32.1
Education (PhD)	21.9	47.2	58.1
Engineering (PhD)	0.4	3.9	8.7
Humanities (PhD)	24.2	41.3	46.5
Law (JD)	7.1	32.0	42.9
Life sciences (PhD)	14.5	25.5	38.7
Mathematical sciences (PhD)	7.8	15.4	18.7
Medicine (MD)	9.1	25.0	35.9
Neurosciences (PhD)	—	32.5	36.8
Physical sciences (PhD)	5.9	11.8	18.3
Sociology and anthropology (PhD)	19.7	40.0	49.5
Veterinary medicine (DVM)	7.8	36.4	57.2

Source: Pion et al., 1996.

options, and increased economic power have together helped alter male-female relationships in ways that the grandmothers (and perhaps the mothers) of today's women would likely find difficult to grasp. With new choices have come increased uncertainty and, in many cases, alterations in role structure, as today's young women and men, without models from the past to draw upon, grapple with changing ideals and evolving notions of personal and interpersonal fulfillment.

Nowhere is the social upheaval of the last two decades more apparent than in family patterns and relationships, as fewer and fewer American families conform to traditional stereotypes. Couples marry later and are quicker to divorce. Today's single parents or married dual-earner parents usually spend less time with their children than their parents spent with them, so in many cases they have insufficient time for effective parenting. More children are born to unmarried mothers, and more childhood years are spent in fatherless homes. The majority of African American children already live in single-parent households; increasingly, so do white and Hispanic youngsters. As a result, many school-age children must either care for themselves unsupervised as they return home each day to an empty house or depend on day care until a working parent arrives to fetch them. The noteworthy contemporary change in family life is that these children may not necessarily come from poor homes, as in the past, but instead may have affluent, professional parents who pursue careers for long hours away from home.

From a contemporary perspective, it no longer makes sense to refer to a typical American family life. Accuracy requires us to consider various types of families, with diverse organizational patterns, styles of living, and living arrangements. The idealized, nostalgic portrait of the American nuclear family depicts a carefree, white family with a suburban residence, sole-provider father in a 9-to-5 job, and a full-time stay-at-home mother always available when the children return from school. Both parents are dedicated to child-rearing and remain together for life; children are educated at a neighborhood school and attend church with their family on Sunday; plenty of money and supportive grandparents are available. Such a portrait does not depict reality for the vast majority of the population today, if indeed it ever did (Coontz, 1992).

Marriage and Divorce: Some Current Statistics

Consider the following facts and forecasts regarding marriage, divorce, and family life today (Popenoe & Whitehead, 1999b; Mason, Skolnick, & Sugarman, 1998; Saxton, 1996):

- Half of all marriages made this year in the United States are projected to end in divorce (although the rate is currently declining somewhat after hitting a high point in the early 1980s).
- Divorce rates are likely to be higher when a marriage is preceded by a premarital pregnancy or out-of-wedlock birth.
- Age of the spouses at the time of first marriage is a good predictor of marital stability (those under 20 are two to three times more likely to divorce than those who marry in their twenties).
- Married couples are divorcing earlier than ever before (38% within 4 years of marriage, 50% within 7 years); thus, younger children are more likely to be affected by divorce than in the past.
- The percentage of infants born to unwed mothers has increased more than sixfold in the last 40 years. More than one out of three children in the United States (two out of three African American children) is now born to an unwed mother.
- Never-married single women—especially those who are past 35, educated, and economically self-sufficient—are having children out of wedlock at an increasing rate.
- About one in three children under age 18 lives with a single parent at some point growing up.
- Single-parent families, approximately 85% of which are headed by women, now represent more than one out of four families with children; that number has tripled since 1960.
- Divorce is likely to be followed by remarriage (five out of six divorced men and three out of four divorced women remarry).
- More than half the people in the United States have belonged or will belong to a stepfamily at some period in their lives.

None of the family forms we will be describing in detail in the remainder of this book will be entirely atypical or unfamiliar to the reader. What is new is the sharp increase in diversity. Also new is the greater acceptance of flexibility, of lifestyles taking alternative (and alternate) forms, and of greater recognition of these lifestyles by most segments of society. We describe a variety of family forms because they reflect the pluralistic nature of American society and thus undoubtedly represent some of the clients that the reader, as a future counselor, will encounter. Some readers may find certain lifestyles, such as working mothers of preschool children, unacceptable, believing that a mother at home is essential to a child's well-being. Some readers may have religious, moral, or political objections to other patterns (gay couples, young heterosexual couples living together outside of marriage), arguing that married, two-parent families represent the ideal arrangement. Before undertaking any clinical work with such families, the counselor should explore his or her feelings regarding a particular lifestyle. If there is a conflict, the counselor must be honest and straightforward with the clients, clearly stating his or her views and determining, together with the clients, whether they wish to proceed. If not, the family should be referred to a suitable counselor.

Family Resiliency

All families, regardless of lifestyle, inevitably face certain serious problems or crises at some point in their life cycle. While most families become temporarily less functional—in some cases dysfunctional—in response to persistent stress, some have learned to call upon certain internal assets and strengths, allowing them to rebound from adversity. As is always the case, these families, regardless of type, number of problems, ethnic or racial makeup, socioeconomic level, or degree of education, are happier and more stable than others—more competent, showing greater recuperative ability despite misfortune, more flexible, more collaborative, adaptive to changing external conditions, purposeful in pursuing satisfaction for all members and in successfully carrying out developmental tasks. While there is no single blueprint for how "the resilient family" functions, family counselors are paying increasing attention to precisely which *interactional processes* within diverse family arrangements contribute to such **resilience** (McCubbin, McCubbin, & Thompson, 1993; Hawley & de Haan, 1996). Identifying and helping to fortify those processes aids in empowering all client families to withstand and rebound from disruptive challenges (Walsh, 1996).

Resilient families are not problem-free but have developed the ability to survive and regenerate even in the midst of overwhelming stress, misfortune, hardships, and life-altering transition points (a sudden job loss, a cross-cultural entry, the birth of a handicapped child, a divorce, the untimely death of a key family member). Emerging hardier from weathering crises or persistent stresses together, such families often strengthen their overall functioning and feel closer to one another, while fostering individual resilience in all family members. For example, poor families are often treated in ways that lower their sense of self-worth and dignity. Their resilience is apt to be evoked if they are given a chance to experience a sense of control over their lives, rather than viewing themselves as helpless victims of an uncaring society (Aponte, 1994).

Walsh (1996) urges that the traditional emphasis on family pathology be rebalanced with identifying competency-based, strength-oriented factors within families. She urges viewing families as challenged (rather than damaged) and for adopting a *relational resilience* perspective, attempting to determine how families in the face of change and adaptation survive hard times and regenerate, even in the midst of overwhelming stress. As Walsh (1996) observes,

> How a family confronts and manages a disruptive experience, buffers stress, effectively reorganizes, and moves forward with life will influence immediate and long-term adaptation for all family members and for the family unit. (p. 267)

All families possess the resources, and thus the potential, for resilience. In traditional families, usually organized according to some form of generational hierarchy, those with greater resilience are able to balance intergenerational continuity and change and to maintain ties among the past, the present, and the future without getting stuck in the past or cut off from it. Clarity and ease of communications also characterize such families; a clear set of expectations about roles and relationships within the family is provided. In whatever type of family form—whether led by never-married mothers, stepfathers, two working parents, or grandparents—resilient families respect individual differences and the separate needs of the family members. These families have mastered successful problem-solving strategies by developing reparative, resiliency-enabling processes that promote endurance and survival.

Changing Families, Changing Relationships

Having just recently passed their prime childbearing years, baby boomers—born between 1946 and 1964, the most fertile period in U.S. history—might have been expected to produce a bumper crop of children themselves. In fact, though, the baby boomers have not. Reasons may include delayed marriages, career priorities, decisions to remain single because of fears of marital failure, the high cost of child-rearing, fear of bringing children into an unstable world, more reliable contraceptive methods, the reluctance to have children in a risky marriage, or simply the desire to enjoy freedom unencumbered by too many family responsibilities. Clearly, different factors are important for different couples. The percentage of couples without children today is at the highest point in 50 years.

Consider the options available 50 years ago in order to better understand the dramatic changes in traditional life-cycle events. Then, marriage represented a significant *rite of passage,* the transition from parental home to independent household, from economic dependence to shared self-sufficiency, a social and sexual transition into adulthood. Men and women lived with parents until married; most married by age 21; more than likely the woman was a virgin when she married or had begun to have premarital intercourse with the man she eventually wed. The couple began to have children almost immediately; as a rule, childbearing was typically over by age 31; marriages remained intact until the death of one of the spouses; widowhood followed by the middle sixties; and, since remarriage at that point was uncommon, men and women both lived out their remaining ten years or so alone.

Now, after living with parents, people may live alone as never-married singles through much of their twenties, live with a roommate of the same sex, cohabit with an adult of the opposite sex, perhaps marry, have children (in or out of wedlock or adopted), get divorced, live alone again or with a lover of the same or opposite sex, remarry, become a stepparent, perhaps become widowed or divorced a second time, marry for a third time, and so forth. Thus, today's Americans are experiencing transition points in their lives largely unknown to previous generations.

Most people no longer marry in order to experience an active sex life.[6] According to Popenoe and Whitehead (1999b), more than half of today's teenage girls have engaged in their first sexual intercourse by age 17, and most remain sexually active for an average of 7–8 years before marriage.[7] Nor do they marry to start a family since, as we have noted, more single American women are having babies than ever before and many married women are choosing to remain child-free or delay childbearing until their late thirties. Never-married single mothers have thus become more commonplace. Ironically, childlessness has become a more socially acceptable option for married women, who no longer have to be embarrassed or become defensive or otherwise justify a choice of career over bearing children, their parents' possible disapproval notwithstanding.

We are once again experiencing important changes in American family life, as we have done repeatedly over the last two centuries. As the historian Hareven (1982) notes, contemporary lifestyles (cohabiting heterosexual couples, same-sex partners, dual-earner marriages, single-parent-led households, and so on) are not new inventions, but rather have become more visible as society becomes more tolerant of change and alternative living arrangements. Hareven argues that we are witnessing not a fragmentation of traditional family patterns, but an emerging acceptance of pluralism in family lifestyles.

The face of the American family has been altered remarkably as profound social and demographic changes have taken place over the past several decades. Thriving marriages, successful child-rearing, a mature and intimate relationship with another, commitment—these have never been easy to come by and are

---

[6]There are, of course, certain important exceptions. Individuals with strong religious convictions may abide by taboos against premarital sexual experiences.

[7]Once married, however, the vast majority remain sexually faithful to their marital partner, according to a national survey of contemporary sexual practices in America (Michael, Gagnon, Laumann, & Kolata, 1994).

complicated by a lack of many successful models. Two decades ago, Conger (1981, p. 1483) called particular attention to the increased strains on couples, as well as increased challenges:

> Changing sex roles; the rapid increase in women's participation in the work force; the pressure of two-job families; generational differences in values and outlook; continued geographic mobility; relative isolation of the nuclear family; continued age segregation; extremely rapid social, economic, and technological changes and the uncertainty about the future that they create; the economic penalties of parenthood in today's world compared to earlier generations—all of these realities have added to the stresses of marriage and parenthood, as well as to their challenges and exciting opportunities.

In twenty years, adaptations have been made to many of these stresses, but as we reveal throughout this text, solutions to many of these issues remain elusive.

A Family Counseling Sampler

Today's family counselors can expect to deal with at least some of the following situations: married couples attempting in one final way, through joint counseling sessions, to hold a deteriorating relationship together (Chapter 5); single parents, usually women, experiencing the emotional and financial hardship of raising children alone (Chapter 6); stepfamilies desperate to work out an arrangement so that they might live together in some degree of harmony despite major differences in background, experiences, and values (Chapter 7); young people in a nonmarital cohabitation living arrangement, knowing they need to make some decisions about their future but uncertain over what a long-term commitment to another person means giving up (Chapter 8); homosexual couples experiencing the pain of breaking up a long-term love relationship (Chapter 9); overloaded dual-career couples attempting to juggle career and family while seeking to achieve equity in their relationship (Chapter 10); and ethnic and racially diverse families trying to cope with an unfamiliar or hostile environment (Chapter 11).

Consider the following brief descriptions from a typical counseling caseload today.

One partner's withdrawal from the intimacy of a couple's relationship typically alerts the counselor to the likelihood of an endangered connection between the pair. Whether deliberately choosing to work different shifts, or taking separate vacations, or involving themselves completely in activities in which the partner has no interest, one or both participants are signaling interpersonal distress and employing exaggerated methods for trying to cope with unhappiness or unfulfillment. The Internet sometimes provides one such escape. Seemingly innocuously, a man may claim he is working and therefore requires isolation, when in reality he is secretly playing games by himself, watching pornographic web sites, day-trading stocks, chatting with strangers, perhaps involving himself in sexual fantasies with unseen partners. Women may also use the Internet for similar purposes, as in the case of Margo and David.

Margo, born in South Africa, was an attractive, lively young woman who came to the United States in her early twenties and met David, an older unmarried man in his late thirties, who was immediately smitten with her energy and vivacity. They married after a whirlwind romance, had two children (a boy and girl) within five years, and soon settled into life in the suburbs. David, a mechanical engineer, rose steadily in his job at an architectural firm, becoming vice president within ten years. Margo immersed herself in child-rearing, although the transition to parenthood did not come easily: She felt isolated from the other mothers in the neighborhood, was unsure of how best to raise children according to the American way, and had less and less time with her busy husband to discuss her self-doubts. On those occasions when she did bring up questions about the children—and occasionally about their growing apart from each other—he shrugged her off, telling her she was imagining problems that did not really exist.

Margo became increasingly depressed, her former energy and enthusiasm seemingly depleted. As she and David drifted apart, their sexual relationship, which both had previously enjoyed, diminished to the point where it became nonexistent. To relieve any accompanying tensions, she turned to tranquilizers, going to several doctors to obtain prescriptions (none knew about the others) and various pharmacies to fill the prescriptions so that no one would suspect her addiction. After a decade of this practice, she finally admitted her habit to her husband, who became concerned—she finally got his attention!—and helped her obtain treatment from a behavioral psychologist, which seemed to extinguish her craving. However, the lack of intimacy in the marriage never got addressed.

After several years, the children now grown and away at school, Margo found herself increasingly isolated and alone. David was even more busy than before in his job, and thus unavailable, and they had made few friends to whom they could turn for social activities. As Margo, with time on her hands, withdrew into her house, she played solitaire on the computer for hours at a time, eventually graduating to bridge tournaments on the Web. Within a short time, bridge became an addiction, and her now distraught husband felt excluded from her life.

Lonely, isolated, despondent, desperate for companionship, Margo began a romance over the Internet with Arthur, a fellow bridge player from New Zealand. Although she and her husband had never been unfaithful, her hunger for intimacy, coupled with her addictive qualities, made this romance an all-consuming one, although the two did not meet for the first six months. However, no longer able to control her urge to see the man, she told her husband that she was going with a woman friend on a Pacific cruise that included a bridge tournament, and secretly arranged to see Arthur, with whom she spent five days. David, meanwhile, trying to get an e-mail address aboard ship so he could reach her, went into her computer and discovered the saved correspondence detailing the exchange of romantic feelings between his wife and Arthur.

Conflicted over what to do, uncertain about a future with Arthur, and in terror of the impending breakup of her marriage, Margo revealed all to her husband, and together they sought marriage counseling.

Josh and Anne Gottlieb, married 6 months, after having each been in marriages ending in divorce, referred themselves for counseling.[8] Both were computer scientists who met as graduate students at a midwestern university. Since both were married at the time, and both were expressing considerable despair about their deteriorating marriages, they found solace in each other and soon were having a sexual affair. Immediately after graduation, Josh divorced his wife, left his two preteenage children with their mother, and departed for a job on the West Coast. Anne, his wife-to-be, shortly thereafter left her husband, took their 6-year-old daughter, Emily, and by prearrangement joined Josh. Within a year they were married, both employed in rewarding jobs, and living happily with her young daughter in a large urban community. Josh talked by telephone with his own children on a regular basis but saw them rarely, only when he had business in the town where they lived.

Unfortunately, the Gottliebs' honeymoon period was short-lived. For one thing, each of them had been married previously to people of the same ethnic and social class background as themselves, and they now experienced some friction as a result of her Baptist and his Jewish backgrounds. (Anne's effort during their first Christmas together to maintain a family custom by reading aloud from the New Testament upset Josh but was never discussed.) Even more disruptive was the sudden appearance of Josh's daughter, Jennifer, now 13, who had been struggling with her mother and in a fit of anger (and with her mother's encouragement) decided to come out, unannounced, to live with her father. Within a short period, during which Anne was determined to make her stepdaughter feel at home, conflict erupted in the household. The stepmother was especially upset at what she viewed as her husband's overindulgent and overly permissive child-rearing techniques, which she believed led to undisciplined and uncontrolled behavior. In addition, never having experienced living with an adolescent, Anne was particularly offended by her stepdaughter's intrusiveness, as Jennifer behaved as though she had proprietary rights over her father, used Anne's perfume, and wore some of Anne's clothes. Josh, caught in the middle, felt concerned about his wife's increasing unhappiness but also, accustomed to an indulgent child-rearing style, believed he needed to placate his daughter or she would feel neglected and rejected. Besides, he felt guilty about not having seen her much during her earlier years. Another major worry and source of his guilt feelings was that his daughter might begin to believe he favored his stepdaughter, Emily, over his own child. Indeed, Jennifer and Emily did quarrel frequently. Finally, when conflict in the household had reached an unacceptable level, the Gottliebs contacted a family counselor, who suggested over the telephone that the parents and both children come together for family sessions.

Andrea and John could not make up their minds about living together, although they had been having an ongoing (and tempestuous) love affair for 5 years. Both single, in their late twenties, and both employed as salespeople at the same department store

---

[8]Self-referral is actually fairly common with stepfamilies, since one or both parents has had earlier unhappy experiences in marriage and may have received joint counseling or in some other fashion learned to view problems within a family context.

where they met, each claimed to be having too much fun to settle down with one person. Each came from divorced families; John had a bitter, never-remarried mother, and Andrea had a much-remarried father. Both young people had pervasive fears of an intimate relationship, as well as some sense that each would have problems sustaining closeness over any length of time. Filled with misgivings, and after a long series of on-again, off-again decisions, John and Andrea made a change only after circumstances intervened: John had to give up his apartment to the new owner of the building where he lived. Forced to make a move, they determined that they would try living together and decide once and for all whether they should marry or split up permanently. Soon, John moved in with Andrea.

Within a month, it seemed that their worst underlying fears were confirmed. Andrea felt that her territory, which she had carefully and lovingly decorated with objects very personal and meaningful to her, was being invaded. John felt very critical of Andrea's way of doing things—cooking, stacking dishes after they were washed, caring for her car, spending money. Accustomed to straight, direct talk—having been raised in a large family where get-togethers often became free-for-alls with family members fighting loudly and bitterly—John could not understand Andrea's long silences and quiet weeping. She, for her part, an only child raised by a doting mother (who herself had little if any relationship with an increasingly ostracized and then divorced father), could not understand why John had so many complaints about her if, as he claimed, he loved her so much. After living together 2 months, both were depressed and confused and, at the suggestion of a fellow employee, sought professional help.

Celia, 27, and Brenda, 29, had been lesbian live-in partners for 4 years and had talked from time to time about adopting a child together. Celia, from San Salvador, had been married briefly 8 years earlier, but the marriage ended in divorce. She had wanted a child while married, but she and her husband had had such a rocky marriage, with numerous separations, that both decided it would not be wise to bring a child into such an unstable situation. Brenda, Australian by birth, had never married but had been involved in raising two children of a woman friend with whom she had had a previous sexual relationship. Celia and Brenda had been together in an exclusive union since shortly after they met, and both were quite involved in the lesbian community, from which they received considerable social support.

A parenting opportunity arose one day when Dora, Celia's 21-year-old unmarried sister and the mother of a 5-year-old boy, announced that she wanted to return to school and told Celia she was considering putting her son, Richardo, up for adoption. Not wanting the boy to be placed with strangers, and accustomed to coming to the aid of her younger sister in times of stress, Celia offered to adopt Richardo. Dora, who trusted her older sister and felt burdened raising Richardo by herself—he was the result of a one-night stand when she was 16—readily agreed. Celia and Brenda had had a good relationship with the boy since his birth, and they were certain that the transition would be easy, that Richardo would thrive, and that raising a child together would strengthen their relationship and enrich their lives. Unfortunately, this would not ultimately prove to be the case.

Soon after Celia adopted Richardo, she and Brenda began to face the prospects of parenting and the multiple ways in which their lives had begun to change as a result of their new living arrangement. They initially tried to create a new life and identity for Richardo, offering him his own room in their large house and immediately changing his name to Rick. They instructed him to call them "Mommy" and "Auntie Brenda" and to try to feel as if he were a part of this three-member family. Brenda, more experienced with raising children, quit her part-time job at the public library and assumed most of the at-home parenting responsibilities. Celia continued to work full time as a legal secretary in order to support the household. However, the social support previously offered by their network of lesbian and gay friends began to dwindle, as few in the community were involved in raising children.

Celia and Brenda were initially pleased with the parenting arrangement they had worked out together, but after six months or so they both began to have reservations about its workability. Celia grew envious of Brenda's close relationship with her adopted son and became distrustful of her own ability to deal with Rick in the easy manner in which Brenda, more experienced with children, seemed able to use. As Celia withdrew from the parenting role, Brenda became increasingly frustrated, resenting the fact that she was carrying out the day-to-day parenting duties with no legal authorization to make decisions regarding Rick. Moreover, Celia's family of origin treated her with suspicion, refusing to acknowledge Brenda's rights regarding child-rearing decisions.

As tensions mounted, Rick began to exhibit problematic behavior at home and at school. He developed various behavioral signs of increased anxiety (sleeping problems, eating problems, discipline problems), finally stating his fear that he would become "unadopted," that Celia and Brenda would separate, and that he would lose his close relationship with Brenda. His schoolwork suffered accordingly, and at a parent-teacher conference (attended by both Celia and Brenda) the teacher reported that Rick was easily distractible and hyperactive in the classroom and that she thought he needed counseling. Recognizing all the signs of increased dysfunction, but knowing they all wanted to stay together, the three made an appointment with a family counselor for the next week.

Martha was 14 and in high school when she met Trevor, a member of a British rock group performing on a Saturday night at an amphitheater in a large California city 35 miles from the midsize community in which she lived. She and three high school girlfriends had been filled with excitement for weeks at the prospect of driving to the concert to hear their favorite band, and together they convinced the four sets of parents that it would be safe since all four girls would be together, it was not a school night, and they would be back home at a reasonable hour. On the way to the concert, they drank a significant amount of alcohol, and after the performance they waited at the stage door to catch a glimpse of their idols. Martha particularly wanted to meet Trevor, 23, and when he emerged she rushed over to him and engaged him in conversation. After a brief encounter, he invited her to a party, assuring her friends he would take her home. A great deal of alcohol and drugs were consumed at the party, and soon Trevor and Martha were having sexual intercourse, she for the first time. Frightened and confused, she reminded Trevor of his promise to drive her home, but instead he arranged for his limousine driver to take her back. She never saw Trevor again.

When Martha discovered she was pregnant, she was panicked, and for a while did not tell anyone except her closest friend, Sally. Slender, it was not until she was five months' pregnant that her older sister, Claire, suspected; pressed to tell the truth, Martha admitted what had happened to her. Claire, 16, frightened and worried, told their mother. Martha's parents were horrified but ultimately agreed that they would move to another town after she delivered the baby and would raise the child as their own. After Fred was born, the family agreed never to reveal the truth to him, and as far as he knew growing up, Martha was his older sister.

Keeping the secret proved to be a heavy burden on the family. Never discussing what had occurred led to further deterioration of the family members' ability to communicate with one another. When Martha's father had had enough—he complained of the financial and especially the psychological millstone she had imposed on the family—he left. His career dreams frustrated, he had had to work for years at a job far less fulfilling than had been the case in the previous town. Martha's mother also resented the sacrifices of her private life that her daughter's actions had imposed on her. Claire felt neglected because her parents had to spend so much time raising a young child. Martha's guilt and sense of indebtedness were never resolved and continued to be oppressive all during her later adolescence. Growing up, her son, Fred, was aware of constant battles in the house without knowing what they were all about.

Martha finished high school, married early to escape the family, and moved away. Fred did not find out the truth of his parentage until he was 12 years of age. After a failed marriage, Martha returned to her parents' home, and one day, having had too much to drink and no longer able to contain her secret, she blurted out the truth to her son. By now she wanted to try to live with him as a single mother, but she recognized they needed counseling together. Astounded, Fred reluctantly agreed to give it a try.

Richard and Rebecca were both career-minded for as long as either could remember. Both had dreamed of becoming doctors, and when they met at the age of 28, he was a student in an M.D./Ph.D. program and she was in medical school. Both were extremely ambitious and sought academic positions after finishing their training. They took their medical training together, and graduated first (Rebecca) and second (Richard) in their class. The day after graduation, they were married. Richard still needed to complete his doctoral studies in molecular biology while Rebecca sought an internship and then a residency in infectious diseases. Richard received an offer to study with an eminent molecular biologist at a distant university for 1 year, and although Rebecca had easily obtained the residency she sought, she accommodated his plans and accepted a less prestigious offer at that university so that they could be together.

Three years later, with Richard winding up his studies and Rebecca completing her residency training, the couple decided to have a baby. Troubles soon began to mount: They could not find an acceptable nanny for their son; financial problems were a serious strain as a result of two large student loans they now needed to repay;

both were overloaded with responsibilities. Rebecca, unhappy over inadequate child care, gave up her academic dreams and took a job at a health maintenance organization, where she thought her hours would be more regular and she would not have to be on call as she had during her training. Unfortunately, she found herself under other kinds of pressure to see lots of patients every day. Richard, completing his research, was busy lining up postdoctoral training. Both were exhausted from work and family responsibilities, and felt stretched to the limit. Feeling close to the breaking point, Rebecca felt it was her turn and demanded that Richard make some sacrifices; she insisted he seek a teaching job at a medical school near her parents' home instead of at the first-class university that had been his dream. When he argued that it would be a bad move for his career, they were at a stalemate and sought help together from a family counselor to whom they had been recommended.

Indira and Sanjay Singh were sister and brother who came from India to the United States with their parents when they were still of preschool age. Their parents had brought them with the hope that the children's lives would be better than theirs, since neither of the parents had had much education or opportunity in their native land. The parents worked very hard, 7 days a week, in a small clothing store they owned, just managing to make a living, and expected the children to help out as early as 6 or 7 years of age as they, the parents, had with their own parents. Both children were taught to be compliant with adults, to respect their parents' wishes, and to engage in social activities primarily with family or extended family members. Friends from school were discouraged, and Indira and Sanjay, now 17 and 14, respectively, were expected to go places only with each other, never alone or with friends. Television was tolerated but monitored by the parents; for example, the children could not see scenes of people kissing, which was also not permitted in Indian cinema. When the children objected, the parents reminded the children that they were being disrespectful and that if the "insolent" behavior continued, the parents would move them all back to India at whatever sacrifice to the family.

Loyalty, respect, and family obligation were essential parts of the family code. As in other Indian families they knew, extended-family ties were stressed, arranged marriages were the norm, and children were expected to obey their parents, especially their father. The parents did not understand why the children wanted to associate with strangers when family members were available. What class or caste did these strangers belong to? What would happen to her father's plans for her marriage if Indira got into trouble as a result of being in bad company? When Indira asked to go to a party with her high school friends, the parents refused, asking instead why she hadn't proposed helping out in the store so they could get some rest. Despite her protests that she did help but also wanted to have some fun, the parents threw up their hands in despair and told the children how miserable their ungrateful behavior had made their parents.

A teacher who knew something of Indian culture, observing Indira's distress, talked to her about the problems of biculturalism and suggested that such culture conflict was not uncommon between first and second generations in a new country. The teacher suggested family counseling, which the parents first refused to do, expressing shame that intervention by a stranger would be necessary. After the children visited a counselor alone for two sessions, the parents reluctantly came in, and together all four began to deal with the differences between countries and to understand cultural expectations.

Summary

In the changing North American society, the intact nuclear family has become less common and certain alternative family forms are becoming more evident. The high divorce rate; the rapid increase in the percentage of women in the labor force; the increasingly common choice to remain single or to delay marriage; the uncloseted gay and lesbian unions; and the sharp rise in the number of cohabiting partners, childless couples, out-of-wedlock children, single-parent-led households, and stepfamilies—together, these contemporary phenomena have changed our understanding of what constitutes a family and have forced counselors to deal with new sets of lifestyles and family relationship problems. The influx of ethnic minorities in certain parts of the country has also added to the diversity facing today's counselors, who must learn to deal with a variety of family styles and cultural backgrounds as we begin the 21st century.

All families, regardless of type, have the potential for resilience—the ability to withstand and bounce back from a crisis or adversity. Rather than search for signs of family pathology, today's family counselors are paying increased attention to what interactional processes within diverse family living arrangements contribute to family resilience. Compared to previous generations, today's families are experiencing transition points foreign to their counterparts in earlier generations.

CHAPTER

TWO

The Family as a Social Unit: Systems Theory and Beyond

For many years, counselors' efforts to look at family problems focused on a specific family member with a "problem," who was usually blamed for any difficulties the family was going through. A search for the origin or meaning of that family member's behavior typically turned to explanations that focused on that person, particularly his or her internal or **intrapsychic** conflicts. As counselors broadened their horizons to include a focus on family relationships, beginning around mid-20th century, they turned to the study of the recurring patterns within a family **system** and the impact of these patterns on the behavior of individual family members. In the final decade or so of the last century, spurred by the **postmodern** revolution in the arts and sciences, counselors once again widened their view to include the cultural context in which problems occur. Arguing that the systems view is too narrow in viewing problems as emanating entirely from flawed family relationships, postmodernists consider many of the problems for which families seek counseling as mired in the "structures of inequality of our culture, including those pertaining to gender, race, ethnicity, class, economics, age, and so on" (White, 1995, p. 115).

In this chapter we first review systems theory, which has provided the theoretical scaffolding for much of family counseling research and practice. Systems theory itself is embedded in a **modernist** orientation to human behavior—observing, describing, quantifying, assessing, hypothesizing, explaining, treating—used by a detached, objective counselor expert in human relationships. In contrast, as we elaborate later in this chapter, the counselor with a postmodern orientation is no

23

longer the outside expert who knows how couples and families should solve their problems. Rather, he or she helps clients bring forth, illuminate, and amplify their knowledge, honoring the clients' abilities to forge new directions based on new interpretations of their own experiences (Weingarten, 1998).

Behavior in Family Context: Understanding Family Systems

Within the social sciences, beginning in the late 1940s, first researchers and then clinicians began looking beyond the past for explanations of current, ongoing behavior. Just as their counterparts in biology, for example, were beginning to comprehend the complex ecological system in which different forms of life (people, animals, plants, birds, air, soil) share a common environment, affecting one another so intimately that it would be naive and foolish to consider them separately, so social scientists began to wonder whether it might be useful to consider an individual as existing in a similar kind of ecological system—namely, his or her family. Seeking a scientific model, family counselors were attracted to **general systems theory,** proposed earlier by biologist Ludwig von Bertalanffy and others, with its emphasis on the unity of living systems, especially its attention to the interaction of component parts. Von Bertalanffy's (1968) theory offered a comprehensive model, suitable to all living systems, intended to be applicable to all behavioral and social sciences alike.

Soon, systems concepts became a useful language for conceptualizing a family's interactive processes. If a family is more than a collection of individuals but instead a whole larger than (and different from) the sum of its parts, then individual behavior is most clearly understood within the context of the whole. The family itself becomes the subject of analysis (Worden, 1994). How the family reaches agreements and negotiates differences tells us a great deal about the nature of the family system. Within such a family framework, the individual's disturbed or troubled behavior (anxiety, depression, alcoholism, an eating disorder) is seen as representative of a system that is faulty, not due to individual deficit or deficiency. That person's current difficulties might then be viewed more accurately as signaling a social system in disequilibrium. The **identified patient's** current difficulties might then be recast as representing a family social system that has become destabilized or is in a state of (perhaps temporary) imbalance.

Turning from exclusive attention to the internal conflicts of the individual to a focus on family patterns, the systems outlook has profound implications for the ways counselors view, think about, and ultimately intervene in human social phenomena (Koman & Stechler, 1985). Systems thinking is not so much directly translatable into specific counseling techniques, but rather provides the counselor with a way of organizing his or her thinking about people and the origins of their dysfunctional behavior. That way of organizing data and conceptualizing problems between people has implications for how to intercede most effectively with troubled families. Viewed from today's vantage point, systems theory lays the foundation for treating individuals, couples, and families within the cultural and ethnic contexts in which they are embedded, offering the counselor a **paradigm** from which to view multiple causes and contexts of behavior (Mikesell, Lusterman, & McDaniel, 1995). From a systems perspective, every event within a family is multiply determined by all the forces operating within that system. Disordered or symptomatic behavior of any individual within the family is understood to be an expression or manifestation of the interactional processes currently taking place within the family system as a whole.

Such a global view, in which the fundamental unit of study is not the individual but rather the system itself, turns our attention to a family's established behavioral sequences or patterns. Families form repetitive patterns over time; this patterning over time is the essence of the family system (Segal & Bavelas, 1983). As Constantine (1986) points out, the family is a good example of the organized complexity for which the systems view is the most appropriate approach. What, then, constitutes a "problem family" likely to be seen in a counseling situation? According to Constantine, the determining factor is neither the number nor severity of a family's problems but rather the family's response to the problems and the extent to which their problems disable the way their family system operates.

Linear and Circular Causality

Presystems theories tended to be reductionistic; that is, they explained complex phenomena by breaking the whole down and analyzing the separate, simpler parts. Thus, ever-smaller units were investigated in order to get a fix on the causes of larger events. In this simple Newtonian view of the physical universe, it made sense to think in terms of **linear causality:** A causes B, which acts upon C, causing D to occur.

Within psychological theory, such an outlook took the form of stimulus-response explanations for complex human behavior. From this perspective, all current behavior is seen as the result of a series of outside forces that build on one another in sequence and ultimately produce the behavior in question. To the psychoanalyst, such forces are likely the result of childhood experiences; to the behaviorally inclined, the causes are more apt to be found in past and present learning experiences. By attending exclusively to the individual, however, both viewpoints fail to examine both the context and the process of the current behavior. Thus, they fail to understand fully the complex dynamics of a family system.

The systems view, by comparison, is more holistic, is better attuned to tangled interpersonal relationships, and stresses the reciprocity of behaviors between people. **Circular causality** emphasizes that forces do not simply move in one direction, each event caused by a previous event, but rather become part of a causal chain, each influencing and being influenced by the others. Goldenberg and Goldenberg (2000, p. 11) offer the following contrast between statements based on linear and circular analysis:

Linear: A bad mother produces sick children.

Implication: Mother's emotional problems cause similar problems in others.

Circular: An unhappy middle-aged woman, struggling with an inattentive husband who feels peripheral to and excluded from the family, attaches herself to her 20-year-old son for male companionship, excluding her adolescent daughter. In turn, the daughter, feeling rejected and unloved, engages in flagrant sexually promiscuous behavior, to the considerable distress of her parents. The son, fearful of leaving home and becoming independent, insists he must remain at home because his mother needs his attention. The mother becomes depressed because her children do not seem to be like other "normal" children, and she blames their dysfunctional behavior on her husband, whom she labels an "absentee father." He in turn becomes angry and defensive, and their sexual relationship suffers. The children respond to the ensuing coldness between the parents in different ways: the son by withdrawing from friends completely and remaining at home with his mother as much as possible, and the daughter by having indiscriminant sexual encounters with one man after another but carefully avoiding intimacy with any of them. Her symptomatic behavior serves not only to draw the family's attention to her, but also leads her parents to draw closer to each other in order to help their distressed daughter.

Implication: Behavior has as least as much to do with the interactional context in which it occurs as with the inner mental processes or emotional problems of any of the players.

Gregory Bateson (1979), a cultural anthropologist by training but with broad interest in **cybernetics** (the study of methods of feedback control within a system), provided many of the theoretical underpinnings for the application of systems thinking to human relationships. He labeled the stimulus-response paradigm a "billiard ball" model—a model that describes a force as moving in only one direction and affecting objects in its path. Consistent with his anthropological outlook, which attempted to ferret out the "rules" of various cultures, he called for a focus on the ongoing patterns and processes between interacting family members. These connective patterns, which reveal the family's implicit rules, rituals, and role assignments for living together (such as who has the right to say or do what to whom), are the fundamental components of the system. Bateson called for the development of a new descriptive language, consistent with cybernetic thinking and systems theory, that emphasizes the relationship between parts and their effect on one another. While A may evoke B, it is also true that B evokes A, as we have just seen. A marital counselor is likely to hear the following exchange from a quarreling couple, each partner feeling put upon and blaming the other for his or her feelings of unhappiness:

Wife: You never seem to talk to me and let me know that you notice I exist.

Husband: It's true. You become so heated and intense at times that you frighten me and I clam up.

Wife: You don't get it! The reason I become so upset is that I get frustrated by your withdrawing behavior. The more frustrated I become, the more persistent I become.

Husband: You're the one who doesn't get it! The more you persist, the more intimidated I get and the more I withdraw.

A counselor working with an entire troubled family, many of whose members blame their woes on one another, is even more likely to confront such a circular situation. These examples illustrate the causal chains that tie together family behavior and communication. Shifting to a perspective that emphasizes circular causality helps us conceptualize a family's collective behavior in current transactional terms—as a network of circular loops in which every member's behavior affects everyone else. People mutually affect one another; there is no specific cause of any single behavioral event. The counselor needs to analyze the various repetitive links that keep the loop locked in place (and thus maintain the mutually defeating interaction patterns) and that prevent the individuals who make up the family system from moving on to more productive or fulfilling activities (Koman & Stechler, 1985).

Cybernetics, Feedback Loops, and Homeostasis

If anthropologist Bateson was primarily responsible for providing the philosophical framework for viewing families as rule-governed systems, it is fair to credit mathematician Norbert Wiener (1948) for coining the term *cybernetics* and for elaborating on **feedback** mechanisms as the basis for controlling communication patterns and information-processing systems. (The cybernetic metaphor would soon be adopted by some family-oriented clinicians interested in explaining why some families become "stuck" in repetitive, unproductive, and often destructive behavior patterns from which, unaided, they seem unable to escape.) Zeroing in at first on how machines receive information that enables them to self-correct and stay on course toward reaching a preprogrammed goal, Wiener focused his attention on how such self-governing systems maintain stability and control by means of **feedback loops.** He defined feedback as a method of controlling a system by reinserting into it the results of its past performance. Stated another way, information about how a system is functioning is looped back (fed back) from the output to the input, thus modifying subsequent input signals. Thus, feedback loops are circular mechanisms whose purpose is to reintroduce information about a system's output back to its input in order to alter, correct, or ultimately govern the system's functioning.

Systems tend to seek equilibrium, or **homeostasis,** by means of feedback information. This balance-seeking pattern serves to maintain stability. Whenever a family's equilibrium is threatened, feedback mechanisms are typically activated by family members in order to bring balance back into the family system (to get members to stop shouting, to not leave angry, to shake hands, to say they're sorry, perhaps to kiss and make up). This attempt to recapture equilibrium or return to the status quo (reduce deviation) is called **negative feedback.** This cybernetic term does not imply something is bad, nor does it connote any value judgment. The term simply means the system is receiving information as a result of some error-activated, excess-activated, or deviant behavioral sequence or pattern within the family process that has just occurred; the system is attempting to introduce self-correcting information in order to maintain homeostasis and return to a steady state. Perhaps the actions of negative feedback can be more graphically described as attenuating loops (Constantine, 1986).

All of us are familiar with such error-activated causal events in our daily lives. The attentive driver does not simply hold the steering wheel steady, but in fact continuously makes slight corrections to keep the car traveling in a predetermined direction. Automobiles with cruise-control devices allow the driver to set a desired speed; if a temporary problem arises, say a sudden sharp incline causing a momentary reduction in speed, that information activates the system, acceleration follows, and the preset speed is once again achieved.

Positive feedback (the use of amplifying loops, in Constantine's [1986] terms) has the opposite effect: It causes further change by augmenting or accelerating the initial deviation. In some cases positive feedback may reach runaway or destabilizing proportions, forcing the system beyond its limits to the point of chaos or self-destruction. The car is oversteered and goes out of control; the cruise control continues to accelerate to ever higher speeds and disastrous consequences; the family, caught in a vicious cycle, cannot stop the feud among members from accelerating, so each side ceases contact with the other for lengthy periods of time.

Both negative and positive feedback loops abound in families. Negative feedback or attenuation may occur with a remarried couple like this (Goldenberg & Goldenberg, 2000):

Husband: I'm upset at the way you talked to that man at the party tonight, especially the way you seemed to be hanging on every word he said.

Wife: Don't be silly! You're the one I care about. He said he had just come back from a trip you and I had talked about going on, and I was interested in what he could tell me about the place.

Husband: OK. But please don't do that again without telling me. You know I'm touchy on the subject because of what [ex-wife] Gina used to do at parties with other men that drove me crazy.

Wife: Sorry, I hadn't thought about that. I'll try to remember next time. In the meantime, you try to remember that you're married to me now and I don't want you to be jealous.

In a less-blissful situation, in place of the previous attenuation, positive feedback or amplification occurs:

Husband: I'm upset at the way you talked to that man at the party tonight, especially the way you seemed to be hanging on every word he said.

Wife: One thing I don't appreciate is your spying on me.

Husband: Spying? That's a funny word to use. You must be getting paranoid in your old age. Or maybe you have something to hide.

Wife: As a matter of fact, I was talking to him about a trip he took that we had talked about, but I don't suppose you'd believe that. Talk about paranoid!

Husband: I give up on women! You're no different from Gina, and I suppose all other women.

Wife: With an attitude like that, I'm starting to see why Gina walked out on you.

Positive feedback, in this illustration destabilizing, may also be beneficial and change the system for the better if it does not get out of control:

Husband: I'm upset at the way you talked to that man at the party tonight, especially the way you seemed to be hanging on every word he said. Can you help me understand what was going on?

Wife: He said he had just come back from a trip you and I had talked about going on, and I was interested in what he had to tell me about the place. Maybe I should have called you over and included you in the conversation.

Husband: No need to invite me. From now on I will come over so I'll know what's happening.

Wife: I'd like that. Keeping in close contact with you at a party always makes me feel good.

While most transactions can probably be characterized by the predominance of one of these two loops—one attenuating a possible conflict, the other amplifying it—both may occur between the same players under different conditions or at different points in their relationship. Moreover, *homeostasis* does not mean "static"; as a relationship grows and develops, stability may call for acknowledging change, and change often comes about in a family through breakthroughs that push the family beyond its previous homeostatic level (Goldenberg & Goldenberg, 2000).

Despite the potentially escalating impact of the runaway system described in the second example, we see in the third example that not all positive feedback need be considered damaging. Counselors may at times encourage positive feedback to motivate clients to break out of existing but stultifying family behavior patterns, such as the use of one member as a scapegoat in order to hide or obscure other, more pressing but unresolved family issues. At times it may be advantageous to push a system with untenable behavior patterns beyond its previous homeostatic level. Encouraging family members to make those breakthrough changes that will help the family system function at a new level might be more therapeutic in the long run than restoring equilibrium. The counselor with a systems perspective needs to determine whether to help the family return to its former level of functioning (from which they may have deviated because of a temporary stress) or to seize an opportunity to help promote discontinuity and choose new options (for example, to reexamine family rules as an independence-seeking child reaches adolescence, or to change the family's interactive pattern so members might function in a new and more harmonious way together). The latter, the result of positive feedback, helps the family system adapt to changing family circumstances and thus helps ensure stability and the survival of a functioning family system.

Open and Closed Systems

All families' systems are selective in their availability to new information and in their willingness to incorporate such information (Guttman, 1991). Such systems may be relatively open or closed, depending on the degree to which they are organized to interact with the outside environment. An open system permits input—new information—from its surroundings and sustains itself by continually interacting with those surroundings. Theoretically, closed systems are not able to participate in such transactions; in point of fact, however, systems are rarely if ever completely isolated or closed off from the outside world.

Theoretically, for a family to be truly operating as a closed system, all outside transactions and communications would have to cease—hardly a likely prospect.[1] Nevertheless, some families, sometimes newly arrived immigrants or members of insular ethnic groups, do exist in relative isolation, communicating only among themselves, suspicious of outsiders, and fostering dependence on the family. Children may be warned to trust only family members, nobody else. Regulated predominantly by deviation-attenuating (negative) feedback, such families seek to hold on to the traditions and conventions of the past and avoid change. Other immigrant families, eager to assimilate into the predominant culture of their new homeland, may make efforts to adapt to the values and behavior patterns of their adopted country.

New ideas, new information, new outlooks are all seen as threatening to the status quo in closed systems. In their extreme form, some families may attempt to impose rigid and unchanging behavior patterns, sealing themselves off from exchanges with the outside world. These closed systems tend toward **entropy**— gradually regressing, decaying because of insufficient input, possibly becoming disorganized and destined for eventual disorder. Sauber (1983) describes such entropic families as maintaining strict taboos regarding who and what should be admitted into the house, limiting the introduction of news and certain forms of music, screening visitors, and so on. A similar example in Chapter 1 concerned the generational conflict within an immigrant family.

Closed family systems force individual members to subordinate their needs to the welfare of the group. Family loyalty is paramount; rules are absolute; tradition must be observed; any deviation in behavior can lead only to chaos. As White

---

[1] Some religious cults do attempt to close out the world beyond their borders, specifically to halt the flow of outside information. Countries that do not permit foreign newspapers, radio or television broadcasts, or access to the Internet or World Wide Web are also systems deliberately closed to better control citizens' behavior.

(1978) portrays closed family systems, parents see to it that doors are kept locked, that family reading matter and television programs are screened, that children report their comings and goings scrupulously, and that rigid daily schedules are kept as closely as possible. Stability in such an arrangement is achieved through the insistence on maintaining tradition.

Open systems use both negative (attenuating) and positive (amplifying) feedback loops. Thus, they are considered to be operating on the systems principle of **equifinality,** meaning that the same end state may be reached from a variety of starting points. To appreciate how a family functions, we must study the organization of the family system—the habitual or redundant way in which they interact, regardless of topic or situation—rather than search for either the origins or outcomes of those interactions. Thus, whether they bicker over the children, money, sex, in-laws, or who takes care of the dry cleaning, their interactive pattern is likely to be the same.

In open systems, where a variety of inputs is possible, the family's feedback process is an overriding determinant of how it functions. Since a number of pathways lead to the same destination, there is no single "correct" way to raise children, to ensure a happy marriage, and so on. Uncertain beginnings do not necessarily doom a relationship; a shaky start—perhaps as a result of an early marriage—may be compensated for by the introduction of corrective feedback as the relationship matures. By the same token, an apparently congenial marriage of many years may become stale or turn sour for a variety of reasons. As we saw in our discussion of causality, a linear description in which A inevitably leads to B overlooks the central role played by the family interactive process. The concept of equifinality means that the counselor may intervene with a family at any of several points or through any of several counseling techniques to obtain the same desired results.

Most family systems strike a balance between openness and closeness. Some individuals find relatively closed family systems safe and secure and never stray too far, physically or psychologically. Members may on occasion be called upon to sacrifice their individual needs for the good of the family, but in the long run may get most of their important needs met through participation in the family group. Of course, one problem is that a closed structure may become rigid; family members may run away or otherwise rebel. Or families may feel isolated; for example, a young, never-married mother, alienated from her unaccepting parents, may find she has little opportunity for exchange with the outside world. Open family systems, desirable as they may appear to be, run the risk of having free expression turn ugly and perhaps divide the family into warring factions. Incompatibilities may surface—over discipline within a stepfamily, for example—and excessive strains may result. The open family system may become entropic, and the stepfamily may disintegrate into warring factions and ultimately break up.

In gauging the degree of openness of a family system, the counselor needs to evaluate how (and how well) the family deals with new information, particularly if that new input provokes a family crisis (for example, discovering a teenager's drug addiction). To what extent do the family members realistically perceive and appraise the problem? How well are they able to delay closure until sufficient information has been sought and discussed and a family plan formulated? To what degree are they able to coordinate their individual responses so that the best possible family action can be undertaken in this unfamiliar situation?

Under ideal conditions, open systems are said to have **negentropy:** They are organized to be adaptable, open to new experiences, and able to alter patterns and discard those that are inappropriate to the present situation. Through exchanges outside their own boundaries, open systems increase their chances of becoming more highly organized and developing resources to repair minor or temporary breakdowns in efficiency (Nichols & Everett, 1986). The relative lack of such exchanges in closed systems decreases their competence to deal with stress. Limited or perhaps nonexistent contact with others outside the family may lead to fearful, confused, and ineffective responses to crisis. In extreme cases of rigid systems, persistent stress, or both, chaos and anarchy within the family may follow.

Subsystems and Boundaries

Subsystems are the parts of an overall system assigned to carry out particular functions or processes within the system in order to maintain and sustain the system as a whole. Every family has a number of such coexisting subdivisions, formed by generation, gender, interest, or role and function within the family (Minuchin, 1974). The most enduring are the spousal, the parent-child, and the sibling subsystems.

The spousal (husband-wife) unit is basic. It is central to the life of the family in its early years and continues to play a major role over the life span of the family. There is little doubt that the overall success of any family depends to a large extent on the husband and wife's ability to work out a successful relationship. (The absence of one parent, more and more common, may have a particularly damaging effect on the remaining parent as well as the children, as we shall see in subsequent chapters.) Any dysfunction in this subsystem is bound to reverberate throughout the family, scapegoating certain children, co-opting others into alliances with one parent against the other, and so on. The way spouses together make decisions, manage conflict, plan the family's future, meet each other's sexual and dependency needs, and much more provides a model of male-female interaction and husband-wife intimacy that will surely affect the children's future relationships.

The parent-child subsystem teaches children about child-rearing; nurturance, guidance, limit setting, and socialization experiences are all crucial here. Through interaction with the parents, children learn to deal with people of greater authority, developing in the process a strengthened or weakened capacity for decision making and self-direction. Problems in this subsystem—serious intergenerational conflicts involving rebelliousness, symptomatic children, runaways, and so on— reflect underlying family disorganization or instability. The following case reflects dysfunctional behavior extending over several generations.

Jill Clemmons, now 40, had a history of unstable relationships with men. An only child, lonely and unhappy, she lived in poverty and on welfare with her mother, who was herself bitter at having been deserted by her husband a decade earlier. Finally feeling unable to bear the boredom and frustration of her life, Jill (with the tacit encouragement of her mother) ran off at 16 and married her high school boyfriend. Their marriage—stormy, without much affection or intimacy, filled with daily fighting—lasted several months before Jill met and moved in with Dave, an older single man of 40, whom Jill was sure would take care of her. Divorced at 17, she married Dave immediately. However, their marriage soon proved to be a nightmare: Dave was verbally and physically abusive and occasionally beat her severely, especially when he came home drunk. On some nights, he would bring home a man he had met at a bar, often insisting that Jill have sexual intercourse with the stranger while Dave watched. Jill finally managed to escape after 3 years, even though she had no place to go.

Drifting from one menial job to the next, Jill managed to survive and live a relatively uneventful life for several years. She dated on and off, and when she met Tom, at 27, she thought her life had finally turned around. He seemed intelligent, caring, and sensitive to her needs. They married after a brief time together, and for a while the relationship was the best Jill had ever known. They had two children together and seemed to be living a relatively tranquil and conventional existence for several years. Soon, however, Jill found herself feeling bored and restless because of having to stay home with her youngsters. She had few child-rearing skills—her mother had been such a poor model—and more and more Jill began to view the children as a burden. Correspondingly, as the children grew into adolescents, their conflicts with their parents (especially Jill) increased sharply. As well, Jill and Tom found less and less to do or talk about together; all they seemed to agree about was that something needed to be done about the children, although neither one knew exactly what. Neither had the ability or the experience to work out problems together, nor did they consider getting professional help.

Soon Tom and Jill realized that there was nothing to stay together for, and they separated. Nora, 16, and Tom, Jr., 14, remained with their father, and Jill moved to another state to "start life again." Nora found that she could not get along with her father and brother, and as her mother had earlier, she left home, ultimately finding her mother and moving in with her. Although she had considerable misgivings, Jill still believed she and her daughter could work things out. Not surprisingly, they could not, and within 4 months Nora had run away from home and begun living with a series of men in a nearby city, contacting her mother only in emergencies. Occasionally, when Jill was at work, her daughter would return to the house for some clothes, food, or whatever money she could find.

The parent-child subsystem, beginning with the wife's pregnancy, expands the boundaries of the previous husband-wife spousal subsystem. The arrival of children vastly complicates family life, particularly when a first child is involved. With subsequent children, as the family expands, the system multiplies in complexity. Alliances and coalitions—some along age lines, some by sex, some by personality characteristics or attitudes—may make an impact on the spousal subsystem, sometimes to the point of threatening its existence, as parents experience their own conflicts about growing up and taking responsibilities. The relatively sudden shift to child-related issues, as Nichols and Everett (1986) point out, may be especially taxing on young adults' marriages, challenging each spouse's own degree of individuation and dependency. A facilitating effect may result, consolidating their parenting efforts; on the other hand, some may retreat back into alliances with their own parents or perhaps move out of the marriage.

Siblings represent a child's first peer group. Through participation in this sibling subsystem, a child may develop patterns of negotiation, cooperation, competition, mutual support, and later attachment to friends. Interpersonal skills are honed here and, if successful, may develop further in school experiences and later in the workplace. Although the future impact of this subsystem is not always clearly discernible when the children are young, its influence on overall family functioning is to a great extent dependent on how viable the other subsystems are. Especially noteworthy for overall family functioning is the extent to which alliances and intergenerational coalitions exist in the family.

Other subsystems, most less durable than those just described, exist in all families. Father-daughter, mother-son, father-oldest son, mother-youngest child are only some of the common transitional alliances that can develop within a family group. The overdevelopment or protracted duration of any of these to the detriment of the spousal subsystem should signal to the counselor that instability and potential disorganization exist within the system.

Goldenberg (1977, pp. 350–351) offers an illustration of the possible impact of a father-daughter alliance on family functioning. In this case, the coalition between the two had destructive results for all family members.

Lisa Ash, a 5-foot, 260-pound, 13-year-old girl, was brought to a residential treatment center by a distraught mother, who complained that she couldn't control her daughter's eating habits and was alarmed about the danger to her health. Lisa, a junior high school student, was the oldest of three daughters in a lower-middle-class family. Both the father, a moderately successful shoe store owner, and his wife, a housewife, were overweight, as were various other uncles, aunts, and, to a lesser extent, Lisa's two younger sisters.

The mother-daughter conflict was evident from the intake interview. In particular, both agreed that they battled frequently over discipline or any restrictions imposed by Mrs. Ash on Lisa's eating behavior. Whenever this occurred, Lisa would lock herself in her room, wait for her father to come home, and then tell him how "cruel" the mother had been to her. Usually, without inquiring further or getting the mother's story, he would side with Lisa and countermand the mother's orders. Occasionally he would invite Lisa out for a pizza or other "snack."

Needless to say, the mother-father relationship was poor. They had not had sexual intercourse for several years, and Mrs. Ash assumed that her husband was impotent, although she was too embarrassed to ask him. She had become increasingly unhappy and had seen a psychiatric social worker a year earlier for several sessions, although then, as now, her husband refused to participate in counseling. He also

Mexican farm workers who had come to California illegally 50 years earlier, Emilio was no stranger to the services offered by the Department of Veterans Affairs, continuing to receive treatment for neurological damage suffered during wartime combat two decades earlier. As a result of his disability, he showed a significant loss of cognitive functioning, and he was irritable, easily perplexed, and given to explosive outbursts when thwarted. When he applied for counseling, he revealed that he was separated from his wife, Miguel's mother, and that he had physical custody of Miguel because, in his words, she was "emotionally unfit to be a mother."

The parents had been separated since Miguel, an only child, was 7, and Miguel visited his mother perhaps once every 2 or 3 months for the day, although she did not live very far away. Emilio offered no explanations as to why the mother, Maria, did not live with her husband and son, but Emilio made it clear that she was unavailable for family counseling. When the female student intern counselor pressed the point, indicating that the entire family should take part, Emilio revealed that Maria was a prescription drug addict, ingesting a variety of painkillers each day, and her behavior would be unpredictable and erratic, if indeed she appeared for the sessions at all. With Emilio's permission, the counselor telephoned Maria to invite her participation, but the woman refused, and in her notes the counselor indicated that Maria appeared confused, frightened, and anxious to end the telephone conversation.

Making an initial assessment based on what she had learned before actually seeing the pair, the student speculated that the father-son relationship seemed to be approaching a crisis stage and required immediate intervention. Consequently, she decided, in consultation with her supervisor, to see this dysfunctional pair without the mother; it was a less than ideal situation, but she hoped Maria might join the counseling at some later date. She reminded herself in her notes that she must remain aware of the possible relevance of the Mexican American background of the pair and in her ongoing assessment throughout counseling to try to ferret out the pair's strengths and the family's resources along with appraising their limitations and deficiencies.

It was clear from the first session that Miguel did not trust the counseling process. He appeared frightened of being exposed, and as a consequence tried to seize control of the situation by demanding that the counselor not take notes, that she not discuss the case with her supervisor, that the microphone (they were in a one-way mirrored room so the supervisor and other student interns could observe) be turned off, and so forth. He refused to offer any information about himself or their relationship, and when Emilio mentioned that Miguel was in individual counseling (as a result of what the father described as sexual molestation by one of Emilio's friends), the youngster, feeling further exposed, became furious and needed considerable comforting before he could continue.

Some glimpse of Miguel's upbringing did emerge during these meetings. It was apparent that he missed his mother and a family life, although Maria was apparently inconsistent in her child-rearing practices, unpredictably available and giving or distant and withdrawn. Miguel had learned to care for himself for long periods of time while his mother was not there, and as a consequence he was unaccustomed to being controlled or directed. Since his parents' separation (they had not divorced) five years earlier, Miguel had become increasingly undisciplined, and when his father had tried to impose some structure—homework time, a reasonable bedtime hour on school nights, cleaning his teeth and showering regularly, helping with the dishes—Miguel rebelled and did what he could to thwart and frustrate his father. The counselor recognized that this was not customary in most Mexican American homes, where the father is typically the esteemed head of the household, the disciplinarian, and the mother more nurturing and the caretaker and overseer of everyday family activities. Here Emilio, a single parent, was trying to be both mother and father to his son.

It was evident from the initial contact that Miguel was bright, resourceful, and desperately needed to structure his environment. He boasted of being tough, standing up to the older boys in the school, and of always being able to come up with the right answer in class so that the teacher did not realize he had not done his homework. A considerable amount of time during the early sessions was spent by Miguel urging his father to buy him some gadgets such as a cellular telephone. Emilio tried to respond, but he was often confused and seemed to become particularly enraged whenever he felt Miguel was "outsmarting" him. Nevertheless, his love for his son did emerge, as did the boy's affection for his father. Before the conclusion of the first session, Miguel reverted to being a little boy, clinging to his father and at one point climbing up on his lap for comforting.

Unhappy and unsuccessful at work, and with few friends, Emilio focused his effort on improving Miguel. He expressed considerable concern over what would become of his son, what he was doing wrong as a father, why Miguel did not see that his father was trying to direct him as best he could. His anger at Miguel appeared in part to reflect his underlying anger at Maria for her neglect as a mother, forcing Emilio to take on an unaccustomed single-parent role for which he felt unprepared. During the counseling sessions, he seemed to be looking to the female counselor for help in completing his family.

Having provided a bare-bones version of the basic relationship patterns in this case, let us assume the counselor adopts one of the approaches we are about to outline (see Table 4.1 on pages 86 and 87). How counselors choose to enter into the family system is usually determined by their theoretical training, personality, and counseling style, as well as the nature of the case. As you learn more about the theories and practices of some of the current models of family counseling, consider which is most appropriate for this family. What combination of theories and techniques would, in your opinion, be most successful?

The Experiential Model

Experiential approaches have as their major theme the humanistic notion of free choice and self-determination. Practitioners are apt to intervene actively in order to encourage clients to overcome those impasses that impede their personal and interpersonal fulfillment. This model is the least theory-bound of all the proposals we describe; advocates tailor their interventions very specifically to the unique conflicts and interpersonal patterns that obstruct or inhibit clients' growth-enhancing behavior.

Experientially oriented counselors focus on the present, the so-called here and now, as it unfolds from moment to moment in the therapeutic encounter between counselor and couple or family. Rather than offer insights or make interpretations, counselors actively provide clients with an opportunity—an encounter—in which both counselor and client seize the opportunity to open themselves to spontaneity and freedom of expression. Thus, as the name suggests, *the interpersonal experience is the primary stimulus for change.* The counselor acts as a facilitator, confronting clients to seek greater self-awareness of their immediate experiences, leading to choice, taking responsibility for actions, and ultimately change. In addition to addressing the ongoing family processes, counselors also direct attention to the separate, individual, subjective needs of each family member.

Virginia Satir (Satir, Banmen, Gerber, & Gomori, 1991) and Carl Whitaker (Whitaker & Bumberry, 1988), although very different in intervention style, represent the major architects of the experiential approach. Satir's **human validation model** and Whitaker's **symbolic-experiential model** both attempt to unlock suppressed feelings and impulses that block growth and fulfillment. Concerned with increasing the self-esteem of all the family members, Satir helped them learn to communicate more clearly, more directly, with greater clarity, more honestly and effectively. She often modeled clear and effective communication for her clients. Satir had a positive, health-oriented view of how best to capture people's potential, rather than searching for signs of their deficiencies or pathology. By establishing a safe therapeutic environment, she set the conditions by which clients could recognize and accept their feelings more fully, build self-esteem, and make better use of their inherent capabilities (Lawrence, 1999). Although the thrust of her therapeutic efforts were toward the future, Satir did attempt, when appropriate, to learn how a family's history imposed limitations on current functioning, all in the service of unlocking dysfunctional patterns stemming from families of origin.

Whitaker, more unorthodox and iconoclastic, helped family members give voice to their underlying impulses, at the same time that he himself searched for similar underlying impulses and symbols within his own fantasies. He attempted to dislodge rigid and repetitive ways of interacting by helping clients substitute more spontaneous and flexible ways of accepting and dealing with their impulses. He too attempted to depathologize human experiences, typically calling upon the personal, unconscious, and subterranean (symbolic) that determine the expression of impulses in each person. Both Satir and Whitaker paid special attention to the therapeutic **process**—what transpires during the family session— and how each participant uses the opportunity to reactivate any dormant but innate process so that it can grow.

Engaging the Alvarez family, an experiential counselor—part teacher, part coach, part challenger—would assume the family was emotionally "stuck"; family members need to learn to recognize their underlying feelings and to express what they are experiencing so that they can learn to function in a more collaborative and connected manner. To that end, the counselor would act to prompt more direct and honest communication between father and son. Recognizing Emilio's limitations and low self-esteem, the counselor would nevertheless encourage

Table 4.1 A comparison of major approaches to family counseling

General model	Major theme	Derivation model
Experiential	Free choice; self growth; self-determination; personal fulfillment	Human validation Symbolic-experiential
Transgenerational	Current problems arise from family relationship patterns extending over two or more generations	Family systems Contextual
Structural	Individual symptoms rooted in family transactional patterns	Structural
Strategic	Current problems maintained by ongoing, repetitive behavioral sequences between family members	Strategic MRI brief therapy
Milan	Dysfunctional families caught up in destructive "family games"	Systemic
Social Constructionist	Families use language to subjectively construct their views of reality and provide the basis for how they create "stories" about themselves	Solution-focused Narratives

Table 4.1   (*continued*)

Leading figures	Key theoretical concepts	Key interventions and goals
Satir	Self-esteem; clarity of communication	Building effective communication; overcoming blocks to personal growth
Whitaker	Symbolic factors represent family's inner world and determine meaning given external reality	Interpersonal encounter to develop openness, self-awareness, and spontaneity
Bowen	Fusion; differentiation of self; multigenerational transmission process	Genograms; increasing self-differentiation in individuals leads to family system changes
Boszormenyi-Nagy	Relational ethics; family ledger; obligations and entitlements	Examining and rebalancing family obligations; restoring trust, fairness, ethical responsibility
Minuchin	Boundaries, subsystems, coalitions, roles	Family mapping; joining family; reframing to change inflexible family structure
Haley, Madanes	Power issues; use of symptoms for controlling relationships while claiming it to be involuntary	Use of directives, including paradoxical interventions; devising strategies for symptom reduction or elimination
Watzlawick	Mishandling normal difficulties by imposing unworkable solutions becomes the problem	Learning new solutions through changes in family interaction patterns in place of repeating failed solutions
Selvini-Palazzoli, Boscolo, Cecchin, Prata	Circular nature of current problems; family following a set of rules or beliefs that does not fit its current reality	Positive connotation; circular questioning to transform family relationship patterns
deShazer	No fixed truths; multiple perspectives of reality; focus on expectations for change	Collaboratively designing situations with expectations for change
White	Problems redefined as external and oppressive	Rewriting problem-saturated assumptions about themselves; searching for unique outcomes in which solutions were achieved

Emilio to ask for what he wanted from Miguel and to listen to what his son needed from the relationship. Acting as a model of clear communication, the counselor would urge the clients to engage in straight talk about their living arrangement: what worked and didn't work for each, and how to give both more of what made each happy to be with the other, so that the relationship would flourish and there would be increased mutual respect.

Followers of Satir would pay special attention to the communication styles Emilio and Miguel had developed and would help them extinguish indirect, distorted, or inappropriate methods for dealing with each other. Active, provocative, confrontational, such counselors would try to help clients recognize and learn to accept the legitimacy of their feelings. Recognizing their need for, but fear of, closeness to each other, the goal would be to increase self-esteem in each participant, so that each would feel safe to express his true feelings in a direct manner. The ultimate goal would be to help the two eliminate destructive repetitive sequences and replace them with more growth-producing and fulfilling patterns as they learned to take charge of their lives, separately and together. Maria would be urged to attend at least one session (and preferably more) in order to enable the counselor to see the communication styles and relationship patterns that exist among these three people.

Whitaker's followers would advocate openness, spontaneity, and self-awareness, urging both Emilio and Miguel to experience feelings, expose vulnerabilities, share uncensored thoughts, and learn to be themselves. Recognizing Emilio and Miguel's unspoken ties to each other, the counselor would focus on the encounter taking place during the session, shaking up old dysfunctional ways of interacting and reactivating their dormant but innate individual processes of growth and connectedness. The mother would likely be invited in (perhaps in a consultative role if she insisted she did not want counseling) for one or more sessions so that unfinished issues between the three could begin to be resolved. For symbolic-experiential counselors, the particular technique chosen arises from the relationship the counselor and clients are able to create; their personal involvement and investment in the therapeutic process provide the key to developing individual autonomy along with a sense of belonging to a family.

The Transgenerational Model

Unlike the model just presented, advocates of the transgenerational model approach attend to family relational patterns in the past as a way of better grasping the origins of current functioning. Current problems are viewed as arising from both explicit interactional and behavioral patterns, and implicit, value-laden patterns formed gradually over generations, especially during periods of family upheaval, and passed along into current ongoing behavior if unresolved (Roberto, 1998). To understand an individual's present problems, it is necessary to comprehend the family's role as an emotional unit, its expectations and demands, and the degree to which each participant in an ongoing relationship feels tied or obligated to finish the business of earlier generations. Unresolved issues from earlier generations may be passed along and result in symptomatic behavior in later generations.

Two influential theory builders are key players here: Murray Bowen (1978) and Ivan Boszormenyi-Nagy (1987). Bowen offered an elaborate family theory, called the **family systems model,** that emphasizes the role of the family's emotional system, extending over several generations, in the etiology of individual dysfunction. (We describe in Chapter 3 Bowen's use of *genograms,* extending back at least three generations, worked out with families during early sessions, in an attempt to trace recurring behavior patterns.) Because Bowen viewed family members as tied in thinking, feeling, and behavior to the family's relationship system, he believed the key to personal maturity and well-being called for a balance between belonging to one's family and developing a sense of separateness and individuality. Bowen assumed this pattern of demarcation was transmitted from parents to children, but not to the same degree in each child. To gauge the degree to which such a **differentiation of self** occurs in a family member, Bowen sought to determine the extent to which that person was able to resist becoming overwhelmed by the emotional reactivity taking place in the family. Those less well able were considered by Bowen to have lost, in varying degrees, a separate sense of self in family relationships; individuals with the greatest **fusion** to the family's emotional system were most apt to experience dysfunction.

According to Bowen, severe dysfunction occurs after several generations as individuals who have not adequately differentiated themselves from their families of origin marry each other, their least well differentiated offspring marries someone of equally poor differentiation, and so forth. Bowen thought that this **multigenerational transmission process** results after several generations in a severe mental disorder in a family member or results in a seriously dysfunctional family. Working with families, Bowen might see individuals separately or work with a couple even if the presenting problem was difficulties with a child or adolescent. Emphasizing the importance of not becoming caught up in the family's emotional system, Bowen attempted to increase each individual's level of differentiation, assuming that such an achievement would ultimately change overreactive emotional interactions throughout the family and lead to greater self-differentiation among all nuclear family members.

Boszormenyi-Nagy's major concern is **relational ethics**: the overall long-term preservation of fairness within a family, ensuring that each member's basic interests are taken into account by other family members. His **contextual** model emphasizes how trust, loyalty, emotional indebtedness to one another, and entitlements are worked out in families over succeeding generations. Well-functioning families are characterized by an ability to negotiate imbalances and maintain a sense of fairness and accountability in relationships over generations. Families that fail to work out such a balance, according to Boszormenyi-Nagy, are burdened by lifelong feelings of indebtedness; he argues that symptoms may appear when trustworthiness and caring within a family break down.

Each family maintains a *family ledger*—a multigenerational accounting system that keeps track of what has been given and, psychologically speaking, who owes what to whom. Whenever perceived injustices occur, the expectation is that later repayment or restitution is due for the party undergoing the injustice. Problems may develop within families, according to Boszormenyi-Nagy, whenever justice is too slow or comes in too small an amount. Thus, dysfunctional behavior in an individual cannot be fully understood without looking at the history of the problem, particularly the transgenerational family ledger, and helping families examine unsettled or unredressed accounts. Family counseling efforts are directed at the family context—those dynamic and ethical interconnections and obligations, especially from the past—that bind families together. Essentially, the counselor guides family members as they work together on their relational commitments to one another in an effort to help rebalance obligations and settle old family accounts, all in the service of restoring trustworthiness and relational integrity in family relationships.

In the case of Emilio and Miguel, transgenerational counselors would look to the past and especially make note of family relationships extending over several generations. Bowenians would create a genogram with Emilio and Miguel's help; Miguel would be asked to get the information from his mother if she insisted on not participating. Together, counselor and clients might be helped to see patterns (such as previous generations of father-son transactions) that are being repeated, in an unfulfilling manner, in the current relationship. Followers of Bowen would look at the family emotional system, especially the fusion between the participants, and begin to work on creating a greater degree of differentiation of self between father and son so that underlying emotional currents would not sweep them up and lead to provocative, angry, and explosive behavior. Without becoming drawn into the father-son relationship, the counselor in this case would make an effort to reduce the emotional intensity of their interactions and help them develop a more stable and less provocative way of dealing with each other. Heavy emphasis is placed on replacing emotional flooding with reason and intellect, in the service of family members' learning to take "I" positions that characterize differentiated persons.

Followers of Boszormenyi-Nagy's contextual approach contend that what holds relationships together is reciprocal trust (Ulrich, 1998). Consequently, counselors would direct their attention to the family ledger, especially each participant's subjective sense of claims, rights, and obligations to each other, in an effort to resolve conflict and establish a trusting father-son relationship. They would attend to the give and take between Emilio and Miguel, how they balance rights and responsibilities to each other, and what each thought he had the right to expect from the other. Unresolved problems from the past—who owes what to whom—would be examined, including the bitterness and resentments Miguel and Emilio continue to harbor about Maria. Maria would be encouraged to attend in order to clear past obligations and entitlements she felt, including her feelings of loss of family. Building on their sense of caring about one another, all three would be taught to negotiate differences that left each feeling that differences had been resolved fairly and equitably. Learning to trust one another, the three could be more forthright and honest, and more openly discuss claims and obligations each felt in regard to the others. In the case of Emilio and Miguel, there were clearly a number of unsettled accounts: what relationship existed with the mother and why it was a taboo topic; what had actually happened in the alleged sexual abuse; whether there had been any history of sexual abuse in previous generations; what individual each family member held accountable for the event; what secrets each kept from the other (reasons for the mother's drug use, father's medical condition); each person's sense of entitlement as well as indebtedness; and so on. All these topics would require exploration by the three together. The goal would be to restore a fairer and more responsible way for the family members to deal with one another.

The Structural Model

Structural approaches attend primarily to the arrangements, usually not explicitly stated or even overtly recognized or acknowledged, that each family makes to govern family transactions. Structuralists are especially interested in these transactional patterns because they offer clues about how the family organizes itself—its subsystems, boundaries, alignments, coalitions, and so on, which affect the family's ability to achieve a balance between stability and change (see Chapter 2). When ongoing transactional patterns are maintained by an inflexible family structure—for example, an internal organization with excessively diffuse (enmeshed) or rigid (disengaged) boundaries—the family may have trouble dealing with the necessary transitions members must make throughout the family's life cycle in response to changing circumstances. Such dysfunctional structures point to the covert rules governing family transactions that have become inoperable or in need of renegotiation.

Structuralists assess families throughout the counseling in order to identify areas of dysfunction as well as possible avenues for change. More specifically, they attempt to gain an understanding of subsystems, boundaries, the family hierarchy, alignments and coalitions, and the family's adaptability or ability to reorganize in response to changing needs (Kemenoff, Jachimczyk, & Fussner, 1999). Family mapping (see Chapter 3) helps the counselor better understand the family's transactional patterns, whether boundaries are too rigid or diffuse, and which subsystems are especially in need of restructuring.

Symptoms in any family member are rooted in the context of current family transactional patterns. All family members are seen by structuralists as "symptomatic," despite family efforts to locate the problem in the identified patient. Particular attention is directed to the family's hierarchical structure: how husband and wife play out their roles. In dysfunctional families, restructuring must occur—with transactional rules modified, more appropriate boundaries created, new interactive patterns tried out, and alternative problem-solving methods attempted—before symptoms are relieved. Freeing family members from stereotyped roles helps the family mobilize its inherent resources and improve its resiliency in the face of inevitable changes.

Led initially by Salvador Minuchin (1974), structuralists attempt to "join" a family (to enter the system by engaging separate members and subsystems) and to map and accommodate to the family's style, gaining access in order to explore and ultimately help modify dysfunctional aspects of the family system. Active, directive, carefully calculated, their interventions are aimed at replacing rigid, outmoded, or unworkable structures with more flexible ones that call for a rearrangement or realignment of the family organization. The ultimate goal is to restructure the family's transactional rules by developing clearer and more appropriate boundaries between subsystems and by strengthening the family's hierarchical order in which the husband and wife remain leaders of the family but allow children increasing freedom as they develop and mature.

Working structurally with Emilio and Miguel, the counselor would try to redefine the problem as transactional, rather than Emilio's not understanding how to be an up-to-date father (Miguel's position) or Miguel's misbehaving and inability to be trusted (Emilio's position). The counselor might reframe Emilio's behavior to his son in a more positive light ("Your father is not being a pest, but wants to be involved with you"). Similarly, the father might be told, "Miguel is not just being rebellious, but is practicing taking care of himself." Such counselor efforts often help change the context in which the other person's behavior is viewed, inviting a new response to the same behavior.

Joining the family system and accommodating to its interactive style, the counselor might probe current undiscussed family rules: what occurs between Miguel and Emilio in the evening and on weekends, what happens at school and how homework is handled, what role the missing mother plays in their relationship, and so on. Is she really unavailable, or have the pair aligned against her? Miguel's entering adolescence would be examined, with the idea of testing the system's flexibility to adapt to change and transitions. Emilio's role as parent would be strengthened, in the service of establishing some more effective hierarchy in regard to his son. Miguel's changing role in the family would be better outlined, and the father-son behavioral patterns reorganized to become more satisfactory to both. In this approach, the counselor would not work specifically on the presenting problem (intergenerational conflict) but would seek to map and then modify the family structure, clarify family boundary issues, and help family members adapt to changing demands as Miguel enters adolescence.

The structurally oriented counselor might encourage the two clients to enact their conflict during the session so that they could demonstrate how they deal with a problem (say, a dispute over a video that Miguel wanted and Emilio refused to rent). Observing the sequence, the counselor could begin to map out a way of modifying their interaction and creating structural changes. In the same way, the counselor might continue to reframe the meaning of a troublesome interactive pattern, providing a new and more constructive context in which an equally plausible explanation is possible (for example, that Emilio cares about Miguel and wants to know his whereabouts after school, rather than that Emilio doesn't trust Miguel and wants to control his life). Released from outmoded roles and functions, Emilio and Miguel could begin to mobilize their resources and together learn to cope better with stress. At that point, they could come to grips with Maria's place in the Alvarez family. Must there be a closed boundary between her and the two male members of the family? Would she be willing to attend a session so the counselor could map how all three interact?

Strategic Models

Using strategic models, based on the early work in communication theory at the Mental Research Institute (MRI) in Palo Alto, California, counselors devise a strategy for change to eliminate the symptom that prompted the family to seek help. Focusing on the present and assuming that current problems are maintained by ongoing, repetitive behavioral sequences among family members, strategists treat presenting symptoms as a solution to a problem (rather than an expression of some hidden, underlying "real" problem) and go about designing a plan for its extinction. In a sense, strategists take the positive position that problems within a family often represent "love gone wrong"; that is, problems may be expressions of protective efforts to help one another that have failed (Keim, 1999).

Strategists pride themselves on using an approach that is pragmatic, brief, and focused on providing solutions and evoking behavioral change rather than providing insights or offering interpretations. Jay Haley (1976, 1984) and Cloe Madanes (1991), major advocates of the strategic approach, are especially interested in power issues within a family and how members seek control of relationships. In their view, symptoms are not beyond a "victim's" control, but actually represent a strategy for controlling a relationship at the same time as the symptom is claimed to be involuntary. Typically, strategists view problems as involving at least three participants (often two ganging up on the third).

More interested in devising strategic interventions than developing a theory of family pathology, strategists seek to eliminate symptoms through a series of counselor-designed directives. Advice, direct suggestions, coaching, and homework assignments are examples of straightforward directives. Sometimes, alternatively, directives are issued in order to provoke defiance in the family. In effect, these **paradoxical interventions** (for example, "continue to remain depressed") ask for no change for the time being. Tailored to a specific situation or specific symptom, these indirect directives are intended to place clients in a double bind. On the one hand, to obey the directive is to acknowledge voluntary control over the symptom (despite the client's claim that the symptom is involuntary); the client can no longer claim helplessness in changing his or her depressed behavior. On the other hand, to disobey the injunction to remain depressed is to give up control to the counselor. Either way, the counselor has maneuvered the client into eliminating the problem.

Paul Watzlawick and his associates (Watzlawick, Weakland, & Fisch, 1974) at the Palo Alto MRI operate a Brief Therapy Project in which they use a series of systems-based techniques to help clients quickly overcome problems by learning new solutions rather than repeating self-perpetuating, self-defeating attempts at problem resolution that proffer "more of the same" in an endless fashion. These counselors contend that most human problems develop because people have mishandled some of life's normal difficulties and continue to apply the same inappropriate solution over and over despite evidence of its unworkability. By restraining people from repeating the same unsuccessful solution, and by altering the system to produce change, the counselor is able to help the family break out of a destructive or dysfunctional cycle of behavior.

The counselor with a strategic orientation would ask what problem needed to be addressed (perhaps "our constant fighting and tension with each other"), would determine who is involved in the problem and in what way, and then would devise a plan of action for changing the dysfunctional situation and dissatisfied roles in order to eliminate the presenting problem. In particular, the circular nature of the interactive patterns between Emilio and Miguel would be explored, not to provide insight but rather to alert the counselor to the repetitive sequences and patterns in which the two engage. How they communicate (angrily), the nature of the roles and hierarchy they have developed (father often led by son), how each wields power (the father through explosive threats, the son through cagily maneuvering people), what they repeatedly quarrel most about (homework completion)—all these are noted in exploring what behavioral sequences are problematic and need changing. Along the way, the counselor might investigate the solutions (threats from the father, manipulations from the son) the two had tried in the past, assuming the failed efforts have only worsened the relationship.[1]

Because parents and children often develop problems at transitional points in their relationship (such as the beginning of a child's adolescence), strategists, responsible for initiating change, would likely introduce directives to help navigate this transitional period successfully. Careful to gain family members' trust, the counselor would offer a strategy for solving the presenting problem without necessarily revealing why. A straightforward directive—an assignment of a task to be performed outside of the counseling session—is issued in order to get family members to behave differently ("Emilio should go over Miguel's homework each evening before turning on the television set"). If unsuccessful, especially if the two of them resist change, the strategist might try a paradoxical directive ("Instead of doing homework, Miguel and Emilio should argue every evening for 30 minutes before watching television"). Issued by an authority, the counselor, the latter places the two family members in a therapeutic double bind, a no-lose situation in which a positive outcome results no matter what they do (to argue each night will result in their recognizing the futility of such behavior and ultimately ending the pattern; to defy the directive and avoid arguing is to learn to get along better and spend time in more productive activities such as completing homework). Paradoxical interventions, used judiciously, are tailored to a family's resistance to change and represent a way of maneuvering a family into abandoning outmoded and dysfunctional behavior.

Finally, the father-mother-son triangle would be examined, preferably with Maria participating. (She might be asked to come in because her son needs her help.) All play a part in how the problem has evolved, and all must participate in its resolution.

---

[1] Keim (1999) contends that oppositional behavior often involves children who wish their parent(s) would act more parental and parents who wish their children would act more childlike. That is, parents want the children to be more accepting of both their authority and affection, while children wish their parents to be more empathic and effective in making them feel more secure.

The Milan Model

This increasingly popular approach, developed by Selvini-Palazzoli, Boscolo, Cecchin, and Prata (1978) in Milan, Italy, represents an extension of some of the strategic techniques just described. As originally formulated, the Milan group set out to decode the rules of a family's "games": the tactics by which the members struggle against one another while together perpetuating unacknowledged inter- actions in order to control one another's behavior. What appeared to be paradox- ical is that although the family presumably sought counseling in order to change, family members nevertheless continued to behave in ways that prevented any changes from occurring. To counteract these continual "games" that define and sustain family relationships, the Milan group proposed a set of counterparadoxi- cal interventions, placing the family in a therapeutic double-bind in order to counteract the members' paradoxical interactions.

Today, the original Milan associates have split into two autonomous groups (Selvini-Palazzoli and Prata, Boscolo and Cecchin) that pursue different emphases while maintaining a systemic outlook. Selvini-Palazzoli, with a new group of col- leagues (Selvini-Palazzoli, Cirillo, Selvini, & Sorrentino, 1989), continues to explore family games, offering a single, sustained, and invariant intervention in order to break up the game. Boscolo and Cecchin (Boscolo, Cecchin, Hoffman, & Penn, 1987) have attempted to expand on early cybernetic ideas, especially how the counselor becomes part of, and a participant in, that which is being observed. This second-order cybernetic notion—that the problem does not exist independ- ently of observers who collectively define it as a problem—has had a profound effect on postmodern (sometimes called post-Milan) thinking, as described in the next section.

The Milan group developed several key intervention techniques. **Positive con- notation** is a form of reframing in which symptomatic behavior is presented to the family as positive or good because it helps to maintain the system's balance. Behavior formerly looked upon as negative ("Our son refuses to go to school") is reframed by the counselor as positive ("He wants to remain at home to provide companionship for his lonely father") so that the symptomatic child is depicted as having good intentions. It is not the behavior (school refusal) that is viewed as positive, but rather the intent behind the behavior (to help maintain family cohe- sion). Redefining the problem (the symptomatic behavior) as voluntary and well intentioned, the other members are prepared to cooperate to achieve the same result—family cohesion—enhancing the possibilities for changes in the family's interactive patterns.

Circular questioning frames every question to the family so that it addresses differences in perception by different family members about the same event or situation: "Who gets more upset when your sister refuses to eat, your mother or father?" "On a scale of 1 to 10, how would you rate the expression of anger in the family this week?" Asking each member the same question about his or her atti- tude toward the same relationship forces every member to focus on differences in perception without the family members having to directly confront one another.

Beyond providing a useful and nonthreatening tool for gathering information, circular questioning aids the process by which the family starts to view itself systemically, an essential step in recognizing that they must change their interactive patterns in order to become a more functional unit. Thus, circular questioning—neutral, nonjudgmental, accepting of current functioning—may in itself trigger major changes in the thinking of each family member as each hears of the others' perceptions of the same event (Prevatt, 1999).

Returning to Emilio and Miguel, the counselor with a Milan emphasis might hypothesize that the two are caught in a mutually provocative and mutually destructive interactive pattern. Checking out the hypothesis, revising it if necessary, the counselor would carefully introduce positive connotation statements regarding the problematic behavior. For example, the counselor might reframe both parties' provocative behavior as intended to achieve a good result—family cohesion or harmony—not to hurt or punish each other. Maintaining neutrality, but actively questioning the participants, the curious counselor might inquire who enjoys quarreling more and what would each miss if the quarreling ceased. By asking thought-provoking, relationship-focused, circular questions, the counselor might help Emilio and Miguel reconsider assumptions each had made about the other's motives and behavior—or the motives each had assigned to Maria. Here the interventions, supportive in nature, are directed at introducing the idea that together, father and son could redefine their relationship and recognize that they are capable of achieving a different way of dealing with each other. Viewing Maria from a new perspective, they together might make inviting gestures intended to include her in future family relationships.

Social Constructionist Models

Postmodern social constructionist views challenge the assumption that a fixed truth or reality exists and that an outside observer can objectively discover it. Instead, these theorists contend that knowledge is relative and depends on the context of which it is a part. Postmodernists argue that our belief systems merely reflect social constructions or points of view that we make about the world. In their view, there is no "true" reality, only a collectively agreed-upon set of constructions that we call reality. Working collaboratively and in a nonhierarchical way with families, the social constructionist is less an expert on how the system should change than a part of the system with a viewpoint, just like all other members. In other words, the counselor is not objective, but rather inevitably makes assumptions (about what constitutes a functional family, a good marriage, good child-rearing practices, and so on) just as each family member does. Together, counselor and family members hold conversations in which they examine the beliefs and assumptions of each participant regarding the family's problems, acknowledging that no single participant has a monopoly on truth or objectivity. In particular, the counselor is interested in learning what shared set of premises a family attaches to a problem that perpetuates the family's behavior. By examining the "stories" about themselves that families live by, counselor and family members search together for new, empowering ways of viewing and resolving client problems (Goldenberg & Goldenberg, 2000).

Rather than focus on family interactive behavior patterns, counselors with a social constructionist outlook help families examine the assumptions or premises that different family members hold about a problem. Since most of our assumptions about the world arise through conversations with others, these counselors concern themselves especially with language and the meaning people give to events. Engaging families in conversation, counselors help members rethink entrenched beliefs (what they consider to be the unchangeable "truth" about themselves) that account to themselves for how they have lived their lives. Ultimately, counselor and clients together empower the family to recast their stories (or "restory") and actively redirect their lives.

Two outstanding examples of such efforts come from Steve deShazer (1991) and Michael White (1989); the former offers a **solution-focused model,** and the latter concerns himself with family **narratives.** The solution-focused counselor listens to the language families use to describe their situation and then begins from the first session to focus on change by discussing solutions they wish to construct together with the counselor. Without attempting to ferret out why or how a particular problem arose, the counselor aids the family in discovering their own creative solutions for becoming "unstuck." DeShazer describes this approach as providing the family with "skeleton keys": interventions that work for a variety of situations and dilemmas that people find themselves in, not necessarily offering a perfect fit for the particular family's presenting problem. Participants are encouraged to deconstruct a problem by looking for the exceptions to the rule—occasions when they were able to control the problem or keep it from occurring. With the focus on change, skeleton key interventions are intended to disrupt problem-maintaining behavior patterns, change outmoded family beliefs, and amplify exceptions to behavior previously thought of by family members as unchangeable.

From the start, solution-focused counselors would emphasize that changes can be expected and would work collaboratively with Emilio and Miguel to achieve those changes. Unconcerned with explanations for why their problems with each other developed, the counselor would emphasize constructing solutions for the future. They might be asked to describe exceptions—times when they got along well—to help them overcome the idea that conflict between them was inevitable. Perhaps they would be asked to speculate on how their relationship would be different under these circumstances. Small changes would be encouraged, especially those that are self-generated and help the father-son pair believe they have the power to change their relationship patterns.

Michael White helps families externalize a problem (such as anorexia in an adolescent) by redefining it as an objectified external tyrant that family members are encouraged to unite against in combat. Offering a nonpathological view of any symptom, so that no one is to blame, he provides the family with an empowering opportunity to co-construct with the counselor a new narrative that emphasizes an alternative account of their lives. Here the counselor is both deconstructing the history of the problem that has shaped the family's lives and helping the family reconstruct or reauthor a preferred story that reflects their preferred way of being. As does deShazer, White asks clients to look for unique outcomes—experiences they have had that contradict their problem-dominated story about themselves. As they develop new stories about themselves, they are encouraged to engage in new behavior consistent with these alternative stories.

For example, White might encourage Emilio and Miguel to examine the stories they have told themselves about the family (Maria's unavailability, Emilio's failure as a single parent, Miguel's inability to cooperate with both parents) and how these internalized narratives, assumed to be unchangeable, have shaped their lives and given them a self-defeating outlook about the future. Instead, each would be encouraged to think about how things could be, and to construct ways together that help both realize their dreams. Miguel might be encouraged to have a more consistent relationship with his mother—regular visits, telephone conversations, invitations to attend school programs. Those unique outcomes, when things went well, would be emphasized, helping all three family members discover neglected aspects of themselves. Ultimately, they would be encouraged to replace blaming one another with behavior consistent with these alternate stories.

Summary

While various theories of family counseling tend to emphasize their uniqueness, in practice all are likely to incorporate certain core techniques based largely on systems theory. For pedagogical purposes, however, this chapter presents a family case history and proceeds to outline some likely ways each of six theoretical positions might address the presenting problem. *Experiential models,* based loosely on the humanistic notion of free choice and self-determination, focus on the ongoing encounter between counselor and family, providing an interpersonal experience that is the primary stimulus for change. *Transgenerational models* look to the past, seeking through the generations family role patterns that, unresolved, continue to impose themselves on current family functioning.

Structural models search for a family's current transactional patterns as a way of modifying a family structure that is having difficulty making the transitions called for as the family proceeds through its life cycle.

Strategic models, assuming current problems are maintained by ongoing, repetitive behavioral sequences between family members, call for an active counselor to devise a strategy for change, in order to eliminate the symptoms or problems that led the family to seek help.

In the *Milan model,* the counselor attempts to decode the rules of the "family games" that define the relationships between members; by using a series of interview techniques, the family is helped to view itself systemically, the first step in taking responsibility together to become a more functional unit.

Social constructionist models insist there is no "true" reality. The focus is on each family member's perception of the problem and its meaning, to the end of "restorying" the family's lives and giving them new directions.

Intervening in Troubled Couple and Family Relationships

A counselor's choice of intervention technique is likely to be influenced by several considerations: theoretical orientation, the nature of the presenting problem, the counselor's personal style, whether brief or longer-term counseling is anticipated, the expected frequency of counseling, the setting, reimbursement considerations, the possible need for medication, and so forth. More likely than not, as we noted in the previous chapter, today's counselor is apt to adopt an eclectic approach, combining discrete parts of theories and treatment methods into a fuller and more inclusive approach with clients. Having decided that intervention at the family level is the treatment of choice, the counselor must determine what members of the family are available, and whether all or a combination will be seen together for specific sessions.

Evidence-Supported Guidelines: The Use of Treatment Manuals

Despite the growing popularity of eclecticism, which is pragmatic and based upon clinical experiences, there is a parallel movement, developed as a result of research into the counseling process, calling for pure-form manual-based treatment. As society's demands for accountability from its professionals has increased in recent years (Nathan, 1998), some counselors have turned to treatment manuals

(Luborsky & DeRubeis, 1984) that represent empirically supported practice guidelines based on controlled clinical trials, leading to a standardized approach to counseling. These "how to do it" manuals, still few in number, address the issue of *specificity*—what approach works best with what clients or what set of problems. That is, manuals provide an operational definition of a particular treatment, providing instructions for how to carry out the treatment in a standard manner. They result from studies that identify treatments shown to be efficacious in controlled research with a delineated population (Chambless & Hollon, 1998) and, on the surface, would hardly seem to be controversial.

Indeed, empirically supported treatment efforts, and their resulting treatment manuals, have received particularly enthusiastic support from health care policymakers who wish to establish the legitimacy of counseling and psychotherapy, and from third-party payers (managed care groups) that need to be convinced of the demonstrable utility of these procedures before approving reimbursement for the services (Addis, 1997). Advocates (Addis, 1997; Addis, Wade, & Hatgis, 1999) contend that prior to their availability, little could be said about which procedure worked most efficiently with which set of client conditions. Their current dissemination reflects research-based efforts to establish accountability and promote empirically validated procedures to practicing counselors. Since publication, some have paved the way for statements regarding the efficacy of certain treatments, such as the cognitive treatment of depression (Beck, Rush, Shaw, & Emery, 1979).[1]

However, their relevance to real-life clinical situations—where numerous factors cannot be controlled as easily as in a laboratory study—remains controversial. Some critics argue that researchers and practitioners have different (and often incompatible) objectives—the former are interested primarily in generalizations by studying samples, while clinicians must focus their attention on individual clients—so that results from the former do not translate well into the practices of the latter. Some counselors are likely to be resistant to a "cookbook . . . paint by-the-numbers approach" (Silverman, 1996), feeling stifled and uncomfortably restricted with particular clients or problems; they are apt to feel that the use of manuals compromises the therapeutic relationship by overemphasizing technique at the expense of authenticity in the counselor-client relationship. Eclectic clinicians may insist on maintaining flexibility, being innovative, and using their experienced-based clinical judgment in treatment planning; they fear being straitjacketed by the confines of treatment manuals (Goldfried & Wolfe, 1996).

---

[1] The American Psychological Association Task Force (1995), surveying empirically supported psychological treatments, identified three categories of treatment efficacy: well-established treatments, probably efficacious treatments, and experimental treatments (not yet established). The task force found 22 well-established treatments for 21 *Diagnostic and Statistical Manual of Mental Disorders* (DSM-IV) syndromes and 7 probably efficacious treatments for the same number of disorders. Most were behavioral in theoretical orientation, not surprising since behavioral treatment targets specific behavior changes. Garfield (1996), a critic of the report, argues that its conclusions emphasizing validated therapies for specific conditions imply more knowledge of what causes change than is warranted by the current state of research.

They are likely to conclude that while practice guidelines may be necessary, empirically supported treatments are no substitute for on-the-spot clinical decision making in real-world clinical settings.

Despite these concerns, counselors face increasing pressure from outside forces (insurance panels, case reviewers, HMO administrators) to account for why they are treating particular clients, why they have chosen certain interventions in doing so, and whether such choices can be justified economically in terms of outcomes (Addis, Wade, & Hatgis, 1999). Happy with the prospect or not, more and more counselors are being forced to respond to today's economic and political realities, adopting practice guidelines and monitoring outcome results. Advocates insist the new guidelines will lead to a more scientifically defensible approach and will stimulate further research in refining which counseling procedures work best for which sets of presenting problems.

Tailoring Techniques to Couples and Families

"What treatment, by whom, is most effective for this individual, with that specific problem and under which set of circumstances?" This question, first asked by Gordon Paul (1967, p. 111) over 30 years ago, has challenged counselors to develop intervention procedures backed up by empirically supported evidence. The overall lack of progress in answering this question suggests that it poses a formidable, if not a daunting, task for researchers with individual clients and is even more complex and intimidating for researchers in family counseling. As we have just pointed out, one encouraging effort has been the efficacy studies[2] of specific techniques with specific populations under controlled conditions, although demonstrations of their effectiveness in real-life clinical situations has been slow in gaining acceptance among many counselors.

Providing more effective and cost-efficient treatment has led to the development of matching and tailoring techniques for individual clients as well as for families (Carlson, Sperry, & Lewis, 1997). Here, *matching* refers to deciding on a particular therapeutic approach (for example, structural) or modality (for example, couple rather than individual) in planning counseling, in order to increase the likelihood of success. Once matching has occurred, *tailoring,* adjusted as counseling progresses, involves flexibly using techniques after a client-counselor relationship has been established, in an effort to enhance the therapeutic alliance

---

[2] *Efficacy studies* are typically conducted under controlled or laboratory conditions and strive to approximate ideal experimental circumstances: Clients are assigned randomly to treatment or no-treatment groups, treatment manuals define the primary procedures, counselors receive training and supervision to ensure standardization of interventions, multiple outcome criteria are designed, and independent evaluators (rather than the counselor or clients) measure outcomes (Pinsof & Wynne, 1995). *Effectiveness studies* are conducted in the field, under customary consultation room conditions. While most research to date is of the efficacy kind, there is some movement, encouraged by National Institute of Mental Health funding, to investigate effectiveness in real-world settings (for example, comparing the results of alternate interventions in terms of their costs as well as their effects), especially pertinent in the age of greater scrutiny of health care expenditures (Goldenberg & Goldenberg, 2000).

and create an atmosphere in which suggestions or directives are most likely to be followed. Worthington (1992) suggests the following analogy between matching and tailoring: The difference is like that between choosing an appropriate suit off the rack and altering the suit to fit the individual. In a nutshell, tailoring is a client- or couple-centered (rather than theory-driven) orientation to treatment planning and intervention.

Sperry (1992) notes that the increasing number of nontraditional couple and family arrangements today require more individualized and "tailored" interventions. The goal here is to select a set of procedures that best fits the couple or family in order to improve the probability that they will benefit from the intervention.

At least three possibilities for tailoring present themselves:

- Tailoring according to client or family diagnosis (Frances, Clarkin, & Perry, 1984)
- Tailoring according to family members' level of relational conflict (Guerin, Fay, Burden, & Kautto, 1987)
- Tailoring according to a couple or family's level of functioning as a system (Weltner, 1992)

Tailoring by Diagnosis

As an example of linking diagnosis to treatment, Frances, Clarkin, and Perry (1984) propose the notion of differential therapeutics, tailoring treatment strategies to the latest DSM diagnostic categories. Perry, Frances, and Clarkin (1990) suggest that the counselor attend to five axes in determining the best approach for clients:

- setting (inpatient, outpatient, partial hospitalization)
- format (individual, couple, family, group)
- treatment methods (supportive, psychoeducational, and so on)
- duration and frequency of treatment
- need for somatic treatment (such as medication and electroshock)

These authors match these five factors to the client's diagnosis, systematically studying which combinations best fit persons with which diagnosis and offering guidelines for how to make the most effective tailoring decision. This tailoring effort is especially cognizant of the time limit imposed by third-party payers and recognizes the need for accountability and a treatment plan. As such, it is sharply focused and rejects the more traditional therapeutic approach of using a single technique with all clients, regardless of presenting problems, behavior patterns, the separate personalities of individual members, or diagnosis.

Tailoring by Level of Relational Conflict

Another sensible effort at tailoring focuses on family conflict, assuming, for example, that different couples express their marital conflict in different ways, struggle over different issues with different degrees of intensity, and have been involved in such struggles for differing lengths of time. Obviously, a "one size fits all" counseling approach fails to deal adequately with the nuances that often distinguish successful from unsuccessful counseling in such cases. Guerin, Fay, Burden, and Kautto (1987), who are Bowenian in orientation, propose that intervention plans pay particular attention to the intensity and duration of the marital conflict in treatment planning. More specifically, they contend that couples seeking counseling can be differentiated in terms of four stages of marital discord. Careful evaluation, according to specific behavioral indices, is followed by a tailor-made therapeutic plan in which a combination of approaches is offered, depending on the stage of conflict. According to this analysis, the stages of marital discord are as follows:

Stage 1 couples are likely to be married a short time and to have a minimal level of conflict of relatively short duration, probably less than six months. Information on how marriage works, following Bowen's ideas primarily (for example, self-differentiation) is presented in a group format and usually covers typical problems encountered early in a marital relationship. Counseling at this level is essentially psychoeducational.

Stage 2 couples display more serious unrest; however, despite conflict lasting more than six months, they are still able to communicate openly, even if that communication is filled with criticism and projection onto the other partner. Intervention here is directed at lowering emotional arousal, decreasing fusion, and increasing each partner's sense of self, reducing their conflict in the process.

Stage 3 couples have been struggling for a long time (usually longer than six months) without resolving their conflicts, so communication, except for blame and sharp criticism, is by and large closed off. Intervention efforts here—often of limited success because the couple has lost much resiliency—are likely to focus on raising each partner's threshold for emotional arousal, reducing the couple's reactivity. Couples at this level may be unresponsive to counseling beyond its early stages.

Stage 4 couples are no longer able or willing to communicate with each other, fearing that self-disclosure will inevitably lead to further criticism and blame from the partner. By the time a couple reaches this last stage, it is likely that one or both spouses has consulted an attorney to end the marriage, and counseling is typically directed at diminishing further damage to the soon-to-be ex-partners, their children, and extended family members. Remaining adversarial, the couple is likely facing a marriage about to dissolve.

Tailoring by Level of Family Functioning

Weltner (1992) first addresses a family's level of functioning as a system, before offering a corresponding set of intervention techniques for each of three designated levels. He argues that effective intervention calls for the counselor to assess the couple's or family's basic functioning level before planning interventions. The techniques then chosen are likely to combine procedures from various approaches tailored to the clients' specific functioning level. Note here that the counselor must be proficient in a variety of available counseling procedures to choose those that together match the level of the couple's or family's requirements.

In Weltner's (1992) typology, three levels are differentiated:

Level I families are viewed as fragmented and underorganized, their lack of parental competence so severe that they have difficulties managing basic survival tasks (food, medical care, protection of children). Here the counselor may have to act as family advocate and help mobilize the support of outside agencies in order to offer effective help and support (for example, to an overwhelmed single parent) for such problems as alcoholism, drug abuse, or an acting-out adolescent.

Level II families are rigid and idiosyncratic, filled with self-defeating behavior poorly suited to dealing with the realities of their lives. Unlike Level I families, in which a lack of socialization patterns is the rule, Level II families have such skills, but they apply these skills inflexibly and inappropriately. They may be living out multigenerational patterns of behavior and loyalties that no longer fit their current existence. Counseling is apt to be directed at helping Level II families look at their stuck interactions and create new constructions regarding their future options.

Level III families who seek counseling—a smaller group than the previous two—tend to be well organized and are likely to be free from the rigid hold of past irrational loyalties and beliefs. If they seek the help of a counselor, it is likely because they wish to improve the quality of their lives or are experiencing a temporary developmental glitch. Marital and family enrichment experiences are appropriate techniques for such families.

Table 5.1 on page 105 describes the criteria used by Weltner (1992) to determine the family's functioning level. Since the same counseling approach hardly fits families from all of these levels, he has devised a continuum that differentiates three therapeutic stances. As indicated in Table 5.2 on page 106, the *take-charge counselor* views the family as impaired and desirous of help, and not likely to resist direct intervention by the counselor. Taking charge, the counselor uses his or her personal authority to help restructure the family, attempting to organize and build an executive system of family leadership that should result in more adaptive behavior. This approach is especially tailored to Level I families.

The *chief investigator counselor,* most appropriate in dealing with Level II families, helps clients understand their misperceptions, unrealistic expectations, and behavior patterns that are not in their best self-interest. Providing insight and using a set of therapeutic techniques that increases awareness of self-limiting thought patterns and self-defeating interactions, the chief investigator helps families move beyond the "stuckness" of the past.

The *fellow traveler counselor,* most appropriate for Level III families, believes the family has the capacity for self-healing. The fellow traveler thus acts as a facilitator to help the family access their self-wisdom.

Table 5.1   Criteria for determining level of pathology

	Level I	Level II	Level III
Issue	Executive capacity (ego) overwhelmed Cannot nurture Cannot contain	Messing up due to old family beliefs and mandates Faulty expectations (boundary problems)	Preoccupied with issues of meaning or quality of life Existential dilemmas
Boundaries	Who cares?	Achieve generational and personal boundaries	Already mastered
Resistance	No	Yes	No
Strategy	Build a new organization (support the shaky ego) Enlarge the executive system Build a containing coalition	Find alternate ways to view reality Help clients to unstick themselves from old patterns and loyalties	Bypass ordinary ways of thinking Access an inner wisdom, the underground stream

Source: Weltner, 1992.

A common goal of all tailoring procedures, which have only recently begun to be applied to marital and family problems, is to avoid mismatching clients and counselors. Because many counselors have one strong suit that they offer all clients, mismatching is likely unless a schema such as we have described in this section is developed for guiding counselor interventions. Because matching and tailoring are at an early stage of development, procedures must be developed for dealing with very complex variables: the counselor's personality, the clients' personalities, lifestyle differences, individual psychopathology, demographic and cultural factors, and many more. While the tailoring approach offers a promising beginning, we remain a long way from answering the challenging question of what approach is most effective for what problems, treated by what counselors, satisfying what criteria of success, in what setting, and at what cost.

Marriage and Divorce Counseling

Although we are about to discuss marriage and divorce counseling as separate and distinct entities, it is necessary from the outset to offer a caveat: Both occur on a continuum, and both can best be understood within the context of family

Table 5.2   Therapeutic stances and characteristics for three counselor types

Issue	Take charge	Chief investigator	Fellow traveler
View of client	Impaired Has assets	Faulty beliefs and expectations Sufficient assets	Growing, not fixed or limited Has unique, valued life experience
	Wants help	Ambivalent about help	In charge of treatment
View of therapist	Informed and competent	Can recognize pathology Can find patterns Object of transference	Co-learner Facilitator
	Responsible for the success of treatment	Co-responsible for outcome	Helps client connect to inner wisdom
Focus	Conscious	Unconscious	Underground stream
	Present	Past	Future (growth)
Tools	Personal authority	Historical perspective (psychodynamic) (family systems)	Empathy and positive regard Variety of ways to bypass ordinary consciousness
	Structural and strategic theory	Transference Paradox	

Source: Weltner, 1992.

relationships and systems. Marriage and, increasingly, divorce occur as events in the ongoing history of a family. Divorce usually results in a transitional life crisis, carrying with it

> the potential for both acute and chronic outcomes that will influence individual members, intergenerational and social network systems, and even unborn members of the new generation of the family. It involves a reorganization of enormous magnitude for the entire family system. (Everett & Volgy, 1991, p. 512)

Marriage counseling (also referred to as marital therapy) involves intervening with individuals in terms of the marital, family, and other significant contexts in which the couple is embedded (Nichols, 1988). Their separate personality attributes, strengths, and weaknesses are inevitably intertwined with family ties, especially their attachments to one another. Even if the counselor begins working with some subsection of the family, it is almost certain that eventually the marital relationship will be scrutinized, underscoring the decisive role that the spousal relationship or subsystem plays in the family, affecting all family relationships. As we have noted, symptomatic or problematic behavior in a child is frequently a reaction to parental marital conflicts. Divorce does far more than uncouple incompatible partners; it changes the structure of the entire family system.

Demand for professional assistance with marital problems is not new, having begun during the 1920s in the United States when physicians Abraham Stone and Hannah Stone established the Marriage and Consultation Center in New York (Goldenberg & Goldenberg, 2000). The American Association of Marriage Counselors (forerunner to today's American Association for Marriage and Family Therapy) was formed in 1941, comprising physicians, sex educators, psychologists, lawyers, social workers, and clergy, all involved with the then-new interdisciplinary field of marriage counseling.

On the other hand, divorce counseling per se has a shorter history. Until perhaps 25 years ago, marriage and family agencies offered a chilly response to those who suggested divorce as a solution for a warring couple, preferring to judge their success by how well they were able to keep couples together (Brown, 1985). If once considered "antifamily," divorce counseling has now merged with marriage counseling, offering an overlapping conceptual framework and a similar set of intervention techniques. If marriage counseling is a relationship treatment that focuses on maintaining, enhancing, and strengthening the marital bond, divorce counseling can be defined as a relationship treatment that focuses on decreasing the function of the marital bond, with the eventual goal of dissolving it (Sprenkle & Gonzalez-Doupe, 1996). Unfortunately, such a clear-cut dichotomy is not often found in clinical practice.

As Everett and Volgy (1991) point out, it would be hard to imagine a clinical practitioner today for whom the process or outcome of divorce has not affected in some way a great proportion of clients. Considering the prevalence of divorce, then, and the fact that counselors must deal with this issue repeatedly in their practices, earlier resistance to divorce counseling probably has influenced the fact that until the last decade, few published guidelines existed for this form of family intervention. In more recent years, however, a spate of books has appeared (Everett, 1987; Isaacs, Montalvo, & Abelsohn, 1986; Nichols, 1988; Rice & Rice, 1986; Sprenkle, 1985; Textor, 1989), generally offering a family systems outlook for conducting conjoint sessions of divorce counseling.

Although continuing to view the dissolution of a marriage in systems terms may still be appropriate, in some cases—an unwilling, untrusting, or geographically unavailable spouse, an uncontrollably angry or violent spouse, a spouse resistant to further contact with an ex-mate—the counselor may be forced to work with only one member of the dyad. Whenever possible, however, the counselor should make every effort to involve both spouses in any divorce decision-making process, if necessary making a personal appeal to the resistant spouse to attend. By failing to intervene with both partners, the counselor not only hears only one side of the story, but is also open to the charge of aligning with one spouse and thus furthering the polarization already taking place (Rice, 1989).

Should children be involved, as is likely to be the case, the spouses will continue to have contact with each other beyond divorce, and they need to prepare for that eventuality.

Although the term *divorce counseling* implies that the decision has been made to terminate the marriage, so that the procedure focuses on disengaging the couple as easily as the situation permits, in reality the circumstances are rarely so tidy or clear-cut. More likely, marriage and divorce counseling are segments of the same continuum, and where the former ends and the latter begins cannot always be demarcated. Some couples begin marriage counseling without having raised the issue of divorce out loud; indeed, they are determined to make the marriage work and only with great reluctance and a sense of failure may come to realize the impossibility of achieving that goal. Others come reporting a vague sense of stagnation in their relationship or perhaps reporting symptoms in themselves or their children that distress them. At the other extreme, couples may seek counseling after determining that divorce is inevitable, perhaps asking for help in minimizing the pain involved in the process for themselves and their children. Thus, couples begin at differing points in the decision-making process and may drift back and forth while trying to reach a decision. This situation calls for considerable flexibility on the counselor's part. It is essential that the counselor explore and keep track of where each spouse is on this continuum, recognizing that the final decision is a difficult one for any couple to reach.

Married couples, then, enter counseling with a variety of expectations and hopes, to say nothing of varying degrees of commitment to remaining together. One or both may have concluded earlier that the marriage is no longer satisfying, although they are nevertheless prepared to engage briefly in the counseling process as a last resort or perhaps wish to give the appearance of making a final effort before separating and filing for divorce. Others, badgered into coming by an insistent spouse (perhaps with the threat of divorce or even suicide), may be denying their internal sense of hopelessness about the future of the relationship and remain fearful even about saying the word *divorce* publicly. Still others think of divorce as a personal failure, a narcissistic injury, or perhaps something that occurs to other people but not to themselves or their families. For some couples, one partner may attend a joint session in order to announce the decision to divorce in the presence of the counselor, feeling less guilty if a possibly distraught spouse is in professional hands. In some cases, one or both partners have already begun a relationship outside the marriage.

Finally, some couples enter counseling together, hoping to improve the relationship. Such improvement is a good possibility, as we have noted (Guerin, Fay, Burden, & Kautto, 1987), especially if intervention begins early enough in the conflict, when communication is still intact, too much damage has not yet been done, and the partners still wish to strengthen their marital bond (Kaslow, 1995). On the other hand, marriage counseling may force the couple to face the fact that their differences are irreconcilable, their goals unrealistic, and their future together unpromising, despite the positive changes each has attempted. In these instances, divorce may be the most feasible alternative for resolving the relationship conflicts.

Divorce counseling, then, may be the final stage in a sequence of unsuccessful efforts to save the marriage. Or, under other circumstances, divorce counseling may follow the legal divorce proceedings, as ex-mates, individually or conjointly, attempt to cope with unfinished or continuing conflict (for example, over child custody or visitation rights). In the former case, in which the couple seeking to repair their marriage are forced to conclude that it cannot be done, counseling need not be finished once that decision is reached. Even if the decision to divorce has been agreed to, the counselor must help educate both spouses about a number of unfinished tasks: understanding why the relationship failed (as insurance against future failure); how best to disengage (and not continue or escalate the conflictual relationship); how to cope with the sense of loss, acute stress, and perhaps temporary disorganization in personal functioning (in one or both); how best to deal with other members of the family system (children, parents, and others); and how to foster autonomy and personal development for each as individual persons (Rice & Rice, 1986). They must agree on how best to mediate the separation process and how to manage their future, ongoing relationships with the children.

In this regard, Salts (1985) makes a useful distinction among three stages of counseling divorcing couples, along with commensurate tasks and goals for the counselor:

Stage 1. The predivorce decision-making stage: helping couples recognize what made theirs an unhappy marriage and aiding them in determining whether their needs can be met within the marriage or what alternative solutions are possible

Stage 2. The restructuring stage: if the decision to divorce has been made, providing both spouses with an opportunity to reaffirm its benefits or, in the case of an unwilling partner, to accept its inevitability

Stage 3. The postdivorce recovery stage: helping couples rebuild separate lives, deal with loss, develop alternative relationships

Sprenkel (1990) outlines a practical set of goals for counselors helping couples cope with the inescapable pain inherent in the divorce process (Box 5.1, page 110). Dealing with role loss; loss of a partner, family, or lifestyle; loss of self-esteem; and doubts that one has what it takes to be a good or lovable husband or wife—all this forms part of the rebuilding process.

The decision to divorce is never made lightly, even in the most dysfunctional marriages, and can be accompanied by feelings of anguish, despair, shock, and disbelief that this is actually happening. The couple may vacillate between trying one more time to salvage the marriage and wishing to dissolve it. Of necessity, the counselor may alternate between marriage and divorce counseling during this period, and must be especially vigilant to avoid taking sides in the middle of the conflict, as one mate insists on leaving and proceeding with the divorce while the other begs for another chance. It is the counselor's task to help the couple consider all options at this predivorce decision-making stage, without being maneuvered into deciding for them whether or not to remain together.

Box 5.1   Goals of divorce counseling

Partners need to be helped to:
1. Accept the end of the marriage.
2. Achieve a functional postdivorce relationship with the ex-spouse.
3. Achieve a reasonable emotional adjustment.
4. Develop an understanding of their own contributions to the dysfunctional behavior that led to the failure of the marriage.
5. Find sources of emotional support.
6. Feel competent and comfortable in postdivorce parenting.
7. Help their children adjust to the loss without triangulating them or nourishing unrealistic expectations.
8. Use the "crisis" of divorce as an opportunity for learning and personal growth.
9. Negotiate the legal process in a way both feel is reasonably equitable.
10. Develop physical, health, and personal habits consistent with adjustment for everyone.

Source: Based on Sprenkel, 1990.

The counselor must also take great care not to become impatient or intolerant with the vacillation and thereby force a premature decision. As Turner (1985) points out, the counselor can expect indecisive behavior at this stage, often marked by seeming irrationality, a great deal of ambivalence, regressive behavior, impulsivity, and frequent reversals. However, Sprenkle and Gonzalez-Doupe (1996) contend that during this decision-making period the counselor can help the couple consider divorce as an alternative to their relationship difficulties (including an appraisal of the possible consequences of such a major decision).

Granvold (1983) recommends the possibility of a planned structured separation for couples at an impasse, especially if they continue to be doubtful about whether divorce is the best alternative. The therapeutic purpose during the decision-making stage is to interrupt the heated marital conflict in order to enable a more measured, rational decision. Such separation also provides both parties with a glimpse of independent living, a period of value reassessment, and an opportunity for experimentation with other lifestyles. For the children, such a separation may be the first event in the process of accommodating to their parents' eventual divorce. A written contract outlining the length of separation (say, three months) as well as its ground rules (dating others, outside sexual relationships, visits with the children) is common under these circumstances. Typically, the nature and frequency of the partners' contacts with each other are spelled out during this "cooling-off" period, and conjoint counseling on a regular basis is continued. Everett and Volgy Everett (1994) offer a step-by-step guide for achieving a "healthy" physical separation for the couple and their children.

The counselor needs to be particularly attuned to the stage of the individual, marital, and family life cycle of the presenting clients. Divorce at any stage may be agonizing; discontent in one or both partners may be especially acute during a major transition in the family (such as the end of child-rearing years, a pending retirement, a landmark birthday). Divorce at midlife may represent a gradual estrangement, shattered dreams, a recognition of one's mortality, and a rush for fun or novelty or adventure before it's too late. In some cases, a partner may realize he or she has tolerated physical or verbal abuse long enough, or put up with excessive use of alcohol or other chemical substances once too often, or can no longer manage living in a relationship devoid of love or affection or simply some communication. Meeting an attractive potential lover who seems to herald promise of a fuller and more gratifying future may galvanize one partner into pursuing a divorce (Kaslow, 1994).

Grief, mourning for the failed relationship that once held so much promise, and despair at ever weathering the crisis and going on alone are all to be expected. Denial, feelings of anger and frustration, vengeance, rage, fear of abandonment—these, too, are familiar to any counselor dealing with a divorcing couple, especially in the early phases of the marital dissolution. Later, sadness, resignation, regret, and remorse are more common. Rice and Rice (1986) suggest that the counselor, in addition to offering support, be prepared to teach social, interpersonal, and even assertiveness techniques to help individuals regain confidence and learn effective coping skills as a single person. In some cases, a previously sheltered spouse (usually the wife) may need to be made aware of functioning with diminished economic resources after the divorce, selling a house, getting a job, and so on.

When children are involved, parents have the additional task of learning to deal cooperatively with each other over an extended period of time. While most divorcing parents try to buffer their young children from the impact of adult conflict, some may unwittingly (or sometimes quite wittingly) recruit their children into taking sides in order to win an unfinished battle. In the midst of conflict, some parents may abdicate their caretaking responsibilities or perhaps lose confidence in their ability to carry out parenting tasks. Isaacs, Montalvo, and Abelsohn (1986) urge counselors working with such cases of "difficult divorce" to focus on the parents' efforts toward reorganizing their relationships both with each other and with their children. Here the focus is on the family getting divorced, not just the parents. Ahrons (1994) uses the term "good divorce" to describe one in which a family with children remains a family despite dramatic and unsettling changes in family structure and size; divorcing parents in partnership continue to be responsible for the emotional, economic, and physical needs of their children, cooperating sufficiently so that the bonds of kinship—with and through their children—may continue. Characteristically, a couple is unlikely to do better after a divorce than they did during their marriage concerning the resolution of such important family issues as child-rearing, finances, and in-laws.

Having successfully navigated the Stage 1 predivorce decision making, and having both decided upon and accepted the inevitability of divorce, the couple can be helped further to make the legal, emotional, financial, social, and parental arrangements in order to make a smooth transition to becoming a postdivorce family (Sprenkle & Gonzalez-Doupe, 1996). During this restructuring stage (Stage 2), it is the partner who feels "left" or believes himself or herself to have been "dumped" who is more anxious to seek further help following physical separation. One way to have both ex-mates feel they have been treated fairly may be both agreeing to **divorce mediation** (see the next section). During the postdivorce recovery stage (Stage 3), counselors may help now-single people separately develop stable and autonomous lifestyles while continuing to coparent their children.

In the following case, a couple has separated but is stalled in the divorce process. What appears to be a request for counseling directed at reaching decisions regarding their 3-year-old child turns out to be an effort to finish up their divorce.

Harry and Lola, separated for 6 months, called a counselor for help in making joint decisions regarding Meredith, their 3-year-old daughter. They asked to come in together as a couple, without the child; while the counselor suspected more was involved between them than was apparent, she agreed to their plan, hoping that without Meredith they might more readily deal with what was blocking their proceeding with the divorce.

As expected, the presenting problems—arrangements regarding visitation, overnight stays for Meredith, vacation plans for her stay with each parent, nursery school attendance—were indeed easily resolved, the couple spending less than one session on deciding these issues. Although they expressed considerable anger toward each other, they were accustomed to cooperating on issues regarding their child. Later in the first counseling session, however, the counselor began to wonder aloud about the reasons their marriage had failed, observing that Harry and Lola showed little awareness or insight into their relationship. It was soon clear to the counselor that Harry and Lola were covering up a number of unresolved issues between them and that their inability to deal with those issues kept them from moving ahead with the divorce. The counselor suggested that the two seemed to have some unfinished business between them, and she invited them to explore those areas for a session or two. She explained that this was not an attempt to reunite the couple, but to help them understand better what had gone wrong. They quickly agreed and set up the additional meetings with the counselor for the forthcoming week.

As Harry and Lola spoke of their backgrounds and helped the counselor fill out a genogram, it became clear that they had come a long way—socially, culturally, intellectually, and financially—from their working-class beginnings. Now both successful architects, they had met at school, drawn together by similarities in religion and the shared experience of growing up poor and being the first in each of their families to attend college. Both were ambitious and fiercely determined to get ahead in their profession. They married soon after graduation, struggled together to succeed, and put off having a child until they were closer to their professional goals: academic careers as professors of architecture and urban planning at a major university.

Meredith was born when the couple was in their early thirties, and they both adored her right from the start. Aside from their devotion to her, though, they seemed less and less to share their earlier closeness and affection. During the previous decade, each had emphasized work, career, and success and, without acknowledging it, had become highly competitive with the other. While each rarely if ever expressed unhappiness or dissatisfaction to the other, both partners nevertheless realized that something was amiss. Sex between them had become infrequent, and while they blamed it on fatigue, busy schedules, and preoccupation with careers, both had a sense—never put into words—that they had lost much interest in each other over the years. Instead, they viewed their lives as filled with obligations and responsibilities from which they drew little pleasure.

Under these circumstances, it was hardly surprising that Harry met Celeste, a young instructor, and was immediately drawn to her. Astonished by the intensity of his feelings, he became all the more aware of the emptiness in his life at home. Despite a renewed effort to reach out to Lola, he found himself still unable to speak to her about any of his feelings of discontent, nor was she able to do so to him. Thus immobilized in any effort to become more intimate, each pulled further and further away from the painful marital situation. Finally, overwhelmed with guilt—although he and Celeste had not become sexually involved with each other—Harry moved out. Typically, finding himself unable to face Lola, he left behind a note, indicating his unhappiness and despair, and blaming his upset on his "midlife crisis." Devastated, dumbfounded, and internally enraged, Lola nevertheless accepted Harry's decision with outward calm.

The couple continued a civil relationship, especially in regard to their daughter. No anger was ever expressed directly, no bitterness was ever shown by either partner, but their underlying rage at their failed marriage did manifest itself in their inability to agree to the simplest arrangements regarding Meredith. While they never brought up what went wrong or what was missing in the marriage, they continuously disagreed about every detail (school, clothes, activities, lessons) of Meredith's life. The counselor agreed that the rift between them had become too great to be bridged. But she noted that if they wanted to help Meredith, which they did, they would have to learn to express feelings more directly to each other—and, by implication, to any future person with whom either wished to pursue a serious relationship. The block in Harry and Lola's ability to communicate angry or hurt feelings was impeding both from moving on with their lives.

Straight talk was alien to their personal styles or cultural backgrounds. Each had been carefully raised to speak only of pleasant things and to say nothing if one could not say something nice. Nevertheless, the counselor pressed them to get in touch with their feelings, insisting that they learn to put into words what each was experiencing internally and expressing nonverbally through their oppositional behavior. As they did so, the problems they initially presented regarding their daughter were more easily resolved.

The couple terminated counseling after three sessions, as they had originally planned. They continued to practice a more open exchange of feelings, and while it did not seem to come naturally, they did make progress. After 2 months, they returned, having moved along sufficiently that they were ready to see an attorney and reach decisions regarding child custody and the division of their assets. The counselor encouraged their greater openness and helped each overcome feelings of anger, sadness, and disappointment. Both seemed more ready to move on in their lives as separate persons who continued to have a relationship because of their child, as well as their common profession.

They divorced a month later. On the day of their court date, and within 5 minutes of each other, each separately called the counselor to indicate what had transpired and to say they were pleased and relieved. Together they had shared a meaningful experience with the counselor, toward whom they both felt close. Each independently reported that Meredith seemed happy and that the ex-spouses were getting better at working their differences out. Within 2 years, both were happily remarried.

Divorce Mediation

Assuming that a couple has decided to divorce, there remain a multitude of practical problems to face, disputes to be resolved, and differences inherent in the marriage dissolution to be negotiated. As Stier (1986) reminds us, after the divorcing couple has mourned together in divorce counseling, worked through their feelings of disappointment and anger, and perhaps explored their separate fears and hopes about the future apart, they have an immediate need to work out the terms of their dissolution agreement and their postdivorce family relationship. Divorce mediation with the aid of a specially trained, nonpartisan third party (a counselor, a lawyer, or a counselor-lawyer team[3]) is intended to provide precisely such an opportunity. Ideally, according to Ahrons (1994), a male/female team maximizes the skills, knowledge, and gender understandings that a divorcing couple will need in any future cooperative encounters. As children grow older, a divorced couple may want to return to mediation to deal with changing issues concerning such things as schools, camps, college tuition, and wedding plans.

Traditionally, during the legal stage of the divorce process, the spouses separately seek the counsel of attorneys and embark on the *adversarial* procedures of a litigated divorce. Each lawyer sets out to serve the best interests of his or her client, retaining or obtaining as much as possible for that client. While attempting to portray his or her client in the most favorable light, each attorney assumes that the other spouse's interests will be similarly represented by opposing legal counsel. Negotiations are thus primarily in the hands of attorneys or, should they fail to arrive at an agreement, settled by a judge. As Kaslow observes, the resulting fray sometimes becomes a destructive free-for-all, resulting in "long-term embattlement and embitterment in which relatives and friends take sides, children are victimized by the continuing strife, and everyone is left depleted and feeling like a loser" (1988, p. 87).

---

[3] Counselors and lawyers who form an interdisciplinary team maximize the benefits that members of each discipline bring to the mediation. While counselors are attuned to the emotional and interpersonal issues surrounding divorce, lawyers are more familiar with legal issues regarding financial settlements, property distribution, spousal and child support, etc. Together they can offer a comprehensive and integrated approach, although their combined services increase costs to the divorcing couples.

In contrast, divorce mediation, which arose in the mid-1970s and has been made mandatory in some places (such as California in 1981), offers an alternative, time-limited route to resolving potential disputes over custody, visitation rights, child support, the distribution of family assets, and other such issues. When out-of-court settlement terms concerning support and visitation rights are arrived at by the couple together, those terms are more likely to be honored (Emery, 1994). Here the assumption is that they themselves are the experts in their own divorce and that they know better than anyone what they need for a satisfactory postdivorce working relationship. Much as in labor mediation, the divorce mediator, knowledgeable about the substantive issues involved in marital dissolution and trained to provide impartial mediation services, acts as a *facilitator* (rather than a counselor or advocate), helping the couple to examine the pros and cons of various alternatives cooperatively and to arrive at a calmer, more equitable, and ultimately more workable set of joint decisions regarding their continuing family (but separated lives). Mediation, then, is particularly appropriate during the Stage 2 or restructuring phase of the divorce process.

The mediator's role, according to Stier (1986), a psychologist-attorney, is to help reorient the disputing parties toward each other, not by imposing rules but by helping the two achieve a shared perception of the situation and of their relationship. Ideally, if mediation is successful, the new perception will redirect their attitudes and dispositions toward each other. According to Neville (1990), an effective mediator needs the ability to reframe, a structural technique that involves taking messages of anger, jealousy, hurt, and resentment and placing them in a different verbal or emotional context. Thus, negative messages from one spouse are given a positive connotation (a Milan technique) and relabeled as well intentioned. In a case of a manifestly angry spouse, for example, one might express the fear of disappointment underlying the anger. This relabeling transforms the way the message is heard and interpreted by the other spouse.

Divorce mediation is not intended to replace the legal system but rather attempts to circumvent its more negative aspects (Sprenkle & Gonzalez-Doupe, 1996). Most mediation aims at a time span of 6 to 12 hour-long sessions (although sometimes a spouse opposed to the divorce will use the mediation process to delay the divorce action). Successful mediation depends on the skill and style of the mediator, the family system of the clients, the complexity of the issues to be resolved, and the intensity of the conflict (Sauber, Beiner, & Meddoff, 1995). Probably, too, the mediation will be more successful when the ex-partners proceed from an equal power base so that they are equally informed regarding family finances, equally skilled at bargaining, equally able to articulate a position, and so on.[4]

---

[4]Opponents of mediation argue that power is rarely equal and that the more experienced negotiator or financially sophisticated spouse—more frequently the husband—may manipulate negotiations in his favor. To counteract this possible imbalance, both spouses are urged to clear the final agreement through their respective attorneys.

Although mediation involves the possible examination together of the couple's disputing patterns, particularly as these patterns hamper progress in the mediation process, the approach is not the same as divorce counseling. Mediation does not focus on the interpersonal problems that led to the breakup, nor does it seek to modify existing individual personality patterns. Although insights and stress reduction may result, these are fringe benefits, not the major purpose of mediation. However, divorce mediation does provide for an airing of emotional issues, something that rarely occurs in court proceedings, and thus may help resolve these issues so that they do not resurface later in the form of postdivorce litigation (Folberg & Milne, 1988).

Divorce mediation is a multistage process of conflict management or resolution, with a continued focus on the family system rather than the interests of a particular family member. An impartial mediator (or team of mediators), with no previous counseling relationship with the clients, helps the couple identify disputed issues, develop and consider options, and make choices, in order to reach consensual agreements that will realistically meet the needs and concerns of the family. Taylor (1988) distinguished the following seven stages:

Stage 1. Creating structure and trust: The mediator develops rapport with the couple and begins to gather relevant information about each partner's perceptions of conflicts, as well as his or her goals and expectations. The participants begin to understand the nature of the mediating process.

Stage 2. Fact-finding and isolation of the issues: The underlying conflict areas, their duration and intensity, and the expressed and perceived rigidity of positions are identified.

Stage 3. Creation of options and alternatives: Both parties are actively involved in assigning priorities to the remaining disagreements, locating stumbling blocks, and together developing new options that may be more satisfactory to both participants.

Stage 4. Negotiation and decision making: The couple is encouraged to take the risky step of making choices, accepting compromises, and bargaining; the couple is directed from a competitive negotiation to a more cooperative interaction.

Stage 5. Clarification—writing a plan: A document outlining the participants' intentions and decisions is produced and is agreed to in writing by both parties.

Stage 6. Legal review and processing: The family system is connected to larger watchdog social systems and institutions, such as private attorneys or judges, in order to verify the agreement's completeness, fairness, and feasibility.

Stage 7. Implementation, review, and revision: Outside the confines of the mediation sessions, a follow-up is conducted on the participants' ability to match intentions with agreed-upon action and behavior.

Mediation typically reduces animosity and rancor, allowing both partners to separate peacefully so that each may begin building a new life. When each feels fairly treated by the other, future cooperation about the children becomes more probable, and possible subsequent disagreements stand a better chance of being settled amicably without resorting to painful and expensive court battles. Although the mediation process is not acceptable to all divorcing couples, nor necessarily effective under all circumstances for those willing to participate, it does hold promise for many as a way of lessening the anguish of divorce, not only for spouses but for children as well.

Summary

Counselor interventions are typically based on theoretical orientation, the presenting problem, the counselor's personal style, the length and frequency of counseling anticipated, the setting, reimbursement considerations, and the assessment of a need for medication. Counselors must also determine in each case which therapeutic modality—individual, couple, or family—is most likely to be effective. Treatment manuals, based on empirically supported research, are often adopted for specific clients or specific sets of problems, although their use is rejected by some counselors as too confining.

Whenever possible, matching and tailoring to client diagnosis, relational conflict, or level of functioning can help maximize counseling benefits. Divorce counseling, an increasingly acceptable form of family intervention, may be the concluding segment of an effort at marriage counseling or may follow legal divorce proceedings as former spouses attempt to cope with unfinished or continuing family conflict. Divorce counseling may be divided into three phases: the predivorce decision-making stage, the restructuring stage, and the postdivorce recovery stage. Divorce mediation, usually attempted during the restructuring stage, offers a nonadversarial attempt by mediators trained in mental health as well as the law to help divorcing couples work together to reach agreements, minimize future conflict, and, ideally, separate without recrimination so that all family members, children included, may go on with building their lives.

COUNSELING FAMILIES WITH VARIED LIFESTYLES

CHAPTER

SIX

Counseling the Single-Parent-Led Family

Single-parent-led families (84% mother-child, 16% father-child) represent the fastest growing family type in the United States (U.S. Bureau of the Census, 1998). Whether resulting from divorce, separation, widowhood, adoption, or out-of-wedlock birth, the one-parent family is becoming increasingly familiar and now represents more than one in four families in the United States. Figure 6.1 on page 122 illustrates the steady growth in the number of children living with one parent since 1960; that number has more than tripled in 35 years. For the first 60 years of the 20th century, with little variation, approximately 9% of all children lived in single-parent homes, but that figure has risen steadily to now reach 28% of all children (55% for African Americans). Today, close to 20 million children under 18 live with one parent, and it is projected that between 50% and 60% of children who were born in the 1990s will live, at some point, in single-family settings (Hetherington, Bridges, & Insabella, 1998).

Primarily the result of a continuing high divorce rate, the ranks of single parents have swelled in recent years because of a second reason: A significant number of single women have opted to have children. In some cases, as we describe in the following pages, these are unmarried teenage mothers who have decided to carry children to full term and to live as single parents. In other, but fewer cases, older women, often in successful professional careers, financially able, and nearing the end of their childbearing years, but not finding or wishing for an appropriate male with whom to maintain a marital relationship, may choose to become pregnant because they wish to experience motherhood (Miller, 1992).

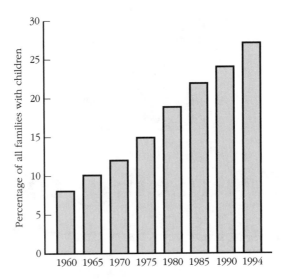

Figure 6.1   Children living in single-parent families: 1960 to 1994

Source: Saxton, 1996.

Recent data show that 37% of the children living in single-family households live with a divorced parent, and an additional 35% live with a parent (almost certainly a mother) who has never married.

Changing Times: Patterns of Marriage and Divorce

A central determinant of the sweeping changes in contemporary American family life is the high rate of marital dissolution. While the U.S. marriage rate has remained stable in recent years, and the rate of divorce has in fact dropped slightly since reaching a peak in the early 1980s, it is nevertheless a fact that the marriages of approximately 50% of couples[1] who marry today will eventually terminate in divorce or permanent separation. The median duration of marriage before divorce is now about seven years (Cox, 1996).

[1] This frequently quoted statistic requires further explanation, since it is often incorrectly assumed by the popular press that it reflects the ratio of number of divorces to number of marriages in any given year (for example, in 1994, 1.2 million divorces and 2.4 million marriages). That would produce a misleading incidence rate, since the same couple's marriage and divorce are unlikely to occur in the same year. Thus, we are talking about separate populations, since most of those divorced must be assumed to have been married in prior years. Sprenkle and Gonzalez-Doupe (1996) contend that a more accurate statistic results from adopting a "cohort" approach, tracking the actual percentage of divorces for marriages that began in a particular year. For example, approximately 30% of couples married in 1964 had divorced by 1980, and over 40% were expected to eventually divorce. Based on similar projections, demographer Paul Glick (1984c) predicted that approximately half the population born between 1946 and 1955 (the baby boom group) will eventually divorce.

A number of individual as well as couple interactive factors have been identified as contributing to marital unhappiness. Unrealistic expectations (for example, that one's spouse will always try to please, never be angry, always be open and honest) based on romantic dreams and false hopes—inevitably unfulfilled—may lead to disappointment and ultimately to despair. Happiness may seem elusive to some partners, who may then withdraw from a relationship and perhaps seek satisfaction in work-related activities or extramarital affairs. Inevitably, too, people change as they age, and a couple (particularly if they marry young) may discover that interests and values diverge to the point that differences are irreconcilable. Some marital partners find that their parents provided poor role models for a successful marriage; others may find themselves too uncomfortable trying to sustain an intimate relationship; still others may become stressed to the point of dysfunction when called upon to care for a newborn child. Serious psychological problems in one or both partners may become exacerbated in the process of living as man and wife. Disillusionment with the relationship, a feeling that one's emotional and physical needs remain unmet, and a sense of growing in different directions may build over time, until a precipitating event—the last straw—or an accumulation of unfulfilled expectations provides the momentum behind the decision to divorce (Milne, 1988).

Beyond personal factors, some of the following interpersonal issues are at the core of most marital breakups:

- ineffective communication patterns
- sexual incompatibilities
- anxiety over making and/or maintaining a long-term commitment
- fewer shared activities
- reduced exchange of affection
- infidelity
- lack of sensitivity or indifference to a partner's feelings or wishes
- conflicts over power and control
- underdeveloped problem-solving skills
- conflicts over money, independence, in-laws, or children
- physical abuse
- inability to respond positively to changing role demands such as those brought about by the birth of a first child or the return to paid work by a partner

John Gottman, perhaps today's most prolific marriage researcher, has offered a number of theoretical papers (for example, Gottman, 1993) as well as empirical studies (Gottman, 1994; Gottman, Coan, Carrère, & Swanson, 1998) predicting marital dissolution or marital stability in couples. Videotaping how couples communicate, verbally and nonverbally, while simultaneously taking physiological measures of each participant during their interaction, he and his associates attempted to identify those behavioral, psychological, and physiological responses essential to a stable marriage and those predictive of divorce. Findings

(Gottman, 1994) suggest it is not the exchange of anger that predicts divorce, but rather the exchange of four forms of *negativity:*

- *criticism* (attacking a partner's character)
- *defensiveness* (denying responsibility for certain behavior)
- *contempt* (insulting, abusive attitudes toward a spouse)
- *stonewalling* (withdrawal and unwillingness to listen to one's partner)

In a typical demand-withdrawal transactional pattern, women were found to be more apt to criticize while men were more likely to stonewall, delay, and obstruct conflict-resolving communication.

Typically, several of these dysfunctional transactions, or transition-point experiences, repeated without resolution over a period of time will escalate the growing marital dissatisfaction of one or both partners. One or both partners may then start to compare, unfavorably, their current relationship with that of friends, or perhaps alternative potential partners available to them. In effect, once a spouse concludes that the costs of staying together outweigh the benefits and that divorce is a feasible and acceptable option, then the marriage is in jeopardy.

The Process of Divorce

Separation and divorce are procedures that occur over time and in stages; the entire process usually involves a great deal of stress, ambivalence, indecision, self-doubt, and uncertainty, even when both partners agree to the action. Although they cannot be fully aware of what lies in store for them, in most cases they are about to undergo a painful, disruptive process from which, more likely than not, it may take much time to recover.

Table 6.1 identifies 14 steps in the divorce process, beginning with increasing doubts about the future of the marriage, emotional disengagement from each other, preseparation fantasies of romantic involvements with others or of leaving the marriage (or sometimes of the other spouse's death), and then one partner's decision to move out of the family household. Immediately before separating, or perhaps immediately afterward, one or both of the former pair may experience a sudden sense of loss or fear that they acted in haste and increased anxiety about going it alone. They may feel guilt over what they are doing to the children or concern about friends' or family's disapproving of their behavior. In some cases, the person who left may move back home, and a brief period of stability may follow.

Such a pseudoreconciliation often lasts only a short time; disillusionment sets in and makes the subsequent decision to divorce even more painful. While later doubts and uncertainties may continue to arise, once the decision is made to divorce, much rage and vengeance may follow as the prior bonds between marital partners become severed, and there is little likelihood of turning back (Everett & Volgy, 1991).

In most cases, one person initiates the process, although the other may be equally aware of unhappiness but be less able or less willing, financially or emo-

Table 6.1   Steps in the divorce process

1. Heightened ambivalence
2. Distancing
3. Preseparation fantasies and actions
4. Physical separation
5. Pseudoreconciliation
6. Predivorce fantasies
7. Decision to divorce
8. Recurring ambivalence
9a. The potential disputes—mediation
9b. The potential disputes—adversarial
10. Postdivorce coparenting
11. Remarriage
12. Blended-family formation
13. Second remarriage
14. Dual-family functioning

Source: Everett & Volgy, 1991.

tionally, to act. In far fewer cases, the noninitiating person is taken by surprise, although probably because he or she did not want to know and thus denied what was taking place prior to the initiating act. It is the exceptional couple who mutually and simultaneously reach the decision to divorce.

However the decision is reached, the counselor seeing the couple at any point along the continuum of marriage, separation, and divorce must be attuned to the blows to self-esteem that separation and divorce inevitably cause. To have invested time, effort, personal resources, and youthfulness, all for naught, is to experience a personal feeling of failure and the sense that perhaps one does not possess the necessary traits to ever achieve or maintain a satisfying marriage. Moreover, marriage bestows a sense of identity, maturity, acceptance, and respectability in most segments of society. For many people, then, to have failed at marriage is to have failed as an adult. Yet divorce also has a positive potential—offering a new beginning as much as an ending—that is important for the counselor to impart to the divorcing pair. All families have the potential for repair and growth, and with the collaboration of counselors, resiliencies not previously expressed may emerge and be strengthened during the restructuring that each spouse undergoes following divorce (Walsh, 1998).

Divorce, even when relatively amicable, rarely occurs abruptly. More likely, couples undergo a series of events together before both partners can let go and begin to lead separate lives, as shown in Figure 6.2 on page 126. A useful descriptive stage model framework for conceptualizing the *divorce process* has been offered by Paul Bohannan (1970, 1984), who views the entire circumstance as

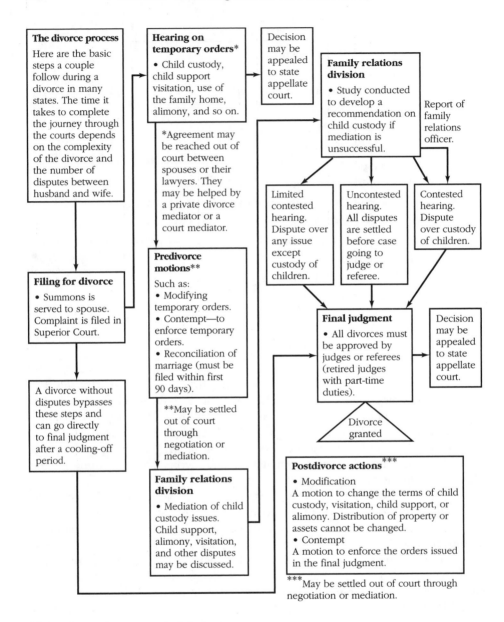

Figure 6.2 Steps in a typical divorce process

Source: Gullotta, Adams, & Alexander, 1986.

usually requiring six overlapping phases before disengagement can be accomplished. These stages do not necessarily occur in an invariant sequence, nor do all persons involved feel the same anguish at each phase, but Kaslow (1988) argues that each stage must be experienced and its stumbling blocks removed before both mates can achieve a sense of well-being.

First comes the *emotional divorce,* which may or may not involve physical separation. During this stage, often at the instigation of one partner, both spouses finally recognize that the marriage is deteriorating. This period may be brief or prolonged, but whatever its length, the couple must deal with the decline of the relationship. If one person gives voice to dissatisfaction or disillusionment before the other, the latter may become alarmed, even agitated, and try to cajole or seduce the initiator back into the marriage. Promises to change, declarations of good intentions, desperate pleas, threats of suicide, even a willingness to begin counseling (if previously resisted) may be offered as inducements to stay. Another common scenario is for both marital partners to use this opportunity to hurl criticisms and invectives, each defending his or her own behavior and denouncing the actions, past or present, of the other.

Kessler (1975) further divides this stage into three phases—*disillusionment, erosion,* and *detachment*—during which each partner focuses on the other's weaknesses and deficiencies, blaming the other for the marital unhappiness. Destructive verbal and nonverbal exchanges, avoidance, lack of attention, withdrawal, and perhaps self-pity characterize behavior at this point, as one or both mates prepare to cope with the future, sometimes by seeking solace through outside sexual contacts or affairs (Woody, 1983). Kaslow (1995) believes that if couples enter conjoint marital counseling at this point—resolving frustrations, ventilating and understanding their suppressed anger, perhaps working on improving the relationship now that it is in jeopardy—they are more likely to work out their marital conflict than if one or both enters individual counseling or psychotherapy.

Returning to Bohannan's stages, secondly comes the *legal divorce,* during which one partner contacts an attorney, serves legal notice on the other, and begins the judicial process. Until a decade ago, it was necessary in most states to justify the action by alleging some ground—adultery, mental cruelty—but today all states allow partners to terminate the marriage without a presumption of fault by either party. While still adversarial, **no-fault divorce** legislation can be interpreted as an encouraging move toward normalizing divorce in our society (Ahrons & Rodgers, 1987). Without determining who is the "guilty party," then, no-fault divorce laws allow judges to grant divorces on the basis of "irreconcilable differences" or following prolonged separation.

The *economic divorce* follows as decisions are made by the divorcing pair regarding the distribution of assets, property, child-support payments, possible alimony payments, and so forth, usually with the help of attorneys and sometimes in conjunction with mental health workers. Divorce mediation (discussed in Chapter 5), a nonadversarial alternative to traditional legal intervention, is a relatively recent, innovative attempt to help the negotiation of these emotion-arousing issues by taking into account the affective as well as the legal dimensions of the marital dissolution.

During Bohannan's fourth stage, that of *coparental divorce,* child custody and visitation rights are hammered out. While custody has traditionally been awarded to the mother, on the unproved assumption that a young child's interests are best served by remaining with the mother, that tradition is increasingly being challenged today. More and more fathers are awarded sole custody now, according to Cox (1996), and shared custody or joint custody, in which both parents retain legal custody, is more the norm. One parent may retain physical custody, the parents may take turns caring for the child, or each parent may be granted custody of one or more children. (We'll return to a fuller discussion of child custody alternatives later in this chapter.) Ahrons and Rodgers (1987) argue that even though a marriage ends and the parents reside in different households, the family (especially with children) continues. These authors prefer to use the term **binuclear families,** rather than single-parent or broken families, in order to emphasize that the two households (including both custodial and noncustodial coparents) continue to form one family system. As Ganong and Coleman (1999) observe, family responsibilities and obligations toward one another (parents toward children and vice versa) continue following divorce and remarriage.

The former partners must next redefine their separate places in the community as single individuals and must also reestablish relations with family and friends. These tasks are handled during the fifth stage, *community divorce.* In many cases, as Weiss (1975) observes, decisions to separate (and especially to divorce) may have been postponed for lengthy periods because of reluctance to face friends and family and make the divorce public. Now, resilience is called for, and needs to be encouraged by the counselor, as the now-single person reestablishes relations with others and attempts lifestyle changes during this difficult transition point. A young divorced person may find it necessary for a variety of reasons (help with child care, finances, feelings of isolation and despair) to move back in with parents, perhaps triggering old parent-child conflicts.

Bohannon's final stage in the divorce process, and for many the most trying one, calls for *psychic divorce,* as each former mate works to accept the fact of permanent separation, redefine himself or herself as a single and unattached person, and begin the often painful process of seeking and being open to new relationships. Identifying and encouraging the expression of each partner's recuperative abilities can be a useful aid in empowering the couple to meet their changing life circumstances.

The entire event is a process with roots in the past, before divorce was contemplated, and carries with it effects that extend into the future. As Ahrons and Rodgers (1987), as well as Kaslow and Schwartz (1987), point out, every family member—children as well as adults—will be profoundly affected. As the family is reorganized, each person must redefine himself or herself as part of a divorced family and must learn new ways of coping with society at large, as well as with other family members. Feelings of abandonment, betrayal, loneliness, anxiety, rage, inadequacy, disillusionment, continued attachment to the person who has left, desperation at feeling unloved (and thus unlovable), mourning—all are likely to appear in some form (Kessler, 1975). Depression, hostility, and bitterness may continue for many divorced people, who may persist in struggling with an ex-spouse or develop dysfunctional parent-child relationships. Others may rush prematurely into new attachments in an effort to reassure themselves of their worth and attractiveness or to cope with feelings of inadequacy or a fear of being alone.

Most divorced people eventually remarry (75% of men, 66% of women), suggesting that the high divorce rate in the United States is less a rejection of the institution of marriage than it is of specific marital partners (Hetherington, Bridges, & Insabella, 1998). The higher percentage for men probably reflects these demographic data: Men are more apt to marry someone not previously married, and they tend to marry younger women and thus have a larger pool of potential partners than do divorced women (Glick, 1984a). As a group, divorced women, typically with physical custody of their young children, have far less chance of remarriage. Census data as analyzed by Glick, a distinguished demographer, indicate that among women in their thirties who have divorced, the likelihood of remarriage also declines with increasing levels of education. While divorced women with no college education are likely to remarry rather quickly, other things being equal, those with more education are not, possibly because they may be more financially independent and also may not have as large a pool of eligible men in their peer group from which to choose.

Most single-parent households are headed by divorced women or women (teenage or adult) who have never married. Widowed and divorced women with custody of their children were about equally numerous in 1960, but by 1983, divorced mothers outnumbered widowed mothers by five to one (Glick, 1984b). In addition, out-of-wedlock births have doubled the proportion of single-parent-led families in the last 25 years. Today, one newborn infant out of four births is to a never-married mother (Saxton, 1996). Very likely, that unwed mother is an adolescent girl (teenagers accounted for 30% of nonmarital births in 1992) or a woman in her twenties (54% of nonmarital births) (Coley & Chase-Lansdale, 1998). Ethnic and racial differences exist: Whites have lower rates of adolescent births than do Hispanics or African Americans. While Hispanic adolescent girls are less apt to have early sexual experiences than the other groups, they are also less likely to use birth control; once pregnant, they are more prone than their white or African American cohorts to give birth rather than choose to abort (Perez & Duany, 1992). (We offer a more extensive discussion of teenage mothers later in this chapter.)

Living Through Divorce

Although divorce has become a familiar and recognized fact of American life—approximately 1 million divorces occur annually in the United States—it is never routine for the family members undergoing the often agonizing experience and its aftermath. Indeed, for most families, the decision to split up is a traumatic event filled with uncertainty about the future and perhaps even dread. Moreover, despite its common occurrence, divorce may still frequently be greeted with shock and embarrassment, if not outright hostility, by family and friends, who may find themselves in the uncomfortable position of having to reevaluate their own marriages. According to Ahrons and Rodgers (1987), who urge that divorce be viewed as an enduring societal institution (much as marriage is perceived in our culture), many people still cling to the long-held attitude that divorce is inherently pathological. If two people are unable or unwilling to maintain a lifelong commitment, goes this argument, one or both partners must have some psychological or moral defect or deficit. Divorcing partners, then, especially if young children are involved, must often deal with a sense of failure, of guilt over breaking up a home, of anguish at being labeled by many as socially deviant or morally weak—all at a time when significant life changes are taking place and important decisions about the future must be made.

Despite these roadblocks, as noted earlier, many couples are less willing today to make emotional compromises or remain in an unhappy situation for economic security, for the sake of the children, or for social appearances. No-fault divorce laws make divorce more readily obtainable, with less stigma or blame attached. Everett and Volgy Everett (1994) offer useful guidelines for achieving a *healthy* divorce, maintaining a sense of stability and security for parents and children alike. Ahrons (1994) takes a similar position, stating that a *good* divorce is attainable once the stigma is removed, the divorced family is redefined as binuclear rather than as a "single-parent" entity, and parents and children establish new roles, rules, and rituals to support the new family structure.

While divorce inevitably disrupts family relationships, most families demonstrate ample resilience in making the many necessary adjustments, and require no counseling. Morawetz and Walker (1984), Ahrons (1994), and Mednick (1987) all challenge a commonly held assumption that single-parent households represent some deviant family form. Their findings indicate that good adjustment, well-being, and satisfaction with life are possible for single parents and their children. Cashon (1982, p. 83), summarizing the published research of the previous decade on female-headed households, concludes that "the majority of families, when not plagued by poverty, are as successful as two-parent families in producing children with appropriate sex-role behavior, good emotional and intellectual adjustment, and non-delinquent behavior." Amato (1993) adds that a child's adjustment to divorce is likely to depend in large measure on whether there is continued parental conflict, the parenting skills of the custodial parent, the involvement of the nonresident parent, economic factors, as well as other unforeseen life stresses. In a more recent review of published studies, Whiteside and Becker (2000) conclude that while parents cannot insulate their children from the dislocations of the divorce process, they are able to actively promote and support positive coping skills. The quality of the postdivorce parental alliance and cooperative coparenting behavior by involved mothers and fathers increase the probability of positive coping by children.

Confirmation for the resilient view comes from an investigation of poor, minority, single-parent-headed families by Lindblad-Goldberg (1989). Her findings reveal that competence building is possible and that many of the social and psychological problems often associated with growing up in a single-parent-led home are more a function of family poverty than of an inevitable breakdown in family structure. Viewing the single-parent-led family as an open system in transformation, she and her colleague Joyce Dukes found, in studying 126 African American female-headed families with incomes well below the poverty line, that successful adaptation was related to the reciprocal processes of three dimensions: *family resources, environmental stress,* and *social network resources.* In this framework, the family's internal resources involve its ability to organize itself and maintain its integration while adapting to changing events. Executive hierarchy headed by a mother with a sense of control or mastery, clear boundary functioning, and workable family communication patterns are especially important. The family's perception of stressful events in the external environment and its subsequent coping patterns also helped determine adaptation. Last, the family's ability to call upon outside resources such as friends and family for network support was critical. Overall, despite an absent mate, the single mother's effort to sustain a sense of family structure while helping children develop coping skills can, with support from others, develop and maintain family competence and stability.

Varieties of Single-Parent Households

Before considering some of the issues encountered in counseling single-parent-led families, we should define our population. For our purposes, the term *single-parent household* is preferable to either *broken home* or simply *single-parent family. Broken home* is pejorative, implying that the family deserves second-class status because of the parental split and that its subsequent vulnerability makes serious consequences inevitable. *Single-parent family* is misleading, in our opinion, in that it suggests that only one parent is involved after divorce. In point of fact, divorce does not mean that the family no longer exists, but only that the marital relationship has ended; particularly where children are involved, some form of binuclear family relationship with the absent parent or other extended-family members probably continues, even if the parents are physically separated (Ahrons, 1994). Counseling such families, the counselor must keep in focus the impact of these outside family members (parent, siblings, grandparents) as much as those who live together under the same roof.

Marital disharmony leading to separation and divorce is perhaps the most easily recognized but hardly the only avenue to single-parent status; also requiring inclusion is a separated or widowed parent, an unwed mother, or a man or a woman who adopts a child. Moreover, although families led by a single parent as a result of divorce have become highly visible in the last decade, such a family structure is not new but actually represents a traditional form of family organization in the United States.

Seward (1978) notes that between the mid-19th century and 1970, perhaps one out of ten families was maintained by one parent, most likely the mother. Especially in the earlier part of this period, death of a spouse and desertion were the most likely causes of parental absence. Only since the early 1970s, as Thompson and Gongla (1983) report, has that pattern changed. Separation and divorce are currently the most common causes of such families. As Figure 6.3 reveals, according to census data, one-parent households have continued to increase in every decade since the 1970s. In the case of African American families, unmarried mothers now outpace separated, divorced, or widowed mothers.

Divorced or widowed mothers themselves are not a unitary group. The counselor must distinguish between women who are temporarily single but will remarry and those who will not. These groups are likely to bring to counseling different economic lives, different expectations concerning the future, and different sets of problems. For example, a temporarily single woman and her children, living for a period in a one-parent household, must later adapt to a stepfamily and to a possible return to childbearing (thus forcing the family to deal simultaneously with an infant or toddler and, say, an adolescent from the previous marriage). She is also vulnerable to a second divorce, and thus new marital transitions and household reorganizations, before returning to single-parent status. The single parent who does not remarry has a shorter period of child-rearing but statistically runs a far greater risk of financial impoverishment, to say nothing of increased feelings of loneliness and despair. She may also find parts of single life unrewarding and find herself relegated to a lower status in the community (Weiss, 1979).

Although still a minority overall, never-married mothers are the fastest-growing group of single parents. As we have noted, more than one out of every four children today is born to an unmarried mother in the United States. Since unmarried mothers as a group tend to be younger, poorer, less educated, and more dependent on welfare than their married counterparts at the time their child is born, the implications of needs for adequate long-term social services and, for our purposes, counseling are staggering.

Teenage Mothers

One of the most striking changes in American family structure in recent decades has been the high incidence of children born to unwed mothers, particularly single female adolescents. Over 1 million adolescents under the age of 20 became pregnant in the United States in 1990, according to the Alan Guttmacher Institute (1994), and approximately half gave birth. Although the birth rate has decreased some in the last decade, the United States still has the highest rate of teenage pregnancy of any industrial nation in the world; the rate is twice that of the next highest country, Great Britain, 4 times higher than Sweden or Spain, and 15 times greater than that of Japan (Coley & Chase-Lansdale, 1998). Teenage girls now

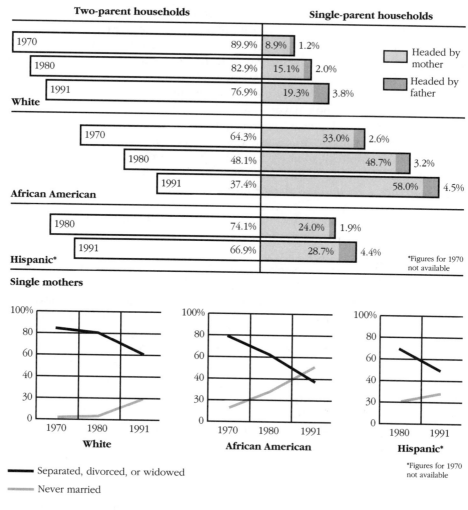

Figure 6.3   Single parents on the rise

account for 30% of all births in the United States. Of these, close to two-thirds of white teen mothers are unmarried when they become pregnant, as are almost all African American teens (97%) (Furstenberg, Brooks-Gunn, & Chase-Lansdale, 1989).[2] Although one in four marries some time between conception and birth of the child, fully half of the first births to teenagers occur out of wedlock.

---

[2] Sexual patterns among American teenagers are not significantly different from their counterparts in other industrialized countries, but American teenagers use contraception less consistently and effectively. As well, the impact of ethnic diversity in the United States to account for the high incidence of teenage pregnancy should not be overemphasized, since the birth rate among white U.S. adolescents easily surpasses that of adolescents in every other industrialized nation (Coley & Chase-Lansdale, 1998).

Teenage mothers frequently come from a background of poverty and are likely to remain locked into a continuing pattern of poverty for the remainder of their lives (Saxton, 1996). In such cases, teenage childbearing adds to their already limited prospects for financial security, steady job expectations, educational attainment, and marital stability. They are apt to drop out of school (sometimes before becoming pregnant), they are apt to become welfare recipients far more often than their peers who delayed childbirth, and they often go on in their twenties to give birth to additional children outside of wedlock. Particularly among younger teenage mothers (15–18 years of age), pregnancy is often the result of lack of information about reproduction and birth control methods, limited access to family planning centers, and sometimes the belief that pregnancy could not happen to them—therefore, contraceptive methods may be carelessly adhered to or ignored completely.

According to Abrahamse, Morrison, and Waite (1988), the individual teenage girl's awareness of what she would stand to lose by becoming an unwed mother is an important tempering factor in whether she protects herself from becoming pregnant. These researchers suggest that this inhibiting effect is apparent at all rungs of the socioeconomic ladder and across all races and ethnicity. Especially among young African American women, those hoping to go to college have dramatically lower nonmarital birth rates than their peers. On the other hand, dropping out of high school increases the risk of pregnancy among teenage girls; of those who did drop out either before or after childbirth in the late 1980s, only 30% eventually graduated (less than half the rate of nonmother dropouts) (Upchurch & McCarthy, 1990). As school policies accept pregnant students, and as additional schooling is required of welfare recipients, this figure is increasing, and more recent findings (Coley & Chase-Lansdale, 1998) indicate that many teenage mothers are now attempting to obtain a general equivalency (GED) high school diploma.

Although pregnancy rates for sexually experienced adolescents have gradually declined in the last two decades, the proportion of pregnant teens who marry before childbirth has sharply decreased, so today the vast majority are unmarried. A reported 40% end their unintended pregnancies through abortion; proportionately, more abortions occur among younger than older teens, and more among white than among African American adolescents. Whites, especially those of higher socioeconomic status, are more apt to marry if pregnant or to place their child for adoption (Burden & Klerman, 1984). However, no more than 3% of those white pregnant adolescents who carry to term, and 1% of African Americans, voluntarily choose adoption with unrelated families for their infants. That figure has steadily decreased in the last two decades (Sobol & Daly, 1992). African Americans as a group make greater use of informal adoption, whereby the infant is absorbed into the extended family (see Chapter 11 for a fuller discussion).

Among all groups who place their infants for adoption, typical reasons given include providing the baby with a family, feeling unprepared for parenthood, wanting to finish school, or lacking financial funds for proper care of the infant.

Family pressures or pressures from physicians or social workers may also contribute to the decision. Although the long-term effect of such an important decision has not yet been adequately researched, Sobol and Daly (1992) note an enduring sense of loss as a recurrent theme. This sense of loss is no doubt exacerbated by society's blocking of open grieving and the biological parent's restricted opportunities to participate, even indirectly, in the life of the child.

Puerto Ricans residing in the U.S. mainland show the highest level of households headed by unmarried female adolescents among all Hispanic groups and, correspondingly, have the highest rate of families living below the poverty line in that subgroup. Unexpected teenage pregnancy is likely to precipitate a crisis in the Puerto Rican family, such an event flying in the face of cultural legacies and traditional values. Gutierrez (1987) reports that initial parental rejection is typically followed by intense turmoil (emotional outbursts, threats of murder or suicide), as issues of family honor predominate. Ultimately, especially with the aid of counseling, some accommodation is reached, the inevitability of the situation is accepted, and practical issues of living arrangements and financial support, and later child care, are resolved.

Teenage girls with low academic ability from poor female-headed families are many times more likely to have a child out of wedlock than are those with high academic ability from upper-income, intact families (Abrahamse, Morrison, & Waite, 1988). As Coley and Chase-Lansdale (1998, p. 153) observe,

> Life experiences associated with poverty, such as alienation at school, prevalent models of unmarried parenthood and unemployment, and lack of educational opportunities and stable career prospects all serve to lower the perceived costs of early motherhood.

It is not uncommon for the teenage mother to call on parents or grandmothers for financial help, coparenting, housing, and support with child-rearing responsibilities and to rely on public assistance. Furstenberg, Brooks-Gunn, and Chase-Lansdale (1989) contend that early childbirth is a potent predictor of long-term welfare dependency, particularly because dropping out of high school is a common result, and the probability of finding stable and remunerative employment is slim. Their long-term investigation reveals that adolescent fathers[3] are usually less adversely affected, economically and scholastically, by early parenthood, although as a group they tend to have negative attitudes toward marriage, to doubt their parenting skills, and to drop out of high school. Many never admit paternity and refuse to provide emotional or financial support, even if able, which often they are not. Others do continue to visit and show interest in the children and their mother, even if remaining unmarried. In many cases, as with teenage mothers, these adolescent fathers come from poor backgrounds and continue a family tradition of teenage childbearing and low educational achievement (Lerman, 1993).

---

[3] Not all men who father children of adolescent girls are teenagers themselves. Cox (1996) suggests that contrary to popular opinion, more are likely to be men in their twenties.

Assessing Single-Parent-Led Families

In assessing single-parent-led families, the family counselor needs to explore the following factors:

- How single parenthood came about (through death, divorce, desertion, or never married)
- At what stage in the marriage that the parent became single (for example, after 12 months of marriage or after 15 years)
- The apparent precipitating factors of a marital breakup (for example, infidelity, chronic quarreling and dissatisfaction, in-law intrusions, immaturity of one or both partners, sexual incompatibilities, financial problems)
- The number of children, the age of the children as well as the age of the parent at the time of becoming a single parent, and the presence and degree of involvement of grandparents or other parts of an extended family
- The specific pile-up of stressor events preceding family dissolution (for example, constant fighting between parents about to separate, forcing the children to choose sides, threats and counterthreats between parents)
- The specific pile-up of stressor events following dissolution and family reorganization (for example, moving to a new location, job, or school; making new friends; establishing a self-identity as a single person or as a member of a single-parent-led family)
- The unfamiliar roles family members have been called upon to play (for example, as head of a one-parent household or as a child called upon to take on more adult responsibilities in the absence of the same-sex parent)
- The role of the absent parent or other significant adult figures in the current single-parent family system
- The quality of relationships within the nuclear family, between the former mates and the family of origin, prior to the events leading to the dissolution of the marriage
- The nature and effectiveness of the single parent's coping skills and resiliency, sense of mastery, and ability to organize and lead the family while adapting to new circumstances
- The single-parent family's relationship with broader social systems (schools, church, welfare, or legal systems)

In addition, the counselor needs to be aware that one-parent households led by fathers are likely to experience different sets of problems and different lifestyles from those led by mothers. Although fathers may have more money, as a rule, they also experience a drop in income and are more likely to have to buy housekeeping and child-care services, because they generally have less experience at these tasks and feel less competent to deal with them. Moreover, fathers may need to resume a dependent relationship with their parents for help with raising the child, something many men (and women, too) consider regressive and distasteful.

Counselors also need to attend to clients' social class, as well as to their racial and ethnic heritage, since these may provide clues as to how effectively and in what manner (for example, with extended-family involvement and community support) such families function. Standards for acceptable social behavior vary between social classes as well as between ethnic groups, and the counselor needs to be careful not to impose his or her own reference group standards on others.

The counselor also needs to appreciate that while families led by a single parent may or may not share a common lifestyle, the more relevant point is that they probably share certain experiences. For example, families led by one parent— whether as a result of separation, divorce, or widowhood—all have experienced some loss. Thus, feelings of loneliness, sadness, guilt, and anger are inevitably present in some degree and in some combination. Morawetz and Walker (1984) report that women in such situations recount the same sets of problems: feeling overburdened, unsupported, and guilty over not being up to the task of raising a family alone. Finding adequate day care or making dependable baby-sitting arrangements, especially for very young children, almost always presents a problem and often becomes a worrisome issue. If the father severs contact with his ex-wife and his children, perhaps paying child support sporadically or not at all— as is frequently the case—the hardship and despair are multiplied. Although the widowed person may dampen or even mute these wearisome feelings in time— indeed, may even comfort herself by exaggerating the positive memories of a previous spouse—the divorced person is far less likely to do so (Weiss, 1979). Part of the reason, of course, is that the divorced couple, especially if children are involved, may continue their conflict (now in the form of wrangles over child-support payments or child visitation) long after the legal divorce is final. In addition, as Getty (1981) points out, if the divorce was initiated by one spouse against the wishes of the other, then the latter, in particular, may be filled with feelings of failure, unworthiness, self-doubt, or perhaps even revenge.

Consider, for example, the differences between the situations of an upper-middle-class, middle-aged widow with adolescent children and a young, working-class, divorced woman, briefly married and with a 2-year-old child. Whereas both may encounter problems trying to raise children on their own, differences in available resources may greatly influence their adaptation to a single life.

Margaret and Ted were married when they graduated from college. She worked for several years as an elementary school teacher while he continued into medical school and through an internship and residency program in ophthalmology. Once Ted established a practice as an ophthalmologist, however, family income was sufficient and they decided to start a family. Margaret had no hesitation in discontinuing her teaching job, since she had long looked forward to having and raising children. Together they had three children—two boys and a girl—and for 25 years Margaret and Ted lived a generally fulfilling and economically comfortable life. However, sudden disaster struck the family when Ted had a massive heart attack at work one day and died instantly, at age 50.

Unlike many single-parent-led families, Margaret and her children did not suffer severe economic upheaval, since Ted had provided for their financial future, although their income was reduced. However, Margaret's loneliness was at times almost unbearable, particularly after the initial period when friends rallied to her side and invited her to their social get-togethers. After six months, few such invitations were forthcoming, and Margaret found herself, at age 49, depressed and alone, not knowing where or to whom to turn. One thing she was sure about, however, was that she must allow her children to lead their own lives and not make them feel obligated or burdened by taking care of their mother. She nevertheless felt responsible for offering them guidance to the best of her ability, although she often bemoaned the fact that she had to be both mother and father to them, and the strain of solo decision making was taking its toll on her health.

As she slowly began, at the urging of her children, to socialize with old friends, she found herself being asked out on dates. Quickly she realized that she had had few experiences with men, having married Ted at such an early age, and that contemporary sexual mores were confusing and frightening. After 6 months, she had not found anyone to match her husband, whom she now missed more than ever.

Despite her good intentions, she did find herself leaning on her children. Margaret's sister, Beatrice, a social worker, became concerned about Margaret's continued unhappiness and growing dependence on the children. Recognizing that they all needed to deal with their grief over their father's death in order to go on with their lives, Beatrice urged them to go together as a family for counseling sessions. With the counselor's support, after several months Margaret resumed dating with men from her church, and with a no-interest loan from a family friend she returned to her undergraduate school for graduate work to obtain training as a school psychologist.

By way of contrast, now consider the case of Lynne, a young divorced person with few personal or familial resources, little education, few job skills, little in the way of social or emotional supports, and solo responsibility for raising a young child:

Lynne, at 22, was the mother of a 2-year-old child. She had married Tom 3 years earlier after a brief romance, and their relationship had been filled with problems from the start. Ever since high school, Lynne had thought about settling down and being a housewife like her mother. She had managed to graduate from high school but had few marketable skills, and she had to take waitressing jobs in order to make some money. The work was unrewarding, and she was unable to afford her own apartment. Living with her mother was difficult since she did not get along with her mother's boyfriend. When Lynne met Tom, an auto mechanic, she moved in with him after knowing him 1 month, in order to get out of the house, and shortly thereafter they were married. Despite their frequent quarrels, they were always able to "kiss and make up"; sex between them was very satisfying and frequently followed one of their prolonged arguments. After a year of marriage, Lynne found she was pregnant. Tired of her job, and sure that caring for a child would be more rewarding, she was pleased about the pregnancy, convinced that it would strengthen her marriage.

The arrival of Lisa, their daughter, stressed the family resources. With Lynne no longer working, Tom was more worried about money now. Frustrated, he complained that Lynne turned more of her attention to the baby than to him. Lynne, on the other hand, could not understand why her husband spent so little time with Lisa and why he was so impatient when the baby cried or in some way interrupted his plans. She was exhausted at the end of the day and expected his help with child care. The couple bickered more than ever, and their sex life, once a certain way to reduce conflict and drain off tension between them, became infrequent and mechanical. When Tom began staying away from home to talk to friends at work, ignoring her and the baby, it became clear to Lynne that nothing was left in their marriage, and she sued for divorce.

Although Lynne was awarded physical custody, with visitation by Tom, and a small amount of child-support money monthly, she soon realized that she needed to make some immediate decisions: Where to live, how to get a job that paid enough so she could supplement the child support, how to get adequate child care on her meager income. Tom soon got laid off from his job, and Lynne's fears concerning Tom's ultimate inability to pay child support soon proved to be well founded: His payments became late and then stopped. His visits with Lisa became less and less frequent, primarily because of his guilt and anger at the situation, and finally stopped after a year during which the two had argued constantly over child-support money.

Lisa soon began to show signs of stress, frequently waking at night and crying until Lynne took her to sleep in her bed for the rest of the night. When Tom told Lynne he was engaged to another woman and planned to leave town for a new job and remarry, the blow to her self-esteem was indescribable. The strain on Lynne became unbearable, financially, emotionally, and socially. Within eight months she had moved back home with her mother. Her mother reluctantly assumed daily child care for her grandchild, although she said with some bitterness that she had assumed she was done with this stage of her life. Lynne's nighttime job as a cocktail waitress allowed her to be with Lisa during the mornings, afternoons, and early evenings. Lisa was cared for by her grandmother at other times. Lynne's work schedule made dating all but impossible for her, although she occasionally went out with a customer when the bar closed.

Common Problems in Single-Parent-Led Families

Inevitably, divorce and its immediate aftermath lead to a series of stressful life events that affects the entire family system (Simons, 1996). No one is immune; the functioning and interactions of all of the members are changed permanently. Where both parents together formerly attempted to take on child care, household, and financial responsibilities, now the custodial parent is likely to feel overloaded by the various tasks she (or sometimes he) is called on to handle alone (Hetherington & Stanley-Hagan, 1997). As we describe below, the noncustodial parent also must establish a new residence, develop a social network, cope with loss of daily contact with the children, arrange visitation, seek new intimate relationships, and maintain some level of coexistence with his (or her) former spouse. Considering these multiple stressors, divorcing parents are apt to remain under significant stress prior to divorce and immediately thereafter as they attempt to deal with separation and redirecting their lives, and as a result may have reduced ability to be helpful to their children during this crucial time of change and readjustment.

As we have emphasized, divorce is a process, not an event occurring at a single transition point between being married and being divorced. Rather, an extended transition is usually required, for parents and children alike. Moreover, in some families, the sequelae of divorce (emotional distress, denial, depression, anger, loss of self-esteem) occur immediately following parental separation; for others, these effects may increase over the first year and then abate; for still other families, such signs may not emerge until a considerable period of time has passed. In the long run, however, according to Furstenberg and Cherlin (1991), a child's adaptation to divorce depends primarily on the extent to which the custodial person is seen as a source of support and on the level of conflict that continues between the ex-spouses.

For pedagogical purposes, we will consider the impact of divorce separately for the various family members—the custodial parent, the noncustodial parent, and the children, In point of fact, of course, the different parts of the family system cannot be so easily separated; each affects the other. All changes associated with marital transitions must be considered from the perspective of changes in the entire family system and its various subsystems. Moreover, the responses of all participants will be affected by the larger social milieu in which they function: peer groups, friendship networks, schools, neighborhood, workplace, and extended families (Hetherington, 1993).

There is great diversity in the responses of both parents and children to separation and divorce. Our intent is to alert the counselor to common responses from all family members to the divorce process and its immediate and subsequent aftermath.

The Custodial Parent

The most glaring difference between two-parent families and families headed by mothers only is the disparity in economic well-being (McLanahan & Sandefur, 1994). Mother-child families, especially with young children, are, generally speaking, worse off financially than any other family type (Cox, 1996). Saxton (1996) characterizes women who head single-parent households[4] as by far the most eco-

---

[4] Although the percentage of children living with fathers has increased rapidly in recent years and now represents about 16% of single-family households, research on custodial fathers remains relatively meager, especially in regard to very young children. In general, the issue of the importance of fathers in children's lives is still in its early research stage (Booth & Crouter, 1998). For the discussion to follow, then, we will assume that the mother has physical custody of the children.

nomically disadvantaged women in the United States, although recent increased enforcement by the states of child-support payments[5] by noncustodial fathers as well as increased participation in the work force by single mothers has probably lessened the problem somewhat for some. However, while these single mothers with children may not experience the drastic decline in living standards that was evident a decade or two ago, they do receive only perhaps a quarter to a half of their predivorce intact-family income. Beyond dollars and cents, this loss is usually accompanied by an increased workload for the solo parent in the home, heavier responsibilities, frequently a move to a poorer neighborhood with worse schools and often a heightened crime rate, and generally downward mobility (McLanahan & Sandefur, 1994).

It is hardly surprising that money problems pose a severe stress for people. Of more significance, psychologically speaking, may be the mother's *change* in economic standing and the subsequent fear of losing control over her life, as well as the lives of children for whom she feels responsible. As Mednick (1987) notes, the sense of control over income and the feeling of being effective as a self-supporter represent significant predictors of life satisfaction and reduced stress. Together, they help diminish the inevitable sense of powerlessness to which custodial mothers are so vulnerable, particularly in the period immediately following the divorce.

Single custodial mothers typically experience considerable stress in balancing the multiple responsibilities of work and family (Burden, 1986). Part-time and unemployed women workers are, of course, even worse off. Sometimes, as we saw in the case just presented, a woman may move back to her parents' home as an adult and custodial parent, although this makeshift solution may itself add other sources of stress. Taking in lodgers to share expenses or moving in with other women in similar straits is another possible solution, again with potential problems. Custodial fathers usually experience less of an income loss, and thus less financial distress, although Meyer and Garasky (1991) report that close to a fifth of father-only-led families live in poverty, and fathers rarely receive child support from an ex-mate.

According to Henggeler and Borduin (1990), the financial impact of the divorce may contribute to a number of psychosocial problems within the family, including the mother's depression and withdrawal from friends, the children's relative lack of interaction with their peers, and disturbances in the mother-child relationships. (We present a checklist of some typical problems faced by custodial single parents in Box 6.1 on page 142.) Solo responsibility for the management of child discipline often becomes an overwhelming task for an already harassed single parent, especially if the child evidences increased behavior problems in response to the stress and conflict surrounding the divorce.

---

[5] Many nonresident fathers still do not pay child support or do so sporadically, despite being mandated to do so by the states, in compliance with federal regulations. The problem with such so-called "deadbeat dads" is especially severe for single mothers who were never married.

Box 6.1 A problem-appraisal checklist for custodial single parents

---

Custodial single parents may experience problems in the following areas:

- Change in economic status (for most, especially women, this translates into economic hardship)
- Grief, self-blame, loss of self-esteem, and depression
- Role overload (attempting to play a multitude of roles—such as organizing a household, caring for children, producing income—previously divided between both parents)
- Social stigma and disapproval over being divorced
- Disruption of customary living arrangements (may include change in residence, community, school district for children, and return to work force)
- Loneliness, feeling of social isolation, loss of friends (especially married couples), the need to develop new social circle
- Lack of adequate support system (formerly provided by mate, in-laws, friends in old community)
- Strain from solo decision making (taking major or perhaps full responsibility for family decisions, unlike past experiences in which such judgments were likely to have been shared or at least discussed)
- Child-care arrangements (depending on the age of the child or children of the parent working or returning to school, this may require considerable planning, energy expenditure, and flexibility in schedule, particularly in the case of illness of the child or parent)
- Interpersonal conflict (with children, ex-spouse, parents and former in-laws, baby-sitter, lovers, roommates)
- Sex and dating (new person introduced into family circle, decisions regarding resumption of a sex life, concern over reactions of children)
- Custody and visitation (continued relations with ex-spouse, concern over child's loyalty, upset as children are introduced to new friends or lovers of ex-spouse)

The Noncustodial Parent

Nonresident parent roles vary widely, from a cessation of contact with ex-spouse and children, to intermittent contact, to remaining a vital part of the family despite living separately (as in the binuclear family). Where any one person fits on this continuum depends largely on his or her previous role in the family system, interest, and availability, and on the freedom of access permitted by the custodial parent. That role is likely to undergo changes over time in any case, and is not always predictable from the father's predivorce behavior. Braver and associates (1993) find the most powerful factor determining continuing involvement to be the noncustodial parent's perception that he or she has some control over the child's upbringing.

Generally speaking, if the parent living outside the family retains some sense of influence over the children's upbringing, he (or she) remains involved in visiting them and contributing financially to their support. On the other hand, if feeling disenfranchised and without input into how the children are raised, the excluded parent is less likely to continue contributing child support and may ultimately relinquish any emotional involvement with the children (Braver et al., 1993).

In some cases, as Morawetz and Walker (1984) report, the level of fury by the custodial mother toward the noncustodial spouse, who is seen as abandoning or betraying the marriage, is so great that the counselor will meet strong resistance when attempting to help family members work through their feelings about the divorce. In such situations, the absent spouse may be kept from the children on one pretext or another, or may be scapegoated or called names ("untrustworthy," "cruel," "crazy") by the custodial parent. The custodial parent may attempt to coerce the children into sharing her rage as a sign of their loyalty. Not only does this place the children in conflict, but it may also force the nonresident father to become marginalized. His reaction, in defense, may be to distance himself from the family, thereby perhaps confirming his indifference and irresponsibility in the other's eyes. (The reverse may also occur: The noncustodial father may provoke the children into angry, rebellious behavior toward the at-home mother.)

Box 6.2 on page 144 is intended to alert the counselor to the possible problem areas to consider with noncustodial parents. Beyond the divorce itself, which may be a prolonged and often embittering process, the result in a great many cases leaves the nonresident parent feeling deprived of ongoing involvement with the children. (The negative consequences of the separation for the children will be discussed in the following section.) From his survey of available research, Hodges (1991) concludes that although women are more likely than men to articulate their distress about marital conflict prior to the separation, men have more difficulty recovering after the divorce than do women. The pervasive sense of loss of daily contact with the children is likely to be especially painful. However, one consolation is that a man is more apt to define himself through his work, and because his job and work contacts remain relatively unchanged after divorce, a major part of his life remains stable (Wallerstein & Blakeslee, 1989).

What of fathers who had limited contact with their children while the family was intact? Wallerstein and Kelly (1980a) have discovered that the predivorce father-child connection is a poor predictor of the postdivorce relationship. In many cases, these fathers become closer to their children and more involved in their children's activities than they had been before the family reorganization. For most children, especially the younger ones, these researchers find such an increase in closeness to be particularly beneficial. The finding that warm, authoritative postdivorce fathering is associated with better child functioning is confirmed by Whiteside and Becker (2000), who emphasize mutually supportive coparenting.

In general, most nonresident fathers maintain a friendly, egalitarian, companionship relationship with their children, hesitant to assume the role of disciplinarian or teacher, and eager for their visits together to be pleasant and entertaining. Hetherington, Bridges, and Insabella (1998) suggest that these fathers are less

---

Box 6.2   A problem-appraisal checklist for noncustodial parents

Noncustodial parents may experience problems in the following areas:

- Change in economic status (lowered living standard due to contributing to the support of two homes)
- Diminished relationship with their children (pain over loss of day-to-day sense of what's happening in their lives)
- Feeling of devaluation as a parent (no longer feeling important and necessary in the lives of their children)
- Disruption of customary living arrangements (change of residence, feeling of starting over, loss of friends)
- Necessity of learning to cope with new tasks (especially for men, having to provide own care, feeding, cleaning, and other services formerly provided by mother or wife)
- Development of new connections with children (including visitation activities, providing a space for children to spend the night, making purchases unilaterally that may provoke the ex-mate)
- Social stigma and disapproval over being divorced
- Necessity of dealing with recurrent memories whenever returning to pick up children
- Grief, self-blame, loss of self-esteem, and depression
- Loneliness, feeling of being at loose ends, the need to develop new social circle
- Interpersonal conflict (with children, ex-spouse, parents and former in-laws, lovers, roommates)
- Necessity of learning to deal with events to which parents in intact families go together (school open house, graduation, weddings, funerals), especially when former partner has new mate
- Sex and dating (decisions regarding resumption of a sex life, concern over child meeting new lover, especially if that person has children)
- Custody and visitation (planning activities may be an unfamiliar experience, being sole caretaker may be difficult if young child is involved)

---

likely than nondivorced fathers to criticize, control, or monitor their children's behavior, or to help them with tasks such as homework. Those who participate in various activities with their children, spend holidays together, and act as more than mere "tour guides" during visitations with their children are apt to aid in their children's sense of well-being (Clarke-Stewart & Hayward, 1996).

The Children

When divorce occurs, the odds are that it will take place prior to the seventh year of marriage; therefore, young children are almost certain to be involved. Children, at least as much as and often more than their parents, experience impaired functioning during and after a divorce. For many children, parental separation and divorce mean exposure to a series of marital transitions and household reorganizations that often proves to be disruptive (Hetherington, Stanley-Hagan, & Anderson, 1989). Although generally speaking, the child's adaptation is related to the parents' adjustment and behavior, in some cases the decision to divorce may improve parents' well-being while having a detrimental effect on their offspring. About two of every five white children (three of four African Americans) will experience parental divorce before reaching the age of 16 (Cherlin, 1992); half will have a stepfather within 4 years (Furstenberg, 1988).

Children are apt to be resilient, however, despite living through their parents' divorce and the adaptations required in its aftermath; the vast majority ultimately grow into competent, normal, functioning adults (Emery & Forehand, 1994). Hetherington, Stanley-Hagan, and Anderson (1989) report that despite initial distress, most children adapt to living in a single-parent household within two or three years if their new situation is not compounded by continued or additional adversity. Nevertheless, during that period they may display aggressive, noncompliant, acting-out behavior, or perhaps experience academic or other school-related difficulties or disruptions in relationships with peers. Despite these difficulties in some children, overall, the researchers found that children ultimately adapt better to a well-functioning single-parent-led family or stepfamily than to a conflict-ridden family of origin. Counselors whose clients are deciding whether to stay together for the sake of the children need this information.

Box 6.3 on page 146 outlines some of the possible consequences of divorce for children. Age at time of separation and divorce offers clues regarding eventual adaptation in children. The emotional impact of the experience is perhaps most telling for younger children (elementary-school-age and younger), precisely because they are not able to comprehend the events unfolding around them, while at the same time they sense the emotional upheaval in their parents, on whom they depend for their security. Severe reactions are likely to occur in those cases where young children are not given an explanation regarding the disappearance of their absent father. Such distress is likely to continue for a considerable time as the parents go through a period of mourning for the lost marriage. Frequently, parents can profit from counselor guidance at this point about how to tell children of the parents' decision to divorce, as well as how to manage their own grief.

In a pioneering, comprehensive longitudinal research undertaking, the California Children of Divorce Project, Wallerstein and Kelly (1974, 1975, 1976) studied the reactions of 60 divorced families over a 5-year period. In all, 131 children, ages 2 to 18, took part. While preschool children tended to react with denial ("It's not happening to me"; "When is Daddy coming home?") and on the surface appeared to be untroubled, on closer inspection many were found to be anxious and self-blaming for the breakup of the family. Fears of abandonment, regression in toilet training, clinging behavior, temper tantrums, and fantasies regarding parental reconciliation were common, although, according to a follow-up 10 years later by Wallerstein, Corbin, and Lewis (1988), children had few memories of earlier fears and suffering.

Slightly older children (7 or 8 years of age) were more apt to become withdrawn and uncommunicative about their feelings and to become depressed.

Box 6.3   A problem-appraisal checklist for children of divorced parents

Children may experience problems in the following areas when their parents divorce:

- Shame, embarrassment, lowered self-esteem
- Diminished relationship with noncustodial parent
- Self-blame for parental split
- Depression, sadness, moodiness, emotional withdrawal
- Conflicting loyalties (upset and anger over being caught between feelings for both parents)
- Continuing fantasies of parental reconciliation
- Anger and rage at both parents (blame of custodial parent for the other parent's absence; blame of noncustodial parent for leaving)
- Anxiety over an uncertain or unfamiliar future
- Parentification (prematurely pressed to act as an adult, overattached to custodial parent, and pressed to act as a surrogate parent to younger children)
- Lowered economic status
- Disruption of customary living arrangements (new school, new home, new friends)
- Antisocial behavior, poor school performance
- Adaptation to visitation activities
- Response to parent dating (diversion of parental attention to person outside previous family; fear of being replaced by parent's new friend)
- Fear of loss and abandonment if custodial parent is absent

School problems and difficulties in making new friends were common reactions. Children aged 9 or 10 at the time of family dissolution were more likely to be angry and ashamed and to verbalize blame at the parents for what they felt they were being put through. Adolescents as a group were more successful at making sense out of what had happened and why the marriage had failed; in many cases, they resolved loyalty conflicts and even saw the decision by their parents to divorce as a good one.

In a 5-year follow-up of all the children, Wallerstein and Kelly (1980b) discovered considerable differences in how well the children had resolved their earlier experiences. In those instances where bitterness and interparental conflict continued (or perhaps even escalated), and where a parent sought alliances with the children against the ex-spouse, postdivorce adaptation was seriously impaired. In such cases, children's disturbed behavior patterns were more a reaction to what was going on at present than what had transpired in the past, when the family was intact. On the other hand, to the extent that acrimony between ex-spouses could be reduced and the nonresident parent could remain involved and offer support to the ex-spouse, the children could get on successfully with their lives (Braver et al., 1993; Whiteside & Becker, 2000).

Child Custody, Child Support, and Visitation

The dissolution of a marriage by no means needs to signal the dissolution of the child's relationship with the nonresident parent. Increasingly, for a variety of legal, financial, and also psychological reasons, including recognition of the father's pain regarding separation, the courts have deemed it best for all concerned that a shared or coparenting custody arrangement be worked out between divorcing parents, if at all feasible. In this way, the child continues to have the benefit of frequent contact with both parents; bitter, drawn-out custody battles are moderated; the nonresident parent is more apt to remain involved (and to continue child support) rather than drift away or be kept away from the children; and there is a substantial reduction in the incidence of kidnapping by a disgruntled, embittered parent who feels his or her only choice is to run off with a child. Pressures on an overburdened single parent, possibly leading to child neglect or abuse, can be lessened when the responsibilities for child care are shared. Changing custody arrangements also permit women choices beyond the traditional ones of custodial mothers. The social stigma or personal guilt formerly inflicted on women who chose to give up or share custody of their children is less severe today, but still exists for many women, especially if they choose to yield sole custody to their former husbands.

Counselors called upon by the court or by an attorney for one of the ex-partners in a divorce action to evaluate and recommend custody decisions[6] to the judge need to be cognizant of the impact of divorce on all family members involved and to assess all participants (mother, father, children) carefully and objectively. Engaging in a dual role—assessor as well as personal counselor—usually precludes such impartiality and should be avoided since it entails the risk of an ethics violation and biased choices. Particularly in **forensic** work with bicultural children, cultural factors need to be considered: norms for any given ethnic group, differences in parenting practices when assessing parenting competencies, and the appropriateness of assessment instruments for people from different cultural backgrounds. The parents' level of acculturation, language proficiency, and generational status all require the counselor's attention (Campos, 1996). The American Psychological Association (1994) has issued a set of guidelines for child custody evaluations in divorce proceedings.

Historically, before the 19th century, women and children were considered part of a man's property. From the time of early English common law, the father as household head had been awarded child custody after a marriage breakup unless it could be established that he was an unfit parent. Such reasoning was based on fathers' better ability to provide economically for their children, since women rarely worked outside the home (O'Donohue & Bradley, 1999). That standard began to change in the latter half of the 19th century, when women were

---

[6]While we emphasize the issues involved in custody decisions connected with divorce, it is important to note that there are other circumstances (allegations of child neglect and abuse, death of a child's guardian) in which counselors might be called upon to provide expert opinion in helping to resolve custody disputes or in helping evaluate the adequacy of child placements (Mason, 1994).

allowed to own property and the criterion of *tender years* was introduced into custody decisions (Mason, 1994). As the focus began to change to what was best for the child, rather than the parents, mothers were now considered to be in a better (more nurturing) position to provide for their children's welfare, particularly in the case of minor children of tender years. By the 1970s in the United States, the gender-based bias favoring maternal custody had begun to change once again, and judges began to exert a great deal of discretionary power in determining what custody arrangement was in the child's best interest (Hall, Pulver, & Cooley, 1996). These *best interests of the child* standards have now replaced the tender years criterion. Each state establishes its own criteria of what constitutes the child's best interests, and there is little consistency across states (O'Donohue & Bradley, 1999).

Such changes came about through two sources: lobbying for men's custody rights by the men's movement (both the Father's Rights of America and the National Congress of Men) and the widespread passage of no-fault divorce laws, now the law in all 50 states. By granting a divorce without imputing wrongdoing or assigning blame for the no-longer-viable marriage, divorce is acknowledged by the state to be an acceptable part of a pluralistic society—like marriage, a matter of individual choice—thus, its dissolution need not inevitably lead to finger pointing (one innocent party, one guilty one) and subsequent acrimony (Emery, 1999). Without accusing either partner of any offense, the marriage is simply declared to be unworkable because of undefined irreconcilable differences and then dissolved. Child custody remains based on the now gender-neutral principle of who serves the best interests of the child. Despite these efforts at parity, however, Bray (1988) contends that many men still insist that a sex bias exists favoring women as custodial parents.

Child support involves financial payments made by the noncustodial parent to the parent with whom the child lives, usually until the child is 18 years of age or through with schooling. Most likely it is the father who makes such support payments to his ex-wife, although nowadays the income of both parents is taken into account by the court in making the calculation. These payments may be in addition to *spousal support* (previously called *alimony*), intended to help equalize the living standards of the ex-spouse. The child-support payments are supposed to be based on the needs of the child, although the ex-partners may disagree on what the child needs, how much it should cost, and who should pay for what. School costs, food, clothing, and shelter, but also such things as piano lessons, sports equipment, and entertainment, are typically included. What complicates matters is that issues of what the child should be receiving (private school? religious education? summer camp?) may themselves have been points of contention during the marriage and are thus unlikely to be settled easily during the divorce action. Moreover, the unresolved conflict that resulted in divorce is commonly carried over into struggles between former partners over money. Should the husband remarry, the conflict over sending checks each month to his ex-wife is likely to be a source of irritation and sometimes deprivation to the new wife and to lead to increased stress in the new marriage. Many ex-husbands cease visitations and stop sending child-support payments after a period of time. In recent years, Congress passed the Child Support Enforcement Act to help state agencies enforce court-ordered child-support payments through withholding wages and tax refunds (Aulette, 1994). In some cases, men can go to jail for withholding payments, although, of course, incarceration prevents them from earning money for further payments. In recent years, enforcement has become more strict, and as a consequence delinquent child-support payments are regularly withheld from any federal income tax refunds otherwise due resistant fathers.

About two-thirds of ever-married custodial mothers (one-fourth of never married) have a child-support award; perhaps half actually receive the full amount, one-quarter receive partial payments, another one-quarter no payments (U.S. Bureau of the Census, 1995). Women whose child-support payments were court ordered are much less likely to receive the full amount than those who receive voluntary payments; similarly, those with court-ordered payments are much more likely to receive no payment at all than if the ex-spouse voluntarily agreed to send money (Saluter, 1989). In some cases, especially among lower-income fathers, food, diapers, gifts, labor around the house, baby-sitting, and some small financial assistance are offered in lieu of child-support payments. The alert counselor can sometimes anticipate a problem over child support and suggest the couple settle the issue and amount voluntarily and cooperatively, helping ensure regular payments (Nord & Zill, 1996).

In some cases, visitation with the nonresident father (perhaps every other weekend or one month during the summer) is (illegally) denied by the custodial mother in retaliation for nonpayment; in other cases, payments are withheld over disputes regarding visitation. In either case, child support and visitation rights are often bound together as the previously married couple tries to work out the details of visitation rights, which are usually specified by courts only as reasonable visitation (Lasswell & Lasswell, 1991). Different definitions of what constitutes "reasonable" to each of the bickering ex-spouses frequently add fuel to an already potentially combustible situation.

Child Custody Alternatives

Child custody decisions, along with determinations of child-support payments and visitation rights for the nonresident parent, are made during the divorce process (see Figure 6.2 on page 126). Because no-fault divorce laws eliminate any determination of guilt over the breakup of the marriage, child custody is no longer automatically given to the presumably aggrieved party (the one who sued) as in the past. In prior years, women were expected to remain at home to care for the children, so they typically were considered the "innocent" party, brought suit, and were awarded child custody, child support, plus a property settlement. Today, women are no longer expected to, or are often not economically able to, stay home and care for the children while men work away from home. As a result, a number of alternative child custody arrangements, established by parental agreement or judicial decision, are now possible, including the following:

- *Sole custody:* One parent is awarded total physical and legal responsibility for the children. The noncustodial parent has no legal right to make decisions regarding the children but is usually awarded visitation rights.
- *Joint legal custody:* Both parents share legal responsibilities and together participate in the major decisions regarding their children, such as religious upbringing or choice of school.
- *Split custody:* Each parent is awarded the full legal custody of one or more of the children (for example, girls with mother, boys with father), or the children alternate, living with the noncustodial parent on weekends or during vacations.
- *Custody awarded to someone other than the parent:* Grandparents or other close relatives gain custody due to the court's decision that parental custody would be harmful because of a poor home environment.

Sole custody, in most cases by the mother, remains the most common pattern (65–70%) (Cox, 1996) despite recent increases in some divorced fathers' efforts to participate jointly in child-rearing. The father retains visitation rights plus any additional rights or privileges agreed upon between parents in the divorce settlement (such as overnight stays or vacations). **Split custody** is less probable, since such an arrangement may compound a child's sense of loss of brothers and sisters (Hodges, 1991), although split custody may be recommended if the children are chronically destructive toward one another. Awarding custody to someone other than the parent is the least probable custody determination and would occur only if the court believed the parents incompetent or potentially harmful to the children (for example, if the parents were drug abusers).

Joint legal custody is an increasingly popular shared arrangement[7] in which both parents have equal authority in regard to their children's general welfare, education, and parenting, just as they had when they were married. Generally speaking, the most common plan is for the children to reside in one parent's home and for the other parent to have access to them, thus avoiding sudden termination of the children's contact with the nonresident parent. Obviously, this arrangement works best when the ex-mates are each caring and committed parents, can be cooperative, have relatively equal and consistent parenting skills, and are able to work together without renewing old animosities. In some states, such as California, joint legal custody is presumed in all divorces unless a ruling

---

[7]Most feminist groups, such as the National Organization for Women (NOW), supported joint custody efforts in the early years as an issue of equal rights. Recently, however, they have begun to question whether joint custody is fair to women from an economic standpoint, claiming that women receive less child support in joint custody decisions than in cases where they are awarded sole custody, yet continue to carry the same responsibilities. Ahrons (1994) observes that as parental responsibilities have become more evenly divided under joint custody rulings, each partner may be responsible for expenses incurred when the children are with him or her, but since women do not yet have equal economic earning power as a rule, they may face more of a financial hardship.

to the contrary is made. As noted previously, under this arrangement each ex-spouse retains legal rights, privileges, and responsibilities as a parent. Joint legal custody does not necessarily mean shared parenting on a daily basis, however. The child's primary residence is likely to remain with one parent, but the child may also live with or have access to the other parent at specified times.

In a variation of joint custody called **joint physical custody** (sometimes con-fused with joint legal custody), both parents take part in the day-to-day care of their children and all necessary decision making, although the parents may live separately. The children may move between households every week or every month, or perhaps spend weekdays with one parent and weekends with the other; in some cases, they may even alternate during each week, spending three days with one parent and four days with the other, who usually lives in the same vicinity so that the children are able to attend the same school. In relatively rare cases, the children remain in the family home while the parents take turns mov-ing in or staying at another residence.

Although legal and physical custody arrangements may be jointly agreed upon, in practice they might not work quite as neatly or be as conflict-free as we have outlined. Not unexpectedly, in some cases the arrangements made for custody, visitation rights, and child-support payments simply provide additional arenas for battle between combatants, particularly those who remain intensely angry and bitter over what they perceive to be past injustices. Since anger associated with divorce can persist many years after dissolution of the marriage and even into remarriage, such chronic bitterness can continue to infuse interactions with the ex-mate in regard to the children. Such sustained antagonism is not inevitable, of course, depending on how well previous problems can be resolved once the couple is apart or whether problems can be accepted and lived with in order for both people to continue to be effective parents.

Ahrons and Rodgers (1987), discussing the binuclear family (two households, one family), depict five distinct types of relationships between former marital partners:

1. *Perfect pals:* Still friends; jointly decided to live separate lives but retain mutual respect, in earlier generations would probably not have gotten divorced; may have had some anger during separation, but now each con-siders the other a responsible and caring parent; still in some conflict at times, but accommodating to each other overall.

2. *Cooperative colleagues:* No longer good friends but able to cooperate suc-cessfully as parents; may no longer like each other in many ways but recog-nize need to compromise for the sake of the children and to fulfill their own desires to be active and responsible parents; some current disagreements but able to avoid escalating power struggles.

3. *Angry associates:* Still bitter and resentful about the marriage and the divorce process; continuous fights over finances, visitation schedules, custody arrangements; each continues parenting, but children are often caught in ongoing loyalty conflicts.

4. *Fiery foes:* No ability to coparent; intense anger, even years after divorce; perceive each other as enemies; each parent may have limited parenting ability; continuing legal battles; children are caught in the middle and forced to take sides; noncustodial parent probably sees children with decreasing frequency over the years.
5. *Dissolved duos:* Discontinued contact between former partners after divorce; one partner may leave geographic area; kidnapping by noncustodial parent may occur; truly single-parent family.

These authors offer the following illustrations of the reactions of each of the relationship types to a child's high school graduation: (1) perfect pals plan dinner out together, sit together during the ceremony, perhaps give one joint gift; (2) cooperative colleagues both attend the ceremony but, if sitting together, do so under some strain; (3) angry associates celebrate separately with the child, sit separately at the ceremony, and avoid contact as much as possible; (4) in the case of fiery foes, one parent is excluded from the celebration and perhaps from the ceremony itself, and feels hurt and angry; (5) in dissolved duos, the custodial parent does not bother informing the ex-spouse of the graduation; the noncustodial parent would not acknowledge the event if aware of it.

Some Counseling Guidelines

Families headed by one parent are frequently formed as a result of crisis: a failed marriage, widowhood, an unexpected pregnancy in the life of an unmarried teenager or young adult. As a result, an early family task frequently involves organizing (or reorganizing) the family unit and beginning the process of stabilization by learning effective coping strategies that may be used to deal with the uncertainty ahead. One central issue apt to require immediate attention is the definition (or redefinition) of family boundaries, as family members take on many new and unfamiliar tasks and responsibilities.

The custodial mother must learn to establish family rules, must delineate responsibilities, and often must learn to impose child discipline single-handedly and deal with other psychosocial problems almost certain to erupt in the children, all at a time when she herself is in a weakened and perhaps overwrought and depressed state. She must learn to live in her same society, which probably was organized around two-parent families (for example, in interactions with schools), cope with the children's often unstated but felt reactions to the separation and the absence of their father, and at the same time try to develop a plan for earning money while providing adequate child care for her offspring. In Burden's (1986) survey of employees at a large corporation, single female parents described their greatest stress as over multiple work and family responsibilities; they spent an average of 75 hours per week trying to balance job and family duties, typically with little or no financial or emotional assistance from others.

In the case of low-income families, the single mother frequently has the choice of only minimum-wage jobs. She must learn to initiate and ultimately cope with the welfare system, obtain employment training, and get affordable housing if not living with her extended family. As Hodges (1991) notes, the lack of another parent to serve as a buffer or provide social support means that single mothers are more vulnerable to the hurt and anger experienced by their children. Inevitably, this increases the pain associated with parenting and may lead to inappropriate problem solving.

Counseling frequently calls for a careful assessment of the mother's work situation, her relationships with fellow workers and job supervisors, and even the work/family policies of her employer in regard to such issues as schedule flexibility, child care, absenteeism, and personal time off (Carlson, Sperry, & Lewis, 1997). Finding and retaining adequate child care, along with an understanding and flexible supervisor, can be vital factors in a single mother's ability to cope with work and home responsibilities (Pelavin, 1995).

Children living with one parent need to adjust to the often painful prospect of not seeing one parent on a daily basis. At the same time, they may have to make an additional series of adjustments to a changed school, new friends, a changed relationship with both parents and any possible new mates, self-consciousness about the divorce, reduced money and activity—all while grieving for the breakup of the family as they knew it. (Some, of course, may relish the new peacefulness, the more relaxed parent at home, the absence of parental conflict.)

Because the family structure has changed, an absent adult member leaves a void, and a child may attempt to fill it. A **parentified child** may be forced into an adult role that the overburdened parent cannot manage alone. The counselor must carefully appraise the needs of the family here, before disturbing the structure; however, the counselor must not lose sight of the fact that a parentified position can be costly to parent and child alike. The counselor needs to help the family restructure itself so that the parent regains the leadership position in the family and the children play more subordinate but supporting roles.

Working therapeutically with a single-parent-led family, the counselor must never lose sight of the psychological presence of the other parent even if, as is likely, that person is physically absent from the consultation room. To ignore the "ghosts" of the earlier marriage by focusing on the parent-child dyad alone is to ignore the considerable influence the absent person (or the memories of that person) may continue to exert on what transpires between those presently attending. The following case illustrates the possible continued "presence" of the absent parent:

After a bitterly fought divorce, in which Linda would settle for nothing less than sole custody of Craig, a 12-year-old only child, with minimum visiting privileges for Craig's father, she soon found that the boy was simply adding to her unhappiness. He was a constant reminder, in appearance, mannerism, voice, and behavior, of his father. To make matters worse, the more she vilified her ex-husband, the more Craig defended him and complained about not having him near anymore. Whenever Craig was with his father, he told Craig what a miserable person his mother had been to live with, attempting to justify his departure to his son. The pressures from both parents for his undivided loyalty began to take their toll on Craig, who became sullen, angry, and withdrawn. Soon a battle began to rage between mother and son; he became increasingly defiant, and she continued issuing gloomy forecasts to him about how he would turn out to be just like his father. Counseling for the two focused on working through previously unexpressed feelings about the divorce on both their parts and creating a less bitter home environment. The father attended several sessions, and while his relationship with his ex-wife was no more loving, they were able to tolerate each other better and not use Craig to get back at each other.

On the other hand, the ghost may be the spouse who met an untimely death:

Hilda and Charles had had a solid and loving marriage for 14 years when he succumbed to cancer. Although the death was by no means sudden—his dying stretched out over a year and a half—Hilda felt devastated when it actually occurred. Beyond missing him terribly and trying to cope with life without him, she felt unprepared to manage by herself. Charles had made few household demands on her and had taken care of many household decisions—servicing the car, paying bills, banking, repairs around the house, vacation planning, and so on. Hilda, on the other hand, had been primarily involved in a small business selling quilts she made. Confused by her new responsibilities, she began to rely more and more on her 12-year-old son, Paul, a mature and competent child, as a partner, often blurring generational boundaries and questioning him about decisions far beyond his capacity or experience to make. In one sense, she was keeping her husband's memory alive, but at the same time she was not allowing Paul to play with his friends in his sports activities, for he felt he must hurry home after school to be with his mother. Finally, Hilda's aunt, a retired schoolteacher, recognizing the evolving problems, was able to intervene, recommending that Hilda attend a counseling group for widows run by a psychologist at the local clinic.

The counselor understood the sudden burden thrust upon Hilda and also the fact that Charles's death had somehow brought mother and son closer. The counselor also helped Hilda to see some negative consequences from Hilda and Paul's enmeshed behavior patterns, however. Both needed to complete their mourning and get on with their lives. Parent-child boundaries needed to be clarified; remaining intertwined hampered the process. Finding a new friend in the group, a younger widow with similar interests and a 10-year-old daughter, Hilda began to see other possibilities and choices. She began to gain self-esteem and take on responsibilities as family head that she previously had done with her small business.

As a result of her regaining control of family leadership, she and her son were able to let go of each other sufficiently so that they could remain available to offer mutual support and encouragement but at the same time begin to pursue independent lives.

The first case illustrates how some formerly married couples may be legally and physically separated but are hardly finished fighting with each other. As we can see, the children of these "angry associates" often feel caught in the middle—loyalty to one means disloyalty to the other—and are in a no-win situation until the parents resolve not to use them to diminish their conflicts. Otherwise, the children remain the long-term recipients of any unfinished business between their parents and years after the divorce may find themselves still caught up in the middle of their parents' conflicts. In other cases, they choose sides, isolating themselves from the other parent, often for many years.

In the second case, we are dealing with a parentified child needing to give up his childhood experiences to take on parental executive responsibilities without the knowledge or ability to carry them off successfully. These burdens may weigh heavily, whether the child is appreciated or not, and as the recipient of confidences inappropriate for his stage of development, he is confused and distressed. Important opportunities to explore relationships with peers are often sacrificed.

These cases also point up the fact that the counselor is most likely to see a custodial mother and her child when the latter is in trouble (with the school, the police), becomes symptomatic (sullen, withdrawn), or when parent-child conflicts become chronic and seemingly unresolvable. Otherwise, the woman's everyday life may be too burdened with work, child-care arrangements, and domestic as well as financial pressures to allow her the luxury of counseling. The earlier the intervention, however, the better the odds of conflict resolution.

In addition to a single mother's lack of knowledge, money, or simply energy for counseling, a number of other roadblocks hinder easy entry by the counselor into the family system. With an intact two-parent family, as Fulmer (1983) points out, the family counselor can rely on the inherent strength or excitement of a revived or reunited parental dyad to alter the rules of the family system. Here, however, no such relationship exists. Instead, a rebellious adolescent, likely to mistrust adults, may be difficult to reach at first, while a younger child has fewer resources to call upon. Neither is helpful in establishing a therapeutic atmosphere at the start of the experience. So, more often than not, according to Fulmer, the counselor must begin any clinical interventions with the mother, who has little inclination or wherewithal to take on new (counseling) projects outside the home. The mother's exhaustion and depression, noted earlier in this chapter, thus become a problem to be addressed early in the counseling if progress with the family is to be made.

Adolescent mothers deserve special attention here. As a group, they rarely seek out available counseling or other services on their own, tending to isolate themselves from others during and after pregnancy and confining their social contacts to members of their families of origin at home. Weatherley and Cartoof (1988) maintain that traditional counseling strategies are likely to be less effective with pregnant and parenting teenagers than a combination of supportive counseling, home visiting, and offers to help with concrete tasks. For those who are amenable to counseling, Jemail and Nathanson (1987) suggest the rationale advanced by Weltner (1992), which we described in Chapter 5, in which a counselor's interventions are tailored to a family's level of functioning. Level I interventions might be directed at a teenage mother and her infant, both of whom lack the basic necessities of food, shelter, and medical care; the goal might be to mobilize family members, friends, agencies, or community helpers in an effort to support, teach, and act as advocate for the ill-prepared young mother. Correspondingly, Level II families might require interventions providing structure, limits, and safety for the child, while helping the mother to continue her education and learn to once again socialize with peers. If a teenager-headed family is functioning at Level III but still seeks counseling, the interventions can focus on strengthening family boundaries and promoting clarity between generations. Overall, counseling should include efforts to keep her in school—if necessary, in special programs designed for pregnant teens—so that she can maintain social contact with peers and receive her high school diploma, without which future economic hardship is all but inevitable.

A number of specific approaches to counseling a single-parent-led family have been proposed: brief strategic family counseling (Bray & Anderson, 1984), structural family counseling (Weltner, 1982), a combined psychodynamic/strategic approach (Morawetz & Walker, 1984), and a skills-building psychoeducational approach (Levant, 1988) (see Chapter 4 for more details on selecting approaches). Bray and Anderson (1984) contend that a brief technique is especially applicable to single-parent situations because their problems usually represent difficulty in making a transition from one family life-cycle stage and structure to another. Because finances are usually limited, short-term treatment is particularly cost-effective. These authors offer several examples (overburdened families, families with unresolved divorce issues) of successfully reframing family problems in a more constructive and acceptable perspective to change the family's perceptions of the presenting problem.

Weltner (1982) points out that the single custodial mother faces numerous problems, as we have noted throughout this chapter, and that their combined weight may overburden her, undermining her competence and sense of self-esteem. Thus, he argues, the counselor's first concern must be to make sure that she adequately performs her executive function as family head. Recognizing that her countless tasks (providing family meals, maintaining family routines, protecting the children, managing the budget, disciplining and guiding her offspring, and so on) may collectively be beyond the energies of a single parent (particularly if, as is likely, she must work outside the home), Weltner urges that help be directed at aiding her to expand the executive function.

In the following case, an ex-client of the counselor contacts him again several years after the termination of counseling. See Figure 6.4 for the genogram of this case.

Rosemary and Jack met at church when each was 20 years old, and after going steady for a year they married. Both had few social experiences with others and seemed to be drawn to each other primarily as a means of escape from barren family experiences. Jack lived with a widowed mother who drank and was physically abusive to him when she was drinking. Rosemary's parents were together, but were blue-

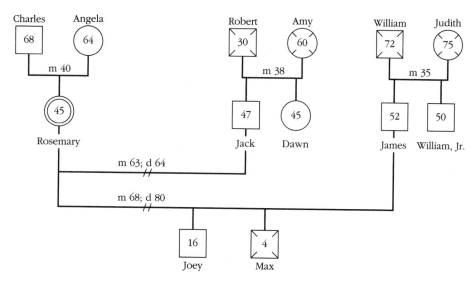

Figure 6.4   Genogram of Rosemary's case

collar workers who often worked extra shifts and had little time for her. Because of their demanding work schedules (and a less than adequate marriage), they neglected her and provided poor models for her regarding parenting.

Jack and Rosemary had a brief and conflict-ridden marriage. Each had an insatiable need for attention, and those needs being unsatisfied, did not understand how to show attention or give love to the other. By the time they contacted a counselor, their relationship had deteriorated to the point where little was left of the marriage, and after five sessions they agreed to separate and obtain a divorce. No children or property were involved, so with the help of the counselor they quickly effected the divorce.

The counselor did not hear from either of them for 2 years, at which time Rosemary called to say she had met someone at work (both were newspaper reporters) whom she wanted him to meet. Recognizing that she appeared to have unstated questions about the relationship, the counselor encouraged her to come in with him. James, age 30, turned out to be an intelligent, hard-working, driven person who seemed to neglect his appearance and, for that matter, his health. Although he seemed to care a great deal for Rosemary, he admitted to her and the counselor that he had a drinking problem, and while he had stopped drinking for the last 6 months, he could not guarantee that he would not start again. Rosemary claimed that it made no difference, that his love was all she cared about, and that because they loved each other she was sure the drinking would not become a problem. Despite efforts by the counselor to get them to explore some of these issues further, Rosemary insisted she had met the man she wanted to marry. The drinking issue, to plague their marriage later, thus was not resolved. The counselor, recognizing the counseling was unfinished, encouraged them to keep in contact.

Rosemary sent the counselor Christmas cards and, over the years, announcements of the birth of her two children, Joey and Max. In one note she mentioned that James had tired of newspaper reporting and, in order to pursue his interest in fine wines, had bought a liquor store that he would run. Several years passed, and the yearly notes stopped. The counselor lost touch with them, although he continued from time to time to wonder what had happened to them, and especially if James could handle being around liquor all day.

A full 10 years passed before Rosemary once again called for help. She seemed to have aged considerably over that time—not surprisingly, considering the story she had to tell. She had endured a number of hardships, but two in particular were devastating. The first concerned the death of Max, at age 4, when a baby-sitter failed to stop him from running into the street after a ball and he was hit by a car. This had happened 6 years earlier; Rosemary had never fully recovered from the loss and continued to grieve. James's periodic drinking, also stimulated by his loss and grief, became more serious after Max's death. Their marriage, already weakened by James's drinking and neglecting his business, could not survive the added stress of the death of their child, and several months thereafter both agreed that James should move out. By this time, he was unable to control the drinking, nor was he able to hold a job. He lived with various friends or family members for several days at a time and held odd jobs for short periods between bouts of drinking.

Rosemary's presumed reason for calling was to bring the counselor up to date and to seek help for her loneliness. She was desperate for companionship but at the same time fearful of involving herself with a man again. She blamed herself for her situation and said she could understand if no man would ever want to be with her. She felt very much alone in raising Joey (now 16) and had few friends to turn to for support. Her parents, with whom she had never repaired her relationship, were now elderly and ill and even less available than before. With the counselor's help, she did begin to socialize by attending Parents Without Partners meetings. While the depression seemed to lift, she began to tell of her problems with Joey, especially her feelings that she did not know how to raise him by herself, did not have sufficient parenting skills, and wished James or someone (the counselor?) would rescue her.

Evidently, Joey was a school truant, spending countless days looking for his father along skid row. He had also been in trouble with the police over numerous speeding tickets he had failed to pay. Rosemary insisted it all was beyond her ability to cope and that Joey could drop out of high school and go off on his own if he wanted to, as long as she did not have to take care of him. The counselor wanted Joey to attend the sessions with his mother, but he refused, and Rosemary could not influence him to participate. He stayed away from home some nights, took money from her purse, emptied his bank account to spend money on his friends. Rosemary felt incompetent to control the situation.

The counselor began by helping her explore her relationship with her parents, in an effort to gain some understanding of why there was a deficit in the parenting she received growing up. As counseling proceeded, it became clearer that the parents, like Rosemary herself, lacked nurturing skills but were not uncaring, as she had believed. Caught up in the same situation, she was able to understand them better and to begin to forgive them. On a more practical note, she was also able to call on them to help her in small ways with Joey, especially when she was away from home on a work assignment. Her newly enhanced relationship with them made her feel less alone.

The counselor thus focused his efforts on building family resources and helping Rosemary develop a support network, while also providing aid in reestablishing her as family head. The counselor and Rosemary worked on improving her coping skills and gaining a sense of control or mastery over what was happening to her and Joey. As she began to reorganize the family, she began to monitor his activities more closely, to demand that they do more things together, that they eat their meals together every night, and that she go to his school to determine just what was happening there. She no longer left her purse out for him to open and remove money, as she had done before, thus taking back adult responsibilities. She talked to Joey about her new social life and brought her new boyfriend for him to meet. She encouraged Joey to talk to her about his problems, to go with her to meetings for children of alcoholics, to bring his friends home if he so wished. For the first time she told him about her life with James, something she had deliberately kept from him before in order to protect his image of his father, and invited Joey to tell her about his feelings concerning the divorce.

As Rosemary assumed an executive function as family head, she began to divide family responsibilities with her son. However, she was careful to maintain generational distinctions and not to cross generational boundaries with him. Although there were only two of them, a hierarchical structure was established and maintained. Her newly developed sense of empowerment seemed to help Joey understand the new family organization and his place in it. Each learned to respect the other's privacy and not to intrude. After 8 months of counseling, the workable alliance established between Rosemary and Joey was holding, and counseling terminated. The damage done to Joey was significant, however, and did not bode well for his future relationships.

In this case, as in others, the single mother may need therapeutic help in developing a functioning support system. She might, like Rosemary, be encouraged to restructure the family by enlisting her children's help with tasks or chores around the house, each according to age and appropriate skills. Other restructuring, as in this case, may involve extended-family members such as a grandparent or family friends or church members, the mother continuing her parental function but with support. Returning to a grandparent's home may be difficult, since the mother may run the risk of losing her executive function to the more available grandparent. Under these circumstances, it is often beneficial for the counselor to include the grandparents in some family sessions, to help define roles and place the mother back in charge of her children.

The one-parent-led family should also be encouraged to seek the help of resources beyond the family. Friends, social service agencies, school-related organizations, members of church congregations, co-op baby-sitter groups, single-parent groups such as Parents Without Partners,[8] employee-sponsored child-care groups, and various women's (or men's) organizations may all offer exactly the kind of aid that a beleaguered single parent needs. An even minimally involved ex-spouse who helps out in emergencies or on weekends can provide considerable comfort and support.

Single-parent families pass through a number of predictable phases, according to Morawetz and Walker (1984): (1) the aftermath of the divorce, (2) the family subgrouping or realignment, (3) the reestablishment of a social life, and (4) the successful separation of parent and child. In their therapeutic work with these families, the authors found that families who seek help in the wake of their divorce—Phase 1—frequently experience rage, despair, overwhelming anxiety, and a sense that they will not be able to cope with the problems they must suddenly confront. The counselor can offer some first aid in stabilizing the family system at this point by joining the system temporarily as it regroups and strengthening the parent's position. The risk of the counselor's stepping in as family rescuer (replacing the missing parent) is greatest at this phase of counseling; nevertheless, intervention of this type is sometimes necessary. The counselor may be most helpful here in supporting the family members as they attempt to reconstruct the story of the marital breakup and help complete the mourning process for the loss of the family.

The success with which the family can deal with its grief and bitterness in the aftermath of the divorce and the speed with which it can be helped to develop self-esteem and overcome feelings of helplessness set the stage for Phase 2: realignment. Now, with the counselor's assistance, the family must learn to adjust to the new reality brought about by the absent parent. The counselor can play a key role at this point, usually a stormy period, as the family members are helped to accept that the painful and unwelcomed dissolution of the family as they have known it is permanent. Morawetz and Walker (1984) describe as common the surfacing of anger and violence, often on the part of the children, during this therapeutic phase; this anger may provide a symptom that serves to pull the custodial parent out of a depression or to signal to the noncustodial parent that the family needs his or her return.

By now, if counseling is successful, the children have learned to live with one parent or to accommodate to two households, and the custodial parent has abandoned any strong hope of reconciliation. In Phase 3 of counseling, the family begins to look toward the future and to seek new social relationships. Dating by the single parent may prove disruptive to the children, who are apt to view this new development as a further loss of parental availability and possibly as behavior disloyal to the absent parent. By phase 4, the counselor is likely to be attempting to expedite the successful separation of parent and child from the

---

[8]A number of organizations offer social as well as educational events for divorced persons and their children. The largest is probably Parents Without Partners, with more than 1000 chapters in all 50 states and in a number of foreign countries, and a membership of 200,000 single parents.

enmeshment that followed the divorce so that each may move on with his or her life. This unloosening of parent-child attachments may lead to an unbalancing of the family system, and the counselor may expect a period of intense feelings. Morawetz and Walker warn that truancy, delinquency, and perhaps even teenage pregnancy may occur; these are all efforts to disrupt change, delay separation, and ensure a return to the earlier parent-child involvement.

In a somewhat different therapeutic approach, a number of counselors, such as Levant (1988), have designed psychoeducational and skills-training programs to remediate specific family problems and, in the process, enhance aspects of family living. Generally brief or time-limited, didactic or experiential programs such as Levant's Fatherhood Project aim to promote family functioning by teaching fathers, often single custodial parents, how to improve their communication skills with their children. In particular, men wishing to develop a more nurturing role, but with few previous experiences or with poor or nonexistent role models from their own fathers, are offered an opportunity to enroll in courses where they learn various communication skills such as listening and responding to their children's feelings and expressing their own feelings in a constructive manner. A basic understanding of child development and child management is also taught, from the perspectives of both child and father.

Levant (1988) employs a skills-training format in which participants role-play situations from their own family experiences, are videotaped for instant playback and observation, and fill out workbook exercises at home with their children. The program is voluntary, offered as an educational experience for men who wish to improve their empathic sensitivity to what transpires in their interactions with their children. The Fatherhood Project thus provides a combined didactic and experiential series of group meetings that aims to help fathers undergo a cognitive restructuring regarding their views of ideal family life. The program is currently being expanded to include single parents of either sex, divorced parents with joint custody, stepparents and their spouses, and couples about to become parents.

In our final example of counseling a single parent, an unwed working-class mother calls for help:

Tammy contacted a counselor in the small university community in which she lived, ostensibly for guidance with her stepchild, Jolie. The counselor suggested that both Tammy and her husband come in together, and after some hesitation Tammy agreed. Although she and Brad gave different last names, it was not until 10 minutes into the interview, during which the counselor was taking a history, that she realized the couple was unmarried. The "stepchild" referred to over the telephone turned out to be Brad's daughter, Jolie, age 7, from a previous marriage, who visited them during summer breaks from her school. In addition, Tammy and Brad had a child together, Rebecca, age 4. Before the close of the first counseling session, it was clear to all three participants that Tammy had a more serious problem in mind than the one regarding Jolie; she was forcing a showdown with Brad regarding his degree of commitment to their relationship, especially whether he intended to marry her.

Subsequent sessions revealed that Tammy's and Brad's backgrounds could hardly have been more dissimilar. She was from a large, working-class family from West Virginia, had dropped out of high school after 1 year, and had traveled to California on her own at age 17 to get away from an abusive father. After a series of odd jobs, she found work as a waitress at a restaurant near the university. Brad, on the other hand, came from an upper-middle-class northeastern WASP family, had been educated in private schools, and was now about to receive his doctorate in public health. Soon after they met at the restaurant, they began dating, and within 3 months were living together. Rebecca was born about 1 year later.

Although Tammy and Brad had now been together for 5 years, his parents knew nothing of Tammy's existence, nor of their grandchild. Brad had also taken great pains to hide her from all but his closest friends at school, telling himself that he was embarrassed by her poor grammar, her lack of sophistication, and her lack of a college education. While Tammy did complain from time to time about such treatment, she was not someone who expected very much from life, and seemed more than willing to accept Brad's explanation that he was trying to work things out with his parents and that it was only a matter of time before they married.

Tammy was able to articulate her anger and resentment early in the counseling sessions. She was furious and hurt that Brad denied her existence to his family and friends and that he never publicly claimed Rebecca as his daughter. Although she loved Brad, she expressed her bitterness over feeling tricked into having a baby when he apparently had no intention of ever marrying her. Brad responded somewhat intellectually at first, trying to appear modern and thus not hampered by marriage certificates since "they were nothing more than useless scraps of paper." He did acknowledge his love for Tammy but expressed his bewilderment over how to satisfy her as well as his family. After 2 months of joint counseling, Brad reluctantly agreed to marry Tammy and to tell his parents that Rebecca was his child, despite his anticipation that they would never approve. Tammy, however, by now was sufficiently angry and disappointed by his behavior and past unkept promises that she insisted they separate.

Tammy lived alone with Rebecca, and the counselor saw them together for two sessions. Rebecca, who carried her father's name, was not aware of her parents' conflict about marriage. They lived in a community where divorce was fairly common, and she was not the only child in her class without a father at home. She did not know that her parents had never married. Brad did send money to support her and visited her regularly before he graduated and took a job at a midwestern university. Within a year, however, he had met a woman with two children and married her, and the money he sent to Tammy and Rebecca, never very much, was reduced further to adjust to the demands from his new family.

Tammy continued to see the counselor from time to time and was eventually encouraged to return to school. She obtained the equivalent of a high school diploma before registering at a local junior college to become a licensed vocational nurse. She did expand her social life and did manage to place Rebecca in a good child-care facility after school, but life for Tammy continued to be hectic. She had periodic bouts of depression and felt particularly alone and desperate at these times. Despite the counselor's support and encouragement, Tammy found herself with few options, little money, and no apparent prospects for a brighter future. She eventually moved to North Carolina, where her cousins lived, and found a job at the local hospital. She never told anyone that she had never married, nor did anyone appear to assume that to be the case. Although her life was far from being fulfilled, she was managing—according to the periodic letters sent to the counselor—to support herself and her child and had regained some sense of self-esteem.

In this case, the counselor initially helped the clients determine the underlying problems they were having, which was necessary before they could begin to resolve their conflicts. By offering support and understanding, largely absent in Tammy's life, the counselor strengthened her client's growing self-sufficiency. Such support seemed essential to the counselor if she was to help Tammy think out important life decisions. The counselor encouraged Tammy to develop marketable skills in order to help her build self-esteem. Finally, Tammy was helped to reconnect to another family system that would offer the support of an extended family. The overwhelming survival issues faced by many single parents are such that counseling may at times be primarily supportive, while the parent gains the wherewithal to reunite with a more real and more permanent support system.

Summary

Single-parent-led families are today's fastest-growing family type, primarily the result of a high divorce rate and unmarried motherhood. Such families now account for one in every four American families. Despite the fact that divorce has become a familiar phenomenon of American life, many members of society still view divorce as failure, and single-parent-led families are often seen as flawed even though many are as successful as two-parent families. Families headed by single parents are not necessarily a homogeneous group. Such families are formed by death, desertion, and birth out of wedlock, as well as separation and divorce, although in recent years separation and divorce have become the leading causes for the formation of these families. Teenage mothers, who account for 30% of all births in the United States, are likely to have a high rate of poverty and a low level of education and to be from minority groups.

Divorce is, by definition, disruptive to all family members. The custodial parent, still most likely to be the mother, faces a wide range of practical problems (finances, role overload, child-care arrangements), as well as emotional distress connected with grief, loneliness, and loss of self-esteem. The nonresident parent must cope with many changes surrounding his or her customary living arrangements, although the most probable adjustment difficulty revolves around a sense of loss of the children, loneliness, and loss of previous social supports. Impaired functioning of children is common following divorce, with elementary-school-age or younger ones most vulnerable to distress. The extent to which the parents remain involved and offer support to each other largely determines the extent to which the children make a successful adaptation to the divorce and get on with their lives.

Although sole custody, usually by the mother, remains the most common outcome of a custody determination, shared parenting arrangements are gaining in popularity. Joint custody allows both parents equal authority in raising their children; such an arrangement may or may not involve joint physical custody.

Counselors must help newly formed single-parent-led families establish boundaries as different members take on new tasks and responsibilities. In addition, such families must come to terms with the psychological presence of the absent parent, whether dead or divorced. Otherwise, they run the risk of creating a parentified child as an absent parent's substitute. The counselor may also have to deal with the single parent's depression and fear of reentering both the social and work worlds outside the home. Several counseling approaches (brief strategic family counseling, structural family counseling, and a skills-building psychoeducational program) have been proposed for working with single-parent-led families. In general, these approaches attempt to strengthen the executive function of the family head, to restructure the family by helping the children take on supportive tasks, to help develop an outside support group, and to teach custodial and noncustodial parents alike new skills aimed at remediating specific family problems. Teenage mothers, if amenable to counseling, can most likely benefit from interventions tailored to their specific level of functioning.

Counseling the Remarried Family

Americans seem to demonstrate an inherent "marriage bias." They enter first marriages at a greater rate than people in most other countries; they also appear to have higher expectations of the marital unit, so much so that they are prepared to abandon the relationship if it proves unfulfilling and to try again to find satisfaction, as evidenced by a higher remarriage rate than couples in other Western nations (Ihinger-Tallman & Pasley, 1987). In what Furstenberg (1987) refers to as American society's general acceptance of "conjugal succession," many couples today expect to stay together only as long as their marriage is emotionally gratifying. If one or both mates find that this is no longer the case, the partners are permitted—or sometimes even encouraged (particularly when the couple is childless)—to break the marriage contract and search for people who might provide greater emotional gratification.[1] As Bray (1995) observes, the social revolution that started in the 1960s in the United States and contributed to the steep jump in divorce, single parenthood, and remarriage rates has helped make stepfamilies a normative family form.

One out of every three Americans today is a stepparent, stepchild, stepsibling, or some member of a stepfamily (Booth & Dunn, 1994), and over half of all Americans will eventually be in one of these situations at some period in their lives (Larson, 1992). Thus, Bernstein (1999) prophesizes that stepfamilies (including first

---

[1] Samuel Johnson, 18th-century essayist and social critic, once characterized remarriage as the "triumph of hope over experience."

marriages of single parents and long-term cohabitation of heterosexual or lesbian and gay partners) will be the most prevalent family form in the 21st century. The recent outpouring of books on the subject (Pasley & Ihinger-Tallman, 1994; Ganong & Coleman, 1999; Hetherington, 1999; Burt & Burt, 1996) all attest to the interest of social scientists in this rapidly accelerating phenomenon.

Because birth mothers continue to be awarded physical custody in the over-whelming number of cases, stepfather (rather than stepmother) families are today's most prevalent form of stepfamily arrangement (Bray, 1995). Contrary to television-inspired expectations that stepfamilies would resemble *The Brady Bunch* (with young children from both former marriages residing together), most stepfamilies are likely to be composed of a husband living with his wife and her children from a previous marriage. If he has children from an earlier marriage, now living with their mother, who retains sole custody, his visitation with them may become steadily less frequent and irregular after his remarriage (and decrease even more dramatically after his former wife is remarried) (Weitzman, 1985). However, while the unraveling of a marriage does sometimes lead to an attenuating relationship between the nonresident father and his children, this need not be the case (Arditti & Kelly, 1994). According to Braver and colleagues (1993), the best predictor of long-term involvement is the father's feeling of remaining "parentally enfranchised" (sharing control with his ex-wife over child-rearing issues). These researchers found that feeling enfranchised leads to feeling less alienated and thus remaining involved, while those who feel left out (or pushed out by an angry ex-spouse) often begin to sense that the children are no longer theirs and distance themselves from them. Thus, when conflict between ex-spouses is low and the noncustodial father feels he has some control of deci-sions in his child's life, then parental contact—and child-support payments—are likely to be maintained (Hetherington, Bridges, & Insabella, 1998).

For most divorced people, single life is short-lived. They tend to remarry quickly; the median interval before remarriage for previously divorced men is 2.3 years; for divorced women it is 2.5 years.[2] In reality, the interval before reentering an intimate relationship may be even more brief if the couple first lives together in a cohabiting arrangement (Cox, 1996). Almost 30% of divorced persons remarry within 12 months of becoming divorced, suggesting short courtships or previous relations with their future partners (Ganong & Coleman, 1994). Age is an important factor in determining the likelihood of remarriage, especially for women. Whereas three out of four women (whether white, black, or Hispanic) who divorce in their twenties will probably remarry, the likelihood drops sharply as women get older; fewer than half who divorce in their thirties remarry, and far fewer with increasing age (Norton & Miller, 1992). For men, income appears to be a key factor, since those earning more money are more likely to remarry than those with lower incomes (Day & Bahr, 1986). Not surprisingly, remarriage after widowhood occurs considerably later—on average, at age 53 for women and age

---

[2] These data suggest that divorced people are not against marriage, only against being married to the person they previously married.

61 for widowers who remarry (Wilson & Clarke, 1992). Clearly, the likelihood of remarrying is greater if the earlier marriage ended in divorce rather than through the death of a spouse.

According to Bray (1995), there are more than 11 million remarried households in the United States. In approximately a third, the wife had been married before; in a third, only the husband had been previously married; and in the remaining third, both spouses had previously been married and divorced. Better educated and financially well-off men are most likely to remarry quickly; on the other hand, the higher a woman's educational level and income, the less likely she is to remarry (Saxton, 1996). (Remarriage is apt to be the fastest way out of poverty for single mothers; on the other hand, autonomous and economically self-sufficient women may not feel the need or pressure, and for that reason may choose not to remarry.) A decade ago, Glick (1989) estimated that if the current trends continued, as many as 35% of U.S. children would be part of a stepfamily before reaching 18 years of age. A more recent analysis (Ganong, Coleman, & Fine, 1995) suggests that figure was probably an underestimation.

Remarried families or stepfamilies are neither inherently problematic nor necessarily a poor substitute for an intact or "natural" family unit (Walsh, 1995). Most members, adults and children alike, report being satisfied and content with stepfamily life (Kelly, 1993). Resilient, well-functioning families are more the rule than the exception. Although born out of a series of disruptive transitions to a family system—from intact family to single-parent-led to stepfamily—that inevitably generates a series of structural and relationship shifts and role changes, reorganization and adaptation are possible, and successful remarriage is achievable. If it is successful, remarriage has a great deal to offer adults and children alike. For adults, the experience can help rebuild self-esteem and a sense of being a worthwhile person capable of loving and being loved. Wiser as a result of the earlier failed experience, the adult has a second chance to form a more mature, more stable relationship and, as Crohn, Sager, Brown, Rodstein, and Walker (1982) point out,

> an opportunity to parent and to benefit from a supportive **suprasystem.** . . . Children can learn to appreciate and respect differences in people and ways of living, can receive affection and support from a new stepparent and the new suprasystem, and can observe the remarried parent in a good and loving relationship, using this as a model for their own future love relationships. (p. 162)

After witnessing a destructive marital relationship, children may now observe positive and mutually enhancing interactions between adults.

On the other hand, a failed second try can lead adults to a renewed sense of defeat, self-blame, and frustration. Children may confirm for themselves that good and caring relationships are short-lived, if they exist at all. Without a doubt, many adults enter a second marriage with fewer illusions or romantic expectations, and they presumably experience some internal pressure to work harder to make the marriage go this time. Yet despite a personal familiarity with the possible anguish and family upheaval brought about by the dissolution of a marriage, remarried people divorce at a somewhat higher rate than partners in first marriages.

If the problems that led to the breakup of a marriage are not successfully understood or worked out, then divorced people may choose new partners who turn out to be all too similar to their ex-mates (for example, alcoholics) or, more accurately, partners with whom they develop and maintain similar interactive patterns. Perhaps they have been psychologically fortified by their earlier experience to go through with what must be done to dissolve an unhappy union, or perhaps they are unwilling, having forged a sense of independence between marriages, to relinquish or compromise their position or accede to the demands of a new mate for too little in return. In many cases, the higher probability of divorce simply reflects the complexities involved in adjusting to a family structure that includes stepchildren and adults who must deal with two households (Jacobson, 1987). In other instances, troublesome ex-spouses or financial burdens aggravated by the need to help support two households, including spousal-support or child-support payments, may prove the ultimate undoing of a remarried relationship. Approximately 10% of remarriages represent a third marriage for one or both partners; as a consequence, about one in ten children will experience a second divorce by the custodial parent before they reach 16 years of age (Cox, 1996).

Varieties of Remarried Family Structures

Remarriage following divorce has become a familiar marker event in the lives of many people in recent years.[3] Although remarriage itself is hardly a new phenomenon, in the past its main purpose was to mend families fragmented by the premature death of a parent, restoring the domestic unit to its original nuclear or intact structure. Today, most remarriages follow divorce rather than death, and thus the surrogate parent augments rather than supplants the biological parent. In most cases, as we have noted, minor children are part of today's remarried families (Bumpass, Sweet, & Martin, 1990).

The blending together of two families is a complex and difficult process at best; the absence of clear-cut ground rules (for example, how to discipline stepchildren, whether loyalty to one parent means disloyalty to the other, what to call an absent parent's new spouse) vastly complicates the merger. Addressing this issue, Bray (1992) observes the following:

> The structure and membership of stepfamilies create important differences from first married families. These include a lack of socially defined role relationships, problems with defining and maintaining family boundaries, developing affection between new family members, and the challenge of negotiating relationships within the binuclear family system. (p. 60)

Remarried families (variously referred to in the literature as Rem, blended, second, binuclear, reconstituted families, or stepfamilies) come in a variety of forms (see Table 7.1), although for simplicity's sake we can divide them into three major

---

[3] Three recent presidents of the United States (Clinton, Reagan, Ford) were members of stepfamilies.

types: those in which the wife becomes a stepmother, those in which the husband becomes a stepfather, and those in which both become stepparents. It is important for the counselor to understand that remarriage connotes far more than joining a simple dyadic relationship. On the contrary, as early stepfamily researchers Sager, Brown, Crohn, Engel, Rodstein, and Walker (1983) point out, each adult entering such a developing dyadic system brings a plethora of attachments and obligations. That person's gender, previous marital status, and custodial or noncustodial children must be considered. For example, as noted in Table 7.1, the previously single woman who weds a formerly married man with children (combination 10), and is thus thrust at once into the unfamiliar role of stepmother, undoubtedly has considerably different expectations, experiences, and possible areas of conflict than does a previously married woman with children in the same circumstances (combination 12).

Table 7.1   Twenty-four possible remarried family combinations

	Woman previously single	Woman previously divorced or widowed, no children	Woman previously divorced or widowed, custodial children	Woman divorced or widowed, noncustodial children	Woman divorced or widowed, both custodial and noncustodial children
Man previously single	n.a.	1	2	3	4
Man previously divorced or widowed, no children	5	6	7	8	9
Man previously divorced or widowed, custodial children	10	11	12	13	14
Man divorced or widowed, noncustodial children	15	16	17	18	19
Man divorced or widowed, both custodial and noncustodial children	20	21	22	23	24

Source: Sager et al., 1983.

The following example illustrates combination 10. We present a case of a father who divorces, obtains joint physical custody of his minor children, and then remarries, although this situation is still more the exception than the rule.[4]

Alan had been married for 9 years to Joy, and together they had had 2 children, Deidre, age 5, and Todd, age 2, by the time they consulted a marital counselor. Married in their senior year—they had both attended a large midwestern university—they had continued for several years after graduation to live relatively unburdened lives not unlike their student days. Alan, the more serious and scholarly of the two, had soon tired of his job as an accountant, however, and with Joy's encouragement had begun graduate studies leading to a Ph.D. in economics. Joy had worked at assorted jobs before signing on as an assistant to the head of an insurance agency, a position that took her away from home for long hours each day. After the birth of their children, Joy, advancing in her job, had continued her work, sometimes barely managing to come home for dinner before returning to see clients in the evening. More and more, Alan had taken over the care of the children, a task he found he did successfully and enjoyed.

By the time they saw the counselor, they had grown apart sufficiently—emotionally, intellectually, socially—that little if anything was left of their marriage, and they decided to get divorced. By mutual consent, reflecting their previously agreed-upon living arrangement, they shared joint custody of the children, but Alan retained physical custody. Over the following 5 years the children saw less and less of their mother, although she would occasionally call them and promise to see them as soon as her busy schedule allowed. As the children learned to predict, that promise was rarely kept. However, their mother did not disappear entirely; rather, she would arrive at their home occasionally, usually unannounced, arms loaded with expensive gifts.

When Alan met Sara, a fellow doctoral student, they discovered that they shared many values in common. As their relationship blossomed, they also found that they were emotionally compatible, and soon they decided to marry. The children, now 10 and 7, liked Sara well enough at first, and Sara was enthusiastic about having a ready-made family. She was good with children, and since she was a bit younger than Alan and herself childless, Sara was anxious to prove to him that she could cope. However, she found it particularly hard to adapt to this instant family despite her efforts to be a good mother. She resented their demands, their intrusions, their possessiveness of their father. Without a honeymoon period in which to develop greater intimacy with her husband, Sara felt thrust into a series of child-rearing tasks for which she had no experience and from which she received little reward. Her husband expected her to relieve him of some parental responsibilities and could not understand

[4]As we noted in the previous chapter, father-only households (Greif, 1995), while still relatively uncommon compared to those led by mothers, are nevertheless approaching a sizable number (3 million) of today's 20 million children under 18 living with a single parent (U.S. Bureau of the Census, 1998). The likelihood of remarriage is actually substantially greater for a custodial father (41%) than for a custodial mother (23%), but it is not clear from census data what percentage of remarried fathers obtained custody before or after they remarried (Meyer & Garasky, 1991). In many cases, fathers wait until they have remarried and established a stable home before seeking physical custody of children living with their ex-wives.

her resistance to becoming an instant parent. The children, for their part, soon refused to listen to any rules she tried to impose, insisting she was not their parent and therefore did not have any rights to discipline them. Sara felt that she was on the receiving end of all the abuse from the children, who resented her closeness to their father, without any of the pleasures, satisfactions, or displays of affection due a parent. Although Alan and Sara had both believed she would make a wonderful mother—she actually had very good success with caring for their needs early on—all four family members were soon involved in considerable turmoil.

Recognizing that the new family system was in trouble, Alan sought out his previous family counselor and along with Sara, Deidre, and Todd began a series of visits as a family. In the process, Alan learned to offer support to his wife and to help her out of the no-win situations in which she often found herself. By relinquishing some of his ideas about what constituted a good parent, he learned to reduce whatever rescue fantasies he had been experiencing of marrying someone who would be another perfect parent. Before the family counseling sessions, he had believed that only if she were perfect, according to his definition, could he relax and entrust the children to his new wife.

Through counseling, Sara was able to acknowledge and ultimately express her frustration and resulting bitterness, often directed toward Alan, at his insistence that she be the mother he would have liked Joy to have been. As this unreasonable expectation became clear to them—they both had bought into it—Alan relaxed his demands in this regard and Sara made an effort to stop competing with the children's natural mother to win their love. She slowly began to recognize that affection and acceptance from the children would come out of their daily living patterns and that the verbal expression of such feelings from children the ages of Deidre and Todd is commonly limited, even in intact families. Particularly if the boundary around her and her husband became stronger, the children would respond to their father's feelings for her and would start to treat her as their parent.

The children were helped to deal with their loyalty conflicts regarding their own mother and to accept that although Sara was not their biological mother, she was in fact the person who was willing to carry out the day-to-day tasks of mothering. As the children became aware that loving Sara did not mean abandoning the tenuous hold they had on their natural mother, the relationship with their stepmother became closer and the family overall became a more cohesive unit.

The counselor held two closing sessions with Alan, Sara, and Joy, but without the children. Together the trio, in a relatively calm way, first dealt with Joy's intermittent extravagant behavior toward the children. Joy acknowledged her guilt feelings over neglecting the day-to-day parenting, recognizing that she attempted to compensate periodically for these feelings by lavishing expensive gifts on the children. Alan and Sara, although resentful of Joy's indulgent behavior, came to understand it better and themselves recognized that they ignored Joy's ideas regarding child-rearing and could be more open to her suggestions. A more inviting attitude on their part led to an arrangement for more regular and more consistent visitation schedules on her part. As they began to treat Joy as a mother entitled to be in on decisions affecting her children's lives, she felt more enfranchised and more a part of their daily lives. When she planned on giving a particularly expensive gift, she discussed it beforehand with the other two parents. Over several months, the relationships began to improve for the children, parents, and stepparent alike.

A remarried family into which both partners bring children from previous marriages (combination 12) presents a different set of problems. Especially when each child has lived in a single-parent arrangement for a period of time, that child's role and position in the family are usually severely altered when his or her parent remarries. In the case we are about to present, building a stepsibling relationship was complicated further in that each was an only child and thus accustomed to a special intimate bond with the previously single parent.

Both Marlene, 29, and Dan, 32, had been married briefly before terminating their first marriages. Each had ended that marriage with a joint custody arrangement in which they were awarded physical custody—Marlene of her 2-year-old son, Robert, and Dan of his 3-year-old daughter, Christine. Each adult had remained a single parent for several years until they met at a church social, fell in love, and decided to marry. In their haste to connect with another adult in a loving relationship, however, the two neglected to talk through differences in child-rearing values, expected household rules, remaining financial and emotional ties to former spouses, and a host of related issues involving the transition into the new family structure. As one indication of their lack of planning, the children, now age 7 and 8, respectively, did not meet each other until two weeks before the wedding ceremony.

The early period in a remarried family's life is usually a time of considerable reorganization and inevitable disequilibrium. In this case, chaos would be a more accurate assessment. The children, in particular, fought over space in the new house, which previous family routine (dinnertime, bedtime) was to be followed, and who could be disciplined by whom. Each child aligned with his or her own parent to the point of seeming at times to represent two warring camps. Robert was vigilant in measuring how much attention Christine was getting, and Christine was equally on the lookout for any special benefits that might come her stepbrother's way. Needless to say, little bonding took place between the children, nor between each child and his or her stepparent. Marlene and Dan were dumbfounded, both having wanted to believe that because they loved their new spouse, they would automatically love (and be loved by) their spouse's children. For the first hectic year, nothing seemed further from the truth.

Nor was the conflict restricted to the children. Each of the parents often ended up defending the action of his or her own child against the other and exchanging open criticism about the other spouse's child-rearing practices. On occasion, usually after a visit by a child with his or her nonresident parent, that parent would call to criticize or complain about the child's alleged mistreatment; this typically had the effect of stirring up old conflicts between the ex-spouses. By the end of the second year of marriage, both Marlene and Dan had many doubts about the possibilities of ultimate success of their marital union. Their earlier plan to have a child together was put on hold, and as a last resort, they sought the help of a family counselor.

The counselor saw all four stepfamily members together and helped them to redefine their conflicts in interactional terms as a systems problem to which each participant contributed. In place of factions based on their earlier experiences living as two single-parent households, the counselor emphasized the family's wholeness as an expanded system, in which each person's needs as well as responsibilities had to be addressed. The counselor suggested that rather than cling to earlier parent-child patterns, here was an opportunity to create new family guidelines and traditions. For example, both children could now give up being partners to their respective parents and return to being children again, something each seemed to desire. Family boundaries were slowly redrawn, and the children began to refer to each other with their friends as brother and sister, despite some awkwardness over their different surnames.

After 2 months, the counselor began working with Marlene and Dan alone, strengthening their bond and helping them work as a parental unit. At several sessions, the ex-spouses were brought in to help reduce friction, as well as better coordinate activities with the children. After 6 months, Marlene announced that she was pregnant and that she and Dan were ready to terminate treatment.

Despite their seeming differences, both cases illustrate that the basic integrative tasks for stepfamilies, as Visher and Visher (1988a) point out, are twofold: (1) maintaining existing parent-child and ex-spouse relationships, but redefining them for a new context; and (2) developing new relationship patterns to build trust within the household as a means of achieving a solid identity as a new family unit. Figure 7.1 (page 174) depicts an intact functional nuclear family (top of the figure), a new stepfamily (middle), and a mature stepfamily (bottom). If successful, the new stepfamily progresses from its early formation, in which little connectedness exists between members, to the mature stepfamily, in which links among all members are strong and binding. As these authors (themselves stepparents) note, the process of establishing the new family as a viable and integrated unit is often a lengthy one for most stepfamilies, since they usually have to overcome a combination of built-in parent-child alliances, problematic generational boundaries, influences outside the household, and a lack of family history or loyalty.

Working with stepfamilies, the counselor needs to bear in mind that the remarried pair are part of a larger social system that includes children, two sets of nonresident parents and their extended-family systems, and each stepparent's extended family system. Within each there is a history of relevant issues from previous marital and divorce experiences, many that more than likely involve unresolved emotional problems and attachments, as well as issues that date back to the different families of origin (Bray, 1995; Visher & Visher, 1996). As stepfamilies struggle over a period of time to develop a family identity, they must address such important issues as the following (Ganong, Coleman, & Fine, 1995):

- developing rules for the new system
- determining what roles will be performed in the new family and who will perform them

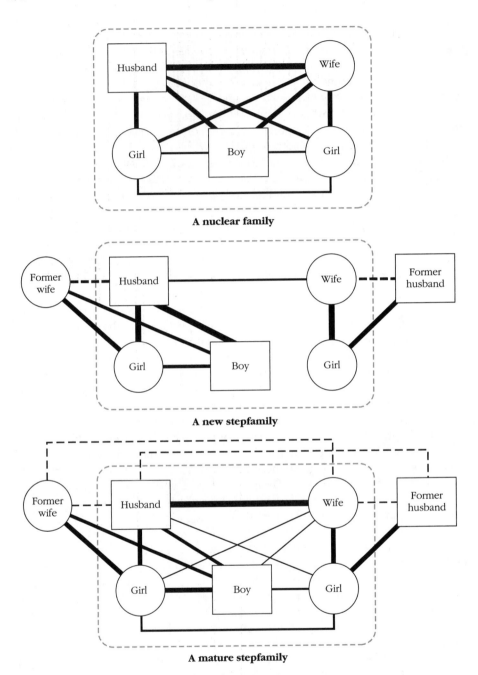

A nuclear family

A new stepfamily

A mature stepfamily

Figure 7.1   Interactive networks in three family configurations

Source: Visher & Visher, 1988a.

- establishing an altered hierarchy in decision making in contrast to the single-parent-led family
- creating new internal boundaries (for example, around the newly formed marital subsystem)
- creating new external boundaries (for example, who is and who is not a member of the newly formed stepfamily)
- sorting out the greater number of subsystems (for example, the subsystem between stepsiblings, the expanded parental subsystem)
- determining how emotionally cohesive they intend the stepfamily to be

In a pioneering study of 88 remarried couples, Duberman (1975) found that stepfamily integration was aided if (1) the previous spouse had died rather than divorced, (2) the new spouse had divorced rather than never having been previously married, and (3) the remarried couple had children of their own together. She found further that parent-child relationships were helped when the wife's children from her previous marriage lived with her and her new spouse. On the other hand, men who left their children with their ex-wife tended to deal less well with their live-in stepchildren. Acceptance by the in-laws and other extended-family members helped strengthen the remarriage. One noteworthy finding was that stepmother-stepdaughter relationships tended to be the most problematic of all stepfamily interactions.[5]

Stepfamily Living Arrangements

A remarried family has been defined by Sager and associates (1981) as one that is created by the marriage (or living together in one domicile) of two partners, one or both of whom has been

> married previously and was divorced or widowed with or without children who visit or reside with them. The couple and the children (custodial or visiting) comprise the Remarried family system. The "metafamily" system is composed of the Remarried family plus former spouses, grandparents, step-grandparents, aunts, uncles, and others who may have significant input into the Remarried system. (p. 3)

Jacobson (1987), in an effort to break away from an approach tied to such conventional terms as *nuclear, intact,* and *broken* families, prefers to conceptualize stepfamilies as *linked family systems.* She believes the term *linked* more accurately reflects the web of interrelationships and the dynamic complexities occurring in such families. Her formulation goes beyond the common phenomenon of a child's living with a custodial remarried parent and his or her spouse (usually the biological mother and stepfather). Instead, Jacobson views the child as likely to be related to two households—the custodial or lived-in household, and the non-custodial or visited household—each of which represents a subsystem of the

---

[5] This stepmother-stepdaughter conflict may have more to do with the absence of the child's mother than it does with the stepparent being a woman (Bernstein, 1999).

dual-household or binuclear family system. In such a setup, the child is a link influencing and being influenced by those in both households.

In such linked families, virtually all members have sustained a recent primary *relationship loss* with which they must cope. One implication we might draw, then, is that the prospect of making a new commitment is likely to provoke fear and apprehension in adults and children alike. Adults may hesitate out of a feeling of vulnerability due to pain from past intimate experiences. Children, too, may pull back from trusting new adults in their lives. Not unexpectedly, they are likely to use the rules and roles of the earlier family life as guidelines for current behavior. Taken together, these factors help explain the often observed fact that satisfactory stepfamily integration is likely to take years to achieve (Bray, 1995; Ganong, Coleman, & Fine, 1995).

McGoldrick and Carter (1988) adopt the useful premise that interactions in the restructured remarried family are likely to be complex, with conflicting and ambiguous roles played by all members. As we illustrated earlier in the case of Sara, a previously unmarried woman marrying a man who had custody of his children, the formation of the new family does not follow any ordinary step-by-step progression; instead, a previously single young adult is often expected to plunge into instant multiple roles as wife and stepmother, for which she has had little if any preparation and in which she cannot expect to be welcomed wholeheartedly.

Unstable and poorly defined boundaries may cause dissension and struggle; intense conflictual feelings on the part of all participants in stepfamilies must be expected, particularly during the early period in the life cycle of any blended family. As McGoldrick and Carter (1988) note, such boundary difficulties often involve these issues:

- *Membership:* Who are the "real" members of the family?
- *Space:* Where do I belong? What space is mine?
- *Authority:* Who is in charge of discipline? Of money? Of decisions?
- *Time:* Who gets how much of my time, and how much do I get of theirs?

Disequilibrium is inevitable, despite the wishes or even the good intentions of all the members of the new family. Ultimately, at least two structural tasks must be accomplished before the participants can be anchored in a truly blended family: (1) the new partners must accept each other as executives in the new family hierarchy, and (2) the children must accept the new stepparent, having worked out the problems of territory or turf that arise from unclear or dysfunctional boundaries (Isaacs, 1982).

The successful renegotiation of boundaries in a stepfamily is essential. Counselors need to help such families restructure their roles within the new unit (biological parent, new parent, and child) and at the same time make certain they do not neglect a similar renegotiation (relinkage) within the larger family unit that includes the former spouse (the child's other parent). The way the process unfolds—it should be started as early in the relationship as possible, even before marriage—can either aid or impede successful blending.

For what problems should the counselor especially screen? Box 7.1 outlines some of the typical interpersonal difficulties likely to restrict, obstruct, or foil the efforts of a remarried family to develop into a functioning unit. As noted, one area of frequent intergenerational conflict involves developing and maintaining rules—a crucial area because these rules help determine the effectiveness with which the stepparent can assume a parenting role. Who sets the rules? Are they the same for both sets of children? If not, then why? Rules regarding discipline, manners, the delegation of tasks and responsibilities, eating and sleeping habits, the form and intensity with which feelings (both positive and negative) are expressed—all need to be established as ongoing family patterns (Ganong & Coleman, 1999). In most cases, rules regarding obligations and responsibilities following changes in family structure can be established only after any underlying fear, anger, and resentment have been cleared up.

Since roles and boundaries are almost certain to be unclear, especially during the new family's formative stages, confusion and disorganization seem inevitable as the family seeks to establish some equilibrium. Einstein (1982) points out the importance of delineating physical boundaries (shared space, property, activities), psychological boundaries (the degree of intimacy, authority, and affection the family members share), and roles (the rights and duties that determine family behavior patterns). For example, a new stepmother of an adolescent learns soon enough that such efforts may require considerable tact, a thick skin, and the ability to tolerate frustration and rejection. (The same virtues may, of course, be expected in a biological parent dealing with his or her own adolescent.) The new stepmother's desire to please her new spouse by rushing to become a much-loved substitute mother is almost certainly doomed to failure and will likely be accompanied by a sense of personal defeat, rejection, and, often, despair.

Box 7.1 A problem-appraisal checklist for remarried families

Remarried families may experience problems in the following areas:

- Difficulties of stepparent in assuming parental role
- Rivalry and jealousy between stepsiblings
- Boundary ambiguity
- Unfinished conflict between ex-spouses
- Competition between biological mother and stepmother (or biological father and stepfather)
- Idealization of absent parent
- Lack of intimacy between parent and nonbiological child
- Loyalty conflicts in children between absent parent and stepparent
- Loyalty conflicts in parent between absent children and stepchildren
- Children's surname differences
- Effects of birth of child from new marriage
- Financial obligations (alimony payments to ex-spouse, child support payments)
- Adolescent issues (change in custody requests; loosened sexual boundaries)

Under ordinary circumstances in an intact family, sibling attachments play a key role in helping children form a sense of identity, a self-concept. Ihinger-Tallman (1987) points out further that "siblings also serve as defenders/protectors of one another; they interpret the outside world to each other, and they teach each other about equity, coalition formation, and the processes of bargaining and negotiation" (p. 164). At times, siblings may serve as buffers against their parents. As contributors to the family "culture," siblings share common experiences, help establish a family history, and play an essential role in intergenerational continuity. Despite occasional disputes and rivalries, they generally feel positively bonded to one another. In stepfamilies, such a history is missing, making attachments and eventual bonding all the more tentative and difficult to achieve.

Relationship problems among stepsiblings may actually promote increased systemic problems within the family. As Henggeler and Borduin (1990) observe, adolescents may resent child-care responsibilities for younger stepsiblings; same-aged siblings may resent unfavorable comparisons regarding grades, appearance, or friends. Thus, integrating stepsiblings into the new family is a major task in most cases, especially (as in the case of Marlene and Dan described earlier) when they have been part of established single-parent homes for any length of time. Under these circumstances—where a special bond with the solo parent has developed, particularly when the child assumed the role of the absent spouse—it is understandable that the child feels betrayed at the very suggestion of remarriage. Data from Wallerstein and Kelly (1980b) on the children of divorce indicate that older children are especially resistant to accepting stepfathers and often require several years before they come to terms with the realities of the remarried situation. In certain cases, it seemed unlikely that such acceptance of the stepfather would ever occur. These findings are consistent with Bray's (1995) more recent studies regarding children's acceptance of stepparents, from which he concludes that "parenting and stepparenting are the most difficult and stressful aspects of stepfamily life, both during early remarriage and in longer-term stepfamilies" (p. 129).

On the other hand, a stepfather who enters a family when a daughter is reaching puberty may, under certain circumstances, find himself in a situation ripe for triangulation among the husband, wife, and adolescent. Although such mother/daughter competition is common, as is some form of triangulation, the competition may take on the character of sexual acting-out in families where problems exist. Without the normal incest taboos that act as powerful injunctions in an intact family, sexual boundaries may be loosened, leading to sexual abuse between a nonbiological parent with poor impulse control and a vulnerable child seeking closeness (Keshet & Mirkin, 1985). Sager and colleagues (1983) describe a range of responses in such an unstructured situation: pleasurable fantasies, repressed thoughts and distancing behavior, angry and violent fighting as a defense against sexual stirrings, and the extreme of sexual relations between stepparent and stepchild. Similarly, sexual involvement between stepsiblings is possible, particularly if they meet at adolescence, during a period of heightened affectionate sexual atmosphere in the home, and when no rules are yet in place regarding their relationship.

Generally speaking, according to Visher and Visher (1979), children do not welcome remarriage for at least two reasons: (1) they may feel split in their loyalties to two sets of parents, and (2) they may continue to harbor the wish that their divorced parents will reunite, a fantasy that is undermined by the remarriage to someone else. Unless such conflicting loyalties can be worked out, however, stepfamily integration will remain incomplete. However, some children are delighted when a single parent remarries, feeling relieved of the burden of offering adult-style companionship. In some cases, the parent's depression may lift with remarriage, there may be more money available, and so on. However, such children may be particularly distressed when they sense a new divorce on the horizon.

Children's initial assessment of their potential gains and losses from the formation of the new family (and the acquisition of new siblings) helps determine future stepsibling relationships (Ihinger-Tallman, 1987). Whether required to share attention and affection from his or her own parent, or friends and possessions (rooms, toys, pets) with a stepsibling, each child may feel shortchanged, as though the losses exceed the benefits of living in a new family. Conversely, in some cases the children may perceive a mutual set of benefits without excessive personal costs, and strong emotional bonds may develop between them. There is certainly a very strong correlation between the ease with which the new parents form a close union and that with which the stepsiblings form a close union, since one process has an impact on the other.

Residues from the former marriage of either or both newly united persons may afflict a remarriage, especially in its early stages of greatest vulnerability. As we have noted a number of times, divorce may represent the end of a marital affiliation, but most often it does not terminate the parenting relationship between former spouses. Thus, remarriage may cause previously agreed-upon custody arrangements, visitation schedules, or financial-support payments to be renegotiated, thereby reopening old wounds between ex-combatants. Or conflict may develop between the stepfather and the biological father—for example, over discipline. Sometimes the child's mother joins in; the child also usually adds fuel to the resulting conflagration. In addition, a biological parent's jealousy about the new spouse and the stepparent's more permanent living arrangement with the biological parent's children may be a threat.

Photographs, furniture, laundry marks, monograms, souvenirs, habits developed during a previous first marriage—all are a part of every remarriage, and thus a constant reminder ("living ghosts") of the time one's partner has spent with another in an intimate relationship. It is not surprising, then, that some divorced couples return to court, sometimes repeatedly, over issues ostensibly involving the children, when in reality they are continuing the battles that led to the divorce in the first place. Particularly when the unmarried ex-spouse did not want the divorce to take place and is now jealous over being displaced by the new marital partner, bitterness may linger and attach itself to any cause justifying litigation and a chance at revenge.

Finally, all remarried families must come to terms with a number of persistent myths regarding stepfamily living. For example, the stereotype of the "wicked," "mistreating" stepmother plagues many women married to men with children (Bernstein, 1999). Being "treated like a stepchild" is a metaphor for neglect and abuse in many societies; endless fairy tales (Sleeping Beauty, Hansel and Gretel, Cinderella) involve an uncaring or abusive stepmother and an uninformed, deceived, or otherwise occupied father. The myth no doubt originated at a time when stepfamilies were the result of death of a parent rather than divorce, and a stepmother was expected to raise her husband's child without much attention from her mate. In many cases, women were chosen by widowed fathers for the express purpose of raising the children, something men were not expected to know how to do.

One consequence of these negative sexist stereotypes is the greater stress found in families with stepmothers than in corresponding stepfather families (Clingempeel, Brand, & Ievoli, 1984). Increased tension in such families is at least in part a function of increased social pressures on stepmothers and the general societal failure to fully accept this family form. For a variety of reasons, society expects more from a woman in her relationship with children than it does from a man with children. This expectation seems to hold whether the children are hers by birth, adoption, or remarriage. A man is expected to provide support or money (less so if his stepchildren are receiving child support from their father); whatever else he provides—and it may be significant—is all to the good, but not essential in the eyes of many people. Visher and Visher (1988a) suggest that many women still derive much of their self-esteem from their role as a good parent, and this connection in turn may help account for more tension between mother and stepmother than between father and stepfather, contributing to increased stress in stepmother families.

Many family counselors believe that the quality of the relationship between stepparent and stepchild may actually be a better predictor of the family's ultimate adaptation to the remarriage than the quality of the new marital dyad. It is entirely possible for a remarried couple to experience marital satisfaction while encountering dissatisfactions within the family regarding stepchildren. In many cases, such chronic problems, unresolved, ultimately erode the marital bond. In other cases, however, the stepparent-stepchild interactive pattern may simply reflect the marital couple's degree of connection and dedication to the marriage. As that connection between generations grows and as each family member adapts to the changing rules and responsibilities of the new family, so grows the likelihood of a successful stepfamily life.

The Developmental Stages of Remarriage

Remarriage is more than a discrete event; it is a complex interactive process, extending over time, in which a group of individuals without a common history or established rituals or behavior patterns attempts to unite and to develop a sense of family cohesion and identity. Such a conversion or redefinition, which must be viewed as going back at least to the disintegration of the first marriage

(McGoldrick & Carter, 1988), typically proceeds through certain predictable developmental phases, from the decision to separate, through the legal divorce and custody arrangements, to the remarriage and possible shifts in custody of one or more children, and ultimately to forging an integrated stepfamily unit. Counseling a family that is about to be remarried, we need to help them understand as best they can the reasons for the failed earlier marriages, the development of the separate family members since the divorce, and the future directions they anticipate as a new family. Above all, they need to be counseled not to expect instant stepfamily unity, but instead to work together to slowly build a lasting identity as a family unit.

As Whiteside (1982) conceptualizes the process, the developmental sequence passes through several key stages: the initial married family, usually with children; a period of parting, as couples separate, divorce, and establish two households; a courting period with plans for remarriage; early remarriage; and finally, if successful, established remarriage. Each stage entails different forms of family organization in terms of boundaries, roles, legal ties, and emotional relationships. Each transition requires significant disruption and change, and Whiteside suggests that counselors can help normalize the process by informing members of common transitional dilemmas:

> Without clear expectations for what is needed or expected in roles such as single parent, non-custodial parent, stepparent, and stepchild, family members cannot easily employ available coping skills, solutions to problems can be less easily reached, and the situation is more likely to be felt as a crisis. (p. 60)

Whiteside's distinction between early and established remarriages is significant for the counselor. Early remarriage involves a transition into marriage and typically entails residual issues from the first marriage and the one-parent period, along with the challenges of forming a functional remarried system. Having just recently worked together to establish stability in the one-parent period, the family is likely to require help from the counselor in dealing with the disruption of that newfound stability. Families in the later stage of remarriage, although established in their interactive patterns, commonly seek counseling because of chronic distress regarding a never-resolved divorce, because a nonresident parent suffers from being cut off from a biological child, or because the stepfamily feels isolated from the family of origin. In some cases, a satisfactory remarriage structure may have been established, but, as in nuclear families, life transitions or unexpected external traumas can strain the family's resources and produce symptoms in one or more members (Whiteside, 1989).

Bradt and Bradt (1986) provide the following colorful description of the stages of remarriage, beginning with the remarriage ceremony and proceeding, optimally, to the emergence of the new, integrated family structure. Progression from one stage to the next is made easier by the successful completion of the prior stage.

1. *Go back!* "What have I gotten myself into?" "Is this a mistake?" "I never thought it would be like this." The couple may be filled with doubt and

apprehension; the children may protest in various ways and attempt to undermine the remarriage; friends and relatives may withhold support.

2. *Making room:* The family members learn to share physical territory and emotional space with others, delineate work/home allocations, and avoid the sense of being an intruder.

3. *Struggles of realignment:* Loyalty conflicts, power struggles, protests, and negotiations occur as former relationship alliances break down and are restructured.

4. *(Re)commitment:* A family identity is established as a budding of family feeling occurs, family mythology and ceremonies evolve, shared experiences are created and defined, and rituals regarding celebrations, vacations, or family meetings are developed.

5. *Rebalancing relationships:* Once recommitment is achieved, the family members can freely move back and forth between the old and new households, defining different membership in each and maintaining loyalty to each, based on the present rather than the past.

6. *Relinquishing feelings of deprivation and burden:* Previously held feelings of being isolated, untrusting, over-responsible, unwilling to collaborate, and so on are given up as each member better defines obligations to self and others.

7. *Growth toward integration:* Having accepted differences, addressed challenges, acknowledged complexity, established commitments, and relinquished feelings of deprivation and burden, the family emerges with an identity and cohesion much like any other functioning family.

8. *Moving on:* Members are free to move into complex networks of relationships focused on problem solving, growth, and interaction with broader systems outside the family.

In each of the stages just outlined, major dislocations must be attended to and major adaptations made. Each stage evokes stress; each provides an opportunity for further growth and family consolidation, but also the risk of relapse and family disruption.

Carter and McGoldrick (1980) regard remarriage as one of the most difficult transitions a family is ever called upon to make. Because most members have experienced recent loss, pain, and a sense of ambiguity, they may wish prematurely for a feeling of closure without understanding that they must confront the built-in complexities of the remarriage process. In most cases, before stepfamily integration can occur, the losses of past family relationships must be mourned, new family traditions must be developed, new interpersonal relationships within the new family must be formed, ties with the absent biological parent must be renegotiated, and children must learn to move satisfactorily between two households. It seems hardly surprising that the remarried family, especially when children are present, may be a fragile entity for a considerable period of time, highly vulnerable to a wide variety of interpersonal, intergenerational, and emotional stresses.

Adopting a developmental point of view, Carter and McGoldrick (1988) contend that separation, divorce, and remarriage each represent significant dislocations in a family's life cycle, calling for additional restabilizing steps before the family can resume its ongoing development. Tables 7.2 (page 184) and 7.3 (page 185) represent these authors' step-by-step outline of the process. In their view, the attitudes listed in the second column of both tables are prerequisites for families to work out the developmental issues regarding divorce and postdivorce adjustment. The counselor who presses families to resolve the developmental issues without first helping them adopt the appropriate attitudes is, in the opinion of McGoldrick and Carter, wasting effort. These authors note further that restabilization calls for an additional ingredient—namely, *the passage of sufficient time.* The counselor needs to communicate this point to families who feel harassed and impatient for change. If the future spouses come from different life-cycle phases (for example, an older man with adult children marrying a young woman with no children or with preteenage children), their differences in experiences and approaches to current responsibilities may delay stepfamily integration still further. The joining of partners at discrepant life-cycle phases calls for a process in which both learn to function in different phases simultaneously. Becoming a stepmother to a teenager before a honeymoon or before becoming an experienced wife or mother is disconcertingly contrary to normal life sequences. In the same way, the husband who is called upon to return to a life phase passed through years earlier—beginning a marriage or raising young children—may find the experience unappealing, especially if his previous marriage had difficulties during this phase. (He may, of course, find it rejuvenating, just as the out-of-sequence experience for the younger wife may prove enlightening and enriching.)

Some Counseling Guidelines

Remarried family life is unique. Stepfamily dynamics are complex, and the counselor who insists on dealing with such families as though they resemble intact biological families has undoubtedly started with false assumptions that require correction. Counselors working with stepfamilies need to be aware of numerous and important structural differences between these families and intact families, bearing in mind that each of these differences may be accompanied by specific stresses and particular developmental tasks.

Common Themes and Counselor Tasks

The counselor attempting to deal effectively with a remarried family will most likely need to provide help in one or more of the following sets of problem areas:

1. *Mourning for losses:* A stepfamily is born of relationship losses, through death or divorce, and the relinquishing of hopes and dreams in the previous family. Special childhood positions in one family (for example, as the only child) may be lost with remarriage, and special household roles (for example, as the parent confidant to a single mother) surrendered. Adults must deal with finding or changing

Table 7.2   Dislocations of the family life cycle requiring additional steps to permit restabilization and further development

Phase	Emotional process of transition prerequisite attitude	Developmental issues
Divorce		
1. The decision to divorce	Acceptance of inability to resolve marital tensions sufficiently to continue relationship	Acceptance of one's own part in failure of the marriage
2. Planning the breakup of the system	Supporting viable arrangements for all parts of the system	Working cooperatively on problems of custody, visitation, finances Dealing with extended family about the divorce
3. Separation	Willingness to continue cooperative coparental relationship Work on resolution of attachment to spouse	Mourning loss of intact family Restructuring marital and parent-child relationships; adaptation to living apart Realignment of relationships with extended family; staying connected with spouse's extended family
4. The divorce	More work on emotional divorce: overcoming hurt, anger, guilt, and so on	Mourning loss of intact family: giving up fantasies of reunion Retrieval of hopes, dreams, expectations from the marriage Staying connected with extended families
Postdivorce Family		
A. Single-parent family	Willingness to maintain parental contact with ex-spouse and support contact of children and ex-spouse's family	Making flexible visitation arrangements with ex-spouse and ex-spouse's family Rebuilding own social network
B. Single-parent (noncustodial)	Willingness to maintain parental contact with ex-spouse and support custodial parent's relationship with children	Finding ways to continue effective parenting relationship with children Rebuilding own social network

Source: Carter & McGoldrick, 1988.

Table 7.3   Remarried family formation: A developmental outline

Steps	Prerequisite attitude	Developmental issues
1. Entering the new relationship	Recovery from loss of first marriage (adequate emotional divorce)	Recommitment to marriage and to forming a family with readiness to deal with the complexity and ambiguity
2. Conceptualizing and planning new marriage and family	Accepting one's own fears and those of new spouse and children about remarriage and forming a step-family Accepting need for time and patience for adjustment to complexity and ambiguity of: • multiple new roles • boundaries: space, time, membership, and authority • affective issues: guilt, loyalty conflicts, desire for mutuality, unresolvable past hurts	Work on openness in the new relationships to avoid pseudomutuality Plan for maintenance of cooperative coparental relationships with ex-spouses Plan to help children deal with fears, loyalty conflicts, and membership in two systems Realignment of relationships with extended family to include new spouse and children Plan for maintenance of children's connections with extended family of ex-spouse(s)
3. Remarriage and reconstitution of family	Final resolution of attachment to previous spouse and ideal of intact family Acceptance of a different model of family with permeable boundaries	Restructuring family boundaries to allow for inclusion of new spouse/stepparent Realignment of relationships throughout subsystems to permit interweaving of several systems Making room for relationships of all children with biological (noncustodial) parents, grandparents, and other extended family Sharing memories and histories to enhance stepfamily integration

Source: Carter & McGoldrick, 1989.

jobs, making new housing arrangements, and relinquishing some old friends and neighbors. Thus, counselors must help stepfamilies address these losses, psychologically disengage from the past, and begin to direct their lives toward future relationships. As an example, a session where the new family listens while the counselor explores the last six months before a mother died of cancer, encouraging the children to express what they experienced during that period and what loss they continue to feel, may have a significant cathartic effect.

2. *Living with differences:* The stepfamily is made up of members with separate family histories and traditions. In addition, each family may come together at differing points in their life cycles (for example, late-adolescent children and preschoolers) and with ways of doing things that seem incompatible. Thus, they are likely to have experiences and expectations significantly different from one another, and the counselor will need to help them negotiate differences that lead to interpersonal conflicts and direct their efforts toward building a new family system. A counselor may, for example, help a 12-year-old girl who feels she should have the same curfew time as her 15-year-old stepsister, or perhaps a 17-year-old boy who sorely resents a 3-year-old's entering his room and messing with his things.

3. *Resolving loyalty issues:* Parent-child relationships precede the new couple bond, and adults may feel loyalty conflicts between love for their child and love for their new marital partner. Children in stepfamilies often feel that loyalty pulls them in two different directions, toward each of their natural parents, while at the same time feeling little loyalty to the stepfamily, especially in its early stages. The counselor may need to direct attention to helping all members learn to trust the new group and develop an identity as a member of a remarried family. For many children, this may mean relinquishing the fantasy that their biological parents will reunite. Helping the remarried parents strengthen their marital bond (without feeling they are somehow betraying an earlier parent-child bond) may go a long way toward helping the child relinquish the fantasy. In this regard, counselors working with stepfamilies are accustomed to helping a child who was used to a close relationship with his or her mother before remarriage and now laments their lost closeness. ("I could always come in and sit on your bed and talk to you, but now you are always with him and the bedroom door is closed.")

4. *Acknowledging the absent parent:* In the case of divorce, the painful effect of an absent biological parent must be recognized; if the previous struggle between the biological parents remains unresolved, the children will be especially torn between the parents. The counselor must help the family to avoid fostering an adversarial relationship between the new parent and the biological parent of the same sex. Continuing contact with the absent biological parent may actually aid the child's ability to form a relationship with the stepparent. The counselor's responsibility here is to help the family confront the problem. If necessary, the counselor may bring the absent father physically into the stepfamily sessions in order to help resolve the conflict.

5. *Living simultaneously in two households:* Children are often members of two households, frequently with different rules and expectations and different parenting styles. Thus, transitions between the two may be stressful for all concerned,

and stability may take time to achieve. Counselors may need to help children understand that a relationship with the nonresident parent continues to exist despite periodic separations. In general, children should be encouraged to remain in contact with both parents, especially if the ex-mates can work out the details in an amicable fashion. Encouraging each set of parents to allow for tension on reentry into their household is often therapeutic for all concerned.

6. *Developing a family identity:* There is no legally binding relationship between stepparents and stepchildren (although later adoption is possible), and adults may therefore have reservations about getting involved emotionally with someone who may disappear from their lives at some future date. The counselor needs to be aware that stepfamily integration—especially stepparent-stepchild bonding—takes time, perhaps years. Any attempt to fit the stepfamily into a biological family mold is doomed to failure, with the possible rare exception of a stepfamily formed when all the children are very young.

7. *Overcoming boundary problems:* Successfully disengaging from previous marital systems and forming a boundary around the new couple and their household can often be an arduous task, what with regular visitation schedules and the presence of the noncustodial parent. Children may impede progress in the disengagement, which is necessary for forming a new, integrated stepfamily. Counselors need to guide stepfamilies to make the separation as well as to create boundaries within the new stepfamily where new roles and new rules can be worked out together.

8. *Learning coparenting:* In most cases, the counselor should encourage the maintenance of an open system with permeable boundaries between current and former spouses and their families. An open coparental relationship is extremely desirable, especially if the former mates have worked out their emotional divorce and any lingering bitterness between them is kept to a minimum. Children should never have the power to decide on remarriage, custody, or visitation, since that would violate the parental boundaries and responsibilities; however, their input into such parental decisions does deserve attention.

Stepfamily Stages and Counselor Interventions

Recognizing that the stepfamily's ultimate goal is greater self-definition as a new family unit, counselors need to appreciate that stepfamily cohesion and ultimately integration require time and occur in stages. Each stage in the process of solidifying a remarried family's attempt to achieve an identity calls for the renegotiating and reorganizing of a complex and dynamic network of relationships. Thus, at each juncture, there is a risk that unresolved issues from the previous stages will reemerge and old feelings flare up, especially if these have been covered over in the rush to form a united remarried family.

Counseling efforts, in addition to persistently supporting the growth and integration of the new family, must address the relationship problems specific to the stage of the family's development. Early on, this may mean directing therapeutic attention to helping members successfully relinquish lost dreams and relation-ships. Stepfamily members may also require help in learning new roles or per-haps in beginning to examine boundary realignments now that a new family entity has been formed. Perhaps new conflict-resolving mechanisms can be encouraged by the counselor and new decision-making structures set in place. Bray (1992) suggests that three key developmental issues are likely to require res-olution during the first years of remarriage: arranging for discipline and parental authority for children, forming a strong marital bond, and developing a workable relationship with the noncustodial parent.

Later in the history of the remarried family, relationship rules may need revi-sion, or a child born to the remarried couple may need to be incorporated into the boundaries of the family. Whatever brings the family to the counselor, prob-lems related to the phase of the family's development and integration must be scrutinized. McGoldrick and Carter (1988) draw special attention to the impact of remarriage in the two possible family life-cycle combinations:

1. *When spouses are at different life-cycle stages:* Family members may experi-ence greater difficulties in making the necessary transitions and are thus like-ly to take longer to integrate into a working family.

2. *When spouses are at the same life-cycle stage:* Stepfamily integration is gen-erally easier, in that family members are dealing with similar life-stage tasks. On the other hand, problems may arise if family members feel overloaded by such tasks as coping with stepchildren, ex-spouses, in-laws, and others.

The early stages of remarriage require interventions that help the new family gradually develop new shared rules and values that feel right to all the members. Strengths carried over from the previous family need to be acknowledged, and feelings of tension, confusion, and frustration accepted as normal and to be expected. Later in the remarriage, unhappy coalitions within the stepfamily may challenge family stability and equilibrium, or perhaps normal life-cycle events (the birth of more children, shifts in custody arrangements at adolescence, chil-dren's growing up and leaving home) may cause disruption in family functioning. At each transition, the counselor needs to help the family reach back into its his-tory, review any past resilient solutions, and clarify and construct relationship pat-terns to meet the current challenge. Searching for new options in dealing with old, familiar patterns may help some families work out solutions never before considered by them as possibilities.

Counseling on Multiple Tracks

Sager and colleagues (1983) argue that the precursor of remarriage has been the simultaneous disruption in three aspects of the life cycle—the individual, the mar-ital, and the family—and that the counselor must consider dislocations in all three to obtain a comprehensive picture of what transpires in the transition to remar-riage. The focus here is on the suprafamily system, composed of functionally related subsystems such as the marital couple, the wife and former husband, and also aunts, uncles, and grandparents. At the beginning of counseling, all members of this suprafamily are seen together so that a therapeutic relationship is formed with all concerned; later, various subgroups are seen, as called for by the stage and content of counseling.

According to the formulation of Sager's group, the conflicts in remarried families are generated in that each spouse has to operate along multiple tracks, dealing simultaneously with possibly incongruent individual, marital, and family life cycles. For example, as a consequence of divorce and remarriage, individual life cycles are lived out over the course of two or more marriages. As these authors observe, husbands and wives may be simultaneously biological parents and stepparents; conflicts may exist in a father, for example, between loyalty to his natural children and to the stepchildren with whom he resides on a daily basis. With remarriage, the man must cope with the complexities of not only being part of an old family life cycle and perhaps of an old marital cycle with an ex-wife but also beginning a new marital cycle and a complicated new family cycle with stepparent-stepchild relationships! The counselor needs to remain alert to the array of tracks on which the systems and their members are likely to be operating, and to ascertain if developmental needs are being sufficiently met in the different systems.

By the time a man or woman contemplates remarriage, he or she has gone through a number of powerful structural life changes in all three life-cycle areas. Sager and associates (1983) offer as illustration the case of Amy Greenson (Table 7.4 on pages 190 and 191), a middle-class white[6] woman, as she separates from her family of origin, marries, has children, separates, divorces, lives as a single parent, and then remarries, beginning a new family life cycle. Note how previous and new marital and family cycles are current and overlap, and how new life-cycle tracks are added to her life, rather than merely replacing old ones.

Reading the table vertically provides a longitudinal view of her life along each life cycle; horizontally, the reader gets a cross-sectional view of what is transpiring simultaneously in her individual, marital, and family life cycles. For example, we see at ages 45 to 50 that by remarrying she has added an additional marital-cycle track to her existence, not merely moving from one marriage to another. Hence, she must deal at one and the same time with difficulties allowing herself to love again (individual cycle), coparenting her daughters from her first marriage through adolescence as well as entering a new marriage (marital cycle), and restructuring her family to now include a stepson as well as her new husband, in addition to caring about her aging parents (family cycle). As is undoubtedly clear

---

[6] There are relatively few studies of nonwhite stepfamilies to date. The situation is beginning to be addressed, although the results are inconclusive. Fine, McKenry, Donnelly, and Voydanoff (1992) contend that African American stepfamilies share a lot in common with white stepfamilies, although Crosbie-Burnett and Lewis (1993) maintain that the transition from intact family to stepfamily in the former group is easier as a result of long-established kinship networks that help with stepfamily integration. Watt-Jones (1997) is critical of the use of the standard genogram for African Americans, contending that its underlying assumption of "family" as strictly a biological entity is not culturally valid, since African Americans have a long history of defining "family" in both biological and functional (significant nonfamily members who play parts in family life) terms. We return to the issue of kinship networks among African Americans in Chapter 11.

Table 7.4 The individual, marital, and family life cycles in a remarried family

Age	Individual life cycle	Marital life cycle	Family life cycle
18–21	Pulls up roots. Develops autonomy. (Amy M. moves out of family's home and attends college in another city.)	Shift from family of origin to new emotional commitment. (Amy meets George Greenson, and they begin to date exclusively.)	During college, Amy still financially dependent on her family of origin; her old room is kept for her at home.
22–28	Provisional adulthood. Develops occupational identification. (Amy graduates and works as a teacher; shares apartment and then lives alone.)	Provisional marital commitment; stress over parenthood. (Amy and George engaged when Amy is 23; marry at 24.)	Self-sufficient vis-à-vis family of origin; her room at home is converted to study.
29–31	Transition at age 30; decides about commitment to work and marriage.	Commitment crisis. (Married six years, George is questioning the relationship. They receive marital counseling.)	Pressure from her family to stay together and have children; her father retires.
32–39	Settling down, deepening commitments. (Amy feels committed to George and desires children; she stops working with birth of first child.)	Productivity: children, friends, work for George. (Their daughters are born when Amy is 32 and 34.)	Family with young children: need to accept new members, take on parenting roles.
40–42	Midlife transition; searching for fit between aspirations and environment. (Amy questions homemaker role, is restless and dissatisfied. After an impetuous sexual misadventure, she avoids dating.)	Couple is summing up: success and failure evaluated. (Amy and George again receive counseling; George has affair; decision to separate is made when children are 6 and 8 years old.)	Postseparation family: two households are set up. Amy returns to live with her parents; there is a resurgence of dependence on her family of origin as she returns to the job market. She has custody of children, who visit father. Grandparents very involved with children while Amy works and begins to date.
43–45	Middle adulthood: restabilizing and reordering priorities; struggle to reestablish autonomy from her family of origin; dealing with work advancement. (Now begins to desire a loving relationship with a man.)	Continuing coparenting relationship although marriage is dissolved. Beginning to date. Testing out new ways of relating to men.	Double single-parent stage: girls are now 11 and 9 and are part of both parents' households.

Age		Marriage	Family
45–50	Tasks of middle adulthood continue. Emotional divorce from George sufficiently complete for her to contemplate idea of marriage again. (Difficulty allowing herself to trust again as love relationship develops.) Remarries to fulfill coupling needs. Simultaneously continues coparenting of her children with first husband while taking on coparenting role with second husband.	*Marriage #1* Need to coparent the girls through their adolescence. Dealing with ex-husband on issues around the girls such as dating and their desire to visit father less often. *Marriage #2* 1. Entering new relationship with Steve. 2. Planning and conceptualizing new marriage. 3. Remarriage. 4. Making new commitment. 5. Commitment crisis: questioning choice. 6. Resolving conflicts and stabilizing remarriage.	*Old family* Allowing adolescent children to individuate. Launching children and moving on. Dealing with aging and illness of her parents. *Remarried family* Restructuring family to include new spouse and stepson (age 10) who lives with Rem couple. Providing a nurturing environment to prepubescent child. Dealing with Steve's ex-wife. Family with adolescent child. (Cycle repeats what Amy experienced with her girls.)
50–59	Looking ahead to enjoying the later years. Dealing with her own aging process.	*Marriage #1* Coparenting relationship is less important. Establishing a workable relationship with George around their adult children. *Marriage #2* 7. Supporting and enjoying friends and activities as children begin to leave home.	Launching child and moving on.
59+		*Marriage #1* Little contact with George except for milestone events of children and grandchildren. *Marriage #2* 8. Continuing support; retirement, pursuit of interests, individually and together with Steve.	*Old family* Relating to her children's spouses and children. *Remarried family* Relating to stepson's spouse and children.

Source: Sager et al, 1983.

from this example, and as Sager and associates (1983) point out, the conflict and stress felt by many dysfunctional remarried couples arise from attempting to deal with the multiple tracks that are by definition part of the remarried family suprasystem.

Multiproblem families exist in all social classes, of course, although some are especially burdened by the stresses of poverty, joblessness, immigrant status, chronic illness, lack of education, and so forth, often leading to feelings of despair and hopelessness about future change. Counseling in all cases starts by involving as many members as possible, establishing a working alliance with each, and beginning the process of making each feel safe in the counseling environment. Sager and colleagues (1983) strongly recommend the early use of three-generational genograms (see Chapter 3). Since such a large amount of data need to be organized, the schematic drawing provides information about previous marriages, the length of any single-parent-household periods, and possible shifts in children's living arrangements. A clearer picture of the complexity of the suprafamily system is likely to emerge, offering some basis for understanding why the members are experiencing stress and confusion at this time. Later, sessions with various subgroups can be arranged for further assessment purposes, and a treatment plan directed at specific problems in the individual, marital, and family life cycles of the particular remarried family can be developed. Overall, the process is intended to refocus and redefine the family's problems in terms of the whole remarried system and its needs and individual responsibilities (Ganong & Coleman, 1999).

Whom to See and When

Visher and Visher (1988b) contend that although the type of problem or specific characteristics of the remarried family are important in determining what combination of members to see, the major determinant is the remarried family's stage of development. Families are unlikely to contact a counselor during an early *fantasy stage* (see Table 7.5), preferring other media of information, self-education, or support group sources for help. Should they seek counselor aid during the following three stages (*pseudo-assimilation, awareness,* and *mobilization*), it is likely that the stepparent has begun to recognize that something is wrong and changes are required. Here the authors recommend the counselor see the couple alone in order to strengthen their relationship; if counseling is successful, children may not need to be seen or can be seen, if necessary, after the couple's relationship becomes viable.

Once the couple has formed a cohesive unit, various combinations of family members working conjointly with the counselor are possible. During the *action stage,* appropriate subgroups may meet together with the counselor in order to manage specific family problems. If working well, relationships between all stepfamily relatives may deepen (*contact stage*), and *resolution* may be reached as the stepfamily strengthens its sense of identity.

The counselor's immediate task, according to this formulation, is to assess the stepfamily's stage of development as a preliminary step toward determining

Table 7.5 Determination of whom to see in therapy

Stage	Characteristics	Productive therapeutic contacts
I. Fantasy	Adults expect instant love and adjustment. Children try to ignore step-parent in hopes that he or she will go away and biological parents will be reunited.	1. Couple 2. Stepfamily household (unlikely to see anyone except for education)
II. Pseudo-Assimilation	Attempts to realize fantasies. Vague sense that things are not going well. Increasing negativity. Splits along biological lines. Stepparents feel something is wrong with them.	1. Couple seen individually and/or conjointly 2. Children if disturbed
III. Awareness	Growing awareness of family pressures. Stepparent begins to perceive what changes are needed. Parent feels pulled between needs of children and new spouse. Groups divide along biological lines. Children may observe and exploit differences between couple. Usually takes outside push—reading, stepfamily group, support from a friend, therapy—to get to Stage IV.	1. Couple seen individually and/or conjointly. 2. Children if need help urgently
IV. Mobilization	Strong emotions begin to be expressed, often leading to arguments between couple. Stepparent clear on need for change. Parent fears change will bring loss. Sharp division between biological groups. Stepparent with no children is in isolated position and lacks support.	1. Couple seen individually and/or conjointly. 2. Children if need help urgently
V. Action	Couple begins working together to find solutions. Family structure changes. Boundaries are clarified. Children may resist changes.	1. Emphasis on couple 2. Appropriate subgroups 3. Suprasystem subgroup combinations
VI. Contact	Couple working well together. Closer bonding between stepchild and other steprelations. Stepparent has definite role with stepchildren. Boundaries clear. More ability to deal with suprasystem issues.	1. Any suprasystem grouping (depends on issues)
VII. Resolution	Stepfamily identity secure. When difficulties arise, family may regress to earlier stages, but moves ahead quickly. Usual difficulties are around nodal family events involving the suprasystem.	1. Any suprasystem grouping (unlikely to come in now)

Source: Visher & Visher, 1988b.

which subgroups should be seen first and whether certain individuals or sub-groups need to be seen at once or can wait until after the couple has achieved adequate stability to join the counseling.

The case studies that follow illustrate some variations in stepfamily patterns. First, we consider a remarried family with a stepfather.

Juan and Maria had known each other growing up in a poor, rural part of El Salvador, but were not close friends. Both were members of large families, and both lived among large extended-family networks. Since the families needed their help in earning a living, both were taken out of school after 5 or 6 years and labored along-side their parents and siblings as farm workers.

When Maria's parents realized that more money was needed to support the family of six children than they could possibly earn, her father headed north, crossing the border illegally into California and making his way to the Central Valley to earn cash as a farm worker and send the money back to his family. Hoping to find work since there were few opportunities in El Salvador, Maria joined him when she reached 16, and together they shared a small apartment near the fields. When she was 18, hop-ing to escape life with her controlling father, Maria married a Mexican laborer, Luis, and a daughter, Isabella, was born the following year. However, the marriage was shaky from the start. Luis drank heavily and frequently became sexually involved with other women. Moreover, when drunk, he was physically abusive to Maria and Isabella. When he left one day to take a job in another part of the country, Maria felt relieved to be rid of him and drifted into a series of relationships with men, in part to relieve her loneliness and also to gain some financial support. She became the mother of Elvira as a result of one such union.

Juan, too, had migrated to the United States as soon as he was 17. For the most part he worked at odd jobs as a parking lot attendant, busboy, delivery man—until he was told by a friend about a job as a carpenter's assistant at a construction site. Applying himself to the work, which he enjoyed, he stayed with the construction com-pany, ultimately joined the union, and now worked on a more or less regular basis, depending on available work, in the home construction business.

When Juan and Maria met at a friend's house, they remembered each other and immediately began dating. After several months, Maria divorced Luis, and she and Juan were married. He seemed willing to take on the role of stepfather to the two girls, and they felt happy finally to have a "real" family with a mother and father. However, consistent with his cultural background, but also due to his lack of experience, he dis-ciplined the children in a heavy-handed manner. Problems between Juan and the chil-dren soon developed, and Juan complained that the children did not accept his strong authority.

Maria and Juan were reasonably happy for a short period of time, although they did quarrel from time to time over what she perceived as his need to control her. He was jealous of her contact with other people and suspicious of her whereabouts if she was late coming home from marketing. While he insisted that she have no secrets from him, he refused to tell her how he spent his paycheck. Whenever she complained that their 700-square-foot house was too crowded—besides the parents and children, Juan's brother now lived with them—he shouted at her, threatened to hit her, and told her to get a job if she wanted more money. Ridiculing her religious beliefs, he sarcastically told her on more than one occasion to pray for a job—perhaps that would help.

When Maria learned about the availability of counseling from a neighbor, she asked Juan to go with her, but he refused. However, after the initial session with her, the counselor called Juan on the telephone and persuaded him to attend joint sessions, which he agreed to do only if it would help Maria to stop complaining about him. Together they attended six counseling sessions.

Realizing that their number of visits would be short, the counselor tried to help them redefine their relationship as a partnership in which each could benefit. Maria was urged to support and back up Juan in taking on coparenting authority with the children, which he desired, and Juan was advised that Maria would be more responsive to his needs if she did not feel so controlled and imprisoned by him. They were urged to listen to each other's suggestions about the children's problems. Together they were counseled to strengthen their marital bond by defining the boundary between themselves and the children. With no interference from Maria's former husband, Luis, whose whereabouts they did not know, they were able to proceed to build and strengthen the stepfamily structure. While by no means problem-free, at the conclusion of counseling they left better prepared for working together as a family.

Unlike the stepfather family just described, in the following case a newly formed stepmother family ran into trouble almost from the beginning. See Figure 7.2 for a structural depiction of the Oliver family before and after counseling.

Joyce and David Oliver had been married only 8 months when they contacted a family counselor as a last resort. Both in their late twenties, Joyce had never been married, establishing a career in business, while David, previously married, had been

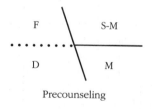

Precounseling

The diffuse boundary between father and daughter indicates they have formed an overinvolved or enmeshed relationship; the stepmother is isolated and excluded, as is the absent biological mother.

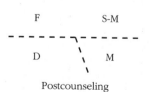

Postcounseling

A restructuring has occurred, and a clear boundary now exists between the united parents and the daughter, as well as between the daughter and her biological mother.

Figure 7.2   Pre- and postcounseling structural mapping of the Oliver remarried family

divorced for about a year when they met at a ski resort. They had a great time together, and after seeing each other daily for several months when they returned to the city, they decided to marry. David had spoken briefly of Kiri, his 4-year-old daughter who lived with his ex-wife in another state, but Joyce did not see the child as having much to do with her since Kiri lived with her mother. She had met her future stepdaughter only once before the wedding ceremony.

The family problems began shortly after the wedding, when Rhonda, David's former spouse, announced that she was having some personal problems, including some with Kiri, and was sending her to live with David and Joyce. For David, who took his parental responsibilities very seriously, this was a welcome opportunity to see Kiri on a regular basis and take an active part in her upbringing. At last he would have the perfect family he had always dreamed of, the perfect harmony that he had failed to achieve in his previous marriage. Having had no experience with children, Joyce wasn't sure what to expect but was eager to share parental responsibilities if it would make her new husband happy.

Unfortunately, David's dreams failed to materialize, in no small part due to his own behavior, as well as Kiri's. She was not an easy child to live with, having been suddenly whisked away from an over-close mother. Confused and frightened, she clung to her father, quickly becoming overattached to him, and excluded her stepmother. David, in turn, feeling guilty over his child's obvious upset, became very attached to Kiri, so much so that at times it felt to Joyce that he preferred the child's company to hers. Instead of learning to live with her new husband, Joyce soon felt she was saddled with an instant family in which she felt like an outsider in her own home. David would call Kiri daily before coming home from work to see if she needed him to bring anything home. When his wife objected and complained of feeling "frozen out," he defended himself as merely acting as any concerned parent would, adding that Joyce's jealousy forced him to do even more for Kiri than he might have if Joyce had done more.

Evenings, David would put Kiri to bed; if he stayed more than the 10 minutes he had promised Joyce, she would get depressed, withdraw, and not talk to him the rest of that evening. According to David, Joyce was a spoiled child herself, competitive with a 4-year-old, and he was losing respect for her. During their joint sessions with a family counselor, he spoke of being raised by a widowed mother as an only child, and how central to his life was the feeling of family closeness. Joyce, on the other hand, insisted that David did not allow her to develop a relationship with Kiri, expecting her to instantly love someone because he did, but doing nothing to instill in Kiri that they had to reorganize the family to include all three of them. She herself had been raised by a divorced mother in a relatively disengaged family where all three children lived relatively separate lives.

The conflict between them had reached the boiling point by the time the couple contacted the counselor. David labeled his wife a "wicked stepmother" whom he threatened to leave unless she "corrected her behavior." She, in turn, accused her husband of having a "romance" with his daughter, strongly implying that there might be more to the father-daughter relationship than was evident. Neither was willing to listen to what the counselor was saying, each apparently eager to win his favor and favorable judgment regarding who was right. Joyce would hear of nothing short of sending Kiri back to her mother; David insisted he would not be given an ultimatum regarding how to deal with his own child. While the counseling was in its early stages, Rhonda announced that she had gotten remarried, to Mel, and that she was pregnant.

The counselor began by indicating he was not there to judge who was right, but to help them gain some tools for understanding what was happening to them. It was clear that both were miserable, as Kiri undoubtedly was also. If they continued this way, they would almost certainly get divorced, an unfortunate circumstance for both of them since their marriage had not had a chance.

In order to reduce the white heat between them so that counseling might proceed, the counselor attempted two early interventions. One was to reduce the tension by asking them to describe their own histories of child-rearing. The information would be useful later, and for the moment would help each begin to grasp that they had come into parenting with different experiences and expectations. As another initial intervention ploy, he asked whether they would be willing to listen to what the other had to say without condemning it, getting defensive, or resorting to name calling. The counselor thus appealed to their rational selves; since each spouse was anxious not to be labeled the difficult or unreasonable one, the two agreed.

Each proceeded to discuss his or her view of child-rearing. They had clear disagreements based on different experiences of their own, and the counselor helped each to listen and try to understand. Joyce's rejecting behavior toward Kiri was reframed by the counselor as inexperience rather than wickedness; David's overinvolvement was reframed as eagerness to be a good father. Joyce acknowledged she could learn from David, since she had known little parental attention and affection growing up; however, she insisted he would have to try to be less critical of her if he really wanted her to make the effort. David acknowledged he might be overdoing the parenting, since he had not had a father of his own at home as a model. The counselor helped him understand that fathers who obtain custody often have unrealistic expectations of how a stepmother should behave. In this case, he was willing to relinquish some parenting chores as he became convinced that she was willing to try. He was encouraged to avoid any coalitions with Kiri against Joyce.

The next phase of the counseling dealt with reestablishing boundaries. The counselor explained that stepfamily blending does not come automatically or instantly, but only through a gradual rearrangement of the new family's structure. It was agreed that David would allow Joyce to do more of the parenting in the best way she saw fit—even if it differed from his way—and that he would explain to Kiri that Rhonda was still her mother, but Joyce would be taking over the day-to-day job, with his approval, while Kiri lived with them. That is, Kiri was told that Joyce was not replacing her biological mother, only supplementing her while Kiri remained with them. Kiri could visit her mother whenever it could be arranged, something she expressed an interest in doing, especially after her stepsister was born. Kiri was told by David and Joyce together that she was a member of two households; she could feel free to move between the two without loyalty conflicts.

David and Joyce had their own loyalty issues to resolve. As he came to understand that he had given his daughter his first loyalty, primarily out of guilt over the impact on Kiri of his failed marriage, he recognized that he was contributing to the diminution of his current marital relationship. Joyce, too, recognized that because she felt as if she were in a secondary position, she struggled against the child excessively, forcing David to defend Kiri; thus, she also contributed to the deteriorating marriage. The counselor helped them untangle these difficulties, focusing them on working to strengthen their separate identity as a couple and their primary loyalty to each other. They were encouraged to spend more time alone as a couple, sharing activities that did not include Kiri. As this occurred, their bond grew; differences between the couple, although still present, began to be negotiated in a more open fashion rather than through a father-daughter versus stepmother conflict. New rules and happier solutions followed, as David, Joyce, and Kiri began to develop their own traditions and to define themselves as a family.

Note the counselor's goals in this case:

1. Reduce the accusations and blame-fixing between the adults.
2. Reframe or relabel the behavior each finds objectionable in the other as well-intentioned, thereby diffusing some of the self-righteous rage and indignation.
3. Appeal to each adult's wish to be seen as reasonable and fair in hearing out the spouse's contentions.
4. Define the problem as a systems one to which each member, including the child, is contributing.
5. Strengthen the spousal subsystem, encouraging their loyalty to each other and their common purpose and family identity.
6. Consolidate parental authority and unity in regard to the child without her experiencing loss of her biological mother.
7. Help reduce loyalty conflicts for the child and adults.
8. Keep the remarried system an open system with permeable boundaries so that the child derives a sense of security from the home where she lives, but also retains membership in her other household.
9. Help the family members to tolerate differences among themselves or from some ideal intact family model.
10. Encourage the development of new rules, behavior patterns, and family traditions.

With the Oliver family, as with all stepfamilies, the counselor's overall task is to help the fragmented family become more cohesive and better integrated. In addition to helping family members develop a sense of identity as a family unit and strengthen the new marital bond, the counselor needs to pay attention to fortifying the sibling bond when stepsiblings exist. Pasley (1985) advises that helping stepfamilies build generational boundaries within the new stepfamily system, rather than supporting original family boundaries, will aid stepfamily integration.

She further suggests that counselors invite both households to participate in the counseling process in order to provide greater clarity regarding the roles and responsibilities of the various members of the enlarged stepfamily suprasystem.

In the following joint custody case, the counselor meets with all four main adults in the suprasystem—the custodial parent, the nonresident parent, the spouse of the custodial parent, and the spouse of the nonresident parent—though the identified patient is one of the preadolescent children.

Kevin, age 11, was doing extremely poorly in school. The teacher complained that he was hyperactive in class and seemed unable to sit still or attend to class activity for more than 3 or 4 minutes at a time. The older of two children, Kevin, along with Mark, age 8, lived in a joint physical custody arrangement, generally staying at his remarried father's home 3 days a week and at his remarried mother's 4 days. When the teacher contacted both parents, each angrily blamed the other for the problems Kevin was having, but ultimately their physician persuaded them to take him to a university-affiliated pediatric clinic for an evaluation.

It was clear almost immediately to the pediatrician who worked on Kevin's case that more was involved than simply what was going on inside the boy. He was aware that the continuous fighting between both sets of parents was having a damaging impact on Kevin, so before he prescribed medication (in this case, Ritalin) for the hyperactivity, he recommended that the four adults seek family counseling. Although they initially resisted the idea, he finally insisted that he could not go ahead with treating Kevin until the family conflict had been reduced. After two weeks of further bickering between the couples, they agreed to see a family counselor the pediatrician had recommended. However, each couple expressed doubts about the wisdom of working together since their prior efforts in conciliation court (over issues regarding finances, visitation schedules, and custody changes) had proved pointless and unsuccessful.

The counselor made it clear from the start that she would see them only as a foursome. When she greeted them in the waiting room, she could see that they were poised to fight, an impression that was confirmed as soon as they entered the consultation room. They immediately attempted to set the counseling agenda along the lines of their previous conciliation court experience, each couple pulling out divorce settlements to back up their claims. The counselor spent some time dissociating herself from the legal process, and the current counseling from their past experiences. The first session was spent identifying the players—Suzy had recently married Clark, Kevin's father; Stanley and Jane (Kevin's mother) had been married for 4 years and had a newborn child—and filling out a genogram (Figure 7.3, page 200). Subsequent sessions revealed that although each former spouse believed that the other's new spouse had initiated the trouble between them, the truth seemed to be that the new spouses had simply empowered their mates to stand up and fight: Clark to limit his financial contribution to the support of the two children, previously given generously, now that he had remarried; Jane to demand that the boys' father help more in picking them up from school and take them more often on holidays, now that she had the additional responsibility of caring for her newborn, Lizzie.

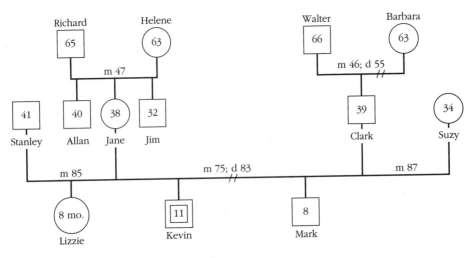

Figure 7.3   Genogram of Kevin's suprafamily

Rather than deal with these difficult issues right away, the counselor refocused their attention on the presenting problem of Kevin's school performance, asking each couple how they understood what was happening to him at school. As each spoke, they began to be aware that Kevin showed similar behavior at home and that, what was more, each experienced him in the same way. He was obstreperous, irresponsible, fidgety, and forgetful about doing his assigned chores, and he frequently fought with Mark. Whereas each couple had assumed previously that they were burdened with his problematic behavior and that the other couple was spared, they now began to recognize that both sets of parents were having identical experiences and that neither was being handed a problem created by the visit to the other, as each had assumed.

The counselor's strategy of getting them to work together on solving their common problem seemed to pay off. Each ex-spouse started to view the other's new spouse as a real person: someone who did indeed create some difficulties but, contrary to what had been assumed, was not responsible for certain other problems. With greater insight came greater sympathy and less scapegoating. Rather than remaining angry with one another, they started tentatively to work together on helping Kevin. As they spoke together in the counselor's office weekly, they recognized that each set of parents was alternating between being too rigid in its demands on Kevin—asking for more than he could give and thus creating an inevitable failure situation—and then giving up in defeat and frustration and becoming too lax and undemanding. The counselor helped them work at being consistent, offering specific suggestions ("You are asking him to perform too long a chore"; "Make sure he is expected to do the same thing in both homes") that, coming from a neutral authority, all four seemed to accept.

The consistency was not lost on Kevin either. Instead of getting a weekly bombardment in each home about the shortcomings (or evil intent or craziness) of the other set of parents, Kevin now heard the parents talk in more supportive terms about one another's efforts. His relationship with Mark improved as he became less competitive with him for parental approval. Both sets of parents seemed less tense with one another and better organized, and that was comforting to Kevin. He became less confused at school and less agitated, although his short attention span continued to be a problem.

By strengthening the coparental coalition, the counselor had helped create a more secure set of home environments. Kevin was sent back to the pediatric clinic, where he was put on a trial run of Ritalin. Although it was dramatically effective at school, all four parents were frightened of keeping him on drugs and began to compete at home over which set of parents was able to keep him off the medication longer while he resided with them during the week. After consulting with the pediatrician, the counselor persuaded the parents to accept the drug use, since it helped greatly in focusing Kevin's attention first at school and later at home.

All four parents were thrilled by Kevin's progress, as well as their ability to discuss issues about the children with one another without quarreling. Slowly they ironed out the final issue to be resolved: their financial differences. The counselor asked them to come a half-hour early for their next appointment and to meet in the waiting room to work out solutions to practical issues (for example, scheduling the time and place of pickup) between them. They did so successfully, and when the counselor was away on vacation, they met at the neutral territory of a local recreation center to continue talking.

The counseling dealt with such powerful issues as competitiveness and jealousy between the biological mother and stepmother, as well as economic and social conflict between the father and stepfather. The system in which both sets of parents participated remained open and the boundaries permeable. The parents felt an increased sense of self-esteem, considerably different from their earlier feelings of anger and helplessness regarding child-rearing. Together they learned negotiating skills, vital in remarried family situations.

Some issues remained unsettled. Anger surfaced occasionally over money, and both of Kevin's parents continued to feel some injustices left over from the original marriage. However, they did agree to put aside their differences in the service of their newly developed family stability. Kevin became increasingly attached to his stepsister, Lizzie, and helped out with her when he could. Suzy and Clark, having survived a crisis over a stepchild that nearly wrecked their marriage, were feeling more optimistic about the future and were planning to adopt a baby.

Psychoeducational Programs

Helping family members through psychoeducational programs to understand common stepfamily relationship patterns (and especially their differences from those in intact families) is often an effective way to aid them in dealing with the unique aspects of stepfamily life (Bray, 1995). Stepfamilies can often profit, too, from reading about the experiences of other stepparents and stepchildren (for example, Kelley, 1995; Boyd, 1998). Michaels (2000) has described a pilot multi-couple stepfamily enrichment program, directed at early intervention for recently formed stepfamilies, in which didactic presentations, group discussions, and experiential exercises are carried out. Her efforts are intended to normalize the stepfamily experience, strengthen the marital bond, and help nurture both the step- and biological-parent-child relationship, making certain that they make a place for the noncustodial parent.

One important psychoeducational resource is the stepfamily awareness movement, led by the Stepfamily Association of America.[7] This national nonprofit organization, founded by Emily and John Visher, has state and local chapters that offer a variety of educational programs (training for professionals, referral to counselors who work with stepfamilies) and provide a network of mutual help services (survival courses in stepfamily living). Its quarterly publication, *Stepfamilies,* is intended to act as an advocate of stepfamily life while keeping readers, many of whom are themselves stepfamily members, informed on the latest studies and events that affect the stepfamily. Visher and Visher (1986) have developed a stepfamily workbook manual (an excerpt from which is shown in Box 7.2) to aid in discussion groups aimed at structuring new suprafamily systems.

Finally, a word about the positive benefits of remarriage and stepfamilies. Clearly, the heavy burden of single parenting is reduced. Not only are economic pressures on the single parent lightened, but the presence of another adult provides essential feedback information on child-rearing procedures. Further, the danger that a child may be pressured into assuming a spousal role with a single parent is lessened. The participation of grandparents and other extended-family members in a remarried situation is typically a plus for the children. A stepfamily also provides an opportunity for parents to have a larger family; this is especially a benefit if one spouse is childless or has fewer children than he or she desires. An only child is certain to benefit from mingling with stepsiblings. A functioning remarried family elicits all the respect and social acceptance that an intact family does. Finally, doing something helpful and beneficial for someone you love—such as helping raise his or her children—is rewarding in and of itself.

Summary

Remarriage has become nearly as common as first marriages in the United States today. Four of five men and three of four women typically remarry within 3 years of getting divorced. There are estimated to be more than 11 million remarried households today. Such remarried families come in a variety of structural forms, depending on whether one or both spouses were previously single, divorced, or widowed, and whether children are present. Each pattern brings with it a separate set of problems for the counselor to consider.

All members of a remarried family have sustained a recent primary relationship loss. New interactive patterns are likely to be complex and prone to stress, as

---

[7] The Stepfamily Association of America's headquarters are in Lincoln, Nebraska (web site: www.stepfam.org). An advocacy group, the organization seeks to change attitudes about stepfamilies through media coverage of its research-based information and educational materials.

Box 7.2   Tasks that must be completed to develop a stepfamily identity

1. *Dealing with losses and changes*
2. *Negotiating different developmental needs*
3. *Establishing new traditions*
4. *Developing a solid couple bond*
5. *Forming new relationships*
6. *Creating a "parenting coalition"*
7. *Accepting continual shifts in household composition*
8. *Risking involvement despite little societal support*

1. *Dealing with losses and changes*
   - Identify/recognize losses for all individuals
   - Support expressions of sadness
   - Help children talk and not act out feelings
   - Read stepfamily books
   - Make changes gradually
   - See that everyone gets a turn
   - Inform children of plans involving them
   - Accept the insecurity of change

2. *Negotiating different developmental needs*
   - Take a child development and/or parenting class
   - Accept validity of the different life-cycle phases
   - Communicate individual needs clearly
   - Negotiate incompatible needs
   - Develop tolerance and flexibility

3. *Establishing new traditions*
   - Recognize ways are *different,* not right or wrong
   - Concentrate on important situations only
   - Stepparents take on discipline enforcement slowly
   - Use family meetings for problem solving and giving appreciation
   - Shift "givens" slowly whenever possible
   - Retain/combine appropriate rituals
   - Enrich with new creative traditions

4. *Developing a solid couple bond*
   - Accept couple as primary long-term relationship
   - Nourish couple relationship
   - Plan for couple "alone time"
   - Decide general household rules as a couple
   - Support one another with the children
   - Expect and accept different parent-child and stepparent-stepchild feelings
   - Work out money matters together

(continued on next page)

Box 7.2 *(continued)*

5. Forming new relationships
- Fill in past histories
- Make stepparent-stepchild one-to-one time
- Make parent-child one-to-one time
- Parent make space for stepparent-stepchild relationship
- Do not expect instant love and adjustment
- Be fair to stepchildren even when caring not developed
- Follow children's lead in what to call stepparent
- Do fun things together

6. Creating a "parenting coalition"
- Deal directly with parenting adults in other household
- Keep children out of the middle of parental disagreements
- Do not talk negatively about adults in other household
- Control what you can and accept limitations
- Avoid power struggles between households
- Respect parenting skills of former spouse
- Contribute own "specialness" to children
- Communicate between households in most effective manner

7. Accepting continual shifts in household composition
- Allow children to enjoy their households
- Give children time to adjust to household transitions
- Avoid asking children to be messengers or spies
- Consider teenager's serious desire to change residence
- Respect privacy (boundaries) of all households
- Set consequences that affect own household only
- Provide personal place for nonresident children
- Plan special times for various household constellations

8. Risking involvement despite little societal support
- Include stepparents in school, religious, sports activities
- Give legal permission for stepparent to act when necessary
- Continue stepparent-stepchild relationships after death or divorce of parent when caring has developed
- Stepparent include self in stepchild's activities
- Find groups supportive of stepfamilies
- Remember that all relationships involve risk

Source: Visher & Visher, 1986.

unfamiliar roles and rules are worked out and boundaries stabilized. Disequilibrium and conflict are the norm, especially in the early stages of a remarried family, and particularly when children are present. Unfinished conflicts between ex-mates add to the overall turmoil, as does the presence of stepsiblings living under one roof. Loyalty conflicts both in children and adults are frequent. Early in a remarriage is also often the time for rearranging custody, visitation, or financial affairs between ex-spouses, sometimes reopening old wounds; this is a special problem because the newly married couple is at its earliest and thus most vulnerable point.

Remarriage is a process that proceeds through a number of distinct phases. Each has its potential for dislocation; each provides an opportunity for family consolidation. Counselors need to remain aware that disruptions may be occurring simultaneously at three levels—individual, marital, and family—for each member of the remarried family. Thus, members may need help in completing mourning for their earlier losses, in working out new relationship problems, and in forging boundary realignments as they attempt to form a stable, integrated family structure.

Counselors need to remain aware that remarried or stepfamilies are structurally different from intact biological families. They are likely to be far more complex, as two distinct families, with different experiences and traditions, attempt to blend into a stable system with an identity of its own. Counseling efforts must address the numerous relationship problems specific to the suprafamily's stage of development. Psychoeducational programs directed at stepfamily life may provide useful help in achieving stepfamily integration.

CHAPTER

E I G H T

Counseling Cohabiting Heterosexual Adults

About half of all single people in the United States cohabit at one time or another before marriage. For some, this living arrangement provides an intimate sexual experience while delaying a long-term commitment; for others, it means little more than a practical sharing of living expenses; for still others, cohabitation means a trial relationship while the couple tests their compatibility before getting married, able to end the relationship if unsuccessful without the complications of divorce (Cherlin, 1992). Cohabiting adults share living arrangements for a variety of reasons and with varying degrees of success; still, the proposition "Will you live with me?" appears to have replaced the traditional "Will you marry me?" for a sizable proportion of the population (Saxton, 1996).

Having come into prominence in the 1970s, this alternative lifestyle, in which adults of the opposite sex live together in an intimate relationship without the formality or sanction of being legally married (sometimes with children from one or the other's previous relationships), had become a relatively permanent and recognizable family structure at the end of the century (Bumpass, Raley, & Sweet, 1995). The number of such couples had increased by close to 1000 percent between 1960 and 1998 (U.S. Bureau of the Census, 1998), some perhaps having lived through several such arrangements over varying periods of time. The latest available count estimates that over 4 million unmarried couples currently share households. Although still representing fewer than 10% of all American couples living together at any one time, the number of people who have *ever* cohabited without marriage is thought to be considerably greater.

On the basis of data collected from a large national representative sample aged 19 and over, Bumpass and Sweet (1989) found that by their early thirties, almost half the population had lived together unmarried at one time, and the proportion is two-thirds among separated or divorced persons under the age of 35. Taken together, cohabiting couples were found to be a heterogeneous group, their choice of living arrangement likely to reflect a variety of attitudes and motivations. For some, commonly referred to as *prenuptial cohabitors,* marriage is definitely planned, although the precise time of the ceremony is uncertain. For others, marriage is a real possibility, and cohabiting represents an opportunity to check out the relationship before making the big decision. Still others express no interest in marriage, preferring the sexual and domestic freedoms they believe to be more attainable in a cohabiting understanding rather than in a marital arrangement. For this last group, cohabitation is an alternative to marriage.

For those uncertain about their relationship but considering marriage, living together represents a late stage of courtship. For others, anxious to marry but delayed by whatever practical restraint, it represents an early stage of marriage. Others, who see living together as an end point in the relationship and do not seek to go further with a commitment to marry, are likely to view cohabitation as a permanent substitute for marriage. Within this last group, some shrink from marriage as too confining of their freedom; others, such as those divorced and receiving spousal-support payments until remarriage, see cohabitation as a practical financial matter or perhaps fear making the same mistake again. Problems with facing unsolved problems over religious differences, value conflicts, substance abuse in one or the other (or both), parental objections, and so on may also play a part in the decision. In the case of elderly couples, divorced or widowed, anxious for companionship but unwilling to merge financial assets or risk marital failure or the disapproval of their children, cohabitation provides familiar couplehood without legal or religious complications. Whereas no significant number of American couples over the age of 60 were reported to be living together in 1960, by 1990 that number had jumped to over 400,000 (Cheval, 1996).

Nonmarital cohabitation arrangements—whether they represent short-term sexual experiences, long-term love relationships, trial marriages, or permanent alternatives to marriage—are clearly out in the open today, although some segments of the population disapprove on religious or moral grounds. The increase in nonmarital cohabitation is particularly striking among college students and better educated middle-class adults, especially those in urban centers where anonymity is more possible. Buunk and van Driel (1989) suggest that nonmarital cohabitation is gradually becoming an *institutional part of the mate selection process* in the United States and elsewhere. For many couples, because of its timing, cohabitation may actually represent more of a landmark—a transition into an intimate relationship with a member of the opposite sex—than marriage, which may or may not follow such a living arrangement.

Cohabitation itself is not exactly a new occurrence—common-law and other nonlegal unions have long been accepted in many societies, particularly among low-income persons—but what is new is its increased prevalence in a broader segment of American society, the fact that the participants do not consider themselves to be married or necessarily in a permanent relationship, and the increasing acceptance of this dyadic structure by the majority culture (Macklin, 1983). Where such a living arrangement between unmarried couples was once likely to cause strong social disapproval, in no small part because the persons involved were flaunting their sexual intimacy, the issue today has become less significant since premarital sexual relationships are commonplace regardless of living arrangement (Bumpass & Sweet, 1989).[1]

It appears likely that much of the current decline in the rate of marriage, as well as the marriage delay noted in Chapter 1, may be offset by the increased prevalence of cohabitation; conversely, divorce rates might be even higher except for breakups among cohabitors before marriage occurs. Axinn and Thornton (1992) suggest that the increase in cohabitation may be a response, at least in part, to the burgeoning divorce rate, leading couples increasingly to view marriage as a fragile relationship and to question it as an institution. Instead, many opt for nonmarital cohabiting unions, without children or the legal implications of marriage, while they spend time living together and testing out their chances of a successful marriage.

Because cohabitation is still considered unconventional (if tolerable) by the majority of society, few guidelines are available, so roles, interactive patterns, and styles of conflict management are often forged between partners on an individual trial-and-error basis, often at the cost of considerable interpersonal distress. Whether one or both partners has been married previously, whether children are included in the living arrangement,[2] whether financial pressures exist, whether families of origin know about and support the arrangement—all these factors influence the kinds of stressors and levels of satisfaction experienced by each partner in the cohabiting relationship. Without question, counselors can expect to see some couples who live in a cohabitational arrangement seeking help in resolving relationship problems, others attempting to settle conflicts over differences in commitment to a shared future, some perhaps desiring premarital counseling, and others reaching out for therapeutic aid in the emotional upheaval accompanying the pair's breakup.

---

[1] One illustration of how rapidly cohabitation has been accepted into mainstream American life (and especially college life) is the fact that when in 1968 a Barnard College woman student was discovered to be living off campus with a young man attending Columbia University, it was considered extraordinary enough to make the front pages of major newspapers throughout the United States (Saxton, 1996).

[2] Four out of ten couples who cohabit have children who live with them (Bumpass, Sweet, & Cherlin, 1991).

Changing Mores, Changing Lifestyles

Public media awareness of the phenomenon of two young people, more often than not college students, living together without being married began in the latter half of the 1960s, a time of social ferment, changing sexual values, and a willingness to experiment with unorthodox lifestyles. As Macklin (1983) observes, prior to that time

> only the most avant garde or the most impoverished, or those otherwise considered to be on the social periphery of society, were to be found openly cohabiting outside of marriage, and unmarried persons known to be living together could be expected to be referred to derogatorily as "shacking up." (p. 52)

Since that time, as we have noted, growth in the prevalence of cohabitation in all age groups has spurted, resulting in rapid social change relating to marriage and family. In a typical scenario, an unmarried couple cohabits for a brief period—one-quarter marry within a year, half within 3 years, according to Bumpass and Sweet's (1989) survey—during which decisions regarding remaining together or breaking up are made. Somewhat less frequently, a person who has been through marriage and divorce chooses to live with someone, sometimes with, but often without, a plan for future marriage; one member of the pair may harbor doubts and be the stumbling block to marriage. In addition, elderly people, widowed or divorced, may choose to live together as domestic partners without being married; in the case of senior citizens, the primary motivations are often companionship and the opportunity to informally merge financial resources without risking the loss of retirement or Social Security benefits or jeopardizing the inheritance of their children as a result of remarriage (Hatch, 1995). Later in this chapter we present clinical examples of various cohabiting relationships, together with a discussion of their interpersonal dynamics, the problems confronting the counselor, and recommended solutions.

Counselors should certainly concern themselves with what sorts of individuals choose this living pattern, what motivates them, and why they choose cohabiting rather than living alone or marrying. Are specific attitudes—for example, regarding male-female roles or the wish to delay commitment or retain a sense of independence while relating to another—likely to be typical of people in this lifestyle? Are cohabitors more unconventional, more defiant of traditional values? Do they as a group have more liberal attitudes toward sexual behavior? Clearly, the counselor needs to look at the specific dyadic relationship of the presenting couple, but we mention certain common patterns as guidelines in organizing an appraisal.

Why the significant change in social values and behavior since the 1960s, not only on the part of young people, which might be more expected, but also on the part of their elders? Several factors, some of which we have touched on in previous chapters, seem to be operating here. More openness regarding sexual behavior, increased availability of effective contraception, and a growing acceptance of sexual involvement outside of marriage all seem to be pertinent. Moreover, a growing demand on the part of women for equal rights and for the abandonment of the double standard vis-à-vis men is clearly a factor. Women today are apt to be more financially self-sufficient and thus less dependent on a husband for economic survival. An emphasis on a meaningful relationship and on the continued growth of both partners has become more important, as people of all ages explore new ways to achieve fulfillment and escape the many games involved in dating. (This view is contrasted by the Christian religious right and orthodox Jewish groups who oppose premarital sex and therefore any form of nonmarital cohabitation.)

Increasingly, the fear of AIDS or other sexually transmitted diseases has prompted many people to seek a single partner, although they may not yet feel ready to commit to marriage. Delaying marriage in order to establish professional and economic identities has become of paramount interest to many men and women alike, and cohabiting may be seen by some as a viable interim solution. The high divorce rate that we have noted has probably led many to proceed cautiously—to try out an intimate relationship before making a more permanent commitment.

The counselor needs to explore the precise reasons for each partner's choice of cohabiting over marrying, being careful not to make premature assumptions that may later prove to be incorrect. One further note of caution: The factors that one or both individuals cite, early in counseling, as the reasons for choosing, or remaining involved in, a live-in arrangement may turn out, on closer examination, to be only a small part of the whole story. Some hidden or unexpressed reasons may include a fear of a long-term commitment, fear of being formally tied to the partner's psychological problems, an unwillingness to assume a partner's previous debts, or perhaps an unwillingness to share an inheritance with someone of more modest economic means.

Are personal, social, and attitudinal differences likely to be identifiable between those who choose to cohabit and those who do not? Unfortunately, the limited research data available are not sufficiently clear, perhaps because people in these relationships do not represent a unitary entity. Rather, as we have noted, cohabitation is really a general term for a cluster of heterogeneous relationship types (discussed in the following section)—some temporary or simply convenient, others more committed and permanent; some casual, others a trial run; some preparatory to marriage, others a substitute for it—whose only commonality is their living situation.

As for discovering a single path to cohabitation, once again none is likely to fit all participants. Although some couples may carefully plan the move only after considerable deliberation about the pros and cons, others seem to drift into living together without a great deal of forethought or formal joint decision making, as a natural next step after a period of steady and exclusive dating. In the latter case, staying over at the other's apartment on an increasingly regular basis gradually leads to the accumulation of clothes and other personal possessions there as a purely practical matter. Perhaps a job loss or other financial pinch, a lease that expires, a job offer in a new location, an offer to help in child care, or acceptance in a graduate program in another city may then become the precipitating factor leading to the decision to move in together.

The Mythology of Cohabitation

A variety of myths exist around cohabitation, depending on the viewer's outlook. For some younger people, learning that an unmarried couple shares living quarters conjures up an image of two loving and caring individuals—both independent and indifferent to convention, liberal at least in their attitudes regarding sexual behavior—who opt for a monogamous relationship but reject the more traditional ideas concerning marriage. Not hampered by the bonds of matrimony, goes this romantic notion, they are free to explore an intimate relationship while maintaining a sense of independence. They stay together because they choose to, not because they are bound by some legal marriage document.

From another perspective, cohabitors are still viewed by some as rebellious, defiant, and immoral people, without legal responsibilities to each other, unwilling to make a lasting commitment but instead choosing a temporary alliance that is doomed to failure and that will leave both parties feeling heartbroken and guilty, and without legal recourse when the inevitable breakup occurs. If they really loved each other as much as they claim, goes this argument, they would get married and raise a family, something they are afraid to do. Living together weakens the institution of marriage and, furthermore, poses a clear and present danger for women and children (Popenoe & Whitehead, 1999a).

Neither of these views is entirely accurate—or entirely inaccurate. Like most human relationships, living together outside of marriage involves a complex arrangement that is entered into for a variety of reasons, some of which may not be fully understood by the participants or their critics. In any specific cohabiting dyad (or triad, where a roommate or perhaps a child shares in the living arrangement), multiple motivations are operating, including a combination of factors described in the two previous chapters. For example, the stepfamily issues we described in Chapter 7 are present when two individuals, one or both of whom bring children along, enter into a cohabiting family arrangement.

The counselor needs to be aware that whatever the couple seeking help say about their attitudes and values, other personal but unexpressed agendas may be at work, and clients may need help in exploring them. With even minimum probing, it is common to find clear but unstated disagreements just below the surface. For example, one partner may want to get married but be afraid to say so, believing that such a view reneges on the no-strings-attached agreement. In another case, one participant may no longer wish to abide by a previously reached agreement regarding sexual monogamy but may be reluctant to broach that subject. Or, conversely, he or she may wish for a rule change to make a previously open relationship into a monogamous one, but not know how to go about implementing that desire. The counselor has to guide the couple in attending to these underlying but previously unexamined conflicts.

The counselor must also be careful not to take statements at face value or assume that because the couple live in a cohabiting relationship, they fit some preconceived stereotype. For instance, couples who may appear nonconforming because they live in an atypical marital structure may actually live conventional lives (DeMaris & MacDonald, 1993), dividing their responsibilities (for example, who does which household tasks) and priorities (whose career development takes precedence) along traditional sex-role lines. Some authorities question whether living together is actually a losing proposition for many women, limiting their ability to make choices, robbing them of the experience of living alone and caring for their own needs, and delaying finding a suitable marital partner and thus risking later childlessness in the process.

The counselor must also recognize his or her own values regarding what is still an unorthodox living arrangement between unmarried adults. If the counselor's viewpoint is opposed to this lifestyle, the therapeutic process may become biased; in such cases the clients deserve a forthright and explicit statement of the counselor's views on cohabitation. For example, it is only fair for a religious counselor who believes the couple is living in sin to explain that outlook at the start. If the couple, having this knowledge, nevertheless chooses to continue counseling, then they do so bearing that counselor's view in mind. Thus, it is essential that the counselor have an explicit, articulated understanding of his or her own values and how they might differ from the clients'. Effective counseling requires not imposing counselor values on other people's lives.

Types of Student Cohabitation

Nonmarital cohabitation is a popular and acceptable living arrangement among many young people, according to a national survey recently undertaken by the Survey Research Center of the University of Michigan (Bachman, Johnston, & O'Malley, 1997). Nearly 60% of the high school seniors questioned indicated that they either approved or mostly approved of the idea of a couple living together before marriage; close to 75% said they believe such couples are "experimenting with a worthwhile alternative lifestyle" or "doing their own thing and not affecting anyone else."

However, student cohabitation is not a unitary entity, but rather an unmarried heterosexual living arrangement that may take a variety of forms, serve different functions, and come about for a multitude of reasons. Among college students, for example, at least four patterns have been differentiated: the Linus-blanket, emancipation, convenience, and testing types of cohabiting patterns (Ridley, Peterman, & Avery, 1978).

In the Linus-blanket type of cohabitational setup, named after the classic Peanuts comic-strip character who is never too far from his security blanket, the counselor can expect at least one of the partners to need a relationship so badly that it hardly matters what kind or with whom. The primary goal here seems to be the avoidance of loneliness and insecurity.

The following cases, abstracted from our files, illustrate some of the transactional forces at play.

Jason and Nicole met one day at the student union of the college both attended. Nicole, 18, was a freshman with an undeclared major, living in the college dorm, away from home for the first time, 1000 miles from her family. Jason, 20, a junior with a business major, also lived several hundred miles from home, but in his own apartment. Nicole was immediately attracted to Jason's good looks, his intelligence, and especially his seemingly high sense of self-assurance. Jason, on the other hand, in addition to finding her physically attractive, was immediately taken by Nicole's sweetness, vulnerability, and apparent need to be taken care of. They dated for several months and developed a sexual relationship—Nicole's first, it turned out—and soon Nicole was spending more and more time at Jason's apartment. Midway through the spring semester, Jason's roommate moved out, and Nicole moved in. However, she retained her dorm address because the school required dorm living for freshmen and because she tried to hide the living arrangement from her parents.

Problems began soon after they became roommates. Nicole, very dependent on Jason for her emotional security, was jealous of his friends and of any time he spent in activities where she was not invited. She worried about whether he was sexually faithful, despite his repeated reassurances. Also, she lived in constant fear that her parents would discover the living arrangement, would certainly disapprove, and might insist she not return to the school the following year. Jason was bothered by her overdependency, her immaturity, her seemingly few coping skills, and her poor self-esteem. Although he agreed to see a counselor together with Nicole, it was clear from the first session that he was simply going through the motions and wanted an excuse to end the relationship. They separated after three sessions, but Nicole continued on an individual basis with the counselor to work on her personal insecurities.

The emancipation type of cohabiting relationship presents the counselor with a different configuration. Here the young person seeks escape and freedom from parental restraint; the decision to cohabit represents a statement of liberation and independence.

Denise, 18, raised as a devout Catholic, had had few close relationships outside her family before going away to a college with a strong religious orientation. Growing up in a large, well-to-do family and attending the best parochial schools in her community, she had been sheltered from most of the everyday problems of living. Her parents were protective and doting and, despite her being the oldest child, expected little of her except that she earn good grades; not smoke, drink, or get involved with drugs; and stay away from bad company. Denise did not disappoint them, since she was a top student, always had her assignments in on time, and never caused anybody any trouble. When she was ready for college, she consulted her parents as well as her school counselor, and together they decided on a nearby school with a reputation for a religious student body and serious dedication to scholarship.

Denise was driven to the campus by her parents, who expressed pleasure at the dormitory accommodations. They were pleased, too, by her roommate, Alice, also 18, who seemingly had a social-class and religious background similar to their daughter's. By the time they left to return home, some 75 miles away, they felt Denise was in a safe, protected environment conducive to personal development.

Trouble began when Denise, now on her own, soon found herself caught in a conflict between internalized pressures from her religious upbringing, her own emerging need to develop an identity, and peer pressures from her classmates, especially Alice. Although raised as a Catholic, Alice had secretly rebelled against the teachings of the church and in high school had had considerable experiences with drugs and sexual experimentation with several boys. At first, Denise was horrified—and somewhat intrigued—by Alice's accounts of her past exploits. As Alice began to bring some of the college men to the room, Denise became increasingly involved and soon found herself particularly interested in Randy, a young African American student from another part of the country.

Randy, 19, a bright, serious, hard-working student, also Catholic, came from a lower middle-class background. He was interested in going on to law school and had spent the year after graduation working in order to save up enough money to supplement the support from his parents. In Denise, he found a quiet, unassuming but caring person with whom he felt comfortable. He and Denise recognized they both lacked sophistication and a great deal of previous dating experience, and that was a plus, to their way of thinking. Both were shy and modest, and since neither was the kind to use a friend's apartment for a sexual liaison, Randy and Denise soon found an apartment near campus to which they retreated several nights each week and on the weekends. However, when Denise's parents decided to surprise her with a visit one Sunday, they were able to track her down and soon, dumbfounded, discovered the situation their daughter had kept from them. Although they protested that racial issues were not involved but that Denise was too young for such a living arrangement, it was clear that there was nothing about the situation to their liking. They refused to recognize the new relationship, insisted their daughter return home immediately, and insisted that she not bring Randy or ever see him again. Denise refused, told them she loved Randy, and said that if they persisted they would never see her again.

It was the parents who consulted a family counselor. Their dislike of the situation was accepted, but they were directed to examine what issues most incensed them. The racial issue called for special scrutiny, suggested the counselor, because it was essential that they be clear in their own minds just how they truly felt. They also were urged to deal with what was involved for them in letting go of Denise and allowing her to make her own judgments about her life. True, they disapproved of the situation, and, yes, they had every right to let their daughter know in no uncertain terms how they really felt. But beyond that, how much risk were they willing to take of alienating her to the point that she might marry him out of rebelliousness? Perhaps by accepting the situation and getting to know the couple, they might remove the heated, resistant motive that might exist in Denise's behavior. In such a case, they might influence the outcome in the direction they desired, instead of forcing the opposite resolution. Denise might or might not continue with Randy, but at least they would not lose contact with their daughter, and Denise and Randy could decide what to do on a more rational basis.

When these issues had been successfully dealt with in the opinion of the counselor, he suggested all four players come together for a joint family session. Denise spoke of her anger at her parents; she accused them of dishonesty regarding their racial attitudes and of unwillingness to let her grow up out of their control. Because the parents had previously worked through the issues with the counselor regarding their feelings about Randy's color, they were not defensive. Instead, they did discuss some of the complications of an interracial marriage but insisted that was not the primary basis for their opposition. Rather, they were more concerned by her inexperience in other relationships, as well as Randy's. Denise made it clear that she and Randy were far from making any permanent commitments and that they had actually decided to live separately next year precisely because they, too, recognized that each needed opportunities to explore new relationships.

The counselor had helped the parents to see Denise's behavior as experimental and a necessary part of her development. Bringing parental attitudes regarding the racial issue into the open helped clarify for Denise that certain ordinarily unspoken but powerful feelings could be addressed. By not making the conflict one over power, with one side forced to back down, any need to be rebellious or punitive was reduced, and the young people were allowed to get on with their lives. By keeping down the uproar and emphasizing the need for clear and honest communication, the counselor had made it possible for Denise to confront her parents with normal late-adolescent issues and for all four persons to benefit from the encounter.

Turning now to an example of a cohabiting arrangement based on convenience, we find the couple entering a knowingly temporary arrangement but one that offers stability and the safety of a single sexual partner.

Terri, a college sophomore, answered an ad in the college newspaper for a roommate soon after the new school year began. She had decided during the summer break that she would live with a girlfriend from high school, but when that plan failed to materialize—the friend transferred to another school at the last minute—Terri sought other living arrangements. In responding to the ad, she found a situation to her liking, living in a three-bedroom apartment near campus with Nancy and Eric, two people she did not know before but seemed to like on first meeting.

Nancy and Eric, old friends but not lovers, had a lot of friends who visited them frequently, and Terri enjoyed living with them very much. She and Nancy would talk at great length with each other, but Eric tended to be more reserved and aloof. He definitely was not her type, Terri thought; he was 3 years older and too serious for her taste, and the fact that he was Jewish made any long-term involvement with him too complicated. Nevertheless, to some extent because of their proximity on a daily basis, within 6 months they had drifted into a sexual relationship. Nancy was aware of what was happening and did not object, since she was not romantically interested in Eric and was glad two people she liked cared about each other. When Nancy decided to move to her own apartment, Eric and Terri remained without getting a new roommate.

Together they were sexually compatible and enjoyed the luxury of domestic living without the responsibilities of a deeper or more permanent commitment. After 2 months, however, Eric began to find fault with Terri: She was too immature, and she was not serious enough about her studies. She, too, found fault with him: He was too involved with term papers, he had little time for her, and when they were together he would find fault with her "childish" behavior in front of his friends. Both expressed resentment over feeling "tied down" and not able to pursue interests in other people to whom they might feel attracted.

When they went together to the school counselor, she pointed out that they had drifted into their living together at least in part because of convenience and that they had not really made a commitment to each other. Each indicated a lasting fondness for the other that each was afraid to jeopardize, but the counselor observed that they could remain friends while living separately. Reassured that they had profited from the domestic experience together without too much pain, they acknowledged that there were no hard feelings and that each was now ready to go on alone.

As indicated by these examples, the Linus-blanket, emancipation, and convenience types of live-in formats are not conducive to fostering a long-term nonmarital relationship. However, they are characteristic of cohabiting arrangements among college students in that they tend to be short-lived, typically terminating after several months or at the end of the school year. In that sense, they can be thought of as more of a courtship phenomenon (perhaps the next step following steady dating for many couples) than as an alternative to marriage.

In a smaller number of cases, student cohabitation is a temporary prelude to marriage. Both partners tend to be older, more mature, and more ready to make a permanent commitment to marriage. They may have decided to live together because it is more convenient until some roadblocks have been overcome (graduation, low income, parental disapproval). However, they are prepared to enter an intimate relationship with someone they love with an eye toward eventual marriage. Testing whether a conjugal experience will confirm their shared beliefs regarding their future together, this living arrangement has the best potential for both personal development and the achievement of interpersonal fulfillment.

Patti and Michael met during their last year at college and immediately started dating each other exclusively. Both had had a number of earlier dating experiences, and Michael had lived with a female student during his sophomore year. Despite Michael's urging, Patti resisted the suggestion that they move in together since they had known each other for only four months and she feared it would cost her some sense of independence, which she cherished. They discussed the matter at great length and agreed that they would see each other every night for dinner at his apartment or hers, and one would often end up staying the night, but it would be best if they retained their own separate lifestyles for the time being. In that way they could build the relationship slowly and determine whether a long-term living arrangement, perhaps ultimately marriage, made sense.

When Michael graduated, he went on to medical school in another part of the country. Although he wanted Patti to accompany him, he was aware that she had her own career plans, so he did not pursue the matter strenuously. Besides, he said to himself, medical school was demanding, and it would not be fair to Patti or him if she lived with him during the first year or two. Patti also went on to graduate school in rehabilitation counseling, a 2-year program that required a great deal of time and dedication. They did agree to speak together by telephone at least once each week, and to fly to each other's cities to see one another about every 3 months. Although each was lonely and also somewhat apprehensive of losing the other because they no longer were in daily contact, the relationship continued to grow and be strengthened.

Upon graduation, and by mutual agreement, Patti found a job in the city where Michael was attending medical school, and they moved in together. Both worked hard at building the relationship, since the time apart had convinced them both that they wanted to spend their lives together. Cautious to the end, they contacted a counselor for some premarital counseling, more a kind of checkup to make certain that no hidden feelings would mar their future together. Satisfied that they could each retain a sense of independence while gaining much from relating to each other, they made plans to get married the following June.

Adult Cohabitation: Trial Marriage or Substitute Marriage?

In considering unmarried students living together and sharing a bedroom, we are dealing with only one portion of the adult cohabiting population. What of the other portion? Some have opted for a permanent or semipermanent alternative to marriage, which may even include having children together, sharing a joint bank account, buying a house, and so on. For a variety of philosophical or practical reasons, these couples commit themselves to a long-term relationship very much like a marriage, but without the legal or religious sanctions.

Carmen, a 24-year-old native of Puerto Rico, had become pregnant at age 16 and, under extreme pressure from her family, married Roberto, 17, who had recently dropped out of high school. With Roberto working at odd jobs—he really wanted to be a hairdresser but could not afford the necessary schooling—and with whatever money their working-class families could spare, the couple and their child, Alicia, managed for several years, although the strain of continuous financial pressure inevitably took its toll. Since neither parent had completed high school, available work was scarce and what was available was typically at minimum wage. Although both Carmen and Roberto worked hard and allowed themselves few if any indulgences, they were constantly in debt. What money was available, perhaps as an occasional gift from their parents, would go into clothes or a toy for Alicia. The strains of the marriage left little time or room to work at building their relationship, which deteriorated and ultimately collapsed. When Alicia was 7, Roberto moved out to another city to look for work, although he continued sending them money whenever he was able. He wrote to Alicia several times a year and would call her on her birthday and at Christmas, but beyond those occasions there was no contact between Roberto and his wife and child.

Attempting to cope with the task of raising a child by herself, Carmen worked as a teacher's aide in an elementary classroom while Alicia was at school. In the evening, her mother or father, her primary support group, would come by to look after Alicia so that Carmen could finish high school and be in a better position to provide support for herself and her daughter.

While at school, Carmen met a number of other women with similar stories, and together they offered each other support and comfort. In addition, Carmen was introduced to Raul, a handyman, by one of her women friends, and they became friends, occasionally going out after class for coffee and conversation. Raul had recently separated from his wife and two children, and after knowing Carmen six weeks, he expressed his loneliness to her and asked if he could live with her—no sexual pressure intended, he vowed. Worried about the effect on Alicia, but lonely herself for adult companionship, she reluctantly agreed. While she was not looking for a roommate in her small apartment and was not interested in Raul in any romantic fashion, she could use his physical help around the house, and he promised to help out financially by paying his share of the rent and food.

The relationship, as it evolved, was not without problems, but the affection each began to feel for one another grew. Both, having experienced failed marriages, felt vulnerable and were guarded, especially during the first few months. Carmen expressed the fear that she was not worth loving and that Raul would tire of her and abandon her sooner or later, as Roberto had done. She also worried about the effect of another breakup on Alicia, toward whom she felt guilty over her broken marriage. Raul also was fearful of commitment and worried that he would not be able to financially support his new family while still helping his wife and children as best he could.

Despite these doubts and misgivings, the cohabitation arrangement seemed to flourish. Alicia, now 9, had gotten to know and like Raul, and was happy; together, the three formed a blended family that resembled a remarried family, particularly after Raul divorced and he and Carmen began a sexual relationship. They did not marry, however, since neither saw any particular advantage a marital state might offer that they did not already have. They tried talking to a counselor at a nearby clinic for several sessions, to ascertain whether their decision was in everyone's interest, Alicia's included. Satisfied that the choice of living arrangement offered the best of both single and married lives, they continued to live together and thrive.

Women with children may also opt for cohabitation in place of remarriage, since they may be receiving spousal and child support payments from an exspouse and thus may not be in a hurry to marry and relinquish the alimony payments, especially if they do not intend to have additional children. As we noted earlier, middle-aged or even elderly persons may also choose to live in a conjugal relationship, sharing expenses, providing companionship and a social partner to each other, but not be willing to marry again or be particularly interested in doing so.

In the following case, a widow, age 70, chose a nonmarital live-in arrangement with a man rather than the more orthodox way of marriage in which she was raised.

Minna and Milton, her husband of 45 years, lived what appeared to their friends and family to be a perfect existence. They were in good health, had three happily married children and two grandchildren, and were financially comfortable as a result of Milton's successful wholesale produce business. They were both active people, enjoyed being with friends, and loved traveling as Milton's business permitted. When Milton died of cancer, at age 75, Minna, feeling suddenly alone at 70, was devastated, and with the encouragement of her children she moved into a condominium retirement community so that she could be with other people her age but without the responsibilities of keeping up her large home.

Soon after her arrival, Minna met Reese, 72, himself a recent widower who had moved into the community several months earlier. A retired furrier, Reese had been happily married and the father of three before his wife's sudden death in an auto accident. Both lonely and unaccustomed to leading a single life, they began to see more and more of each other and soon moved in together in Minna's apartment. Minna enjoyed having someone to love and take care of again, and Reese adored the attention and renewed opportunity to love someone, since his wife had been taken from him so suddenly.

When Minna's children learned of the arrangement, however, they objected violently, arguing with their mother that she would soon end up caring for a sick and aging man from whom she would receive little in return. When Minna revealed to her daughter, Margo, that "sex had never been better," the daughter became even more upset, said she didn't want to know about it, and dropped the conversation. Reese's three sons also seemed to feel threatened about his new relationship, finally voicing the fear that any money he had when he died would go to Minna and not to them.

Minna and Reese, living up to the cultural expectations of their generation, would probably have married under normal circumstances. However, both sets of children applied such pressure on their respective parents not to marry that, contrary to their upbringing, they decided to live together instead, sharing expenses but keeping their individual monies and investments separate.

Still dissatisfied with the arrangement, and fearing her mother was "acting crazy waiting on a man hand and foot, which she had never done for my father," Margo prevailed upon Minna to go together with her to see a counselor. After three sessions, in which such issues as their evolving mother-daughter relationship, sex among the elderly, and the memory of Minna and Milton's happy years were explored, Margo was better able to understand her mother's need for a relationship, which did not jeopardize the memory of her parents' long and happy marriage.

When Minna relayed these topics to Reese, he recognized that his children probably had similar concerns, and he proceeded to talk to them without a counselor.

Although the children continued to have reservations about the wisdom or propriety of their parents' cohabiting union, they learned to accept it, and Minna and Reese remained living together unmarried.

People of any age, busy forging careers and not ready for children, or established in careers but divorced or widowed and not interested in expanding their families, may look at cohabitation as less demanding than formal marriage (although breaking up after many years together can be just as painful as a divorce). Newcomb (1987), Eidelson (1983), and others point out that for many people, traditional marriage simply does not represent the ideal way to achieve an amalgam of independence and relatedness. For these people in particular, long-term cohabitation offers a preferred structure for achieving the often conflicting goals of autonomy and affiliation with another person. At least one of the partners who chooses permanent cohabiting as an alternative to marriage is likely to view marriage as constraining and ultimately love-draining; as Cox (1996) reports, he or she may argue that "If I stay with my mate out of my own free desire rather than because I legally must remain, our relationship will be more honest and caring" (p. 123).

The magnitude of the cohabiting living arrangement, then, can be explained in a number of ways, and the counselor needs to zero in on which set of factors is at work with any specific couple. Does this couple live together instead of marrying because they are not ready to make a complete commitment? Because they are immature and fearful of the responsibility of making a marriage work? Because one or both fear being alone but do not have the wish or sense of security to form a strong partnership or achieve real intimacy? Because, unless children are involved, they both believe marriage is irrelevant or unnecessary? Because they feel unable to predict how they will feel in the future and thus want to keep all options open? Because they know few if any really happily married people, and want to avoid the legal entanglements and expense of a divorce? Because they can combine all the benefits of both an unencumbered single life (autonomy, independence) and married life (intimacy, sexuality, companionship) by living together? Because they fear parental disapproval of marriage to this person? Because they sense some persistent significant problems in their partner that remain unresolved at this time?

Do they plan to marry? Does one partner want marriage and the other not, or not now? Is their present living arrangement temporary? Are they in a trial marriage because they seriously contemplate a permanent commitment and first want to check out their compatibility and the quality of their relationship? As we have indicated, the proportion of marriages preceded by a period of cohabitation is now greater than ever. Once cohabitation substituted for marriage for many couples, but today it is more commonplace that couples consider living together as a step in the marital process.

Cohabiting couples marry for different reasons. Some may be trying desperately to repair a failing union, probably hoping that the added commitment of a marriage contract will rescue their troubled relationship. (Couples in such a situation typically divorce soon after their marriage, discovering that the conflicts they experienced as cohabitors are likely to become intensified after the marriage.) Others, still of childbearing age, are ready to settle down and have children; conversely, some marry in response to an accidental pregnancy. Some young people may want to make their relationship legal to please a dying parent. Perhaps a landlord or an employer insists on their marriage, or the Army requires a soldier to be married if he or she wants to live on the base. Tax deductions for married couples offer an inducement to some couples. Some partners become possessive or fear the consequences of an open relationship. Others are finally ready to make the commitment to someone they cannot live without.

Do premarital cohabiting couples tend to establish successful marriages? Since cohabitors try out an intimate relationship before deciding to marry and end seemingly unworkable ones before tying the knot, and since they delay marriage by living together and thus are older and presumably more sure of what they want in a marriage after the cohabiting experience, we might suspect that marriages following cohabitation would be more stable. Actually, marriages preceded by couples living together are much more likely to break up than are unions initiated by marriage. According to the Bumpass and Sweet (1989) survey, the proportion separating or divorcing within 10 years is a third higher among those who cohabited than among those who did not. McRae's (1997) more recent survey of published results confirms the strong negative association between premarital cohabitation and marital stability, but points out that much of the research was carried out when cohabitation before marriage was considered as unconventional behavior. She notes some evidence that younger generations do not demonstrate the same strong link between living together before marriage and later marital dissolution, suggesting that as cohabitation becomes the majority pattern before marriage, the link to a future unstable marriage will become progressively weaker.

Does the premarital cohabiting experience weaken commitment to the institution of marriage, thereby diminishing the probability of subsequent marital success? Or is cohabitation initially selected by hesitant people ready only for tentative or trial relationships, or with more liberal attitudes toward divorce, and thus more accepting of the termination of an intimate marital situation? Some authorities (Bennett, Blanc, & Bloom, 1988) argue that cohabitors are drawn disproportionately from the ranks of the divorce-prone, who view divorce as an acceptable alternative, and that this susceptibility to divorce rather than the cohabiting experience accounts for the high rates of marital instability. Another possibility, of course, is that cohabitation produces relationships, attitudes, or values that impact negatively on marital stability (Booth & Johnson, 1988). Living together for a period of time may set up patterns of independence (handling money separately, nonsharing of parenting responsibilities) that later may be difficult to change and may present a problem once a couple is married.

As part of a longitudinal investigation of families, Axinn and Thornton (1992) studied the relationship between cohabitation and divorce using sophisticated statistical analyses. They found that nonmarital cohabiting relationships indeed are selective and that those who choose this lifestyle tend to be least committed to marriage and most accepting of divorce. Moreover, Axinn and Thornton discovered the important intergenerational effect of maternal commitment to marriage and approval of divorce; that is, mothers' attitudes toward marriage and divorce influence their children's subsequent attitudes and behavior. These results suggest that cohabitation may change the way individuals view marriage, perhaps reinforcing the notion that relationships are temporary and need not be expected to last a lifetime. These researchers argue that just as high divorce rates may have led to a declining commitment to marriage and nonmarital cohabitation as a substitute, so the rise in cohabitation itself may have a feedback effect, increasing acceptance of divorce and thereby increasing the likelihood of actual divorce.

Assessing Cohabiting Couples

As a rule, cohabiting couples do not consult a counselor about whether they should live together. When they do seek help from a counselor, they are far more likely to present problems common to all troubled couples (for example, poor communication, sexual difficulties, erosion of their previous love and compatibility). Cole (1988) refers to these areas of potential conflict as *relationship-maintenance struggles;* they may be interpersonally induced (as in the examples in the previous sentence) or situationally evoked by outside forces (for example, emotional cutoff from parents or other relatives). Therapeutically, the counselor needs to treat them as similar to problems occurring between marriage partners.

Living together unmarried also presents a unique set of challenges; however, Box 8.1 (page 224) alerts the counselor to common problems that most cohabiting couples must address as they enter into and attempt to advance an evolving relationship. While the social stigma, for example, may be minimal in the couple's own subgroup (such as among college students), often that is hardly the case in the larger social structure, public media to the contrary. Parents, other family members, fellow employees or an employer, even friends may be kept in the dark about the live-in arrangement, pointing to the couple's self-consciousness. Sometimes the couple maintains two telephone lines in their apartment, each answering only his or her own, to keep up the illusion that each is living alone. In more extreme cases, the pretense goes as far as retaining two apartments while living together in one, in a further effort to avoid detection. If one partner's parents are visiting, the other may move out temporarily, to evade parental disapproval. If the arrangement is discovered, parents may urge a breakup or, in some cases, press for an early marriage. The counselor assessing the strengths and weaknesses or perhaps the durability of the relationship must certainly attempt to help the partners evaluate the degree of discomfort they feel in what is still an unconventional lifestyle.

Another likely area of difficulty is what to call the cohabiting partner. Meet my live-in boyfriend (girlfriend)? The person with whom I share an apartment (bed)? My fiancée? My housemate? My lover? My significant other? My domestic partner?

Box 8.1   A problem-appraisal checklist for cohabiting heterosexual adult couples

---

Cohabiting heterosexual adults may experience problems in the following areas:

- Social stigma
- Term for cohabiting partner
- Unequal commitment between partners
- Lack of legal safeguards
- Dealing with families of origin
- Differing views of roles and lifestyle patterns
- Monogamous versus nonmonogamous sexual relationship
- Division of labor, money, resources
- Parenting of other's children
- Differing views of autonomy and connectedness
- Differing expectations regarding future
- Terminating the relationship

According to 1990 U.S. census jargon, the man and woman are POSSLQ (People of the Opposite Sex Sharing Living Quarters)! Meet my POSSLQ?[3] The confusion, embarrassment, and discomfort at not knowing precisely how to describe the relationship reflect society's lack of clarity about how best to conceptualize what is occurring between individuals who have committed themselves to each other, but in a nontraditional way.

Legal complexities and potentially damaging legal consequences may arise from an unmarried union. For example, a bitter nonresident father may demand that the court overturn an earlier custody ruling because the child is living with a mother who is cohabiting, arguing that such a living arrangement is detrimental to the child's moral and emotional well-being. Thus, the counselor may need to alert a divorced client with a live-in partner to the possible threat to custody and may need to urge the client to evaluate his or her situation regarding conceivable legal action by a vengeful or otherwise outraged ex-spouse.

In a similar way, a divorced custodial mother, particularly one who has been left by her husband in favor of another woman, may retaliate by restricting the father's visitation rights, claiming she wants to shield her child from visiting him because he is living with a woman to whom he is not married. Unfinished fighting between divorced parents often erupts over this emotional issue, as they repeatedly drag each other into court (or the counselor's office, where the former mates need to be seen jointly).

As we have noted, the emotional trauma of separation after a live-in arrangement, particularly one of long duration, may be every bit as painful as after a

---

[3] This awkward term was replaced in the 2000 census by two categories: the nondescript "Housemate/Roommate" for those sharing living quarters primarily to share expenses, and the suggestive "Unmarried Partner" for those sharing living quarters who also have a "close personal relationship."

long-standing marriage. The termination of a relationship that has been intimate and binding is never casual, as any marital or family counselor can attest. Loss of the emotional closeness, the mutual sharing, the daily involvement in each other's lives is always accompanied by considerable anguish and a sense of failure, no matter how far the relationship has deteriorated. Cohabitors may reject traditional ideas regarding marriage, but that is not to say they survive the breakup with any greater equanimity than do divorcing spouses.

In addition to their lives having become entwined, the unmarried couple may have accumulated property together, and promises of marriage may have been made. In the widely publicized 1976 case of *Marvin v. Marvin,* involving the cohabiting couple movie actor Lee Marvin and Michelle Marvin (who legally changed her name although the two remained unmarried), she sought court action to divide the considerable property accumulated by the couple during their unmarried years together. The California Supreme Court finally ruled that a cohabiting couple can make a contract—a **prenuptial agreement**—affecting their property rights, as the Marvins had done, as long as sex is not part of the consideration for signing the agreement. That is, before moving in together, a couple can sign a contract regarding their earnings and property rights as long as the contract does not involve payment for the performance of sexual services, which would in essence be an unlawful contract for prostitution. Not all states have followed the California ruling, although all recognize that legal remedies are often needed to divide property obtained by unmarried cohabiting couples. As Huber and Baruth (1987) suggest, some counselors working with cohabiting adults recommend that relationship interests be formalized, if not by marriage then by binding contract, in the best legal interest of both parties.

Additional legal entanglements, often the source of considerable distress, occur if the cohabiting partners have children together. Beyond that, a cohabiting couple may continually face social discrimination in matters such as buying a house together, obtaining a bank loan, and becoming eligible for the partner's health insurance benefits (although the recognition of unmarried "domestic partners" for insurance purposes is gaining acceptance). Despite signs of increasing judicial acknowledgment of the cohabiting lifestyle, society does not yet grant full recognition of such unconventionality.

Counseling Unmarried Couples

Although we have focused our discussion on cohabiting couples, the counselor should not lose sight of the fact that these pairs are a part of a larger group of unmarried couples, living together or not, who seek counseling. At the Marriage Council of Philadelphia (recently renamed the Penn Council for Relationships), for example, unmarried couples represent 13% of all couples requesting help with their relationships. According to Berman and Goldberg (1986), such couples typically present a wide range of problems: from college students in a relationship that they acknowledge is transient, to couples who have lived together for several years and are undecided about splitting up, to common-law marriages of many years' duration. Berman and Goldberg's survey reveals that those who seek premarital counseling are likely to be couples in their late thirties, one or both of whom have been previously married and have children from the former marriages.

Although any couple, married or unmarried, must deal with similar relationship problems, being unmarried often adds an uncertainty to the character of that relationship. If the couple has been together for a long time, the counselor is bound to wonder what functions are being served by remaining unmarried and, conversely, what would be changed by the couple getting married. Although the pair may live together in a marriage-like manner for many years, there remains an inevitably nonbinding and temporary quality to their union. Berman and Goldberg (1986) suggest that the lack of a public announcement often implies to the couple themselves as well as to others that the partners wish to retain the potential of availability and lessened interdependence. In many cases, however, as we have seen, although remaining unmarried may preserve the illusion of freedom and autonomy, such relationships are often as fused and highly interdependent as any long-term marriage.

Counselors experienced in working with unmarried couples are accustomed to the twosome presenting differences in their levels of commitment, one partner wanting to marry while the other is uncertain or resistant. Aside from marriage, conflicts over commitment may take place over whether to live together (or continue to live together) or split up. Regardless of the married or unmarried state the couple wishes for, Cole (1988) contends that the couple must develop interpersonal commitments to the maintenance and growth of each other's individuality and of the relationship.

In the case of nonmarital cohabitors in particular, counselors can expect ambivalence from one or both partners—wishing for security, attachment, togetherness, commitment, and dependence on the one hand, while simultaneously wishing for autonomy, freedom, independence, and personal growth on the other. Too much of the former can lead to feelings of being trapped in a relationship; too much of the latter can create the danger of feeling alone, unprotected, and insecure. Counselors who aid the couple in finding a mutually satisfactory balance can help resolve what for many is a pivotal and recurrent problem (Buunk & van Driel, 1989).

Premarital and Remarital Counseling

Unmarried couples, previously married or not, may consult a counselor when they are at the point of contemplating marriage, often as a kind of checkup on the health of their relationship. At other times, however, their motivation is different: One or both fear that some underlying conflict remains unresolved and may lead to a future deterioration of their relationship. In cases where one or the other (or perhaps both) has been divorced, such caution is especially apparent in the form of vigilance to spot flaws that may impair their future happiness together. Some states make premarital counseling mandatory for all couples seeking marriage licenses where at least one partner is under 18. The Catholic church has long made premarital counseling within the church mandatory for those seeking marriage in the church. *Marriage encounter programs,* some sponsored by religious groups to meet the needs of their members, others more secular, are currently popular. *Marital enrichment programs,* such as the Preventive Intervention and Relationship Enhancement Program (PREP) (Floyd, Markman, Kelly, Blumberg, & Stanley, 1995), offer couples planning marriage an educational opportunity to improve their communication and problem-solving skills.

From the outset, the counselor needs to be sensitive to each partner's family history (say, one involving parents in an intact marriage, the other parents who have had multiple mates) and to their individual and joint expectations for their forthcoming marriage (Stahmann & Hiebert, 1997). One partner may bear the scars of growing up in a dysfunctional family setting, while the other has been spared the traumatic experience. One may be the offspring of a closed family system, or perhaps an enmeshed one, and be afraid to move too far away from his or her family rules and traditions, while the other may have grown up encouraged to seek new experiences and establish new traditions. In the case of remarriage, the counselor needs to help the couple come to terms with why the previous marriage failed.

When a premarital or remarital couple seeks help, perhaps sensing some unresolved issue (in-laws, finances, alcohol, differences in degree of commitment, physical or psychological incompatibility), one counseling approach (Stahmann & Hiebert, 1997) is to spend four to six 2-hour sessions guiding the couple in examining their interactions and potential conflict areas in some depth. Here the aim is to provide a problem-solving experience that will enhance and enrich their future married lives together. In the process, the counselor may also help the couple discover some previously undiscussed but potentially problematic transactional patterns; as the couple is made aware of them, they can begin to work on new transactions before marriage.

How long have the partners known each other? Have they lived together and for how long? Why have they decided to marry now? Does one of the partners have a stronger wish to marry than the other? How do they think marriage will be different from their current living arrangement? How well do they communicate? Do they experience any discomfort when they attempt to be intimate or emotionally close to each other? How do they manage areas of disagreement? How deep is each partner's commitment to the marriage? Do they agree about having children, the division of labor around the house, handling money, friends of each, vacations, further schooling or career moves, where they want to live, and so on? Are they sexually compatible? How temperamentally suited to each other are they? Do they have any strong religious or political conflicts?

How similar are their socioeconomic backgrounds? Their educational levels? Their ages? Their value systems? Their racial and ethnic backgrounds and religious affiliations? Their life experiences? Does either have any history of medical or emotional problems? What kind of parental models did each have? Were their parents divorced? Any signs of potential in-law problems?

Time is needed to explore these and other factors influencing the likelihood of a stable and satisfying marriage. There will probably be some degree of conflict over one or more of these issues, but by itself this does not necessarily rule out the possibility of a happy and long-lasting union. Early identification of potential problems may actually head off future disharmony if addressed and resolved. On the other hand, significant and irreconcilable differences may be uncovered, and the couple may decide to postpone the marriage while they work out these problems, or even to cancel their marriage plans for an indefinite period. The goal here is not to resolve all conflict, but rather to help the couple become aware of significant issues between them, to give them a new way of understanding those issues, and to teach them some skills in dealing with those issues. One of the counselor's major functions may be to raise questions the two have not raised between themselves, to open up areas they have neglected or avoided, and especially to expand their thinking about the nature of their relationship.

While some degree of conflict is an inevitable part of any ongoing interaction, certain seriously conflicted unmarried couples deserve the counselor's special attention. Stahmann and Hiebert (1987) identified the following transactional patterns that should alert the counselor to potential trouble:

The uncommitted partner: One or both partners may present an underlying inability or hesitation to make a firm commitment to marriage at this time, despite appearing verbally agreeable to doing so.

The passive-inactive partner: In this profile, one partner appears socially inactive, repressed in expressing feelings, passive and dependent in the couple's interactions.

The unresponsive and insensitive partner: Here one person is inhibited and overly restrained, and is typically insensitive, unfeeling, and often hostile and critical in dealing with the partner.

The apprehensive and pessimistic partner: One partner is excessively tense, hyperemotional, and periodically discouraged about the future of the relationship.

The angry and aggressive partner: In this transactional pattern, one or both are intense, argumentative, and frequently verbally or physically abusive.

All the patterns we have just identified should be looked for as part of a transaction with another person rather than as a personality trait or characteristic in one or both individuals. The counselor is trying to determine whether certain potential trouble spots or destructive interactive patterns exist, the extent to which they intrude on the stability of the relationship, and whether, if uncorrected, they contain the seeds of eventual marital unhappiness and breakup.

PREPARE: A Premarital Inventory

Counselors doing premarital counseling often use one or more assessment devices or instruments to appraise the couple's compatibility and look for areas where there is potential for interpersonal dysfunction. David Olson, who was instrumental in developing the circumplex model for identifying types of family functioning (see Chapter 3), has also produced a useful and reliable inventory for evaluating a couple's preparation for marriage (Olson, Fournier, & Druckman, 1986). Aptly titled PREPARE (PREmarital Personal And Relationship Evaluation),[4] this computer-scored 165-item inventory is intended to aid premarital couples to better understand and discuss their families of origin with each other and to help them think about the type of family system they would like for themselves. An updated version (Olson, 1996), significantly revised, is currently available.

PREPARE helps identify and measure relationship strengths and areas where work is necessary in 11 interactive subject areas:

- marriage expectations
- personality issues
- communication
- conflict resolution
- financial management
- leisure activities
- sexual relationship
- children and parenting
- family and friends
- role relationship
- spiritual beliefs

Each partner separately rates each of the items on a five-point scale, from "strongly agree" to "strongly disagree." Typical items in the realistic expectations category are these: "After marriage it will be easier to change those things about my partner I don't like"; "Some of my needs for security, support, and companionship will be met by persons other than my partner." In the personality issues category: "Sometimes I am bothered by my partner's temper"; "At times I think my partner is too domineering." In the communication category: "It is very easy for me to express all my true feelings to my partner"; "When we are having a problem, my partner often gives me the silent treatment." The 1996 revision also assesses four interrelated personality characteristics for each respondent: assertiveness, self-confidence, avoidance, and partner dominance.

In addition, the instrument contains an idealistic distortion scale, an effort to correct for any tendency on the part of either potential spouse to respond to items in an idealistic rather than realistic manner. Fowers and Olson (1992), working

---

[4] PREPARE-MC (Premarital Personal and Relationship Evaluation—Marriage with Children) is a revised inventory that is also currently available and designed for couples, with children, who plan to marry.

with a sample of more than 5000 couples, were able to use PREPARE to statistically differentiate among four pairs of premarital couples. These types are
included in the 1996 revision:

1. *Vitalized couples:* These couples showed a high degree of overall relationship satisfaction. They were comfortable in discussing feelings and resolving
   problems together, and satisfied in their sexual and affectional exchange.
   There was an interest in religious activity and a strong preference for egalitarian roles.
2. *Harmonious couples:* These couples showed a moderate level of overall
   relationship quality. They were relatively satisfied with each other's personality and habits and able to discuss and resolve differences. They did not
   tend to be religiously oriented. They had not yet come to a consensus on
   child-related issues such as number of children or projected parenting roles.
3. *Traditional couples:* These couples showed moderate dissatisfaction with
   their relationship but showed strengths in areas involving decision making
   and future planning. They were somewhat unhappy with the partner's personal habits and uncomfortable discussing feelings or dealing with conflict,
   not entirely satisfied with sexual relationship, and quite religiously oriented.
   They agreed on children and parent roles.
4. *Conflicted couples:* These couples revealed distress on all PREPARE scales;
   dissatisfaction with the partner's personality and habits; and poor ability to
   discuss relationship problems, including sex and how to deal with friends
   and family. They were not religiously oriented but endorsed traditional role
   patterns.

Conflicted couples tended to have the fewest resources: They were younger,
less well educated, and in occupations of lower income and status. Their parents
and friends tended to view their marriage plans less favorably than did those in
the other couple types. Racial and religious differences between the man and
woman were more common than elsewhere. More often than in other couples in
the study, the woman was pregnant. Together, these demographic characteristics
are usually associated with lower marital satisfaction and stability (Fowers &
Olson, 1992).

The PREPARE scale is often used in conjunction with the circumplex model,
assessing information from each partner about his or her family of origin, as in
the following case:

Marian, 38, had a successful career in publishing and devoted most of her time to it,
thus delaying marriage until now. She had lived briefly with men on two occasions in
her late twenties, but those relationships, while they had had a sexual aspect that was
satisfying to her, had not really provided much in the way of emotional closeness.
Each had lasted for approximately 8 to 10 months and then had broken up at her
instigation. In both cases, Marian, an intensely emotional person, had periodically
expressed doubts about continuing the relationship, each time finding fault with her

partner and concluding that they had no future together and should separate. Only after the man pleaded that they continue would she relent, but it took little time before her dissatisfaction resumed.

For the last 2 years, Marian had lived with Paul, a 46-year-old, previously married land developer. In background as well as temperament, Marian and Paul could not be more different. She was from a lower-middle-class family with a Jewish father and a Protestant mother converted to Judaism, and grew up in a large city in the West. He, on the other hand, was from a small Tennessee town, raised as a Baptist (though he no longer practiced his religion) in a well-to-do family, and had never left his home state until he was inducted into the Army during the Korean War in the early 1950s. Paul had married his high school sweetheart when he returned from the service, and that marriage, an unhappy one almost from the beginning, had produced two children, now aged 23 and 20 and living on their own on the East Coast. Unable to verbally express his dissatisfactions directly, Paul had slowly withdrawn from his wife, having less and less contact with her over the years. The couple had stayed married for 24 years, however, after which time Paul, with the support of his children, had initiated divorce proceedings and soon thereafter moved to the West Coast. He met Marian at a party, they dated for several months, and after knowing each other a year, they moved in together.

One day Marian called a pastoral counselor,[5] in this case a rabbi, in what seemed to him an urgent voice, and after she had explained her situation, the counselor set up a joint appointment for her and Paul the next day. Marian was in tears soon after sitting down, explaining that they needed to work out right away whether they should continue together. Paul was quiet, seemed to be listening, and when Marian became upset reached for her hand to comfort her. He indicated that he loved Marian and wanted to marry her, but that she was unsure and was continually changing her mind in what he called a "she loves me, she loves me not" fashion. She stated that two issues were urgent: She wanted children and believed he did not; she also worried that marrying a non-Jew would be unacceptable to her family and friends.

The counselor noted Paul's passivity and Marian's apprehensive style. After hearing each tell of their previous relationships, he suspected that surely there were reasons why Paul had stayed in an increasingly unhappy marriage for so long, and also why Marian had found fault with all previous relationships and seemed to be doing so again. The counselor's working hypothesis at the end of the first session, possibly to be modified or corrected later as he came to know them better, was that Marian had a fear of commitment and possibly of trusting a man in an intimate, sustained relationship; however, she did seem to have access to her feelings, which would be helpful as the couple probed more deeply into their interactions in later sessions. The counselor speculated that Paul was far less aware of his feelings and motives, probably because he felt they were often hostile and therefore unacceptable to others. Paul was

---

[5] In fact, pastoral counselors provide more premarital counseling in the United States than do physicians or mental health professionals.

someone who wanted very much to be liked, and it probably would be difficult for him to own up to feelings or motives he thought Marian would find objectionable. Sensing discomfort with each other but not knowing why, perhaps they had seized upon their differences in background or the issue of children because these seemed tangible and thus reasonable explanations for their growing uneasiness as they approached marriage. In order to check out some of these hunches, the counselor had each take home and independently fill out a PREPARE inventory, to be returned the following session.

During the next meeting the following week, the counselor observed that the couple seemed closer. They spoke of wedding plans, and at the conclusion of the session, the counselor pointed out to Marian that the two issues that had seemed so urgent to her the previous week were not even mentioned today. Were they merely a smoke-screen on her part to cover up her discomfort at getting close to marriage? She acknowledged that their previous session had made her realize that their difference in religious background was a minor factor, especially since neither was particularly reli-giously oriented. As for children, she said, she had been thinking that perhaps her earlier statement represented more of a response to reaching the end of her fertility period than any strong wish to have a baby. Paul, on the other hand, had also been thinking about that first session and had concluded that although he thought his par-enting days with young children were over, he would agree to have a child if that was what it would take to make the relationship work. The counselor urged Paul to fully examine how he really felt, not simply to tell people what he thought they wanted to hear, as he had done in the past.

As for their transactions with each other, the counselor pointed out that Marian's intensity frightened Paul away, keeping him from expressing what he was feeling. Thus, it had the opposite effect from what she claimed she wanted to achieve. Paul, on the other hand, by withholding feelings, especially when he was annoyed or irri-tated, forced Marian to pursue him in the only way she knew, by expressing her feel-ings in no uncertain terms. He, too, through his passive response, was drawing out of Marian the opposite of what he wanted. The counselor's efforts were thus directed at helping them focus on their interaction rather than on individual personality traits in one or the other. If they could modify their ways of dealing with each other, and if each took responsibility for his or her own reactions, as well as some responsibility for what he or she drew out of the other, then future interactions between them would pro-ceed more smoothly.

The following week, the counselor discussed with the couple their families of ori-gin. Filling out the brief Family Adaptability and Cohesion Evaluation Scales (FACES III) (see Chapter 3) separately, each saw his or her family as reasonably well bal-anced (see Figure 8.1). Marian viewed hers as structurally connected and with good communication; Paul saw his as flexibly separated but with less effective communica-tion patterns. She believed hers was strongly bonded—highly cohesive—but not entirely able to accept change. In Paul's view, his family's rules and relationships were more flexible and adaptable to change. Separation from the family had been easier for him than for her. Exploring their families of origin helped each understand that

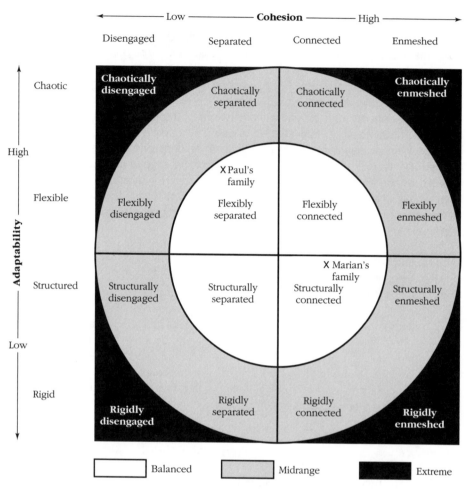

Figure 8.1   Marian's and Paul's circumplex-model scores

Source: Gorall & Olson, 1995.

while some differences existed in their backgrounds, the differences were more apparent than real, and thus not likely to be the source of conflict that they, especially Marian, had feared.

By the following session, the PREPARE profile had been returned from computer analysis; its printout confirmed that no serious or insurmountable differences existed, although it noted Marian's assertiveness in expressing her feelings and Paul's tendency toward avoidance of dealing directly with issues. Both had realistic expectations regarding marriage, they agreed on the personality issues that required attention, and they were generally satisfied with each other's personality and habits. Test results indicated that the couple were congruent in their views regarding finances and their preferences for dealing with leisure time. Marian wanted family to play a larger role in their lives than did Paul, but the differences were not irreconcilable. The two enjoyed spending free time together and were comfortable discussing sexual preferences and interests. They could be classified as a harmonious couple.

Major areas requiring further work involved communicating thoughts and sharing feelings more easily. Paul especially had to work on this, but Marian could help by listening more patiently and by being more aware of the effect on Paul of the intense expression of her feelings. Paul needed to be more prepared to deal with differences between them as they arose, instead of tending to deny or minimize problems. Trust was still an issue for Marian, but the counselor believed that problem would be reduced as she came to have faith that Paul was being honest with her and saying what he felt. They still were somewhat apart in their attitudes regarding the place of religious activity and values in their marriage, but once again the differences were negotiable.

The final session reviewed the couple's outlooks regarding the future together, emphasizing that although they had gained some understanding of the issues between them, considerably more needed to be accomplished. Each needed to continue what had been started, openly sharing thoughts and feelings and clarifying what each believed, even if some resulting conflict then needed resolution. They needed to have a clearer picture of the attitudes and beliefs of the other, and of the issues between them brought up in counseling that were delicate and still unresolved. Marian and Paul left counseling feeling closer than they had before, determined to continue on their own what they had started with the counselor. They still had differences and conflicts to resolve, but they felt now that they knew better what those differences were and how to start working on them.

Summary

Cohabitation, the situation in which two unmarried adults of the opposite sex share living quarters, has increased sharply in recent years among all age groups. Greater public acceptance of this phenomenon reflects changing public attitudes regarding sexual behavior among unmarried adults, increased availability and effectiveness of contraceptive devices, a greater demand for equal rights for women, efforts to abandon the double standard, a trend toward delayed marriages, and a new emphasis on the development of a meaningful relationship between a man and woman where both feel independent while relating to each other.

Cohabitation is not a unitary entity. It takes the form of a variety of relationships: some temporary or convenient, others more committed and permanent; some a trial marriage, others a substitute for marriage. Moreover, cohabitation is entered into for a multitude of reasons, many frequently unknown to the partners, despite their stated motives. Cohabitation among college students, perhaps the most conspicuous participants, is generally of four types: the Linus-blanket type, where the primary quest on the part of one or both is for security and the satisfaction of dependency needs; the emancipation type, where one or both are seeking freedom from parental or societal restraints; the convenience type, usually of short duration, allowing a regular sexual outlet and domestic living without commitment; and the testing type, where both are more mature and are seeking a satisfying intimate relationship while maintaining autonomy.

Cohabitation tends to be more familiar among less affluent parts of the population, probably for economic reasons. Elderly couples may live together in order to share expenses or to offer each other support and reduce feelings of loneliness. Overall, contrary to popular expectations, marriages preceded by cohabitation are more likely to dissolve than are unions initiated by marriage, although this may be changing as cohabitation becomes institutionalized as a common prerequisite to marriage.

Counselors working with unmarried couples may need to help them deal with issues concerning commitment, social acceptance, relatives, the lack of legal safeguards, the decision whether the relationship is to be monogamous, division of responsibilities, expectations about the future, and in many cases termination of the union. Couples seeking premarital or remarital counseling either want to check on the state of their partnership in light of the forthcoming marriage or are concerned that some underlying conflict may mar the future marriage. In the latter case, typically there is an uncommitted partner, a passive-inactive partner, one who is unresponsive and insensitive, a partner who is apprehensive and pessimistic about the couple's future, or an angry or aggressive partner. In addition to focusing on key elements of the couple's backgrounds and their current interaction patterns, the counselor often helps the two examine their communication styles, their motivations, their attitudes regarding marital responsibilities, and their management of conflict. The purpose is less to resolve all conflict than to help the couple become aware of issues between them and learn some skills for resolving them. Four to six sessions are commonly required, with the counselor sometimes using assessment devices or test instruments as aids in the appraisal.

CHAPTER

NINE

Counseling Gay Male and Lesbian Families

Cohabiting homosexuals[1] have much in common with the cohabiting heterosexuals we considered in the previous chapter. Both are part of minority social systems in which couples seek satisfaction of their erotic and affectional needs in an unorthodox and socially different living arrangement. Both may face ostracism from their families as well as the larger social system if exposed and therefore frequently seek anonymity by opting to live in communities where there is an increased probability of tolerance for diversity. Both contain members of all occupational and socioeconomic groups, come from all races and ethnic groups, and, contrary to popular notions, represent subcultures with great diversity in attitudes, values, and lifestyle. For both heterosexuals and homosexuals, the cohabiting couple's union may be short-lived; in other cases, it may be a long-term or perhaps a permanent living arrangement. Both heterosexual and homosexual cohabiting couples often go to extremes to keep the sexual nature of their relationship

---

[1] For the remainder of this chapter, we will use the popular terms *gay* and *lesbian* instead of the more stigmatizing term *homosexual*. The latter has acquired a clinically negative connotation, suggesting to some either psychopathology or immoral behavior, or possibly both. By defining someone exclusively by his or her sexual orientation or preference, the term *homosexual* unfairly excludes or minimizes all other personal or interpersonal aspects in the life of that individual. The prejudice persists, in the use of the term, that love, sensual pleasure, or erotic expressions of affection and intimacy must be achieved in a heterosexual form or they are unnatural, inferior, or sinful. *Gay* and *lesbian*, although not universally accepted, are more neutral terms used more frequently by people who are themselves involved in a preferred erotic relationship with a member or members of the same sex.

secret from those whom they perceive as hostile and disapproving. Although they are gaining some social recognition as *domestic partners,* both lack full legal safeguards enjoyed by married couples since they are not considered by society in general to be part of a lawfully recognized marital union.

Similar as these situations may be, however, they differ in significant ways that the counselor must recognize before attempting to understand **gay** male or **lesbian** clients. Despite the fact that homosexuality has existed throughout recorded history and is present in every society in the world, the idea of two people of the same sex, particularly men, sharing a sexual life together evokes a more negative reaction in general than does the identical behavior by unmarried heterosexuals. Also, unlike other stigmatized minority groups, gays and lesbians can remain "invisible" by allowing others to assume that they are heterosexual; for the most part, they often must keep their private homoerotic behavior hidden.

Thus, the counselor can expect same-sex couples not only to have experienced social prejudice imposed by a hostile and unaccepting society but also themselves to share, consciously or unconsciously, many of these condemning attitudes as a result of having grown up in the same society. **Homophobic**[2] beliefs (excessive fear and hatred of same-sex intimacy and sexuality and of homosexual individuals) within contemporary social mores and cultural attitudes remain widespread among heterosexuals (Herek, 1994). As Malyon (1982) points out in discussing some of the therapeutic issues involved in working with gay males, these clients have themselves likely internalized such attitudes, contributing to a sense of guilt and a desire to punish themselves. Thus, he argues, they require a *gay-affirmative viewpoint* from the counselor. This is in sharp contrast to what Harrison (1987) observes to have been the attitude of most counselors as recently as the early 1970s—namely, that counseling should attempt to change gay clients' sexual orientation.

Halderman (1994) enumerates some of the ways that medical, psychological, and religious counselors have tried, unsuccessfully, for over a century to reverse what they assume to be an unwanted homosexual orientation, including psychoanalytic therapy, prayer and spiritual intervention, electric shock treatment, nausea-inducing drugs, hormone therapy, surgery, and various adjunctive behavioral treatments. He observes that while homosexuality is no longer thought of as an illness, requiring treatment, efforts by some counselors, such as Nicolosi (1991), to reorient gay men and lesbians—usually referred to as *sexual orientation con-*

---

[2] Homophobia manifests itself in a variety of ways in our culture. Externally, it is visible in anti-gay statutes in an increasing number of states and local communities, as well as "gay bashing," in which vulnerable gay men are considered legitimate targets for violence because of their sexual preferences. Internalized homophobia, more subtle, represents homophobic values incorporated by individuals socialized in a homophobic culture such as ours (Brown, 1995). Intense internal homophobic beliefs may serve to mask any same-sex erotic feelings in some men.

version therapy—provide evidence that many earlier outlooks regarding reparative treatment persist today. For the most part, however, today's counselor tries to treat the gay or lesbian client's emotional or interpersonal problems and not that person's sexual orientation or preferences (Fassinger, 1991).

The term *homosexuality* refers to a sexual orientation or form of interactive behavior—seeking and receiving sexual and affectional pleasures with a same-gender partner—and not to a clinical or pathological condition. Nevertheless, men or women suspected of engaging in such behavior are typically treated as outcasts by many segments of society. *Heterosexism* (the belief that heterosexuality should be the only acceptable sexual orientation) has led to prejudice, discrimination, harassment, and violence (Blumenfeld, 1992). Heterosexism involves viewing gays and lesbians exclusively as sexualized beings, so that their sexual orientation alone describes them fully. This is a mistaken idea, as mistaken as judging a person's entire life by the fact that he or she is heterosexual. Calling someone heterosexual or homosexual may say something about his or her sexual behavior, sexual fantasies, and affectional preferences (Appleby & Anastas, 1995), but it says little if anything about the broader issues of that individual's personality, ways of relating to others, and so on. Still, the label *homosexual* has historically stigmatized the individual or couple, often arousing private snickers as well as public ridicule, and may instantly discredit people unless the stigma can be hidden. Until very recently, only by concealing his or her private life could the person with a homosexual preference hope to pass as acceptable in society and thus not be open to scorn and ostracism.

That situation began to change in the late 1960s, as gays became more visible in our society. The Stonewall Riots of 1969, in which a group of gay men resisted police harassment at a gay bar in New York, is usually considered the birth of the gay liberation movement. Although gays and lesbians continued to experience legal and social discrimination (for example, in housing, employment, and military service), many began to recognize their community's potential political clout as they became aware of their size as a minority group and their significance as a voting bloc. Many laws and public policies that discriminated on the basis of sexual preference (such as custody rights in regard to children from previous marriages and foster parenting protection) were successfully challenged in the courts by gay rights advocates. As part of the gay rights movement's emphasis on gay pride, more and more gay people, particularly in urban centers, opted to "come out" (of the closet) and assert their gay identity, insisting on greater social acceptance. However, the advent of **AIDS** (acquired immune deficiency syndrome)— once referred to as the "gay plague"—has once again had a disenfranchising effect on the homosexual population. In many cases, anti-gay heterosexuals have seized on the AIDS scare to practice overt discrimination and even sexual violence and assault (including homicide) against homosexuals (Berrill, 1990). Victimization because of their sexual choices remains a familiar experience for many gays and lesbians from an early age (Savin-Williams, 1994).

Some Basic Concepts and Terminology

Sexual behavior between partners of the same sex can be found worldwide, at all socioeconomic levels, among all racial and ethnic groups, and in rural as well as urban areas.[3] A wide range of lifestyles and various subpopulations flourish within the overall group. Some individuals are married to someone of the opposite sex but have occasional same-sex affairs. Others live together in long-term relationships with a same-sex lover, and still others live alone and engage in casual "pickup" sex. In some cases, men or women have had children in previous heterosexual relationships before assuming lesbian or gay identities, and the children live in their new same-sex relationship; in another scenario, lesbians have given birth after "coming out" (Martin, 1993; Patterson, 1995). Some individuals are contemporaneously **bisexual,** engaging in intimate sexual relations with both men and women. Others are sequentially bisexual in a series of sexual relations with people of both genders. Clearly, there is not one type of gay or lesbian union or lifestyle.

Precise census data are, of course, unavailable, considering the danger of exposure experienced by many gays and lesbians, but some reasonably accurate assessments can be made. Marmor (1980) estimates that the prevalence of exclusively homosexual behavior in Western culture is 5–10% for adult males and 3–5% for adult females. As gays and lesbians have become more visible since that calculation two decades ago, their estimated number, although still far from being exact, has ranged from approximately 5 million men and 2.5 million women in the United States alone who have a predominantly homosexual orientation (Buunk & van Driel, 1989) to 26 million Americans (Sprague, 1999). While we are unlikely ever to have a precise count, it is clear that homosexuality is a widespread phenomenon even in a society such as ours, which strongly condemns the behavior even among consenting adults.

Research on homosexuality—largely a taboo topic until Evelyn Hooker's (1957) pioneering studies—confirms that no essential difference exists in the incidence of mental problems between homosexual populations and heterosexual populations.[4] No single personality profile or unitary set of family or social characteristics has been uncovered that is unique to all gay persons (Appleby & Anastas, 1995). Put another way, lesbians and gay men are more like their heterosexual counterparts than they are different from them; analogously, relationships

---

[3] Before proceeding with this discussion, it is important to note that most empirical research on gays and lesbians has been conducted with white, middle-class respondents. Similarly, research on members of ethnic minorities rarely acknowledges differences in sexual orientation among these members. One useful attempt to correct this biased situation comes from Greene (1994), who examines gay and lesbian life among Latin Americans, Asian Americans, African Americans, and Native Americans, and deals with the subsequent treatment implications for each group.

[4] The American Psychiatric Association declassified homosexuality as a mental disorder in 1973. That decision was at least as much the result of political prodding from gay activists as it was the result of research such as Hooker's investigations. Prior to that decision, a man or woman whose sexual preference was not exclusively for a member of the opposite sex was diagnosed by psychiatric experts as abnormal.

between lovers of the same sex are likely to be similar to those found among het-erosexuals (Scrivner & Eldridge, 1995). However, sexual orientation, once estab-lished, is not readily subject to change (Storms, 1986).

As for etiology, a variety of personality, clinical, biological, and developmental theories have been offered, some motivated by political agendas aimed at bring-ing about preventions and "cures." Warren (1980) cites two opposing viewpoints: (1) homosexuality is an acquired taste (therefore, the result of choice and, by implication, morally blameworthy), and (2) homosexuality is inborn (therefore, the gay person is not subject to blame). She notes that gays favor the inborn pref-erence theory, while anti-gay activists tend to support the acquired taste explana-tion (thereby justifying the firing of openly homosexual teachers, for example, because as role models they may unduly influence young people to make what is viewed as an arbitrary moral choice to become gay). The inborn, or biological, view (looking for genes, prenatal hormones, and neuroanatomy as determinants of sexual orientation) is currently receiving academic attention, as researchers have all but abandoned the search for evidence of specific life experiences that predispose a person toward homosexuality (DeCecco & Elia, 1993). One notable exception comes from the research of social psychologist Daryl Bem (1996), who proposes a controversial developmental theory of sexual orientation based on childhood temperaments that influence preferences for sex-typical or sex-atypical activities and peers. No conclusive research findings are yet available, nor have any specific genetic, intrapsychic, or interpersonal factors been scientifically demonstrated as causal factors in developing a gay or lesbian sexual orientation.

Gay people tend to face special problems regarding self-disclosure in most rural or religious communities, where they are often forced to pretend to others—or even to themselves—that they are heterosexual so as to be accepted in the nongay world. To remain exclusively gay in such communities is to live in fear of discovery and to secretly seek out other gay individuals or couples. Since the number of gays is usually limited, it is common to feel socially isolated; many solve the problem by moving on to larger communities such as the Castro district of San Francisco, the West Hollywood section of Los Angeles, or West Greenwich Village in New York City. Here, gays are far more apt to meet other gays through homophile organizations, bars, or gay churches. As Harry (1988) observes, a number of gay and lesbian organizations devoted to socially integrating the new-comer into the gay world have sprung up in most large American cities within the last 30 years. Among other functions, these organizations provide a social net-work for meeting other gays, offering an alternative social setting to the often highly sexual context of the gay bar. The point, in keeping with the effort to make the gay life more than simply a sexual encounter or series of encounters, is to emphasize social and cultural, rather than predominantly erotic, opportunities.

San Francisco is particularly receptive to this population, having passed the first *domestic partners* bill (now available in a number of urban communities), permitting unmarried couples to register their relationship in much the same way that hetero-sexual couples file marriage licenses. This ordinance permits those who live as "domestic partners" with city employees "in an intimate and committed relationship" (whether of the same or opposite sex) to enjoy the same rights and benefits (such as health insurance coverage for dependents) as do couples who are legally married. As of 2000, California law allows registration with the state as domestic partners, extending health insurance to same-sex pairs and giving partners hospital visitation rights (previously restricted to family members), although it does not extend Social Security benefits, inheritance provisions, or the right to make medical decisions for each other in emergency situations, all part of heterosexual married life.

While over 30 states have enacted laws to prevent same-sex marriages from being recognized, Vermont passed the first "civil union" law in 2000 granting gay and lesbian couples virtually all benefits and protections available to married couples. Licenses for the civil union are certified by a justice of the peace or clergyman, and if the union is dissolved, the matter is handled in family court. Adoptions, joint tax returns, inheritance, and medical decision making are treated as if the couple was married. (The civil union law applies only to Vermont residents, has no impact on federal law regarding marriage, and is not yet recognized by any other state.) In that same year, France became the first European nation to legalize civil solidarity pacts for unmarried gay or straight couples. Several large corporations now offer similar benefit packages to employees in recognition of today's alternative living arrangements.

The preceding emphasis on gay marriage is not to say that "gay scenes"— organized efforts to arrange erotic contact, often between strangers—do not exist. Casual sex has long been a part of gay life, at least for men, and as Humphreys and Miller (1980) note, nearly all American towns have at least one homosexual scene. Bus terminals, freeway rest stops, isolated park bathrooms, stylish resorts, athletic clubs—all have served as places for men to establish contact for instant and impersonal sexual liaisons.

"Cruising" in public parks or restrooms, far more prevalent among gay males than lesbians, constitutes yet another form of searching for brief and anonymous sexual activity with strangers where no interpersonal commitment, intimacy, or responsibility is required. More likely, those seeking such casual encounters visit bars or bathhouses catering to homosexual clients rather than run the risk of arrest or harassment by cruising in public places. More recently, the AIDS epidemic has forced many bathhouses to close down and has prompted many gay men to reevaluate their sexual practices and to discontinue pickup activity in favor of forming a committed couple. Since the start of the AIDS epidemic, gay men in general have adopted safer sex practices, and many single men are increasingly monogamous (Scrivner & Eldridge, 1995). However, as recent medical breakthroughs have extended life for those with AIDS and decreased AIDS-related mortality, complacency has set in for some gay men, especially younger ones, many of whom are once again engaging in greater risk-taking, unprotected by condoms ("bareback sex") (Gold & Skinner, 1992).

Even in cities where casual contacts are easily available, the majority of gay men, like most people, seek the comfort of a more stable union with a loved partner. Typically, most of these extended gay relations last up to 3 years or so, although some continue for decades. Possibly these same-sex relationships, which are similar in many ways to cohabitant heterosexual unions, end more easily than heterosexual marriages because no legal restraints bind the couple together and, in most cases, no children keep the couple involved with each other once problems develop.

Being Gay in a Nongay World:
The Coming-Out Process

On September 22, 1975, in San Francisco's Union Square, a woman moved out of the crowd, raised her arm, leveled a chrome-plated gun, and pulled the trigger. A man standing nearby saw the movement and pushed down on the gun barrel. The bullet missed its target by five feet. Oliver Sipple had just saved the life of the President of the United States. His quick action made him an instant hero. The President wrote him a letter thanking him. Over 1000 other people wrote to him praising him. It should have been a moment of triumph for Oliver. Instead it was a nightmare.

"Within 24 hours, reporters had also learned that the ex-Marine was involved in the San Francisco gay community, and the story became page one—and wire service—copy" (*The Advocate,* Oct. 22, 1975). The *Chicago Sun-Times* called him a "Homosexual Hero" in a headline. The *Denver Post* referred to him as a "Gay Vet." Oliver went into seclusion to avoid the media. He was so distressed at the prospect of his mother in Detroit reading about him as a gay hero that he all but declined to take credit for saving the life of the President of the United States! (Berzon, 1979)

This excerpt poignantly illustrates not only what apprehension some gay persons experience about the unintended discovery of their secret, but also how that fear of disclosure must permeate much of their daily behavior. As Berzon (1979) notes, nearly every gay person with a family is concerned about disclosure to his or her family. Many attempt to conceal the fact by developing a series of obfuscating strategies. Gay lovers, especially in their twenties, may maintain separate residences or, if they live together, may pose as roommates. They are likely to discourage parental visits and, should a visit take place, will maintain the fiction that as roommates they sleep in separate rooms. Repeated visits, sometimes extending over several years, serve to reinforce the illusion that the two are simply very good friends who enjoy being together. Ultimately the pretense wears thin, though, and the parents become aware their child is gay. (In some cases, the parents continue to deceive themselves even if they suspect, denying to themselves what their eyes tell them.) In either case, the term *gay* or *homosexual* is studiously avoided. The couple can never openly express physical affection toward each other in front of the parents and never make explicit reference to the intimate part of their union (Harry, 1988).

In another scenario, the couple may decide, early on or later in the relationship, to "come out" to their parents (LaSala, 2000). Here they risk alienation or long-term—perhaps permanent—rejection. If the parents are strongly religious, both may find the revelation intolerable. If, as is happening increasingly, the parents learn simultaneously that their son has been diagnosed as having AIDS and has been living a gay life without their knowledge, the shock may be doubly devastating.

Coming out—openly acknowledging and describing oneself as gay—is a process that occurs over time and in front of different audiences. "I came out with my parents" may be followed by "I told some of the nongay people at school" or perhaps "I finally came clean with the boss today." First, of course, the gay person must come out to himself or herself, establishing a positive self-definition. In the following case, a young adult struggled with his self-definition.

Sheldon, 29, came to a counselor with a vague assortment of physical and psychological complaints. He reported experiencing anxiety attacks several times a week, without knowing what exactly was disturbing him. He felt dizzy at work and couldn't seem to concentrate on his job as a bookkeeper for a large furniture manufacturing firm. He had gone out with one woman for several weeks but now found himself restless and not really interested in pursuing the relationship much further.

After two sessions of reporting a variety of symptoms of distress, he finally told the female counselor that he had something "peculiar to confess." He then proceeded to describe a series of experiences—beginning in high school—of visiting bathhouses and public parks in a neighboring town in order to engage in impersonal sex with other men. However, he insisted to the counselor that he was not gay, that he actually disliked homosexuals and their "swishy" behavior, and that he planned one day to marry and lead a conventional life. He had been sexually intimate with several women since high school, he contended, and although the experiences had ranged from neutral to unpleasant, he remained certain that through counseling he could learn to enjoy heterosexual relationships.

As Sheldon spoke of his growing-up years, the counselor recognized Sheldon's early patterns of difficulty with his family of origin. He was the youngest of four boys, living in a lower-middle-class family with what he described as a strong, domineering, and difficult mother and a weak, inadequate, and unconnected father. Growing up, Sheldon felt disengaged from both parents, as well as from his brothers. The household was filled with tension among the family members, there was a great deal of confusion, and communication was poor or nonexistent.

The counselor recognized Sheldon's struggle over his gay identity and consulted a gay psychologist from the local gay counseling center over how best to help Sheldon resolve his conflicts about who he was. The consultant urged caution in helping Sheldon come out, pointing out that the client was exhibiting distortions of reality as he fought to deny the nature of his sexual urges. The counselor continued to explore Sheldon's past and present homosexual behavior, including an ongoing infatuation with an alcoholic young man that Sheldon insisted was not significant. She also continued to direct Sheldon's attention to family issues from the past as well as the present.

When Sheldon went back home to another state to visit his family, he was urged by the counselor to talk to his brothers about their sexual experiences. Surprisingly to him, it turned out that two of the three boys were gay but not openly so. The visit seemed to clarify a great deal to Sheldon regarding their upbringing, and he returned to counseling more accepting of himself, although not yet ready to reveal his gayness publicly.

When his parents came to town several weeks later, the counselor recommended that Sheldon invite them to join him in the next session. He expressed considerable discomfort over doing so, afraid something would slip out about his homosexual behavior. After the counselor reassured him that she would not reveal his secret, however, Sheldon finally consented to the parents' presence. The mother's opening words, as she sat down, were these: "I wanted Sheldon to be a girl when he was born, since I already had three boys." By this statement she seemed to be acknowledging at some level that she understood why she had been called to the session, that Sheldon was struggling with his sexual identity. The counselor made no attempt to discuss homosexuality, but instead asked questions about the family's early years. Sheldon's father remained relatively quiet throughout the 2-hour meeting, answering questions in a brief manner, and only when asked.

In subsequent sessions with Sheldon, the counselor helped him recognize that his parents "knew" and that he need not waste so much energy in hiding the truth from them. At first, of course, he needed to be truthful to himself, facing who and what he was. After two more meetings with the counselor, Sheldon terminated the sessions. He had accepted his gayness and had come out on a limited basis, telling his woman friend and some colleagues at work. He never spoke of it with his parents, but he assumed they knew and were able to live with it without acknowledging it in so many words.

Most gay men, in spite of the popular stereotype, are not obviously effeminate in appearance or behavior. Since they pass as heterosexual, giving up the security of anonymity by coming out may be fraught with anxiety. As Harrison (1987) notes, "Every gay man, whatever his age, must decide when to stop asking permission to be himself and to go public about his sexual identity" (p. 226). For lesbians, the secrecy may be somewhat easier to maintain, since our society tolerates open physical affection between women far more readily than between men, and women living together generally raise fewer eyebrows than do cohabiting men. Both minority groups may choose to avoid disclosure and to pass as "straight" within nongay settings by adopting the manner and dress of the majority. In addition to silently putting up with endless matchmaking efforts by well-meaning co-workers, part of that impression management calls for remaining hushed in the face of jokes or other slanderous remarks about homosexuals if they wish to avoid drawing attention to their gay selves.

The process of coming out has usually begun before the gay person contacts a counselor; that is, although no public disclosure has been made, the individual (young or old, single or married) has begun to struggle with same-sex erotic feelings and fantasies. This self-recognition stage may last for a considerable period of time, during which the person may feel confused and may or may not act on the feelings by having one or more homosexual experiences. In many cases this stage leads ultimately to the next stage of self-acceptance: risking rejection by telling carefully chosen others. (We saw in the case of Sheldon that this may be a painful and drawn-out process.) As the individual sets about exploring his or her new sexual identity, there is increased mingling with others with similar sexual preferences. (The amount of sexual experimentation differs between men and women; men are more likely to engage in a series of one-time sexual contacts, although some lesbians may do so also.) As the newly found freedom to sexually explore becomes less intriguing and the need for intimacy becomes stronger, a more stable and committed relationship with a single partner is likely to follow.

There may or may not be much contact with the local homosexual subculture, although access to gay or lesbian identified organizations is often important as the individual seeks help and support in coping with the homophobia and anti-gay discrimination he or she is likely to encounter (Appleby & Anastas, 1995). As we observed earlier, the initial sexual contact with a partner of the same sex may be relatively short-lived and may simply be the first of a number of such coupling experiences.

As for the counselor, it is essential to understand the significance of these stages of the coming-out process. As with heterosexual clients, having relationships with a series of partners may well represent experimental dating and not necessarily failed relationships. We should also note here that the process is often more rapid and more complete if the client's current significant others—including, when appropriate, members of his or her family of origin—participate in the counseling sessions. Exchanging feedback information, exposing family secrets, and dealing more effectively with interlocking problems often have a catalytic effect on hastening the emergence of a gay identity (LaSala, 2000).

Gays and Lesbians: Similarities and Differences

Although we have for the most part written of gay male and lesbian couples as though they shared the same characteristics and concerns, the counselor must understand the ways in which these relationships also differ. Since societal reaction to male and female homosexuality has historically been different, and members of each group are subject to different socialization experiences and gender-role expectations as they grow up in heterosexual families, it follows that lesbian and gay lifestyle patterns are likely to differ significantly and that each group lives in markedly different types of subculture (Buunk & van Driel, 1989).

First the similarities: Both types of couples must face the choice of remaining hidden (denying their true identities to others, losing self-respect and a sense of control over their lives) or lifting the mask and revealing the secret (thereby risking loss of love and support from family and friends, forfeiting jobs or curtailing promotions, and so on). Revealing themselves as homosexual risks verbal abuse or physical attacks or dismissal from work or from the armed forces (Kavanagh, 1995). On the other hand, avoiding disclosure and attempting to remain "socially invisible" (Appleby & Anastas, 1995) may lead lesbians and gays alike to find themselves, in Rochlin's (1979) words, participating in the popular homophobic game "I-know-they-know-and-they-know-I-know-they-know-but-let's-all-pretend-nobody-knows" (p. 162).

As we reported in the case of Sheldon, a gay male may engage in homosexual acts but deny to himself that he is gay, thus pretending that he measures up to the community standard of "maleness" and ensuring that he will not be viewed by society as a lower-status "female." Similarly, as Toder (1979, p. 45) reports, a woman in a same-sex love affair may fear being labeled homosexual by a rejecting society and thus may deny the implications of the relationship ("I'm not a lesbian; I just happen to be in love with this person and this person just happens to be a woman").

Role playing in both gay and lesbian lifestyles may defy stereotypes. The popular media notion of a "butch/femme" gay male couple emulating a traditional male/female married relationship (with one partner masculine, dominant in sexual activity, providing the financial support, the other engaged in complementary household activity) is an improbable one and more often than not an awkward attempt to mimic a heterosexual relationship. Rather, as Harry (1983) points out, gay relationships are more likely to be patterned after a best friends/roommates model than a heterosexual role model. Although butch/femme patterns do characterize some gay male relationships, especially those based on inequality, Harry (1983) contends that masculinity in appearance and behavior is likely to be highly valued in oneself and one's partner, suggesting a "butch/butch" pattern may be even more likely among gay male couples.

The counselor would do well to recognize that both young gay men and lesbian women lack any visible role models (with the recent exception of the few celebrities who risk public exposure) of how a happy, normal homosexual couple operates on a day-to-day basis. Unlike members of other minorities, apt to grow up among members of their own reference group, where culture and tradition can be transmitted in a positive manner, gays and lesbians have heterosexual relationships as their sole paradigms. Many internalize the prevalent concept that same-sex relationships are by definition brief, devoid of deep feelings, and based primarily on sexual attraction. Growing up male often involves learning to dominate, control, and seek power, but not to be nurturant or emotionally expressive; this is often a problem for a gay male couple learning to work at relationship maintenance. Socialized as women, lesbian couples may have problems expressing anger or asserting power or initiating sexual activity, all usually associated with male activity. In this regard, Kurdek (1995) found that gay couples engaged in sex more than heterosexual couples, while lesbians did so less frequently. Lesbians were found to be more likely to value emotional expressiveness in their relationship than were gay men (Peplau, 1991). A lesbian couple, because it contains two women, is twice as likely than its male counterpart to include a survivor of childhood or adult sexual abuse (Brown, 1995).

Lesbian women are more likely than their gay male counterparts to strive for stable, extended relationships (Saghir & Robins, 1980). Although one-night stands or casual encounters do occur, they tend to be infrequent. Lesbians, much like their female heterosexual counterparts, are more likely to establish affectionate bonds with partners over a period of time before becoming sexually involved. In those same-sex love affairs, they tend to value equality, emotional expressiveness, and a similarity of attitudes between partners (Peplau, 1991). Long-lasting relationships of more than a year's duration, with an emphasis on faithfulness, tend to be the rule. Thus, the total number of sexual partners is usually fewer compared to those of gay men. Although sexual fidelity may be desired by gay male couples, it may also be frequently breached by a casual sexual pickup experience by one or the other partner. Among lesbians, casual or impersonal sex is the exception, although, once again as with heterosexual women, affairs may occur and may lead to a breakup of the relationship (Blumstein & Schwartz, 1983).

Although a small minority of lesbians do engage in traditional gender roles (the butch/femme pattern), most are likely to divide household tasks and responsibilities according to talent and interest or by turns, since both are likely to be employed. Socializing is often done at home, usually with other lesbian couples or perhaps gay male pairs. In systems terms, as Rice and Kelly (1988) observe, it makes sense that a subsystem (the couple) trying to relate to a larger system (society) that either ignores or criticizes them will attempt to tighten the partner boundaries, fusing with others like themselves and adopting a self-protective posture against the outside world.

Generally speaking, according to Harry (1983), the social world of lesbians tends to be a world of couples, whereas the world of gay men is one of both singles and couples. As we just noted, among lesbians a sexual relationship may arise from an evolving affectionate relationship, whereas for gay men, in keeping with the socialization of men in general in our society, the sequence is likely to be reversed. Blumstein and Schwartz (1983) found lesbians to have sex far less frequently than other types of couples, often expressing a preference for physical closeness—hugging, touching, cuddling—over genital sex. According to these findings, such activities are likely to become ends in themselves for many lesbian couples, rather than foreplay leading to genital sex activity.

Evelyn, 24, and Anne Marie, 26, both assistant professors of music at neighboring universities in the same large western city, met at a music educators' conference and were immediately attracted to each other. They spent several days together, at mealtimes and between sessions, sharing work experiences and talking over their pasts. They found that they had a great deal in common—both were raised Catholic but no longer practiced their religion, both were brought up in small towns, both had had an early love of music—and when the conference ended, they agreed to continue seeing each other. It was only after 6 months or so that their relationship became a physical one, primarily cuddling and caressing, and only occasionally involving genital play.

As they learned about each other, it turned out that Anne Marie had been a lesbian since her teenage years. A tomboy with an early aversion to girls' activities, she had had her first homosexual experience at 15 with another girl at a summer camp.

Anne Marie had never been attracted to boys or men. Instead, she had had a number of romantic "crushes" on teachers growing up, and one long live-in arrangement with a woman beginning when she was 21.

Evelyn, on the other hand, had had several love affairs with men, beginning during her adolescent years, but had found them unsatisfactory. For 4 years prior to meeting Anne Marie, she had not dated and had been celibate. Socially, she was extremely shy and felt inadequate at conventional feminine tasks, such as cooking, decorating, and choosing clothes. From the start she was fascinated by Anne Marie's sense of style as well as her confidence in social situations.

Together, the women bought a house and settled into a "married" lifestyle. They shared expenses, took turns cooking and doing various chores around the house, traveled to Europe on vacation together, and seemed in general to enjoy their life as a couple. Their friends were primarily people from work, mostly heterosexuals, although they also had gay male and lesbian couples to the house for parties. They were not obviously homosexual, nor did they ever bring the issue up before the university administrators, faculty, or students. While they did not deny their lesbian relationship, neither did they affirm or flaunt it publicly. Monogamous, they seemed to friends like a childless couple with both partners oriented toward furthering their careers. As for family, Anne Marie, an only child, had been cut off from hers since she left home for college. Evelyn's parents were dead, and her two brothers rarely contacted her. When she did hear from them, they pretended Anne Marie did not exist.

After 14 years, Evelyn, now 38, and Anne Marie, 40, began to drift apart. They quarreled more often, seemed to have developed different interests, found they had less and less to talk about, and finally decided to split up. Anne Marie revealed that she had found herself interested in a younger woman at her school and wanted to be free to pursue that new relationship.

Since no strong family or social ties kept them together, they separated, with a counselor's help, without too much bitterness. Evelyn remained by herself in the house for several years, and then she, too, found a young woman of 26 who moved in with her as her lover. Both "married types" who needed the comfort, support, and intimacy of a coupled relationship, Evelyn and Anne Marie, after their "divorce," each ultimately sought and found another long-term relationship.

Assessing Gay and Lesbian Couples

Gay men and lesbians seek professional counseling for the same reasons others do: anxiety, depression, relationship conflicts, dysfunctional families of origin (Isensee, 1991). Although the problems inherent in being gay in a society rejecting of that sexual orientation may lead some to the counselor's office, it is more likely that they come looking for ways to deal with their life problems and not to alter their sexual preferences.

All of us, those who grow up to become homosexual as well as those who become heterosexual, are exposed at an early age to untruths that produce nega-

---

Box 9.1   A counselor checklist of common myths regarding homosexuality

Do you believe these statements?

- Most gay men are effeminate, and most lesbians are masculine in appearance and behavior.
- Most gay couples adopt male/female (active/passive) roles in their relationships.
- All gay men are sexually promiscuous.
- Gay men believe that they are women in men's bodies, and gay women believe that they are men in women's bodies.
- Most gay people would have a sex-change operation if they could afford it.
- Most gay people are child molesters.
- People choose to become homosexual.
- Most gay people are unhappy with their sexual orientation and seek therapy to convert to heterosexuality.
- Counselors report high success rates in converting homosexuals to heterosexuals.
- Most gay people are easily identifiable by their dress and mannerisms.
- Homosexual behavior is unnatural because it does not occur in other species.
- Homosexuality is the result of a hereditary defect.
- Homosexuals have hormone abnormalities.
- All homosexual males have dominant, overbearing mothers and weak, passive fathers.
- Homosexuality threatens the continuity of the species.
- All male hairdressers, interior decorators, and ballet dancers are homosexuals.
- Homosexuality is an illness that can be cured.

Source: Gartrell, 1983.

---

tive stereotypes about male homosexuality (see Box 9.1 above): Gay men are called sexual perverts, queers, sinners against the natural order of life, faggots, child molesters, possibly criminals. It is hardly any wonder that those who become gay are often filled with self-critical attitudes. As Malyon (1982) points out, that negative self-image, along with an inevitable internalized homophobic attitude, is bound to have serious negative consequences for a person's overall self-identity. A common solution is to develop a false identity by suppressing homoerotic promptings and taking on a heterosexual persona. It is hardly surprising, then, to find that gay men and lesbians often secretly struggle with themselves as they grow up, sometimes believing their sexual impulses mean they are mentally ill. For these individuals, accepting society's label that they are abnormal is often less painful than exploring the possibility of adopting a gay identity, which carries with it negative expectations of ever having adult relationships that transcend a sexual or otherwise superficial realm (Brown, 1995).

Achieving a Gay Identity

Closeting themselves helps most gays and lesbians avoid facing the emotions of shame and guilt over who they are. Coming out, as we noted earlier, is risky, and most often there is no turning back once a gay life is exposed. As indicated in Box 9.2, the process of coming out is of major significance, not merely because of the public disclosure, but because it represents self-recognition and the start of gay self-identity. The counselor needs to assess how successfully and how fully this is accomplished and should not be too surprised if further hesitation and stalling follow the initial disclosure to significant others. Also, the counselor should note in working with gay or lesbian couples whether one of the partners is further along than the other in affirming his or her gayness, since greater concealment by one may have detrimental consequences for the relationship and for the couple's social behavior with family and friends.

Estrangement from one's family of origin—emotionally, financially, and interpersonally—is especially painful. Gays sometimes report feeling like minority group members or second-class citizens in their own families, often feeling the need to explain, defend, apologize for, or hide their gayness or else risk ridicule or ostracism. On first learning that their child is gay, parents are apt to be rejecting, perhaps blaming themselves, feeling stigmatized, and wondering what they did wrong in raising their child. Some parents seize the opportunity to blame each other for the "aberration." Often they fear that their child will be the victim of hate crimes, lose civil rights protection, or contract AIDS (Scrivner & Eldridge, 1995). Some despairing or desperate parents may exert pressure on their child to seek psychotherapy, in the hope of turning that person into a heterosexual; some may threaten to cut off support if their child is in college or attempt to take away

---

Box 9.2 A problem-appraisal checklist for gay/lesbian couples

Gay couples may experience problems in the following areas:

- Coming out—concealment versus openness
- Self-acceptance of gay identity
- Family estrangement
- Church acceptance versus condemnation
- Sexual exclusiveness versus nonexclusiveness
- The AIDS crisis
- Long-term versus short-term relationships
- Aging and later-life problems
- Gay fatherhood and lesbian motherhood
- Lack of legal safeguards
- Gender-role patterns in the relationship

a gay person's children, should they exist, unless the homosexual behavior ceases. Ultimately, especially with the aid of counseling, many parents overcome the shock, anger, and guilt, and accept their child's gayness; however, many do not.[5] The person coming out is seeking external validation that he or she is a worthwhile, socially acceptable human being in the eyes of those individuals from whom such approbation is particularly important.

Counselors need to take into account the historical period in which gays and lesbians came of age in understanding the process of achieving a gay or lesbian identity. Different generations meet the greater openness now available to them with strategies carved out of their personal past. Parks (1999) reports that lesbian women of the pre-1969 Stonewall Riots era, for example, were likely to have experienced silence about their (homo)sexuality and an isolation from other lesbians as they struggled to define what they were going through. She found that these women are apt to carry on the legacy of silence even as times have become more open. By way of contrast, young lesbian women growing up in more liberating times may be somewhat more open and deliberate in their behavior and to consider themselves as "normal" even if they perceive that others do not. Geography also plays a role in the identity process; nonurban women, especially those over 45, tend to be more cautious about revealing their lesbian identity and using the resources available to them.

In addition to family and friends, some gays may look to their church for affirmation that their sexual orientation need not be in conflict with their religious beliefs. Unfortunately, until recently all American churches condemned homosexuality, causing a sense of alienation from organized religion on the part of most gays. As noted by McNaught (1979), himself a Catholic, growing up gay and Catholic may be akin to living in Northern Ireland with a Catholic mother and a Protestant father. Loyalty to one seems to preclude loyalty to the other: The Catholic church censures homosexuality, while other gays castigate those who retain ties to an oppressive church. The Judeo-Christian tradition throughout history has been highly critical of same-sex acts, assuming that heterosexuality is natural and that those who engage in homosexual activity do so willfully. Thus, many gay men may experience severe conflict between their homoerotic feelings and their need for acceptance by a homophobic religious community (Halderman, 1994).

Guilbord (1999) contends that most mainline religious bodies, from the World Council of Churches to local congregations, are in conflict as to how they will officially receive and treat nonheterosexual people. The more politically conservative condemn homosexuality as "an abomination before God," and several ministries are dedicated to urging gays to become heterosexual or, short of that goal, to practice celibacy. On the other hand, in recent years churches open to gays

---

[5] One major national organization, Parents, Families and Friends of Lesbians and Gays (PFLAG), promotes the health and well-being of gay, lesbian, and bisexual persons and their families and friends. With over 400 affiliates worldwide, this grassroots network, based in Washington, D.C., represents both an educational group and an advocacy group, disseminating information regarding sexual orientation and gender identity as well as promoting measures to secure equal rights.

have sprung up in most large American cities, thus reducing the alienation felt by many religious gays. For the counselor, the therapeutic task may often include helping an isolated gay client or gay couple reconnect to a larger system such as the church, which in the past may have provided comfort and faith. The Universal Fellowship of Metropolitan Community Churches has over 300 branches world-wide dedicated to serving the spiritual needs of gays, lesbians, and their families.

Sexuality and the AIDS Epidemic

The fear of AIDS has affected relationships between gay men, regardless of age, prior relationships, or history of sexual activity. Sexual exclusivity between part-ners, including those who previously sought sexual experiences outside of the relationship, has now become more common, placing additional expectations on the relationship. Some experience the loss of extra-relationship sex with sadness and anger and may resent being forced into a heterosexual model of monoga-mous coupling. Others see exclusivity as adding an expression of positive self-regard and thus as an important force in the couple's development.

Coming to an agreement regarding the sexual exclusiveness of the relationship is often the single most important decision faced by gay couples (Silverstein, 1981). The point to look for here is not so much whether monogamy or non-monogamy exists, but rather the extent to which the couple can agree on this point. Gay male relationships, in particular, lack the norms built into heterosexual marriage or other long-term male-female relationships, so infidelity is not neces-sarily considered a serious offense or deviation. Since sex with a variety of part-ners is a fact of life in many gay male relationships (Blasband & Peplau, 1985), the counselor should not apply heterosexual norms in evaluating the effect of such behavior on the couple's ability to stay together. Rather, it is important to determine whether the casual pickup or affair has violated one partner's expecta-tions and, if it has, the extent to which the violation impairs the couple's future together.

Casual or impersonal sex has had to be reevaluated by gays (as well as non-gays) in light of the AIDS epidemic. AIDS is an infectious disease caused by the human immunodeficiency virus (HIV); the most common form of transmission is through unprotected sexual contact, allowing the exchange of bodily fluids between an infected and uninfected partner. As a result of the viral infection, the body's immune system is damaged in varying, often progressive, degrees of severity, with the result that the body is vulnerable to fatal opportunistic infec-tions such as pneumonia or tuberculosis, opportunistic tumors and malignancies such as Kaposi's sarcoma, and in some cases AIDS-related dementia caused by central nervous system damage (Green, 1989). Despite the current life-prolonging treatments, death may be caused by one or more of these opportunistic infec-tions. Homosexual and bisexual men are among the highest-risk groups. By the end of 1994, 400,000 Americans had been stricken with AIDS, and an additional 1 to 2 million are estimated to have contracted HIV—the causal agent for AIDS—

although some may remain symptom-free of AIDS for a period of time (Rosenthal, Boyd-Franklin, Steiner, & Tunnell, 1996).

Fear of AIDS has led to changing sex practices (such as increased use of condoms) between long-term partners, the closing of most bathhouses, fewer casual pickups, and sometimes the adoption of celibacy in an effort by gays to protect themselves and their partners. Although most gay men have adopted such safer sex practices, resulting in a decrease in all types of sexually transmitted diseases in the gay community in the last decade (Paul, Hays, & Coates, 1995), the threat of AIDS continues to figure prominently in relationships. For couples, the discovery by one person that he has AIDS is not only personally terrifying but also leads to fear that he may become a dependent burden on his lover or, conversely, that the partner may reject him by leaving. Grief, anger, rage are all common reactions to AIDS-related deaths, and survivors are likely to fear new relationships that may lead to personal infection or further loss. Whatever that outcome, the infected person may have to reveal previously hidden casual experiences with other men to his unsuspecting partner and also face the disturbing possibility that he has transmitted the disease to his partner. Disclosure of AIDS may also lead to job loss, loss of health insurance benefits, loss of sexual freedom, demands that the person vacate an apartment, or rejection by family, friends, or work associates. In some cases, the gay person may feel he deserves the disease, particularly if he has still not fully accepted his gay identity. Within the gay community, members must deal with the grief related to multiple deaths among others in their social network (Scrivner & Eldridge, 1995). Within their families of origin, stigma, shame, fear of contagion, fear of discovery, anger that the infected person has brought such a devastating disease into the family, and similar powerful reactions can tear families apart (Rosenthal, Boyd-Franklin, Steiner, & Tunnell, 1996).

Counselors can also anticipate gay couples who seek help with problems concerning sexual intimacy but who insist they are not frightened that one or the other partner may be HIV-positive. Walker (1987) suggests that these individuals are most likely in denial and thus are seeking a less threatening explanation for their current difficulties. She argues that unless the counselor working with the couple faces his or her own fear of AIDS and is also knowledgeable about the defense mechanism of denial occasioned by the threat of any fatal disease, the counselor may unconsciously collude in the couple's denial and not raise the issue in assessing their presenting problem. Landau-Stanton (1993) has provided a useful sourcebook on the relationships among AIDS, health, and mental health. (We'll return to the important topic of AIDS counseling for the entire family system, of which the couple is one part, later in this chapter.)

Gay and Lesbian Parenting

The exact number of gay or lesbian adults who have parented children is difficult to determine, since many may conceal their current sexual orientation for fear of losing child custody or visitation privileges following the breakup of the relationship. Nevertheless, Silverstein and Quartironi (1996) estimate that there are 1 to 3 million gay fathers; according to Gartrell and associates (1996), perhaps 1 to 5 million lesbians have given birth to children. Add same-sex couples who adopt children and those who have children through **donor insemination,** and it is likely that 12 to 15 million children reside in homes with gay parents in the United States alone (*Not all parents are straight,* 1987). Although such estimates may seem high, a large number, perhaps the majority, are closeted and thus "invisible"; for example, single parents in same-sex relationships may keep their sexual preferences secret out of fear of negative attitudes from neighbors, employers, or fellow workers.

Although parenthood may at first glance seem antagonistic to being gay, the facts are otherwise. Gay men marry for a variety of reasons: They may find their homosexuality personally unacceptable, they may use the marriage as a socially acceptable cover behind which to hide their gayness, or they may marry to avoid continued family pressure. In addition, they may prefer male sexual partners but develop affectionate feelings for a particular woman or simply feel more comfortable around women. Along with all these other factors may be a genuine desire for children. Lesbians, too, may marry and bear children because they wish to have them or because it is expected of women by society. Some may make a transition over time from a self-identification as a previously married heterosexual to a lesbian identity and still retain custody of their children.[6] Crawford (1987) argues that lesbian-headed families must deal with the special challenges to their fitness for motherhood that arise in a homophobic society (and in their own internalized homophobia). Among the myths they themselves must overcome regarding a lesbian's suitability to be a mother, Sachs (1986) listed the following falsehoods:

> Lesbians are women who act like men, hate men, and do not fit the feminine role; motherhood requires a high degree of altruism and nurturance, and lesbians cannot fill the maternal role because they are oversexed, narcissistic, and pleasure-oriented; lesbians are masculine and aggressive, so they cannot assume the feminine task of raising children. (p. 244)

Bozett (1985) differentiates five marker events that may typify a gay father's career: (1) a heterosexual dating period, (2) a marriage during which the man

---

[6]Although homosexuality no longer disqualifies a parent from custody in most states (Silverstein & Quartironi, 1996), judges retain considerable discretion in the matter. Despite the changes brought about by the American Psychiatric Association's declassifying homosexuality as a mental disorder almost three decades ago, many courts remain concerned about the possible stigma for the child, the possibility of peer ridicule, the possibility that the child might grow up to be homosexual, and the possibility that the child might learn inappropriate sex-role behavior (Hodges, 1991). However, available research reveals no evidence that gay and lesbian adults are unfit parents. Nor are lesbian women markedly different in their mental health or in their approaches to child-rearing than heterosexual women. While there are at present more data on lesbian mothers than on gay fathers, the available findings suggest that children raised by these mothers develop patterns of gender-role behavior much like those of all other children. There is no evidence of rates of homosexuality among the offspring of lesbian or gay parents greater than that which occurs in the heterosexual population (Patterson, 1995).

assumes the role of husband, (3) becoming a father, (4) alteration in the spousal relationship (usually separation and divorce), and (5) the activation of a gay lifestyle. Concurrent with these benchmarks, of course, is the man's growing awareness and acceptance of his own gay identity.

Most gay males do not disclose their homosexuality to their prospective mates, although some do. In some cases, rather than being deceptive, these unrevealing men may not consider themselves really to be gay, even if they have had one or more homosexual experiences. The future wife, if informed, may even respond positively, perhaps because she believes that the gay life is a thing of the past or, more rarely, because she prefers nonheterosexual men, or perhaps because she convinces herself that their relationship is strong enough to keep her future mate faithful to her. Homosexual experiences during marriage may be hidden, or again may be tolerated by the spouse for reasons of her own (the couple has grown apart; she does not enjoy sex with him; she likes the social respectability of being married and wants to keep the marriage intact; she wants to protect the children from knowing; she, too, is having an affair; and so on). In most cases, however, a marriage in which the husband is actively and openly gay will likely end in divorce, according to Bozett (1982), since the man will not be able to continue finding satisfaction in a heterosexual marriage, his wife will not be able to live with his homosexual patterns, or both.

Premarital counseling with couples in which past homosexual liaisons have been admitted should explore both the immediate and long-range effect this behavior is likely to have on the integrity of the future marriage. The counselor needs to help both partners honestly explore their abilities to sustain an intimate heterosexual relationship once united. If married, the couple needs help in exploring their options if they wish to continue together (for example, permitting the husband to continue periodic sexual liaisons with men). If children are involved, issues about informing them or issues of custody require exploration. Generally speaking, premarital counseling is rare, the couple being more likely to seek counseling once one marital partner's secret homosexual behavior has been exposed and has become a threat to the continuation of the marriage.

Being a gay man does not preclude being a good husband and father. In the following case, a conventional middle-class professional man, married for 20 years and the father of three children, finally confronted his desire for a gay lifestyle.

Andrew S., M.D., was a practicing physician with an excellent reputation in the professional community. At 44, he was financially successful, appeared to have a happy marriage, and was the proud father of three children—all girls—whom he adored. But Andrew also harbored a secret: Since high school he had engaged in casual homosexual encounters in school restrooms and public parks.

When he met Allison at college, Andrew found her very attractive and dated her off and on for two years. After he graduated and before he went on to medical school, they married. He never told her of his gay past, nor did he ever mention it to anyone else, including some gay friends he had known all his life. After 20 years of marriage, Andrew and Allison appeared to be the ideal couple: They were outgoing, intelligent, sophisticated, well traveled, and excellent hosts, and they had three loving children to whom they were devoted. If Allison felt neglected at times and thought Andrew seemed less interested in sex than she thought he should be, she concluded that he was busy with his career as a doctor and a member of the university hospital attending staff, rather than that anything was wrong between them.

Nevertheless, when Allison decided to return to graduate school after her children did not seem to need her as much as they had earlier, she met a young man 15 years her junior whose company she thoroughly enjoyed. Since her husband was away from home for long periods, she became more and more attached to her new friend, and soon they became sexually intimate. However, she soon felt guilty, knowing Andrew would not do such a thing to her, and she told her husband. At her insistence they decided to see a family counselor.

Andrew was surprisingly nonchalant about the affair. Although he stated that he himself would not do such a thing, he understood that perhaps he had neglected Allison too much recently. With his practice, his hospital work, and his workouts at the men's gym at the university four nights a week, he recognized that he had not been available for her. They seemed to deal with what had happened in a way that appeared to be acceptable to both of them, and after three sessions they terminated counseling.

The male counselor did not hear from them for 6 months, at which time Andrew called for an individual appointment. He said Allison knew about the call and accepted that there were some personal matters he wanted to explore with the counselor. Andrew began by saying that he had not been exactly honest in the joint sessions when he said he had been completely faithful. Actually, he now admitted, he had been sexually intimate with some female patients over the years. He seemed to gain some relief from this disclosure, especially from the counselor's apparent acceptance of his secret behavior. He did not make another appointment at the end of the session, but 2 weeks later he returned. This time he appeared agitated, finally disclosing that he had lied during the previous meeting to test whether the counselor would be nonjudgmental. Now satisfied, he was prepared to tell the truth: He had been having impersonal homosexual experiences since early in their marriage. His workouts at the gym were really excuses to be with men and to have homosexual contacts in the gym's shower room.

Andrew was now torn by his desire for a more open gay life and his responsibilities to his wife and children. He was certain that he was some kind of "freak," because married men should not feel or behave as he had. By coincidence, he spotted an ad in his university's newspaper inviting married men who experienced homoerotic feelings to join a weekly discussion group off campus. With the counselor's encouragement, he met with the group, feeling much relieved to find others in similar circumstances. With their support and the support of the counselor, he finally told his wife, who seemed to receive the news with some understanding and acceptance. Next, he made plans to move into an apartment and begin to associate with openly gay men to see whether he indeed preferred a gay lifestyle. To help him with his children, he sought out the local gay fathers' support group.[7]

Soon Andrew began to integrate a gay identity, feeling more whole and less fragmented than he had in 20 years. As he no longer felt torn by leading a double life, he now appeared more tranquil, and as a result more available to his children. Although they were rejecting at first, refusing to have anything to do with a gay father, they gradually learned to accept the truth of their father's sexual orientation. With the counselor's help, Andrew became more disclosing about his homosexuality to them, despite his fears of losing their love and respect. When he began a long-term relationship with Harold several months later, he did not introduce him to his daughters for a brief period of time. With support from his gay parents' support group, however, Andrew encouraged regular visits by his children, who now seem to appreciate their father's happy relationship.

Gay fathers with custody of their children must deal with certain powerful negative cultural stereotypes: They are sexually promiscuous, not family-oriented; they sexually abuse young children; as men, they do not know how to play a nurturing role in the family; they will encourage their children to become gay. Despite these erroneous notions, all of which have been disproved, many men choosing to lead a gay life after divorce desire to have their children near them and may even seek child custody. In addition, in recent years an emerging group of men, openly gay from the start, have opted to become parents, either through artificial insemination with a lesbian or heterosexual woman, or by means of adoption (in states such as Vermont, where this is allowed). In the latter case, they may live as single parents (sometimes revealing their homosexuality to their child, sometimes not) or as part of a gay coparenting couple, their partner fulfilling a stepfather role (Silverstein & Quartironi, 1996).

Compared to single gay fathers, single lesbian mothers are more likely to tell their children about their sexual orientation (Turner, Scadden, & Harris, 1990). As for lesbian couples, they are even more likely than gay men to live in households that contain children. Several factors are probably operating here: Lesbians are far more likely to have been married before turning to same-sex relationships, and they tend to come out later, increasing the likelihood of having borne children while married. Moreover, despite the hesitations by some judges noted above, courts in general tend not to be hesitant to award custody to a mother (particularly if her sexual identity has not been a contested issue in the divorce proceedings).

It is not at all uncommon for one or both lesbian partners to have their children residing with them. Thus, they face many of the same problems as any blended family (see Chapter 7), where adults and children from different households must reorganize their lives into a coherent new family unit (Carl, 1990). Here that reorganization is complicated by the fact that the union between par-

---

[7] The Gay and Lesbian Coalition International in Washington, D.C., maintains a list of support groups in various cities, along with the names of gay parents in each area willing to offer assistance and guidance in dealing with children.

ents may be temporary or short-lived and may involve more than one such alliance during the children's growing-up years. Coparenting by two lesbians must also proceed without any legal safeguards—regarding custody should the natural mother die, for example—a further roadblock to involvement by the non-parent.

Since the early 1980s, when easy access to donor insemination became available, a sizable number of lesbians have opted to become parents. In this unfolding social phenomenon, a lesbian woman may choose to become a single parent, or a couple to coparent. In the latter scenario, the couple wishes to form a family within the context of their established relationship rather than bringing in children from a previous marriage (Pies, 1985, 1990; Pollack & Vaughn, 1987). Rejecting the notion that they must engage in sexual intercourse with a man in order to bear a child, many lesbians find donor insemination a more acceptable choice, even though they must often face close scrutiny of their relationship or encounter homophobic gatekeepers at sperm banks or family planning clinics (Sparks & Hamilton, 1991).

If donor insemination is chosen, the counselor may need to help the woman decide in advance whether she wants to be impregnated by the sperm of a donor known to her and, if so, whether or not she should involve him as a father who is not a member of the lesbian family. If she opts for an unknown donor, the woman may need the counselor's help to explain to the child in later years the reasons for her choice of an absent father and to deal with the child's possible upset about his or her origins in early adolescence and later. In one national longitudinal study of lesbian families in which the children were conceived by donor insemination, Gartrell and associates (1996) found an equal division between those preferring an unknown sperm donor and those electing to know his identity. Among those choosing the latter, they again were equally divided regarding his participation in parenting, with those in favor believing their offspring would benefit from knowing his or her father growing up, and those who prefer that he remain unknown wishing to avoid possible legal custody conflicts later. Regardless of the choice, Kirkpatrick (1987) contends that children of lesbian mothers have more adult male family friends and relatives involved in their lives than do children of heterosexual parents. Most lesbian couples with children conceived by donor insemination share parenting equally, although relationship difficulties (for example, jealousy regarding the pregnancy or breast-feeding experience) may occur (Gartrell et al., 1999).

Adoption provides yet another avenue for lesbians who want children.[8] Since lesbians usually cannot adopt as a couple, however, the nonadoptive partner often remains invisible as her mate goes through a lengthy adoptive process (in which the person seeking to adopt as a single parent may or may not reveal her lesbianism). Such going back "in" after coming out is frequently a painful process for both partners, who in addition are denied the support customarily offered to heterosexual couples during adoption agency home visits (Shuster, 1987).

[8] In Chapter 1, we presented a case of lesbian partners who adopt a child.

Nevertheless, gays and lesbians are adopting with increasing frequency, particularly in large cities and with hard-to-place youngsters.

Whatever the choice—donor insemination or adoption—the lesbian mother or gay father must help the child, especially as adolescence approaches, to deal with the likely stigma and homophobic slurs from peers and to develop coping strategies for survival in a society that remains generally unaccepting. Sometimes conflict develops between a teenager's self-conscious need for secrecy (about not being like everybody else) and a gay parent's insistent openness about homosexuality as a political statement. According to Tasker and Golombok's (1997) findings, children are more apt to accept their mother's lesbianism if she is an active participant in the lesbian community.

Some Counseling Guidelines

Most authorities (Brown, 1995; Laird & Green, 1996; Perez, Debord, & Bieschkle, 2000) agree on the absolute necessity, as a minimum, of helping same-sex couples accept and value their sexual orientation and to achieve, embrace, and integrate a gay identity. Counselors who feel uncomfortable doing so, despite paying lip service to this goal, would do well to work through any interfering internalized homophobic feelings. Common manifestations of such counselor-internalized homophobia range from a failure to value the couple's commitment ("Gay/lesbian relations never last"), on the assumption that their problems are insurmountable compared to those presented by heterosexual couples, to overglamorizing the same-sex relationship as inherently romantic (the myth of automatic intragender empathy) and courageous in the face of rejection by the heterosexual world. As Brown (1995) observes, denigrating homosexual relationships and placing them on a pedestal both have potential for harm.

In the event that the counselor, having carefully examined his or her internalized homophobia, cannot overcome prejudicial values regarding same-sex intimate relationships, clients should be referred to some other counselor or community group (for example, a gay counseling center) whose attitudes and outlooks are more consistent with developing a positive self-identity. Gay or straight, the counselor must continually appraise his or her own feelings toward the client(s) throughout the counseling, especially as certain erotic, prejudicial, or homophobic **countertransference** feelings intrude on the counseling process and the personal world of both clients and counselors (Silverstein, 1991). To attempt to force gay clients to rid themselves of their homosexuality because of counselor heterosexism is a miscarriage of the counselor's mission.

In some cases, a gay person may insist on seeing a gay counselor, much as a woman client may feel more comfortable with, and better understood by, another woman; an African American may prefer another African American; or a couple experiencing conflict with their children may be willing to talk only to a counselor who is also a parent. Although such a request may simply mean that the client wishes to speak to someone who has had similar experiences, it may also mean a great deal more. In the case of gay clients, it more probably reflects a distrust of straight counselors as members of a rejecting, heterosexist, oppressing group, or perhaps indicates the clients' incompletely worked-through feelings of self-acceptance. Fear of exposure of their secret, loss of privacy, and concern that confidentiality might be broken may also play a part. In the situation where one member of a gay couple is far less open than the other about his or her sexual orientation, and restricts social contacts primarily or even exclusively to other gays, distrust and suspicion may be so great that working with a nongay counselor is ruled out. In less severe cases, a counselor's consulting with a colleague more experienced in working with lesbians and gays may prove useful, both in raising counselor consciousness and educating oneself about lesbian and gay experiences (Scrivner & Eldridge, 1995; Siegel & Walker, 1996).

Whatever the particular set of circumstances, the first phase of counseling gay or lesbian couples involves grappling with issues of trust. As Malyon (1982) contends, the clients must come to regard the counselor as a person of special knowledge, competence, and good will who cares about them, if counseling is to proceed. Values must inevitably be addressed; any counselor bias with respect to homosexuality must be revealed along with the goals of the treatment. For effective counseling to occur, counselor disclosure of attitudes is every bit as important as that same declaration by clients.

As Brown (1995) notes, gay men, as a result of two male gender role socialization experiences in Western cultures, are typically not well prepared to do the work of relationship maintenance and may need help in building good relationship skills. Frequently, the counselor must focus on commitment and monogamy issues, especially important since the advent of AIDS. Competition for power and status, again common among men in Western cultures, may require examination. Brown contends further that lesbian clients, again as a result of female socialization experiences times two, may need help with such issues as sharing power, the expression of anger and hostility, initiation of sexual activity, and boundary maintenance.

As we have observed a number of times, gay couples who come for professional help are not there to seek guidance in changing their sexual orientation. Rather, for the most part they come with problems quite analogous to those presented by nongay couples: sharing power, communication difficulties between partners, differences in commitment to the relationship, handling money, balancing work and home commitments, managing time together, dealing with children, coping with extended family, infidelity, jealousy, sexual problems, intimacy concerns, breaking up, illness, and so on.

Beyond these issues common to all couples, however, are those unique to the experiences of gay partners. These include dealing with such issues as the following (McWhirter & Mattison, 1982):

- their own overt or covert homophobic attitudes, leading to low self-esteem and lack of self-acceptance
- the degree to which as individuals and as a couple they are out in the open with gay and nongay friends, family, employers, and colleagues

- the paucity of role models for their relationship, leading to uncertainty or to the adoption of inappropriate male-female patterns
- communication difficulties, especially overzealous communication of feelings between partners, causing relationship fatigue and distress

Achieving a range of behaviors that allows sufficient closeness but also enough distance to maintain a sense of individuality is difficult for many couples, gay or straight, but may become especially acute for a female pair in a society such as ours, in which women typically learn to define themselves in relation to others. Lesbian relationships are susceptible to what Krestan and Bepko (1980) describe as fusion feelings; they may vacillate between extraordinary closeness and unbreachable distance, as the exhilaration of intimacy gives way to fear of the loss of self.

Sometimes a gay male couple may also need help in negotiating separateness and closeness. In the following case, two men, both with previous gay experiences, turned a casual sexual encounter into a more extended relationship lasting five years. They contacted a family counselor when that union developed signs of dysfunction.

Simon and Alf would probably seem mismatched to most casual observers. Simon, at 45, had established himself as an executive in a large pharmaceutical company, where he was considered to be among the three or four men likely to become chief executive officer in the near future. Alf, 10 years younger, worked as a salesman for a small printing company, barely earning enough to support himself. They had met at a gay bar and after some brief embracing had gone to Simon's house for what they both assumed would be a one-night stand. They found themselves attracted to each other, however, and both wanted to continue the liaison. About 3 weeks into the relationship, Simon asked Alf to move in with him. Devoid of friends and looking for a safe place to live, Alf readily accepted.

Although living together appeared to work reasonably well from the start, both were aware of major differences in background, education, and financial stability. Their social experiences and degree of gay identity also differed. Simon had a large social circle that included prominent gay and nongay men and women. His homosexual behavior was whispered about at work, but he neither denied nor admitted his gayness. He had had two previous live-in arrangements with men prior to living with Alf.

Alf, on the other hand, had had numerous recent same-sex bathhouse experiences, but had not been in any but casual relationships until he met Simon. He had not attended college, but instead had joined a cult right after high school, probably in an effort to avoid dealing with his sexual urgings, particularly his homosexual feelings. When Alf's parents had had him kidnapped from the cult and deprogrammed, he protested at first, but soon was ready to reenter the world outside the cult. His impersonal sexual experiences with men began soon after returning home and became a regular part of his weekly routine after work. He never discussed his homosexuality with anyone at work, and most of his co-workers thought of him as interested in women. Alf was essentially a loner before joining with Simon.

Not surprisingly, Simon dominated Alf, who continued the passive role he experienced in the cult. The older man supplied most of the money, the friends, the travel opportunities. Alf was expected to cook, work in the garden, and in general take care of Simon after his hard day at the office. Their role pattern thus mimicked a traditional male-female one. Simon was always the sexual aggressor, a role he demanded. Alf enjoyed being desired and valued, and felt safe and secure in the relationship.

Before living together, Simon had had extensive individual psychotherapy and as a result felt secure about his gay identity. Alf continued to struggle with his, and after they had been together for several years, he also decided to seek individual therapeutic help. His straight counselor encouraged Alf to find new friends on his own and to develop a stronger sense of self independent of Simon. In addition, Alf was urged to go through a normal adolescence, which he seemed to have skipped while in the cult, including exploring other relationships in the gay community.

As a result of counseling, Alf became aware of previously suppressed feelings of resentment over his subservient position with Simon. He recognized and became bitter over both his emotional and financial dependence on his lover. Alf did not own anything himself, he realized, and now he wanted something in his name from Simon. Also, he felt he had been taken advantage of long enough, having to go to bed when Simon decided, having to socialize when and with whom Simon decided, and so on. He now wanted to meet new men, something Simon opposed, ostensibly because of the danger of AIDS, but more personally because Simon feared Alf would leave him for a younger, more attractive partner.

The couple was now fighting more than ever before. Simon contended that Alf should either contribute more money or, if not, be more willing to contribute more toward housekeeping responsibilities. With increased struggles over sex outside their relationship, in addition to the conflicts over money, the two decided to seek counseling from a family counselor. Both preferred a woman counselor because they felt she would likely have less prejudice against gay men. When Simon called her for an appointment, he said, "My friend and I are seeking couples therapy. He's free after 5 P.M. Are you interested?" Thus providing a clue that the counselor would be working with gays, Simon seemed to be asking whether, as a nongay, she was comfortable enough to work with them. Assured that she passed the initial test, they set up an appointment for the next day.

At the first session, both men presented, in graphic but unsolicited detail, a description of their favorite sex positions. Once again reassured that the female counselor did not appear startled or repelled, they went on in subsequent sessions to discuss relationship issues. For several weeks they discussed issues of power and control, in addition to their differing views of money. After this first phase of counseling, Simon put one-half ownership of their summer home in Alf's name and agreed to a more equitable distribution of responsibilities at home. During this phase, the counselor helped Alf, in particular, work on his homophobic feelings, especially his concern that nobody in the nongay world could accept him.

As Alf developed a stronger sense of his gay identity, he was more willing to come out with his family, as well as with friends at work. In particular, the counselor helped both men assert their rights as a couple. Visiting Alf's parents, who knew they were both gay, they no longer pretended to be merely close acquaintances. When Alf's Aunt Georgia came to town, Simon was no longer identified as Alf's landlord, but rather as his gay partner.

The sexual issues were more difficult to resolve, and they took up most of the next phase of counseling, lasting 2 months. Despite Simon's expressed fear of AIDS, Alf continued his casual homosexual contacts. However, he did agree to join a small discussion group called Safe Sex, where gay men frankly talked over their sex habits. While there was no sex per se in the group, Simon was alarmed, especially when he discovered that some group participants had tested HIV-positive.

As Alf turned more and more to the group for role models, he began to question whether a woman counselor could really understand him or help him with his conflicts with Simon. Although Simon protested that they still needed to work on the issue of sexual exclusiveness, Alf insisted that he would no longer attend the sessions, and they terminated counseling.

Two years later, still fighting but still together, they once again briefly contacted their former counselor. They were at the point of separating and asked for some guidance to make the final split-up as painless as possible. Alf now wanted to try living by himself, something he had never done before. Simon opposed the idea but reconciled himself to remaining friends, to which Alf agreed. After 5 years as a couple, they let go of each other and went their separate ways.

As this case illustrates, working with gay couples does not call for any specific counseling techniques per se, but rather a set of attitudes toward homosexuality and a level of knowledge that help gay clients accept themselves and their life choices. Because internalized homophobic feelings are present in everyone, gays need help in uncovering and working through their own anti-homoerotic biases as a first step toward achieving a sense of self-worth and acceptance of a gay partner. Each partner may be at a different stage of self-acceptance as a gay person, and here the counselor can help bring previously hidden differences to the surface for clarification, reducing dissimilarity and conflict between the pair. As they achieve a better balance between their attitudes, the underlying rejection of self and partner is minimized and resistance to coming out as a gay couple is reduced.

Understanding how the couple define themselves and where they are in the coming-out process is one of the counselor's first tasks. Here a genogram may help the counselor in assessing intergenerational links, the degree of closeness with family members, or, when applicable, what role that spouses or children from earlier heterosexual unions play in their lives (Buxton, 1994). Gay or lesbian self-definition always requires counselor exploration, not merely counselor acceptance; whether to make their relationship as a same-sex couple public may or may not be as important. As in most couple relationships, heterosexual or homosexual, the partners' feelings regarding public exposure may differ, and these differences need examination and resolution.

The counselor needs to act as a facilitator, offering support and encouragement as gay clients affirm their gay identity. To be of maximum help, the counselor should be acquainted with community support systems and local resource services (mental health programs, health clinics, gay parents' groups, church programs, AIDS projects, gay newspapers, gay political organizations) available to gay clients.

In assisting gays to affirm their sexuality, counselors may need to help them find ways to do so responsibly and safely. The emergence of the AIDS health crisis demands that safe sex be learned and practiced; safe sex is especially important for young gays, many of whom, believing themselves invulnerable, may disregard the advice to protect themselves. In most gay communities, casual encounters have been discouraged, and the use of condoms, in addition to other safety measures, has been undertaken as awareness of the risk of AIDS has become more widespread. Most gays know all too well, by experiencing the deaths of many of their gay friends, the dangers to themselves and others involved in unsafe sexual practices. However, some may need help from the counselor in facing the risks so that they do not simply deny or avoid possible consequences. It is vital here to ensure that the counselor's own anxiety does not prevent any discussion or acknowledgment of the risk to one or both partners.

HIV and AIDS Counseling

Considering the impact of the HIV/AIDS epidemic on the functioning of gay couples, it would be safe to say that no counseling with gay men would be complete without a full examination of their attitudes and behavior regarding this issue. AIDS testing is simply a fact of life in the gay community, although some may choose to deny it and believe they are indestructible or else fear the implications of a positive test result. Although advances in research have led to new treatments increasing the life span as well as quality of life for an increasing number of persons living with an HIV-positive or AIDS diagnosis, the fact remains that there is as yet no cure for AIDS. Counselors can play a crucial role in helping prevent the uninfected from infection, mobilizing support of family members for infected persons, helping safeguard the mental and physical health of uninfected family members, and preserving the stability and resilience of millions of American families faced with the onset of HIV/AIDS in a family member (Rosenthal, Boyd-Franklin, Steiner, & Tunnell, 1996).

First recognized as a disease in the United States in 1979, the incidence of HIV/AIDS in the gay population has steadily risen over the last two decades.[9]

---

[9] There are a number of ways to become infected with the HIV virus: unprotected sexual contact, shared use of syringes by HIV-positive drug users, transmission to a fetus by an HIV-positive pregnant woman, or blood transfusions—when the blood supply is not properly screened for HIV antibodies. On rare occasions, health care workers can become infected by accidental needle pricks while treating an HIV-infected person.

Theoretically speaking, to ensure accurate diagnosis and prompt medical treatment, each gay man who is at risk should avail himself of HIV antibody testing. Practically speaking, however, the decision to be tested is a personal choice in which factors regarding medical treatment and legal protection must be considered (Marks & Goldblum, 1989). While acknowledging that medical intervention is helped when the physician knows as much as possible about the patient's health, many gays worry that antibody testing may reveal an HIV infection that will stigmatize them and expose them to discrimination in employment, housing, insurance coverage, and even medical care by health workers who seek to avoid contact with such patients. Thus, each individual must evaluate the cost to himself of the disclosure and weigh that cost against the potential benefits of longer survival as a result of early treatment. Kalichman (1998) offers a comprehensive description of the transmission and clinical course of the disease, its treatment, as well as its psychological, neuropsychological, and social sequelae.

Counselor intervention typically takes one of two forms: pre-AIDS-test counseling and posttest counseling. In pretest counseling, the counselor needs to help gay clients explore the degree of risk in their sexual behavior patterns and to define for themselves their areas of concern. Since testing is a crucial decision, often accompanied by depression, sleep disturbance, and even suicidal thoughts, the counselor must limit his or her input regarding the wisdom of proceeding with testing, although providing accurate and up-to-date information about the tests is in order. Whether or not the client elects to be tested, the counselor needs to provide him with necessary risk-reduction information so that he may lower the chances of either acquiring the HIV infection or passing it on to others (McCreaner, 1989).

In the following case, a 47-year-old psychologist, previously unknown to the counselor, asked for help with certain family issues.

Jay, a successful behavioral psychologist, had had extensive individual psychotherapy over much of his lifetime, starting when he was an adolescent. Although he later recalled that the issue of homosexual feelings did come up in some sessions, he had refused to deal with such impulses, preferring to deny and repress them. Married at 24, he was the father of two daughters within 3 years. Receiving his doctorate around the time of the birth of his second child, he immediately began a series of part-time jobs in several mental health clinics and eventually opened his own practice, dealing primarily with behavioral problems. The marriage developed a number of seemingly insurmountable problems for Jay and his wife, he told the counselor, and after 10 years of marriage they divorced. What he was seeking now, he confided, were suggestions from a family counselor about how best to deal with his children, now grown into young adulthood, with whom he was having problems.

Although during the second visit he described his marriage as "reasonably happy for the first 5 years," he did report occasional affairs with men during out-of-town trips during that period. As he slowly accepted his sexual preference for men, his marriage deteriorated, and soon he moved out and found a male lover with whom he shared an apartment. Over the years, he had lived with a number of men, usually for months or even a year or two at a time. He expressed satisfaction that he had come out when he did and that overall his life as a gay person had been gratifying.

The counselor found Jay intelligent, witty, and sophisticated, but she was unclear as to the exact reason he had sought her services. He did bring up a number of topics over a month of counseling—interpersonal problems with another psychologist with whom he shared an office, conflicts with his children, a decreased sex drive with the younger partner with whom he had shared his home for the last 2 years. The counselor wondered, however, if his life seemed to be what he said he wanted it to be, why was he really there?

After six weekly sessions, Jay tangentially mentioned that he was afraid of AIDS and sensed he might be HIV-positive. Although he had no obvious symptoms and had begun to practice safe sex 2 years earlier by using condoms, he was worried about occasional cold sores around his mouth that were slow to heal and persistent stomach upset. The worry was ever-present, he confessed, and he was frightened he might die. When the counselor brought up the issue of AIDS testing, wondering whether testing would reduce his uncertainty and also reduce his distress, he became agitated. There was no cure, he insisted, nor was one on the way, and the available medication would only prolong his life but reduce the quality of that life significantly. If the results were negative, he continued, he would only feel guilty as a survivor, after so many others had died. No, he would have no part of AIDS testing. He had worked so hard to put his life together and deal with his gayness, and now this had happened. As he continued discussing testing during several sessions, he cursed the unfairness of it all. He and the counselor were able to discuss reducing high-risk sexual behavior with his partner. When she suggested he bring in his current lover, however, so that all three could discuss the issues together, Jay said he was not ready to do that. After several more sessions, Jay terminated counseling and never contacted the counselor again.

About a year later, still bothered that their sessions together lacked closure, the counselor wrote Jay a follow-up note inquiring about how he was doing. He replied in a long, newsy letter that covered the areas discussed in counseling. Relations with his ex-wife, daughters, and lover were all going well. The one area he avoided was AIDS testing.

Approximately three years later, the counselor came across an obituary item in the newspaper announcing that Jay had died of AIDS.

In general, posttest counseling concerns itself with helping those found to be infected with the HIV virus (Green, 1989). AIDS is not the same as an HIV infection, and many people with an HIV infection may feel healthy for an indeterminate period of time, especially if they comply with the often complex (and costly) drug regimen. However, they must remain motivated to continue the drug intake, despite possible serious side effects, while still facing the high risk of developing AIDS. Counseling gays who test positive for the HIV virus or with full-blown cases of AIDS involves helping them deal with fears of all of the following: loss of independence, becoming physically helpless, rejection by a lover, financial problems, disclosure to family or others of homosexuality, punishment by society for being gay, the infection of partners, and their own ultimate death. Here again a multigenerational genogram can prove a useful assessment tool, identifying family members who might be called upon as resources or to offer help (Boyd-Franklin, Steiner, & Boland, 1995).

Harrison (1987) urges counselors to empower gay clients in every possible way: to confront people who withdraw from them, to affirm their right to receive support, to assert themselves in hospital settings, to demand being treated with respect and not as freaks or lepers, to express their anger and frustration, and so on. Even those who seem to have fully accepted their gay identity may regress, feel contaminated, become seriously depressed, or fear negative judgment from others. They may blame their illness on their sexual orientation and thus feel deserving of the disease. The counselor may need to coordinate efforts with other health workers in monitoring the client's condition and in supporting increasingly direct discussions of death.

Counselors should understand that the diagnosis of AIDS is typically catastrophic, the nature of the illness is turbulent, and patients can look forward to repeated hospitalizations and recurrent bouts of illness. Nichols (1986) describes the usual reactions of shock, denial, bargaining, fear, guilt, anger, sadness, and ultimately acceptance—all stages of a grief process similar to that undergone by people with cancer or other life-threatening illness. In addition, AIDS evokes cultural taboos regarding homosexual behavior and thus attaches an additional stigma of an immoral person, a pariah—contagious, dangerous, threatening others' existence. The family counselor needs to remain flexible, perhaps seeing the person with AIDS alone to explore feelings he is not yet ready to share, before bringing in the partner. Similarly, members of the family of origin may require separate sessions as preparation for a conjoint session with the AIDS patient, alone or with his partner.

Family members of people with HIV or AIDS are also at risk for emotional and behavioral problems, and require help in developing adaptive coping mechanisms. Lovers, parents, siblings, children, and caregivers are all at risk for a wide range of psychological reactions, including anxiety, depression, anger, guilt, anticipatory loss, and helplessness, in the face of an unrelenting disease process (Rosenthal, Boyd-Franklin, Steiner, & Tunnell, 1996). Often, educational and support groups led by knowledgeable counselors can be beneficial. Many gay men are cut off from their families either by choice or rejection; a family of origin with unresolved grudges and hurts can often be helped to restructure and learn to work collaboratively in coping with the challenges posed by the discovery of HIV or AIDS.

AIDS counseling also involves caring for survivors of the dying person, helping them grieve the loss. Not just gay partners but also families of origin who have lost someone to AIDS may need help with bereavement. The social stigma attached to the disease may deprive them of the social support they would normally expect to receive when a family member dies. As Walker (1987) notes, what individuals, couples, and families with AIDS problems have in common is that they all have a member who suffers a uniquely stigmatized fatal illness, one where issues of contagion reverberate through the family and into the larger culture. Most families and individuals are wrestling with issues of guilt and shame, blame and anger, betrayal and fear, helplessness and impotence. They are afraid of contagion, of social ostracism, of pain and death. They must care or be cared for in situations where they meet hostility, contempt, fear and inadequate care. They must fight endless red tape for potentially life saving medicine and perhaps be denied it. (p. 2)

Finally, the counselor must sort out and deal with his or her own feelings regarding death and dying. Attitudes toward sexuality in general and sexually transmitted diseases in particular require self-examination. Working with dying AIDS patients can be a devastating experience in itself, and it may be desirable to arrange for some supportive counseling or networking with other AIDS workers for assistance in mourning and to avoid counselor burnout. The counselor must guard against overidentifying with clients (particularly if the counselor himself is gay), judging them, or becoming demoralized by their demise. The experience may also be humbling and richly rewarding as the counselor explores his or her own feelings regarding illness, loss, death, dying, and his or her own lack of omnipotence, and at the same time makes someone's last days more bearable.

Summary

Gay couples have much in common with cohabiting heterosexual couples but also experience some major differences: greater rejection by society, self-condemnation, more determined efforts at concealment, internalized homophobic feelings, and fear of disenfranchisement as a result of the AIDS health crisis.

A preference for sex activity with partners of the same sex is present in all societies, at all socioeconomic levels, and among all racial and ethnic groups. Gays typically gravitate toward larger communities, whatever their place of origin, since meeting other gays is easier there and disclosure is less likely to lead to social ostracism. Gay subcultures exist in most large communities, easing entry into the gay lifestyle.

The majority of gay men seek extended relationships, but casual sexual encounters, particularly among younger gay men, are common. Coming out as a gay person can cause considerable apprehension and is typically a process that extends over time and in front of different audiences. Lesbians are more likely than gay men to strive for stable, extended relationships.

All gays and lesbians must struggle with achieving self-acceptance in a society in which homosexuality conjures up negative stereotypes and rejection from family, church, and nongay friends. Couples must reach an agreement on sexual exclusiveness, especially in light of the AIDS crisis. Gay fathers and lesbian mothers, who care for approximately 12 to 15 million children in the United States, must deal with integrating children into their gay lives; lesbians in particular often have their children residing with them. Increasingly, gay and especially lesbian couples may form families within the context of their relationship, either by adoption or, in the case of women, through donor insemination.

Counseling gays requires providing them with help in achieving a gay identity. In some cases, gays may insist on seeing a gay counselor, especially if they distrust a straight one or if they have not sufficiently accepted their own sexual orientation. Gay couples rarely come for counseling to change that orientation, but rather to deal with relationship issues much like those of their nongay counterparts. In addition, gay couples typically attempt to grapple with such issues as their own homophobic feelings, problems with coming out, and the paucity of adequate role models.

AIDS counseling may take one of two forms: counseling gays before AIDS testing or after testing has found them to be HIV-positive. The former involves helping them assess the risk in their sexual behavior patterns and examining the benefits of AIDS testing versus the cost in possible future discrimination. Posttest counseling requires teaching safe sex practices and helping HIV-positive gay men, their partners, and their families of origin deal with the ultimate loss.

THREE

COUNSELING FAMILIES WITH SPECIAL CIRCUMSTANCES

C H A P T E R

T E N

Counseling the Dual-Career Family

One of the most significant and far-reaching changes in the American family over the last several decades has come about as a result of the large-scale entrance of women, especially married women, into the labor force (Cox, 1996). As we indicate in Figure 10.1 on page 274, maternal employment has now reached the point where the dual-earner situation represents the modal pattern among married couples (U.S. Bureau of Labor Statistics, 1999a). As a result, the relationship between work and family commitments and responsibilities has become more complex, gender roles less clear, power within the family redistributed, family activities and time schedules more restricted, and the care of children more variable as full-time parental supervision is less and less the norm. Work-family conflicts, present throughout our history whenever both parents worked, have become particularly salient, since dual-earner families now work an average of 80 hours per week outside the home compared to 40 hours just one generation ago (Googins, 1991). The social changes occurring over the last several decades have challenged today's families to achieve and maintain a sense of togetherness at the same time that they seek economic stability (Carlson, Sperry, & Lewis, 1997).

Dual-earner families per se are hardly a new phenomenon in the United States; throughout our country's history, many wives have joined their husbands as breadwinners, largely out of economic necessity. Moreover, wives in low-income, immigrant, small-business, farm, and African American families, in particular, have

There were 53.7 million married-couple families in the United States in 1998. In over half of them, both the husband and wife were employed. These dual-worker families accounted for 53.1% of the married-couple families.

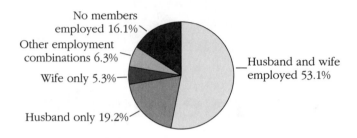

Families in which only the husband worked for pay comprised 19.2% of all married-couple families. In 5.3% of the families maintained by married couples, only the wife was employed.

No one worked for pay in 16.1% of married-couple families. This category includes couples in which both the husband and wife are retired.

Figure 10.1 Distribution of married-couple families by presence of employed members (1998)

Source: U.S. Bureau of Labor Statistics, 1999a.

always contributed money, either working alongside husbands to supplement their income or in some cases as sole support for their families. What is new is that dual incomes are no longer restricted to working-class families, but more and more are becoming the norm for middle- and upper-class families as well. The days when the family relied on a single breadwinner father and a married woman was considered to be neglecting her children if she worked outside the home are a thing of the past. Moreover, the number of children at home no longer determines whether women participate in the work force.

Today, the dual-earner family is the most common family style in the United States; in families with school-age children, this has been the case for more than 20 years (Hoffman, 1989). In such a two-wage arrangement, both partners are employed for pay, the wife typically working outside the home for one or more of the following reasons: because the family needs her income for economic survival, because her paycheck enhances the family's standard of living, or because she finds working away from home gratifying and fulfilling. Not surprisingly, considering the nurturing role traditionally assigned to women in the family, the wife often finds herself torn between the demands of work and family responsibilities. Hochschild (1997) refers to the woman's daytime paid employment as her *first shift;* she then comes home in the evening to begin her *second shift,* about 15 hours more per week than her husband works. Even if her family members do help, which is increasingly the case, the woman is likely to remain primarily responsible for household-related chores (child care, cleaning, and cooking). As long as such a second shift is defined as a woman's problem, a covert struggle between husband and wife is inevitable, intimate relations between the two will be strained, and the family system is likely to be in disharmony.

Two persons dedicated to a single career (traditionally his) represents a familiar if less visible phenomenon today. Here the wife, often well educated but without employment outside the home, channels her talents and energies into assisting her husband's high-achievement, high-commitment career rather than advancing her own occupational or professional development. She offers primarily emotional and practical support rather than household labor; the role structure of breadwinner male and supportive homemaker female goes largely unchallenged by the participants, both of whom appear to benefit from the arrangement. By freeing himself of family-based roles and domestic responsibilities, the man can pursue a productive public career. In this traditional "egalitarian" marriage, benefits also accrue to the domestically based wife. However, her measure of success comes from how successful her husband becomes, with the understanding that her help and support in furthering his career, while simultaneously managing family responsibilities and providing for their social lives, play a key role in his attainments. According to a popular notion, "behind every successful man there is a [perhaps exhausted] woman," or, possibly more accurately, "it takes two people to further one career."

Such a two-person career is one version of a traditional marriage, usually involving mid-level or upper-level executives, in which the wife is committed to management of the home and family, while at the same time giving both technical and social support to her husband (Bruce & Reed, 1991). Hochschild (1989) suggests that the man in such a situation has *backstage wealth,*[1] as in the case of a high-level executive "with a highly educated, unemployed wife who entertains his clients and runs his household; and a secretary who handles his appointments, makes his travel arrangements, and orders anniversary flowers for his wife" (p. 255).

The links among gender, work, and family did not gain the attention of social scientists until World War II, when married women left home in large numbers to seek employment in offices and factories. Although most women returned to the home at war's end, a sizable number did not. When it became clear in the postwar period that married women's role in the workplace was not merely a wartime phenomenon, "working wives" became the target of studies investigating the impact of a wife's work on her children and her marriage. Underlying these early

---

[1] We are emphasizing a male executive's backstage wealth here, but sometimes, although less frequently, the roles can be reversed: A man might stay at home and help manage his wife's career (for example, as movie star or politician), providing support and backup as together they work at advancing her professional achievements.

studies, as Walker and Wallston (1985) contend, is the assumption that the family's viability depended on sex-typed divisions of roles and that women pursuing careers were somehow entering into a deviant lifestyle that could threaten society's well-being.

Initially more the exception than the rule (except among working-class people), families in which both parents work outside the home have grown in number enormously within a single generation, to the point where, as we have noted, they are now the rule rather than the exception. The majority of married women have now joined their husbands in the work force; the more affluent the family, the greater the likelihood that the mother works (Saxton, 1996). By 1996, as we showed in Figure 1.1 in Chapter 1, 3 out of 4 married women with children under the age of 18 were employed outside the home; well over half of the mothers with children younger than 3 years of age, with a husband present in the household, were employed, as were 6 out of 10 mothers with children under 6 years of age. As Silberstein (1992) observes, this rapidly developing social and economic phenomenon offers a window onto the changing landscape of gender roles and relations in contemporary society.

The preceding brief background is important in understanding one of the most dramatic changes in family structure and relationship patterns to have occurred over the last two decades: the emergence of substantial numbers of dual-career families, in which both spouses pursue professional or managerial careers characterized by strong commitment, personal growth, and increasing levels of responsibility (Bruce & Reed, 1991). This relatively new phenomenon, unlike dual-earner marriages (where work is essentially for the purpose of providing money to pay bills), represents a variation of a nuclear family in which both partners simultaneously seek intellectual challenges from careers as well as emotional fulfillment from their family lives.[2] Dual-careerists tend to seek career paths involving progressively more power, responsibility, and financial remuneration, and are apt to view their careers as an essential and integral part of their self-definition (Stoltz-Loike, 1992).

Dual-careerists also differ from couples in two-person careers in that the latter necessitates a second person in an emotionally supportive role—a spouse at home—to make a single career work. The liability carried by dual-careerists is precisely the lack of such a necessary auxiliary partner. In the view of Hunt and Hunt (1977), the greatest challenge of two careers lies not in the required juggling of family and work responsibilities nor in the necessity for a new division of domestic labor between husband and wife, but in the lack of a nonworking spouse at home that both require as a necessity for support and success.

---

[2] Much of the momentum for this social development arose from the feminist movement and the related fact that women were entering the professions. Sandra Bem (1998), a feminist and a psychologist, provides an illuminating view of her efforts, along with psychologist husband Daryl Bem, to "function as truly egalitarian partners and parents and also to raise children in accordance with gender-liberated, antihomophobic, and sex-positive feminist ideals" (p. x).

Dual-Career Marriages:
Balancing Work and Family Life

At the core of every dual-career marriage, according to Silberstein (1992), is an attempt to redefine the relationship between work and family, the two primary spheres of modern life. In a traditional marriage, in which the husband is away at work and the wife cares for the children and takes household responsibilities, sex-linked role assignments to single spheres are easily made. Most work outside the home is viewed as masculine, and the husband is assigned to care for the family's instrumental needs; caring for the family and its expressive needs is viewed as the wife's responsibility. Only when women entered the work force in large numbers, and especially as many pursued careers, has this notion of men and women living in neat, gender-determined divisions of work and family been challenged so extensively as it is today.

In the 1960s, a period of heady optimism concerning the possibility of significant changes in the structure of American life, many women, including those with young children, entered the professional work force. By 1974, according to Klein (1975), close to 5 million women were in career-level positions, a sudden jump of 68% over the previous decade. Close to half (about 2 million) were married and residing with their husbands, who themselves were likely to be pursuing careers.

By the mid-1980s—a time of swollen university enrollments with women pursuing career-oriented goals, greater career opportunities for women, two-career couples living together outside of marriage, and greater public acceptance of the two-career phenomenon—there were probably 5 million dual-career couples (Goldenberg & Goldenberg, 1984). Bruce and Reed (1991) suggest that by 1990, dual-careerists made up more than 20% of all dual-earner couples. The percentage is likely to be even higher as we proceed into the 21st century.

Gilbert (1985, 1988) describes the changing attitudes and expectations of women in dual-career relationships over the past three decades. According to her studies, women of the 1960s, encouraged by the growing women's movement, could be characterized as willing to continue traditional household and child-care responsibilities while *adding* the opportunity to have a career. As Hunt and Hunt (1982) point out in describing this earlier period, the work world largely excluded women but had special rules for those allowed to enter. Those rules permitted men in dual-career marriages to continue to lead lives similar to those of other career men, while women in dual-career marriages were expected to engage in a balancing act that allowed a measure of career involvement as long as it did not inconvenience the family.

Women in the 1980s, according to Gilbert (1985), made a more conscious effort to share both home and work roles with their spouses. However, it was still true that although both careerists may have declared a willingness to share power and domestic responsibilities and to support their partner's career aspirations, in practice their efforts frequently fell short of the mark. Although progress was made toward reaching egalitarian goals, women in general were still likely to assume a larger proportion of child-care and household responsibilities than their husbands, to defer career aspirations in favor of their mates' career advancement, and to cut back career activities during critical periods of family development (Farber, 1988).

Some of the attraction of pursuing a career while simultaneously maintaining a family had been replaced, for many women at the close of the 1990s, by a greater awareness of problems stemming from the changing family lifestyle. Counselors today can expect to see many dual-career couples seeking help with work-overload problems, gender-role conflicts, struggles over power and dependency in the marital relationship, conflicts over achievement and competition, patterns of role sharing, tensions over child care, and relationship difficulties. How a couple adapts to these challenges, according to Shellenberger and Hoffman (1995), will determine the quality of their family life and in many cases the survival of their relationship.

Achieving a workable balance—a more or less smoothly functioning interpersonal system in which each partner maintains a sense of independence, uniqueness, and wholeness, all within the context and security of the spousal relationship—is never an easy task for any couple. As Goldenberg (1986) observes, the task is made all the more difficult for contemporary dual-career couples by the lack of prior role models from which to draw support. He argues that significant changes in the role structure between men and women are required to make a dual-career marriage work, and very few road maps for this journey presently exist. Young women for the most part are just now beginning to have models of mothers who pursued major careers.

Conceptualizing the Dual-Career Lifestyle

In a dual-career family, according to Rapoport and Rapoport (1969), who are generally credited with coining the term and are themselves a two-career couple, both the husband and the wife pursue active professional careers as well as active, involved family lives. By the term *career* these authors mean, rather precisely, "those types of job sequences that require a high degree of commitment and that have a continuous developmental character" (Rapoport & Rapoport, 1976, p. 9).

Obviously, many noncareer jobs may be performed with considerable commitment, although they may bring little personal development or advancement in status or salary. These authors argue that careers typically have an intrinsically demanding character. They are likely to require educational preparation and related professional work experience. Gilbert (1985) emphasizes continuous full-time commitment by both partners in her definition of a dual-career family as "a variation of the nuclear family in which both spouses pursue an uninterrupted lifelong career and also establish and develop a family life that often includes children" (p. 6). A less strict and probably more realistic definition is offered by a number of authors, including Shaevitz and Shaevitz (1980), who regard couples as dual-careerists when both spouses have made a "significant commitment full or part time to a role outside of the home" (p. 12).

Unlike partners in a two-person career, one of whom (in most cases, the wife) derives vicarious pleasure, achievement, and status from helping the other advance in a career, dual-careerists each pursue separate and distinct work roles, presumably offering support and encouragement to the career aspirations of the other. Ideally, the wife's career, no less than her husband's, is an integral part of her identity, representing a professional commitment that is more than a way to supplement the family income. Greater intellectual companionship, more adult contacts, increased financial freedom, added stimulation, better balance of power and decision making, more opportunity for self-expression, sharing of the provider role, an expanded sense of personal fulfillment, escape from household drudgery, and a possible closer relationship between father and children as a result of his greater participation in their upbringing are some of the potential benefits. The possible danger is in overlooking the numerous sources of stress and naively assuming that dual-career families have the best of it all: plenty of money, fulfilling family relationships, satisfying careers, an exciting and filled-to-the-brim lifestyle. To imagine typical dual-career marriages to be composed of the brilliant but sensitive nuclear physicist husband who enjoys changing diapers and the hotshot female lawyer balancing a briefcase on her knees while nursing a newborn child is to engage in a fantasy that often bears little resemblance to real life.

In reality, making a two-career marriage work requires the ability to challenge traditional views about the rights and roles of men and women in our society. Tension often results as each spouse attempts to transcend earlier social conditioning in order to take on tasks ordinarily associated with the opposite sex. As Silberstein (1992) points out, the tension is caused not simply by performing out-of-role behavior, but also by not performing in-role behavior (for example, a mother's not getting a chance to stay home for very long to nurture her infant). Successful adaptation to a dual-career lifestyle involves changing gender-role expectations and inevitably changes the system context and subsequent lives of men as much as it brings more obvious changes to women's lives.

Professional Women in Dual-Career Marriages

Not all dual-career couples are the same. Each maintains a relationship that is constantly in flux, evolving over time as careers develop and diminish, children grow and leave home, and marital compatibilities wax and wane. Some start out together at college, preparing for careers that they then both pursue in an uninterrupted fashion. Some prepare together, but the woman stops to raise a family while her husband continues his career. In the past, especially, some women did not think of careers until later in life, perhaps after their children were grown or they were divorced or widowed. One partner in a couple (most likely the woman) may work part time at a career throughout the child-rearing years. The point is that no "one-size-fits-all" pattern exists, especially for women. Nor are all professionals, men or women, equally committed to their careers or equally involved with their families. Most likely, dual-careerists can be considered to be high-status dual-earner families (Crouter & Manke, 1997) characterized by high levels of occupational prestige as well as temporal and emotional involvement in work for both husband and wife.

In an early longitudinal study carried out over an 8-year period, Poloma, Pendleton, and Garland (1981) examined the consequences for a group of married professional women of having a dual-career marriage. In particular, they were interested in the relationship between careers and stages in the family's life cycle. What effect do marriage and motherhood have on career development? How well are professional women able to coordinate their careers with those of their husbands? In the vast majority of cases, these researchers found that women who had children limited their career involvement, turning down promotions with increased responsibilities and opting for part-time employment instead of full-time work, as well as foregoing geographic mobility.

For example, a female professor might turn down an opportunity for an administrative promotion (a demanding 11-month job) in favor of a more flexible teaching assignment geared to the normal academic year (hers and her children's). A woman physician choosing between work and family responsibilities might decide to work half time (or perhaps in a group practice or for a health maintenance organization in which being "on call" is shared with others). A woman attorney with a bright future in a prestigious law firm might find it necessary to relocate to another city in order to enhance her husband's career opportunities, perhaps finding it necessary in the process to forfeit her specialty and substitute legal work less to her liking. In each case, career development is curtailed and possible marital and family tensions heightened. Most couples in Poloma, Pendleton, and Garland's (1981) sample chose to combine a career with child-rearing; inevitably, this was associated with some reduction of career involvement for the women, depending on age, stamina, and child-rearing philosophy. (Many women today challenge these compromises but as a rule still make them.)

These researchers were able to differentiate four major career types among professional women. The first, pursuing what is termed a *regular career,* begins her career before marriage, right out of college or shortly thereafter, and may continue in her work with minimal interruption, possibly stopping for brief periods to bear children or to engage in part-time employment during early child-rearing years. Although this career pattern resembles men's in the same profession, being a mother as well as a professional has its costs, especially when the children are younger (for example, allowing less evening work, less travel).

A woman's *interrupted career* begins as a regular career but is halted, possibly for several years, so she can be with her children; eventually, she resumes professional work. In this case, professional growth or opportunities for promotion may be reduced. On the other hand, there may well be a gain for some women who look forward to taking such a sabbatical from their careers. A brief hiatus after early career demands may be most welcome, although there is a risk of resentment from a husband not customarily granted such an opportunity for an inter-rupted career.

The woman with a *second career* usually receives her professional training near the time when her children are grown or after they leave home. Thus, the heaviest demands of early child-rearing years are behind her before she embarks on professional training and a future career. Although she gets off to a late start and is likely to be behind age cohorts in income and status for a long time (per-haps permanently), in most cases she ultimately pursues a career pattern much like regular female careerists.

A *modified second career* begins earlier: The woman obtains training and sub-sequent career development after the last child is deemed no longer in need of full-time mothering (perhaps when entering kindergarten). Family demands are still present, so this woman may begin her career slowly, increasing the momen-tum of her work involvement step by step as her child-care responsibilities lessen over the years. Like the regular careerist, but with her child-rearing years behind her, she may seek full-time or part-time work, but might need to be available for family demands for a period of time.

These patterns indicate that even with help from their husbands or live-in housekeepers or nannies, married career women with children have serious diffi-culty in following career paths like those of their male counterparts. Attempting to combine career and family is possible, of course, but it is a pressure-prone situa-tion that frequently leads to conflicts over the multiple and sometimes conflicting demands.[3] Despite these drawbacks, most women careerists today remain in the work force more or less continuously, attempting to simultaneously care for their families and hold a job outside the home, taking time off only briefly to bear chil-dren (Schwartz, 1992).

A number of innovative family-friendly employment policies and procedures for balancing work and family responsibilities have been introduced, largely in recognition of the considerable proportion of women of childbearing age in today's work force (Hudson Institute, 1988). In addition to family-leave benefits offered to men as well as women, affordable on-site day care at places of employment may relieve some dual-careerists (as well as single parents and other dual-earner couples) of the never-ending search for reliable care for their children while the parents are at work. When on-site day care is unavailable, parents must try to find dependable baby-sitters or private high-quality day care facilities where they can drop off their child and pick him or her (or them) up after a day's work. Today, fully one-half of all preschoolers spend at least part of their day under the care of adults other than their parents (Catton, 1991). In many cases, employed parents of preschoolers must devise a combination of creative child-care arrange-ments in order to remain working (Folk & Yi, 1994).

Beyond that, flexible working arrangements may often be adopted, making use of *flextime* (adjusting the times at which the workday begins and ends, as

---

[3] Hochschild (1997) offers a number of case studies describing how different couples cope with these work-family issues.

well as the number of workdays per week—for example, a working week may consist of 4 10-hour days), *flexiplace* (working out of one's home and communicating with the office by telephone or computer), and *job sharing* (two part-time employees fulfilling the duties ordinarily performed by a single employee). These options are often seen by women careerists as preferable to part-time professional work, in which there are usually few opportunities for advancement. Bruce and Reed (1991) view flexible work arrangements, leave policies, and on-site day care as effective strategies for retaining qualified employees (although they may not be available in many workplaces). Work-family conflict remains a problem for many working women, however. In this regard, Pelavin (1995) found that more than the obvious time pressures involved in trying to do both jobs, her interviewees voiced frustration that many male managers were intolerant when a woman on occasion put her family's needs ahead of her career demands.

Changing Domestic Role Patterns

Flexibility in defining and learning new roles and in accommodating family-rule changes are essential elements in making a two-career relationship work. Establishing a new division of labor based on available time, interest, and skills is necessary if the couple is to avoid **role overload,** a frequent complaint of couples seriously trying to meet all work and family demands. Basic child care, meal preparation and cleanup, shopping, laundry, doctors' appointments, bill paying, monitoring children's homework and attending school conferences, directing baby-sitters and housekeepers, arranging for maintenance of cars and household appliances, indoor and outdoor cleaning, travel planning, pet care, maintaining social relationships, staying home with a sick child—these are just some of the tasks every couple must deal with that can become especially taxing when the couple is already overcommitted.

As we indicated earlier, most of these responsibilities are ordinarily handled by a stay-at-home wife, a key player lacking in a dual-career family. In the past, for the small number of women working away from home, relatively inexpensive and reliable female domestic help or cheap baby-sitting was available to help ease some of the burden, but as more women enter the workplace, fewer of them are willing to work at the low salaries these jobs command. Nor are female relatives (mothers, grandmothers, sisters) as likely to be at home or nearby as in the past; they may also be working outside the home. Some men prefer to be househusbands, or perhaps work out of their home and assume the major household responsibilities, but their number is relatively small. To pay for child care means that the couple must work harder or more hours, increasing fatigue and reducing family time together. Time becomes a highly valued commodity for dual-careerists, especially the wife, and particularly if there are children at home (Cox, 1996).

What impact has the entry of women into paid employment had on their husbands' participation in household chores and child care? Over a decade ago, Hoffman (1989) suggested a modest increase, particularly if the mother is employed full time, there is more than one child, and there are no older children, especially daughters, at home. Today, while husbands are more likely to be willing participants, the division of labor remains unequal; married women who are employed full time continue to have a greater total workload than their husbands (Lundberg & Frankenhaeuser, 1999). Those men who are better educated or who are married to higher-earning wives tend to share more domestic responsibilities at home (Ross & Mirowsky, 1994).

Interestingly, although working wives may do two or three times the amount of domestic work than do their husbands, fewer than one-third of the wives report the division of labor to be unfair (Hawkins, Marshall, & Allen, 1998). More than time and task are involved here; the symbolic value of domestic labor is typically a factor in determining a couple's sense of fairness in dividing household chores. Hochschild (1997) suggests that couples are less likely to struggle over who does what chore than whether what is done is received with recognition and appreciation. A husband's availability, respect for, and understanding of the hard work involved in carrying out domestic chores, and the listening to her concerns about family work, symbolically help determine his wife's sense of fairness. Thus, as Lennon and Rosenfield (1994) confirm, the working woman's *interpretation* of the help she is receiving from her husband is far more important than the actual splitting of domestic labor tasks. They add that with generally fewer economic resources and with limited options outside of marriage, some women may be induced into defining an objectively unequal situation as just. That is, it may be more workable for some working women to believe the household division of labor is fair than to acknowledge any unfairness when one doesn't have the power to do much about it (Hawkins, Marshall, & Allen, 1998).

How much actual change has occurred in dividing responsibilities for household tasks in recent years, as two-career families have become more commonplace? Using data from two national studies concerned with how husbands and wives allocate time to household responsibilities, Pleck (1985) determined that the nature of employed wives' overload and husbands' response to their wives' employment are both changing. Although such overload for women still exists, it is declining as "men's time in the family is increasing while women's is decreasing" (p. 146). Moreover, according to this research, not only have husbands with employed wives increased their domestic involvements (child care, housework), but so have husbands whose wives do not work outside the home. Overall, Pleck concludes, a value shift in our society is occurring—no doubt stimulated in part by the surge of married women into the labor market—toward greater family involvement by husbands as well as a greater sharing of breadwinner responsibilities. Men and older children are carrying out more household and child-care duties than ever before, although their efforts still remain considerably less than those of the working mother (Manke, Seery, Crouter, & McHale, 1994).

According to Gilbert's (1985) research, husbands who perceive their wives as highly committed to careers are especially likely to participate in domestic work. She found dual-career husbands more willing to take on child-care tasks than to do housework; indeed, her results indicate that one of the motivations of men who choose dual-career lifestyles is the desire to nurture their children. However, household tasks are likely to be divided in a sex-stereotypic manner. Gilbert (1988) suggests that when a husband contributes to domestic work, it is often with the understanding that he is operating in female territory, and he is apt to undertake the task jointly with another family member. Hochschild (1997) indicates that although men may choose household tasks they like to do, women are far more apt to attend to tasks that need to be done.

Silberstein's (1992) survey concludes that the arrival of children often propels dual-career couples into more egalitarian role sharing. Her data reveal that the contributions of both parents are approximately equal on certain school-related tasks and some household chores. Nevertheless, women still tend to shoulder more of the responsibility for meal-related tasks (planning meals, grocery shopping, cooking dinner) and child-care tasks (getting children ready for bed, taking children to appointments, staying home with a sick child), whereas men take primary responsibility for traditional male tasks such as arranging car repairs, lawn and garden maintenance, and doing home repairs. She concludes that resistance to household chores on the part of men stems partly from the fact that these are by and large undesirable duties. Although women may also find them uninviting, they are more likely to have been socialized to believe such chores are an inevitable part of adult life, and whether they work outside the home or not, they anticipate responsibilities inside the home. According to Silberstein's respondents, men's early experiences, which are deeply socialized and often resistant to change, lead them to assume that these tasks will be done for them.

Despite these gender-role socialization experiences, Silberstein found that times are indeed changing: Approximately one-third of the 20 dual-career couples in her study (ages 32–42) were engaged in a significant attempt to recalibrate their work and family assignments. Succeeding generations, growing up in families with two working parents, are likely to go beyond this group (just as this group has gone beyond its parents) and to achieve even greater equity in the division of labor.

Sources of Stress in Dual-Career Lifestyles

Beyond changes in the division of labor, often calling for significant role restructuring within the family, all two-career couples must deal with a number of other issues that are potential sources of interpersonal conflict and family tension:

- What is the division of labor in the household? Are tasks rotated or assigned?
- Will household help be necessary? How much? How is it budgeted?
- If there are children, who will be the primary caretaker? Who will be available in emergencies?
- Whose job can better accommodate childhood illnesses, special school events, teacher conferences?
- Are there differences in income? If so, how have these differences created power imbalances?

- How does the couple deal with competitiveness and gender expectations?
- Who controls the money? Separate or joint accounts? What are the rights of each in spending the money?
- How does the couple deal with overload or burnout?
- How do they allocate their time in order to nourish their relationship?

Frequently, the counselor's first task is to help two-career couples distinguish which of their problems are caused by the makeup of their specific marital relationship and which are problems inherent in a dual-career lifestyle. The issue is complex, and the two causes of problems are clearly interrelated. Box 10.1 offers the counselor a list of strains that may result from the dual-career lifestyle. Role overload, as we have noted, is a common complaint of dual-careerists, who assume responsibilities for multiple roles while lamenting the fatigue, the limited leisure time, and the drained energies caused by their chosen lifestyle. This is particularly true of those superachievers, men or women, who insist on having it all—successful careers, fulfilling marriages, prize-winning children, glorious vacations, and complex social lives.

However, women are more likely to experience role strain as they attempt to add career roles to their traditional gender-related roles. Who of the working pair is more willing to stay home with a sick child or pick him or her up at school—the mother or father? Which of the parents should defer the day's work plans to stay home if no trusted outside support (a housekeeper, a baby-sitter, a grandmother) is available? Most likely it is the woman, perhaps unable to mobilize her husband, who has not been socialized to give child care his highest priority. Her conflict, as a result of loyalties to both work and family, may lead to considerable strain and resentment toward her spouse and children (and also the "uncaring" employer). Or, in some cases, she may try to deny the feeling of resentment at being primarily responsible for certain family activities. In such instances, some more conventionally oriented women may berate themselves that a good mother

---

Box 10.1   A problem-appraisal checklist for dual-career couples

Dual-career couples may experience problems in the following areas:

- Role overload
- Career demands versus personal and family demands
- Competition between spouses
- Achieving equity in their relationship
- Division of labor
- Job-related geographic mobility
- Child-care arrangements
- Time allocation
- Establishing social networks
- Maintaining a personal identity

should be able to do whatever her family requires without complaining. Even those women less invested in motherhood may withhold any complaints, fearing that their husbands may suggest that if it is too difficult for them, then perhaps they should consider less involvement in their careers.

It has been common (far more in the past than among younger dual-careerists) for a woman to deal with the conflict between career demands and family needs by adjusting the former to accommodate the latter. As we noted in an earlier section, she was likely to interrupt a career to have children, work part time while her children were young, or perhaps even delay starting a career until her children were self-sufficient or fully grown. She and her husband may have chosen not to have children or to have put off their arrival. If they opted for children, the couple might have arranged to work at different hours so as to take turns with child-care responsibilities (although seeing each other only in passing is hardly conducive to a fulfilling relationship). While these options remain, priorities have shifted for many dual-careerists. In the past, the decision on who must make the accommodation was simple: Probably the man's career took precedence; he was almost certainly the major breadwinner and accustomed to making fewer adjustments to family needs than his wife. Today, the solution is not always so cut and dried, and a number of factors beyond gender and economic gain (personal gratification, potential for the future, the other person's turn to develop a career) may prevail.

In the following case, both partners began their relationship with high degrees of career involvement, but the situation changed.

Tony and Abby had each been married before when they met at a business conference. Tony, 45, had divorced 4 years earlier, having been married for 20 years to Florence, a homemaker. Their marriage had been unhappy for many years, and although both had agreed to stay together for the sake of the children, they had found it increasingly difficult to stick to their plan, and they had divorced as soon as their three children (Ben, 19, Howard, 18, Gillian, 16) were well into adolescence. Tony, a successful executive, had agreed to a generous spousal and child-support settlement. After the "miserable" marriage and "painful" divorce, Tony had vowed not to remarry.

Abby, on the other hand, had been married three times, briefly each time, and at age 36 believed she did not want children and thus would have no reason to marry again. Because she was quite self-sufficient financially, as vice-president in charge of labor negotiations for a large firm, she had not sought nor did she receive any alimony from any of her failed marriages.

When they met, Tony was immediately smitten by Abby's intelligence and vivaciousness. She was extremely attractive, he thought, and her independent and non-clinging behavior was a welcome relief from Florence's overdependency. He respected her as an ambitious career woman, earning an impressive salary and eager to advance in her company. She, too, appreciated his no-strings-attached attitude, and together they enjoyed travel, going to the theater, and socializing with friends. Except for the irritation of paying large amounts of money to his ex-wife, Tony was content, and Abby had never been happier.

After living together for 3 years without being married, the two needed to make a serious decision when Abby discovered she was pregnant. She now had a change of heart and wanted to marry and have the baby. At 39, this was probably her last possible pregnancy, and she felt for the first time that a child of hers would have a father she respected. Tony was conflicted about the idea of marrying and especially of becoming a father again. He remembered well the demands of an infant and felt he was getting too old to deal with them comfortably. He also felt that he deserved to have some free time with his wife, after the heavy demands of their two careers, and the infant would interfere with that. Wanting to please Abby, he acquiesced on the condition that Abby take major responsibility for raising the child. He insisted that they hire a housekeeper to look after their child so that their lives would be interrupted only minimally and they could enjoy their pleasurable life as before.

Tony and Abby married, and Abby continued to work while pregnant. Toward the end of her pregnancy, however, her firm decided to cut back on personnel in her department, and she took that opportunity to resign but continue working for the company as an independent consultant from her home. In addition to enabling her to work convenient hours, this seemed like a good opportunity to build a labor consulting business of her own at home while raising their child. The housekeeper she hired was helpful in freeing her from many domestic chores.

Unfortunately, soon after their son Donny was born, Abby's contract with the firm expired and she had trouble getting more accounts. With their combined income now seriously reduced, she fired the housekeeper; although Abby enjoyed being with her child all day, the drop in income was troublesome to both Tony and Abby.

Abby now began to resent quite intensely the spousal and child-support money they were sending to Florence and her children each month. Tony, too, was becoming more and more annoyed at Abby's loss of income, and especially with her requests that he do more with their child in the evenings and on weekends. Their relationship began to deteriorate, with a great deal of acrimony and blaming.

Abby complained that Tony indulged his children from his previous marriage with money: He was helping with college tuition and extra spending money. She thought this financial arrangement was unfair to her and would have to stop; the children should get part-time jobs. He demanded she become more frugal, and began to control her expenditures. She claimed to have fired the housekeeper in an economy move, but kept secret from him her hiring of a cleaning woman to come in two or three times a week. When he asked her to get a baby-sitter and join him and his business associates for dinner at a gourmet restaurant one evening, she agreed but showed up with her year-old son. The event turned out to be miserable for all concerned, and Abby swore she would not go out with him under those circumstances again.

When they contacted a counselor, it was readily apparent that both were misusing money to fight with each other. Each spouse was bitter and felt betrayed. The counselor chose not to deal with specific issues at first, but instead to focus on the inappropriateness of maintaining their premarital agreement on the kind of life they were to live and to reopen negotiations about a new arrangement. Abby, in particular, no longer believed in what she had agreed to before Donny was born, namely that she could handle matters at home, continue working, and not bother Tony with the day-to-day operations of the home. Tony remained angry at her because he believed she had reneged on her earlier promises in an unfair and uncaring way. Slowly they began to renegotiate a new contract based on a more realistic appraisal of their current situation and what each wanted from the relationship.

During counseling, Abby decided to return to full-time work, leaving their son, now 2, with an older neighborhood woman with whom she felt comfortable. The housekeeper had never been her idea, and the baby-sitter provided a more homelike atmosphere. Tony was persuaded to become more involved with Donny, who now was more responsive to his dad. The couple was encouraged by the counselor to return to many of the things they had enjoyed before, with recognition that the circumstances of having a child required some modification of earlier patterns. The parents began to take brief weekend vacations alone, leaving Donny with the baby-sitter, to whom he was now attached. Tony reported before counseling terminated that Abby had once again become more attractive to him and that he was enjoying parenting for the first time in his life. Abby stated that being a successful working woman and a good mother did wonders for her self-esteem. She no longer felt she needed to placate her husband by being "supermom," able single-handedly to care for job, husband, and child without missing a step or experiencing exhaustion and occasional despondency. She remained an independent individual, which he admired, and he was the strong, consistent family man she had hoped for when she first learned she was pregnant.

Redistributing household and child-care responsibilities and renegotiating an outdated contract were key elements in making this marital system functional once again. Successful counseling involved not so much helping the couple achieve complete *equality*—an equal division of roles and work opportunities—but rather accomplishing greater *equity* through a fairer and more flexible distribution of roles. The goal here is for each partner to experience, over time and across situations, a sense of fairness, trusting that the opportunities and constraints of each partner's role will balance out. In our example, Abby felt better when she believed that her needs were being heard and that she had some choices in the roles she chose to play. Even if a major portion of the responsibility for caring for her son fell on her, for example, she came to feel that her husband recognized her contribution, did what he could to help, and took greater responsibility in other areas, such as earning a living. Tony felt less exploited in his temporary role as sole breadwinner when he understood Abby's conflict between career and family demands. He also came to realize that she was committed to a career and not planning to become a dependent individual like his first wife. Having resolved her dilemma over satisfactory child care, which was central to her sense of being a good mother, Abby no longer viewed the work role as incompatible with her maternal role and was able to return to work. Together, the two had achieved a greater sense of equity.

Money was an important issue with Abby and Tony, as it is with all dual-career couples. The ability to earn money represents power, and any change in the amount contributed to the family changes both the power balance and, inevitably, the family's well-being. Money going outside the family to ex-wives, children, or even old debts[4] creates stress, especially if it has not been discussed or agreed upon beforehand. A change in status (power) from being a self-supporting woman to receiving lower pay as a part-time worker often damages a woman's sense of confidence, since she is no longer contributing her share, and the change unbalances the family system. Similarly, a man experiencing economic problems at work also suffers a loss of self-esteem. The counselor must address these money issues with couples rather specifically, even if such topics are often taboo in social situations. Female counselors, because of early socialization, may agree with the wife not to bring up money and embarrass the husband, and thus may miss dealing with an important manifestation of the central power issue in any relationship.

The decision to have children is a key one for working parents. The birth of a child puts a strain on any marriage, as the dyadic family system changes to a far more intricate triadic form. Husband-wife relationships inevitably change as new forces operate within the system. In the case of dual-careerists, the presence of children further complicates their lives, especially if both are heavily committed to career development and advancement. Time allocations must be restructured, less leisure time is available, and professional and domestic responsibilities need to be renegotiated. Juggling work and child care is rarely easy, and feelings of guilt or resentment are often the result. Parents worry at times that being a good parent and being in a career are incompatible, or that choosing the career may have a serious negative effect on a child's well-being. They may feel guilty over their resentment that the child has somehow infringed on their time, careers, or marital relationship. In many cases, unable or unwilling to deal with the causes of the increased pressures, parents search for scapegoats to blame: overcommitment to friends and work or too much time spent with relatives (including, in the case of remarrieds, time spent with children from the previous marriage).

Men and women inevitably worry about whether they are providing proper parenting. Quality day care for youngsters is essential if parental anxieties are to be kept in check. In the absence of high-quality organized workplace facilities— which are still relatively rare, although increasingly more common as employers recognize the need for a stable work force—grandparents, trusted and dependable baby-sitters, and part-time or at-home work by one parent may fill the need. Each of these makeshift solutions carries positive and negative consequences. Parents who take turns in shifts caring for their children at home manage to provide them with at least one parent at home at all times, a definite plus, but often do so at the expense of feeling exhausted and of minimizing adult time together for the sake of the children, a negative result. By doing so, they also deny the children the opportunity to experience parental interaction and interaction of the family unit as a whole.

---

[4] Dual-career couples frequently enter marriage after long periods of schooling, and one or both often bring college loans and other debts into the new marriage. Much of the early stress may revolve around paying off such debts and striving to catch up with their peer group (buying furniture, a house, a car) after having delayed gratification for many years.

Bringing children to day care provides the stimulation of other children, a plus for the child, but often involves complicated pickup and drop-off arrangements, to say nothing of having to keep a sick child at home, for which stress-inducing last-minute adult plans must be made. Day care also robs the child of a needed chance to be alone for periods of time. Hiring a full-time child-care person can be more convenient and less disruptive, but it is often expensive and adds another person to the family system, changing possible alliances and coalitions. Grandparents, especially grandmothers, may help out, but their input regarding child care may introduce conflict; adults who relinquish a parental role to their own parent may feel reduced to children themselves. Besides, many grandparents themselves are now part of the non-child-care workplace.

Some child-care plans (for example, driving children to and from schools in a carpool with other parents) are easily worked out, although parents may run up against scheduling problems with other parents or, worse, people with whom it is difficult to be compatible. Nevertheless, barring unforeseen emergencies, which may require cutting into work responsibilities, such joint efforts are relatively anxiety-free for most working parents. Caring for a sick child, on the other hand, is a far more difficult matter to resolve. In general, men are more willing to pick up and deliver than to stay home and minister to the sick. On the other hand, serving only as a backup parent for emergencies or routine activities (for example, chauffeuring children) may not feel right for some men, who may wish to be more central to their child's daily emotional life. This is especially so if their wives get to do the satisfying, fun things (for example, going to the school play, attending "Mommy and Me" classes). Since many of these trade-offs are typically made covertly, the counselor may need to bring the issue of gender and responsibility into the open for joint discussion and resolution.

Dual-career couples must be helped to work out an emergency backup system, a secondary group of caregivers who can be turned to when extraordinary events (a sick child, a school holiday) require a change of plans. Without such a secondary support system, stress on one or both dual-careerists is inevitable, and a frequent result is conflict and competition over whose work plans are more important and thus less subject to interruption.

Finally, one barrier to intimacy and marital harmony comes from feelings of competition between two high-achieving and ambitious people who happen to be married to each other (Vannoy-Hiller & Philliber, 1989). This is especially the case if one or both feel insecure or anxious or frustrated in their careers. Even if the two deny the feeling, insisting they are completely supportive of each other's career, some competition may lurk below the surface and intrude on the relationship. Especially if the two are in the same field or at the same career stage—or, worse yet, both—comparisons of success and recognition are inevitable. Although the competition may not be fierce, the counselor will need to explore its presence with the couple, attending specifically to when and under what circumstances it occurs. Even when couples are supportive of each other's professional strivings, feelings of competition may be exacerbated by scarcity (for example, when both spouses, just out of graduate school, apply for the same job opening). Competition over who earns more (presumably a measure of who is more successful) is ever present; men in general still feel their salary should exceed their spouse's (which in most cases it does). Women are increasingly less likely to accept this inequality as the natural order of things. Dual-career couples need to accept that competitive feelings are a normal part of being high-achieving people and are not necessarily destructive. Counselors might encourage each partner to voice, and thus help exorcise, any lingering guilt that might surround normal feelings of competition.

Whatever the sources of stress, the goal of equity based on mutual trust represents the ideal, if not the most easily achieved, solution for dual-career partners. As Hall and Hall (1979) recognized two decades ago, "One of the factors that strengthens a relationship is the feeling of equity for both parties—the feeling that each partner is benefiting from the relationship as much as he or she is contributing to it" (p. 154). The couple, as well as the counselor, must bear in mind that equity is not achieved through a perfect 50/50 split in work-family responsibility—never a real possibility—but rather is attainable only through a sense that both partners are striving toward a common goal, not reachable at the expense of either one.

Commuter Marriages

For most people in North America, intact marriages are assumed to involve two spouses sharing a single residence. In the past, when the man was offered a job opportunity in another city, his wife and children followed him, thus maintaining the intact household. Many two-career couples also follow the man's relocation, frequently because his work usually commands a higher salary. Yet, with the growth in the number of dual-career families today, it should not be surprising that an attractive opportunity for career advancement in another locale may lead one person to move away from his or her spouse and children without altering or upsetting the family's location. How to maintain separate residences and pursue independent career paths while retaining an intimate relationship with a spouse and connection with one's children from a distance becomes the problem to be resolved by the commuting couple (Lang, 1988).

Known as **commuter marriages,** such arrangements entail the maintenance of separate residences by spouses who may live apart and independently for periods ranging from several days per week to months or even years at a time (Gerstel & Gross, 1984). Unlike couples geographically separated in the past, contemporary commuter marriages have a number of distinctive characteristics: Each partner has chosen not to allow the marriage to force him or her into sacrificing individual achievement and success; they live at a great enough distance from each other to establish separate households; they make the choice without setting a specific time by which the two households will be reunited; and they are not separated by choice, since they would like to be together (Carlson, Sperry, & Lewis, 1997).

Needless to say, such an arrangement contains many built-in sources of stress, as couples strive to adjust to feelings of loneliness or mistrust, and learn to maintain intimacy and emotional continuity on a long-distance basis. Couples who have a stronger and more established relationship, are older, and are free from child-rearing responsibilities are usually in the best position to deal with the tensions of the commuter lifestyle. According to Gerstel and Gross (1984), the couple tends to fare better when at least one spouse's career is well established than when both partners at the same time must contend with the demands and uncertainties of new professional and marital identities. Older couples have a backlog of experiences together to better cushion the impact of separation; in some cases, where a husband's career has had priority in the past, both spouses accept the fact that it is now only fair and equitable that the wife have her turn. Unfortunately, it is often the newly married, not yet having established a solid foundation for the marriage but eager to begin careers, who represent many of today's commuter couples.

Commuters—sometimes called "married singles"—live apart precisely because each simultaneously wants to pursue a career, not because one or the other has an occupation that requires living separately for periods of time. (Examples of the latter include merchant marines, professional athletes, politicians, and entertainers.) Nor are they likely to commute for reasons of financial gain alone. While two active professional careers may yield high family income, that combined income often fails to compensate for the additional expense of maintaining two residences, travel back and forth to see each other, and large telephone bills. Commuter couples are people intensely committed to their careers, who at the same time value their marriage enough to be willing to put up with the hardship, cost, and effort involved in trying to make it all work.

Although some couples manage to stay together precisely because they only see each other from time to time, most dual-career commuters are committed to their family and wish to keep their marriage strong. Both spouses are, at the same time, strongly committed to their professional identification. Most couples view the separation as a forced choice that benefits their sense of personal autonomy and work achievement, but at the same time generates new tensions in the marital relationship (Walker & Wallston, 1985).

Most married commuters struggle to balance the tangible rewards of professional advancement—money, recognition, status—with the more intangible rewards of a continuing personal connection with spouse and children. Rather than requiring one partner to make a career sacrifice for the other, young professionals in particular may opt for a more equitable solution in which both are willing to give up time together now for the excitement and challenge of advancing their long-range individual careers (Winfield, 1985). Although a commuter arrangement could loosen the marital bond, it may also have benefits for the commuter. He or she may welcome the freedom from family pressures and daily constraints—from having to accommodate to another's mealtime or bedtime patterns or from being interrupted by child-care responsibilities. Kirschner and Wallum (1978) go so far as to suggest that the commuter may actually intensify his or her dedication to career, perhaps to justify having chosen such an unortho-dox living arrangement.

The resolution of issues involving job mobility is essential for many of today's young married couples. An attractive career opportunity, a chance for advance-ment but in another town, or perhaps offers to both spouses from different locales are common dilemmas in which difficult choices must be made. In some cases, a transfer within an organization for one leads to a predicament for others in the family, as they attempt to determine the wisdom of the other spouse's giv-ing up a satisfying job, the children's changing schools in midyear, selling the house, and uprooting everyone. Whose job is more important? Is disrupting a partner's promising career too much to ask for the sake of living together 7 days a week? What stresses are really involved in relocating the family? What about liv-ing apart? For how long? How often and under what circumstances will they reunite? Can the marriage sustain the strain? What about the effect on the chil-dren? Is there a chance that the absent parent will not be easily accepted back into the family? How will the family's customary way of functioning change to adjust to the missing person?

In the following case, two young high achievers, recently married and with a 2-year-old daughter, opted for living apart temporarily as the best solution in a tight job market.

Stacy and John met and married while both were attending graduate school. Both ambitious for careers, they loved the academic life and were certain that as professors they could have it all—intellectual stimulation, a social network of interesting friends, time off for travel, prestigious jobs, periodic sabbatical leaves, and enough income to lead a comfortable life. Both also wanted what a family life would provide, and in her last year at the university Stacy got pregnant, as planned, gave birth to Robin, their daughter, during summer break, and without missing any school time received her Ph.D. in Greek literature on schedule. However, John seemed to be less well organized and became bogged down in his psychology dissertation during his fourth year in graduate school. As a result, he found himself needing to return to the university for at least an additional year when Stacy was ready to look for a university teaching job.

Finding a job proved to be more of a hurdle than Stacy had imagined. Only a handful of universities offered courses she was prepared to teach, and at those schools, teacher turnover was slow and job openings rare. After sending her résumé to 150 colleges and universities, she discovered only 2 had openings, and there were 8 applicants for each one. Fortunately, her outstanding school performance, plus strong letters of recommendation from her major advisor and other professors, helped her land a 2-year contract at one of these schools, a small university 600 miles away.

The job offer stirred up much soul-searching in both Stacy and John. Should she take the one offer she had received or wait until a better one opened up later, per-haps next year, when, presumably, John would also enter the job market? What would she do in the meantime? What were the chances they could ever teach at the same or nearby schools? If she took the job, how often would they see each other? What about Robin?

These and other questions and uncertainties led them to make an appointment with a counselor at the university's student health center. Both appeared very upset by the pending decision, blaming themselves for not having been realistic about poor job opportunities for Stacy when they planned their academic lives together. John also blamed his dissertation chairman for throwing what John considered to be needless roadblocks in his way, delaying progress in completing his study and thus not allowing him to follow Stacy. He admitted to feeling competitive with Stacy for the first time, envying the apparent ease with which she had completed her graduate work in 4 years. Stacy, too, admitted impatience with John's progress, criticizing him for taking on an impossible dissertation topic, choosing the wrong chairman, and in general not moving fast enough. Stacy talked of becoming a housewife and forgetting any academic aspirations, although she soon realized that such an act would be motivated by utter frustration and would ultimately be self-destructive. There was also the issue of money and the repaying of student loans to be considered.

With the counselor's help over several sessions, they decided that Stacy would take the teaching post and that she would take Robin with her. Perhaps with fewer distractions at home, John could devote full time to finishing his dissertation and joining her. They believed their marriage could stand the necessary strain; in any case, they had few choices, and it would only be for a short period. They agreed to talk to each other at least 5 nights per week—after 11 P.M., to keep telephone costs at a minimum—and to plan reunions every 2 months.

Not surprisingly, the separation turned out to be more painful than either had thought. Both became lonely and depressed. In particular, they reported missing the small things that as a loving couple they had taken for granted: the daily exchange of small talk and gossip about school, the shared mealtimes when the three of them were alone together, even studying in silence next to each other in their bedroom. They missed their sexual intimacy, touching each other, being tender. John missed seeing Robin grow up.

Stacy did enjoy her students and colleagues and had begun to make friends. She found a female undergraduate student to help baby-sit when necessary in the evenings and a good day care center near the university where she could leave Robin during the day. John did less well, gaining a great deal of weight, neglecting his household chores, too distracted to devote his limited energies to completing his dissertation. When they spoke on the phone, they frequently bickered, each feeling cheated by the separation. Their calls became less frequent as each began to spend more (nonsexual) time with friends. When they did meet, usually at some halfway point, for the weekend, there was initial tension, and they invariably quarreled. Perhaps they expected too much or wanted to crowd too much into their brief reunion, but the feelings of awkwardness and discomfort with each other never left them.

Six months after their separation, John contacted the counselor once again for individual help. He expressed a deep longing to be with his wife and child, indicating he could not go on this way much longer. Continuing his systems view, although working with one member only, the counselor focused on what John felt was happening to his family. Reviewing the family transactions within the last half year, John was asked to tally up the sacrifices and to see if any benefits might have accrued. He revealed that he was beginning to manage and to look at his manuscript again, but he was frustrated and lonely, and blamed Stacy for the decision that he realized they had made together.

John was asked to clarify for himself how much of the current conflict with Stacy resulted from their present temporary situation and how much represented previously unspoken but never resolved marital issues from the past. He confessed to resenting her apparent ease in graduate school when he was stumbling through and her time away from him devoted to school at first and then the baby. He acknowledged that the friends they had together had tried to help after Stacy left, but he had failed to respond, and soon they had stopped calling.

John was offered a number of techniques for allocating his time better. In particular, the counselor urged him to focus on the primary goal—finishing his dissertation and getting back with his wife and child. While doing so, he needed to rebuild his social life, since friends were essential if he was to avoid feeling lonely and depressed. He needed to strengthen his sense of personal identity, and being by himself while Stacy and Robin were away was a good opportunity to work on that.

Stacy and John came to see the counselor together during her academic breaks and in the summer when she and Robin returned home. As the couple worked out some unfinished conflict from the past, their bond, weakened by the separation, seemed to grow stronger. John said he was proud of himself for learning to carry out domestic chores efficiently for the first time in his life. He still did not like to cook, relying too much on fast-food restaurants, but he was starting to watch his diet better. He said, too, that he was proud of Stacy's accomplishments and her independence, but he was afraid she no longer needed or wanted him. She reassured him that his fears were unfounded and that she had begun making inquiries at her school about possible openings in psychology for him next year. For one week she went back to another state to visit some friends, leaving Robin with her father, a situation John enjoyed immensely.

During their second year of separation, John and Stacy talked less on the phone, saving money in order to meet more frequently. Each tried to make that meeting more relaxed, not expecting that a 2-day weekend would compensate for a month apart. They became physically closer than they had been all of the previous year, and each looked forward to their next rendezvous when parting. John finished his dissertation early in the second year and moved to be with his family. Together, he and Stacy sent applications for common employment to a large number of universities, hoping they might be able to teach at the same place. When they last sent a postcard to the counselor, it was to notify him of their new address at a university town in the Midwest, where both were getting ready to start teaching.

Adaptational Strategies and Family Systems

It should be clear by now that there is more than one way to make a go of dual-career marriage. Hall and Hall (1979) offer a thumbnail sketch of several distinct patterns followed by effective two-career couples—couples satisfied in their homes, their family relationships, their lifestyles, and their careers. From these authors' description it is clear that no single role structure is satisfactory to all dual-career pairs; each one must forge an adaptational style that takes into account both work and family involvements and priorities. These authors distinguished four general types: accommodators, adversaries, allies, and acrobats.

Accommodators have a marital relationship in which one partner is high in career involvement and low in home involvement while the second partner holds the opposite priorities. One assumes primary (but not total) responsibility for family-centered roles, whereas the second takes major (but not sole) responsibility for career development. More than likely, this combination approximates gender-based roles in a traditional marriage. In most cases the main breadwinner is the professional man; it is the professional woman who involves herself more at home. If a move to another locale should become necessary, the family would likely follow him, since his career is paramount. Thus, a part-time or substitute teacher would accompany her computer executive husband if he were transferred to another city.

Adversaries are both highly involved in their careers and only minimally involved in home, family, or parental roles. Each partner defines himself or herself primarily by career while retaining some interest in maintaining a well-run home and smoothly functioning family life. Conflict in such an arrangement may arise over which of the two will perform non-career-related tasks at home (for example, staying home from the office to wait for the repairman). While each wants the support of the other, neither is willing to make major career sacrifices to help the other's career or fulfill family roles. Competition is probably more severe here than in the other transactional patterns (who won the grant, who got the promotion, who will follow whose job relocation). Children, if present, are a problem, since each partner prefers the other to assume major child-rearing responsibilities.

Allies are both either highly engrossed in their careers or in their home roles, but not in both areas. Their priorities are clear. They may view their roles as parents or as a couple as paramount, gaining satisfaction from home and family rather than from career advancement. Conflict tends to be low in this arrangement, since each is willing to support the other at home, and neither accedes to potentially stressful career demands. On the other hand, if both view their careers as all-important, conflict is kept low by minimizing domestic roles and the need for a well-organized home. Those in this category who value careers often choose to be childless. Neither resents purchases by the other—they treasure each other's independence—and together they may rely on a housekeeper or dinner out instead of bothering with fixing meals at home. Commuting marriages for the sake of career advancement are more easily tolerated here than in other configurations.

Acrobats hope to have it all, since they both actively engage in careers and in home roles. That is, they seek satisfaction and fulfillment from playing all roles; they juggle demanding career activities with performing family duties well. High achievement in their careers, a good marriage, happy children, a well-run home, exotic vacations, a reputation as top-notch host and hostess are all pursued, sometimes in a seemingly never-ending, frantic manner. Neither looks to the other to take over; both want to do it all themselves. No speaking engagement is turned down, no call for volunteers ignored, no office in a professional organization allowed to go unfilled, no child's birthday allowed to pass without a large, elaborate party, no soccer practice or musical recital by the children unattended. If conflict is experienced, it is apt to be internal (for example, work overload) rather than adversarial.

Some Counseling Guidelines

Various counseling approaches, ranging from the problem solving to the developmental to the interpersonal, have been proposed in dealing therapeutically with dual-careerists. For example, Sekaran (1986), a management and organizational authority, suggests ways in which counselors can help such couples identify and resolve conflict by providing them with better strategies for decision making, stress management, and time management. In addition to encouraging client couples to clarify (and perhaps reassess) their concepts of success, she offers suggestions for helping organizations change policies (offering parental leave, flexible work schedules, child-care assistance) to more effectively address the needs of employees from dual-career households. Many corporations are beginning to recognize that such pro-family policies not only build employee loyalty but also reduce turnover costs as employee work-family conflicts are reduced (Carlson, Sperry, & Lewis, 1997).

With a similar organizational outlook, Bruce and Reed (1991) argue that the dual-career couple is the prototype of the future employee, struggling to balance the demands of work and family. Addressing public-sector employers, they urge the restructuring of organizational policies, such as the adoption of family-oriented benefits (family leave, flextime, flexiplace, part-time employment, job sharing), the hiring of husband-wife couples (doing away with policies restricting nepotism), and increased supervisory awareness and support for working spouses, in order to maximize the talents of career-oriented men and women with families. Some counselors and organizational psychologists are being recruited to work within larger corporate systems to help resolve dual-careerist (or other dual-earner or single-parent) conflicts between work and family through the introduction of family-friendly policies.

Hall and Hall (1979) suggest that helping each partner confront and resolve his or her own unfinished developmental business is a useful way of beginning to untangle current relationship conflicts. Glickauf-Hughes, Hughes, and Wells (1986) support this effort, arguing that while learning coping skills may help some dual-career couples, others may feel frustrated until more basic issues from each spouse's early development (for example, regarding trust, autonomy, and intimacy) get resolved. For example, these authors contend that power conflicts (over household divisions of labor, career moves, use of leisure time, sex) may reflect each partner's childhood experience that others cannot be counted on to meet his or her needs and that he or she must "look out for number one." Until both spouses sufficiently master the developmental tasks of trust or autonomy (following the schema of Erik Erikson [1963]), their current ability to resolve power dilemmas and thus achieve equity will be seriously compromised.

A more interpersonal systems-oriented view is offered by Goldenberg (1986). He maintains that to be effective, counseling for dual-career couples must be highly focused and must involve both partners conjointly. In his experience, their sessions together may well be the first time that one partner has been forced to attend to the other partner's agenda. When this happens, each partner may begin to become sensitized to the fact that more is happening interpersonally between the spouses than his or her individual unhappiness alone. According to Goldenberg (1986), such recognition is an essential first step in reorganizing the faulty relationship system.

Certain conflict areas increase the probability that two-career families will seek counseling. Gilbert (1988) lists five such problem areas:

1. Managing stress (which may have reached the breaking point)
2. Matching career expectations (not only career expectations and career reality of one spouse but also career accomplishment and satisfaction between spouses)
3. Struggles with role sharing (overcoming resistances rooted in traditional sex roles)
4. Deciding whether or not to have children (if so, at what point in the woman's career?)
5. Accommodating aged parents (as members of the "sandwich generation," middle-aged couples more and more may be caught between the demands of adolescent children and aging parents)

Maintaining their carefully achieved balance may make some dual-careerists especially resistant to change. Even those couples who attempt to live out the philosophy of having an "equal" relationship may find their resolve sorely tested when trying to balance work and family roles. As illustration, Shellenberger and Hoffman (1995) cite the example of a man who appreciates the additional income his wife brings home but who might still expect her to maintain her customary domestic tasks despite her increased responsibilities (and fatigue) as a result of her work outside the home. Such differing demands and differing expectations between spouses are common and add stress to their marital relationship. Men may expect women to share more of the financial load, and women may feel entitled to receive greater understanding and emotional support for their work efforts. These authors suggest that these new role strains may tax or stretch the family's balance and lead to resentments, each partner feeling the other is not making a sufficient contribution.

For many young dual-careerists, having children can frequently compound the problem, for men may feel they must work even harder to support a growing family (now reliant on male income alone for a period of time), and women may feel torn between returning to work as soon as possible and leaving their young child in a child-care arrangement, reducing their workloads to care for the child themselves for part of the time, or quitting a budding career for a (sometimes indefinite) period of time.[5] Men, on the other hand, who perhaps wish to modify earlier career aspirations in order to devote more time to their families, may find themselves penalized at work for becoming less dedicated. In the case of men or women careerists alike, much of the territory remains uncharted, and both family and work environments need restructuring in order to adapt successfully to rapid social change.

By both choosing to focus on achievement and the pursuit of success, the busy couple may shield themselves from acknowledging marital or family strains until they are unavoidable, or an external event (such as an extramarital affair) forces the couple to face their disintegrating relationship. With both accustomed to success in their professional lives, neither is eager to examine their failing marriage. As Price-Bonham and Murphy (1980) observe, dual-career couples often delay entering counseling until their relationship has deteriorated to an almost irreversible point.

Once in the counseling situation, it is essential that the couple be treated evenhandedly. The counselor's approach must not be tied to the values and sex-role assignments of the traditional marriage. Counselors not only must be aware of the dynamic struggles within their client couples, but also must look for similar struggles within themselves that may be counterproductive to the counseling (Goldenberg & Goldenberg, 1984). The dual-careerist spouse who senses a bias in the counselor's attitude toward role stereotypes and gender-related domestic assignments "is likely to withdraw, feel ganged up on and probably pessimistic, if not despairing, about being understood" (Goldenberg, 1986, p. 4).

In the following case, we see two highly successful married individuals, at somewhat different stages of their careers, trying to resolve pressing differences between them that add considerable stress to their already overburdened lives. At the wife's insistence, they contacted a woman counselor.

Marilyn and Frank, both physicians, met when she began her residency training to become a surgeon and Frank headed the department of surgery training program in a large city hospital. Although a mere 5 years older, at 35, Frank was considerably more advanced in his career than Marilyn, who had just finished her internship and begun her training under Frank to become a surgeon. They were attracted to each

---

[5] In a controversial article published in the *Harvard Business Review*, Felice Schwartz (1989) proposed that corporations distinguish between women who are "career primary" and those who are "career and family." The former will not interrupt their careers to raise families and thus should be considered on the same fast track as men in regard to further training and promotional opportunities. The latter group of women should be put on the "Mommy Track," according to this author, staying put in middle management without feeling pressure to compete for promotions. Supporters of Schwartz's argument believe this distinction provides an opportunity for women to devote time to family, if they wish, without penalty. However, critics contend that those who choose the Mommy Track will find themselves diminished as professionals, earning less and receiving less prestige for their efforts. Moreover, they argue that the Mommy Track can legitimize discrimination against women employees, making it easier to justify the hiring of a man rather than a woman who might opt to leave to have children.

other from their first meeting and soon began to date each other exclusively. Within a year of their meeting, they made plans to marry.

While their backgrounds seemed worlds apart—Frank came from a large, working-class Hispanic family, Marilyn from an upper-middle-class WASP upbringing—they felt confident that as intelligent people who had common values and career interests, they could make a go of marriage. Marilyn had been married before, to a man from an Armenian background, and had experienced no strain with his family or friends, so she believed she could overcome any social or cultural differences with Frank. He had been alienated from his family for some time, and although they lived in the same city, he saw them only rarely.

When Marilyn first met Frank, she was dazzled by his intelligence and clinical ability in surgery. While she was immediately attracted to him, she was at the same time taken aback by his reputation as a "womanizer." Within the hospital there was considerable gossip about his sexual promiscuity; he was known as someone who sought out all attractive nurses, as well as female medical students, interns, and residents. She thus distrusted his obvious interest in her, but as she got to know him, this concern subsided somewhat, since he stopped pursuing anyone else. Besides, Marilyn was drawn to the combination of danger and romance he exuded. Frank, on the other hand, found her quick intelligence very appealing, and as he got to know Marilyn, he realized and appreciated her steadying influence on him.

As they got to know each other better, they found they both came from hard-working, achieving families, each with a number of siblings and cousins with M.D.s and Ph.D.s. Moreover, they discovered that problems with alcoholism permeated both families, although neither Marilyn nor Frank had a particular drinking problem. Marilyn was the oldest child in her family, accustomed to caring for her younger siblings. Frank was the youngest in his family, the baby everyone adored and wanted to indulge.

Even before they married, the couple quarreled a great deal. Marilyn was jealous and suspicious when she didn't know Frank's whereabouts for long periods of time, suspecting he was with another woman. Frank protested his innocence but was frequently irritated by her lack of trust. He felt, too, that she never let anything pass, insisting that the smallest issue between them had to be examined and worked out in detail. In his family, he had been allowed considerable latitude—"space"—and he expected the same in this relationship. She had always been the "rescuer" in her family, and her close scrutiny of the basis for any tension between her and Frank was often done in the pursuit of clarification to reduce the stress and make things between them right again.

When they decided to marry, Marilyn persuaded Frank that they should see a professional for premarital counseling. In particular, she wanted them to see a married woman, whom she felt would understand the feelings and potential conflicts of a young professional woman in a dual-career marriage. Together they saw the counselor for a total of six sessions. They seemed to benefit from the experience in that their communication patterns improved and they both felt more free to express to each other what they were experiencing in the relationship.

Frank and Marilyn married about a year after they met. After a brief honeymoon, both plunged back into extremely demanding work schedules, putting off children due to the large debts they had incurred and their desire that she finish her training. Marilyn was determined to be the best resident in the training program, a goal she seemed to reach. However, she was now aware that their unequal status bothered her; Frank seemed to her to be giving off a double message: "We are equal; I am still superior." She also became more sensitive to his behavior with the other residents, feeling that any decision he made that was not to someone's liking reflected poorly on her. He, on the other hand, felt her observing and evaluating him whenever he lectured or demonstrated a surgical procedure, and he became very uncomfortable and defensive whenever he felt she was criticizing him or trying to improve him. Frank now found it harder and harder to maintain his position with Marilyn as her teacher, retaining her admiration and his superior status in her eyes. She still tended to put him on a pedestal, only to become disappointed when he didn't behave as she thought a concerned teacher should, or when he was not as interested in the evening in her cases as she felt he should be, tired or not.

As both devoted themselves to work and career advancement, their social contacts shrank, and their dependence on each other for stimulation and fulfillment deepened. More and more they behaved as "workaholics," without many friends, their careers all-consuming. He no longer went to the gym after work, as he had done several nights each week before their marriage. She stopped seeing girlfriends for lunch or evenings out together.

After 1 year of this regime, both felt overburdened, put upon, and quarrelsome. Their pressure-cooker lives now became further complicated when Marilyn was offered a chance to move to another, more prestigious surgery training at a university hospital in the same city. Both felt ambivalent about making the change: She was tempted to go but wanted Frank to insist that she stay; he would miss her but felt some relief that he would be less open to her daily assessment of his job performance. They decided to schedule a new series of appointments with their counselor to work out some solutions.

The counselor immediately made them focus on exactly what a pressure-filled existence their lives had become. In their drive for success, she helped them realize, they seemed to have neglected nourishing the intimate emotional bond that drew them together in the first place. The counselor suggested they now pause and make some decisions about what precisely they wanted out of their lives together. She stated her belief that they needed to reevaluate how they dealt with time demands, making certain that they left time and energy for fun, play, and relaxation together. They needed time, too, to dream and plan a little for their future. In addition, the counselor asked them to attend to their increasing social isolation, and the couple soon recognized that a network of friends with whom to share work and marital experiences might prove to be a good antidote to becoming insular. Beyond those immediate goals, the counselor indicated that they needed to reconsider the long-term effects of the lessening of differences in their professional status, since without doubt those differences would narrow in the future. By doing so, the counselor helped them focus and begin to work through the issue of competitiveness between them. Could they imagine their lives together 15 or 20 years from now? Would they be together? Would there be children? How many? How far did each expect to advance in his or her career? How did they see the balance of family and career in their future together?

The couple initially contracted for five sessions, and when the counseling series was completed they seemed to be in better contact with the unresolved issues between them. They agreed to work further on their own and to see the counselor again in 6 months. When they did, it was clear that some progress had been made—in particular, they seemed to have achieved a better balance between career demands and time for each other—but significant problems remained between them. For example, there were the differences in cultural background. When Frank and Marilyn went together to the fiesta celebrating his mother's 65th birthday, there was open tension between them. She worried that he would behave in his old macho way in front of his cousins, appearing to ignore and thus dominate his Anglo wife. He worried that she would appear withdrawn, particularly if his family did not welcome her with open arms, a highly likely possibility.

Instead of denying dissimilarities in background, the counselor encouraged them to examine these past differences and to work through their impact on their present lives. The couple became aware that differences in social class and ethnic background led to basic differences in expectations regarding the role of women and the importance of family. The differences in their birth order—she the oldest child, he the youngest—also led to different expectations of roles and entitlements. These dissimilarities might or might not be significant, but they could not be buried or covered up.

The counselor also encouraged both spouses to separate their personal identities, in their case best accomplished by seeking separate work environments. In that way, competition between them would be minimized, although they needed to acknowledge it would not be eliminated completely. As they moved away from the teacher-student roles, each sought recognition in related, but not identical, surgical fields. Frank remained primarily a teacher and trainer; Marilyn became a thoracic surgeon.

The couple planned to have children within 2 years. They realized that the divisions of labor at home would have to be renegotiated when a child arrived, and they now began to plan to add on a nursery room to their house. They also began to discuss how their lives would change with the arrival of a baby and how emergencies at home would be handled, since Marilyn intended to return to her career as soon as feasible. In the process, they started to socialize with other young couples from their places of work and talked with them at great length about family and career responsibilities.

Future sessions with the counselor were left open on an as-needed basis. While Marilyn had learned to become less intrusive and Frank less withdrawn, they both knew that more work on their communication patterns was necessary and that occasional backslides were probably inevitable. In all likelihood, they assured the counselor upon completing the current round of counseling sessions, they would be calling her again.

Many of the rewards and benefits of a dual-career marriage are seen in this case: an opportunity for self-fulfillment for both partners, greater intellectual stimulation, and the chance to lead a more economically enriched life together. At the same time, many of the common problems are also present: competition, restricted job mobility, difficulties with time allocation, and work overload.

The counselor needs to help any dual-career couple understand that they are undertaking a marriage that may well give them both a sense of accomplishment, perhaps even elation, but often at the price of exhaustion and guilt over goals not achieved. To romanticize the dual-career family as "having it all" is to invite inevitable disappointment. Rather, the counselor must aid the couple in exploring their values and priorities, pursuing what is important to both partners, relinquishing experiences to which they assign less urgency, and accepting the limitations of their demanding lives. Stoltz-Loike (1992) offers a number of assessment and skills-training intervention devices, tailored specifically to dual-careerists, helping them recognize their unique situation in which each must tailor family and work responsibilities with his or her spouse. She emphasizes the changing work-family role conflicts that dual-careerists are likely to experience over the course of their relationship, all in the service of achieving a balance in these areas as they continue the process of negotiating career and family equity over time.

Beyond working with couples to help them resolve their career and relationship issues, the counselor may play a consultant's role with employers, furthering their use of the talents of dual-careerists in the workplace. Through single lectures, ongoing in-house seminars, perhaps informal brown bag luncheons, they can offer psychoeducational workshops on one or more of the following: time management, stress reduction, lifestyle management, communication and negotiation skills, stress and sexuality, women's health issues and work, and balancing career, family, and personal life (Carlson, Sperry, & Lewis, 1997).

Summary

The large-scale entrance of married women into the labor force in recent years has resulted in numerous changes in the work and family commitments of both partners, sometimes resulting in work-family conflicts, particularly for women. Although dual-earner families have existed for many years, especially among working-class populations, a relatively new phenomenon—dual-career families— has emerged in significant numbers within the last 20 years. Such families contain husband and wife professionals both actively pursuing work that requires a high degree of career commitment, as well as involving themselves in their home and family lives.

Dual-career couples are not always equally committed to their careers or to their domestic roles. Women, depending on the stage of the family life cycle, may resolve the sometimes conflicting demands of the two roles by interrupting their careers for child-rearing, by seeking part-time or temporary employment, or by restricting their geographic mobility in order to fulfill parental responsibilities. Some may postpone careers; others may return to earlier careers only after their children no longer need them at home or after becoming divorced or widowed.

Several new family-friendly employment procedures, such as flextime, flexiplace, and job sharing, are often chosen by married women careerists as preferable to part-time employment.

To make a dual-career relationship work and to avoid role overload, especially for the woman, changes in who carries out domestic tasks, including child care and household maintenance duties, must be negotiated. Genuine recognition and appreciation by husbands of the work performed by women at home may help add to the wife's sense of fairness regarding household responsibilities. Men and older children are devoting more time to family duties while women devote less than they did in the past, although, by and large, working mothers still shoulder the major domestic responsibilities. A greater sharing of both family involvement and breadwinner responsibilities by the two partners represents a value shift in today's society, although women are still expected to be primarily responsible for family and home-related chores.

Beyond role overload, a number of stresses are potential sources of interpersonal conflict between dual-careerists. Clashes between career and family demands, competition between the spouses, and difficulties in making time available for all their work and family commitments are common. The presence of children may add to their responsibility overload, especially if adequate child care is unavailable or too costly. Whatever the sources of stress, the counselor needs to help the dual-career couple try to achieve the goal of equity: for each partner to feel that, overall, fairness exists both in their role opportunities and in their constraints and responsibilities.

Commuter marriages—in which one adult chooses to live apart from his or her spouse, usually for a job opportunity—place considerable strain on the marital bond, particularly among newly married couples with young children. Such "married singles," who would prefer to be together, must often cope with feelings of loneliness and mistrust as they attempt to maintain intimacy and commitment to the marriage on a long-distance basis.

A number of alternative strategies are open to dual-careerists who attempt to find satisfaction at home and in their careers. Some may adapt to the situation by one partner's remaining high in career ambition but low in home involvement while the other partner adopts the reverse priorities. Others may become adversarial, both pursuing careers with only minimal attention to home, family, or parental responsibilities. In another configuration, the two may become allies in their careers or their home life, but not in both. A final group may resemble acrobats who strive to have it all, seeking satisfaction from playing career and domestic roles fully, while never missing an opportunity to add on another responsibility.

A variety of approaches may be used in counseling dual-career families: helping them manage decision making and time allocation, having each partner separately resolve his or her unfinished developmental issues from the past, or focusing conjointly on their current interpersonal transactions. Managing stress, matching career expectations, struggling with role sharing, deciding whether to have children, and accommodating aged parents are typical conflicts requiring resolution. Whatever the counseling technique—and a combination is likely—the counselor must adopt an evenhanded approach to both careerists that is not bound by the values and sex-role assignments of the traditional marriage. In addition, counselors may sometimes provide consultation to corporations, offering psychoeducational workshops for their dual-career employees to help them better balance their career, family, and personal lives.

Counseling Ethnically Diverse Minority Families

American society is in a state of flux, as rapid social changes add complexities and often turbulence and uncertainty to our lifestyles and value systems. We are, increasingly, a diverse society, a pluralistic one made up of varying races and multiple ethnic groups, with millions of people migrating here seeking a better life.[1] As we observed earlier in this text, one in every four Americans today is a person of color (Homma-True, Greene, Lopez, & Trimble, 1993), and it is estimated that by early in the current century about one-third of the U.S. population will consist of racial and ethnic minority groups (Jones, 1991). California is the first large state in which non-Hispanic whites are no longer the majority (Purdum, 2000); thus, it represents an example of what it may eventually be like to live in a United States in which no one racial or ethnic group predominates. How counselors assess, counsel, and in general communicate with these diverse families is not only screened through the counselors' professional knowledge, but also through their own "cultural filters"—those values, attitudes, customs, religious beliefs and practices, and especially outlooks regarding what constitutes normal

---

[1] More than 10 million people migrated to the United States in the past 20 years, fully one-fourth of the gain in overall U.S. population during that time period (Abe-Kim & Takeuchi, 1996). In the 1980s alone, 8 million immigrants arrived in the United States. The only previous decade in which a greater migration took place was in the first decade of the 20th century, when 8.8 million immigrants arrived (Gelfand & Yee, 1991). A major difference is that the earlier group was almost exclusively European, while the more recent immigrants arrive from all parts of the world (Asia, Africa, Latin America, the Middle East, and so on).

behavior that stem from the counselors' particular cultural backgrounds (Giordano & Carini-Giordano, 1995).

The danger here is of *cultural dissonance*. Unless prepared and informed about the family's cultural history, the counselor might misdiagnose or mislabel an unfamiliar family pattern as abnormal, when that behavior may be appropriate to the family's ethnic group heritage. Or perhaps the misguided counselor might undertake unsuitable intervention measures because of a failure to appreciate that a behavior pattern or family interactive sequence, alien to the counselor's background and in his or her judgment in need of change, might simply reflect the normal range of values, attitudes, and expressive styles that are congruent with the family's cultural forebears.

This final chapter is intended to help the reader become more culturally literate and culturally competent, more aware of the cultural histories of client families before undertaking assessment or intervention procedures. Although no single counselor can reasonably be expected to be aware of the cultural nuances of the wide variety of ethnic groups living in North America today, our aim here is to help sensitize the counselor to the need for gaining greater understanding before initiating counseling with families from unfamiliar cultures. The counselor's task is often a precarious one. Blindly adopting an ethnically focused position, the counselor may display a sensitivity to cultural differences but run the risk of stereotyping by assuming that a cultural group is homogeneous, therefore responding to a particular family as if it were a cultural prototype. As Falicov (1995b) observes, in ethnically diverse groups, a variety of other factors—educational level, social class, religion, stage of acculturation into American society, to name but a few—also influence family behavior patterns. Moreover, family members differ in their degree of acculturation as well as their adherence to cultural values (Sue, 1994). The counselor needs to evaluate the effects of all these factors on client family functioning. No counselor can become an expert in all ethnic groups, but all can learn to adopt an attitude of openness to cultural variability. Adopting such a *multicultural outlook,* the special task for today's counselor is to remain alert to the cultural context in which behavior takes place, as well as to cultural norms, lest patterns acceptable in one culture be pathologized by a counselor who uses an inappropriate yardstick in measuring such behavior (McGoldrick, 1998).

The notion made popular around the turn of the past century, when many European groups flocked to the United States, was that America is a melting pot, in which immigrants from different places of origin mingle and blend into one. In this view, a new and unique American culture continually emerges as each new immigrant group affects the existing culture. However, growing awareness in the 1960s and 1970s of the lack of effective civil rights for some minorities led to the recognition that the melting pot principle had bypassed certain groups, such as African Americans, who had only a minimal impact on a changing America. Furthermore, new immigrant groups, expected to culturally assimilate, were under pressure to relinquish their traditional ethnic values in order to adopt those of the dominant culture, which many found unacceptable.

Together, these realizations led to the view of *cultural pluralism:* that members of diverse ethnic and racial groups retain their cultural identities while sharing common elements with the dominant American culture (Axelson, 1999). Ideally, each group preserves its cultural and historical heritage while afforded equal opportunity in American economic, political, and educational spheres. Rather than a melting pot, Atkinson, Morten, and Sue (1989) use a cultural pluralism viewpoint to liken the United States to a cultural stew, in which "various ingredients are mixed together, but rather than melting into a single mass, the components remain intact and distinguishable while contributing to a whole that is richer than its parts alone" (p. 7).

Cultural pluralism and cultural diversity add vitality and need not lead to irreconcilable divisions between various segments of our society, although differences between groups may lead to misunderstanding and conflict. The rapid assimilation of immigrant groups into the majority culture, accompanied by the elimination of differences among such groups and between them and the majority culture, poses the risk of causing the breakdown of subculture identities and the abandonment of ethnic heritages. In turn, the loss of these cultural attributes results in severe strain on family structures and increased vulnerability to future family dysfunction. Retaining aspects of their separate cultural identities, subgroups can adapt to (and, in the process, help change) American society without the loss or destruction of subcultural norms. The degree and quality of that adaptation or acculturation are likely to be a function of how long ago newcomers arrived, the circumstances of their arrival, the support system they found upon arrival, and the degree of acceptance or prejudice and discrimination they found here.

Family counselors must be culturally sensitive to the values and traditions of their ever-increasing diverse set of clients if they are to deal with such clients in an effective manner (Aponte & Wohl, 2000). They must develop a respectful attitude toward the family's ethnic identity and take great care before using norms that stem from the majority cultural matrix in assessing the attitudes, beliefs, and behavior patterns of those whose cultural backgrounds differ from theirs. Lau (1986) presents a provocative example of the relevance of cultural values to family relationships by describing a stone tableau in a public park in Singapore:

Haw Par Villa was built by a rich Chinese philanthropist who felt that the people needed a public park in which moral parables could be portrayed in stone. One such stone tableau illustrated the cardinal virtue of filial piety. At a time of famine in China, a young woman is confronted with a moral dilemma: does she offer her breast milk to her old mother, who is starving, or does she save her remaining child, given her other child is already dead on the ground? Despite her maternal instincts, she turns away from her crying baby and offers her breast to her mother. Thus, for traditional Chinese, the prescriptive rule is one of unquestionable filial piety, where responsibility to one's parent is paramount and transcends responsibilities to spouse and children. (pp. 234–235)

Most Western readers are likely to be uncomfortable with the young mother's choice, thus reinforcing the point that we are all bound by the cultural patternings of our reference group; we are not free agents, but rather, no less than the young woman in the parable, we are ourselves culturally constrained persons. Lau (1986) reminds us that a counselor may not possess the same world view as his or her clients and thus may be unaware of the cultural norms for those persons: what belief systems are sanctioned by the group of which the client is a part, what is idiosyncratic, and what indicates individual or family dysfunction. Adding to the dilemma of working with families of unfamiliar background, the counselor may not understand what norms govern appropriate sex-role or family-role behavior, what interactive communication styles are appropriate for the culture, the family's degree of acculturation, its English fluency, what cultural traditions are still practiced at home, its familiarity and comfort with the American mainstream lifestyle, or in general how that culture organizes the family's experience of itself, which may differ from the counselor's cultural perspective or life experiences.

In order to provide the counselor with some guidelines regarding the cultural relativity of family life, we have attempted in this chapter to outline the lifestyles and common family patterns of three sets of minority families: African Americans, Hispanic Americans, and Asian/Pacific Americans. Our descriptions are hardly exhaustive, but rather are intended to alert the family counselor to be attentive to cultural differences and to seek consultation or do further research when cultural issues are present. At the same time, we wish to note that many significant ethnic groups are not included here, but need to be approached by the counselor with the same diligence and open-mindedness regarding cultural patterns. McGoldrick, Giordano, and Pearce (1996) have assembled an indispensable resource describing more than 40 groups of hyphenated Americans, originating from all points of the world, demonstrating the ongoing effect of ethnic, racial, and religious influences on family patterns long after the immigrant generation arrived in this country. Of particular value to counselors is their attention to each group's likelihood of engaging in help-seeking behavior, including expectations from counseling.

Adopting the outlook of cultural diversity allows the counselor to expand from an exclusive focus on the transactions within the family to a broader approach that also pays attention to the larger sociocultural contexts that influence family behavior. That broader context should include a consideration of the impact of socioeconomic and political factors (poverty, discrimination, racism, other oppressions) on the lives of many ethnic minorities (Sue, 1994). Counselors make more global interventions when they see families as embedded within the context of larger human service systems (welfare, educational, legal, health, probation) in which many poor, minority "multiproblem" families are often caught up. Imber-Black (1990) urges the counselor planning to work with such families to adopt a macrosystemic perspective, attending not just to who the key actors are in the family, but also to what larger systems interact with the family and what labels, stigmas, and ethnic myths such systems may adopt or impose when working with these families. Inevitably, part of the counselor's job is in teaching ethnic families empowerment strategies, supporting and encouraging them to become their own advocates by mobilizing their ability to deal effectively with mainstream culture (Diller, 1999).

All families are the same, and all families are different. To make effective inter-ventions with families, counselors must try to distinguish among family behaviors that are *universal, transcultural, culture-specific,* or *idiosyncratic.* In other words, counselors need to discriminate among those family situations where basic issues reflect human processes that are similar whatever the ethnic or cultural back-ground, those situations where specific cultural issues are clinically pertinent to family functioning, and those where cultural issues are tangential (Falicov, 1988). To be effective, as Ramirez (1991) contends, counselors need to remain especially sensitive to cultural as well as individual diversity when working with ethnic minority clients, encouraging the development of diverse coping skills as needed. Moreover, as McGoldrick, Garcia Preto, Hines, and Lee (1991) point out, family counselors who appreciate the cultural relativity of family life (including how families identify, define, and attempt to solve problems, as well as seek help) are likely to adopt a broader perspective and thus improve their chances to intervene successfully with families. At the same time, counselors must never lose sight of how their own ethnic identity and subsequent cultural values and assumptions influence the helping process.

Migration, especially from Mexico, Central and South America, and the Asian/Pacific area, accounts in large part for the rapid population changes we are experiencing. Sluzki (1979) points out that migration may involve many families together from a particular country, region, or culture, or perhaps be an isolated experience for a single family. Some families may choose to migrate by their own decision or be forced by the decisions of others or by natural cataclysms; they may leave with truckloads of household items or in many cases no more than a bundle of essentials. They range from those families who arrive by jet airplane seeking better professional opportunities to those who sneak under barbed-wire borders at night to escape oppression. Some look forward with hope; others look backward in fear. Some are thoroughly familiar with, and others completely ignorant of, the situation on arrival in the new land: its language and customs, where they will live, what work will be available. Migration may represent the last hope of asylum for a religious or political refugee, or the doomed move from poverty in the home country to poverty in the new land. Diversity, then, exists both across and within ethnic groups. Whatever the reasons for migration, however, the process is inevitably disruptive for the family; before adaptation is complete, the family must go through several stages that are bound to influence its outlook and test its cop-ing skills. In some cases, that adaptation may take several generations.

Ethnicity, comprising the unique characteristics of an ethnic group, is a funda-mental determinant of how families establish and reinforce acceptable rules, ritu-als, values, attitudes, behavior patterns, and modes of emotional expression; as such, it plays a major role in shaping both individual and family identity (Alba, 1990). Beyond race, religion, and national or geographic origins, important as these are, ethnicity refers to a group's "peoplehood" and provides a sense of com-monality transmitted by the family over generations and reinforced by the sur-rounding community. Ethnicity affords a historical continuity and as such plays a decisive role in shaping our individual and family identities. A powerful force, retained and conveyed over generations, our ethnic background influences how we think, how we feel, how we work, how we relax, how we celebrate holidays and rituals, how we express our anxieties, and how we feel about illness or life and death. The sense of ethnicity unites those who think of themselves as alike by virtue of common ancestry, real or fictitious, and who are so regarded by others in the society in which they live (McGoldrick, Garcia Preto, Hines, & Lee, 1991).

Ethnic origins, whether acknowledged or not, typically play a significant role in family life throughout the life cycle, although their impact may vary greatly among groups as well as within a group itself. In some families who hold onto traditional ways, clinging to cohorts from their religious or cultural background, ethnic values and identifications may be particularly strong and are likely retained for generations. In such cases, as McGoldrick (1982) suggests, second-, third-, and even fourth-generation Americans often differ from the dominant culture in values, lifestyle patterns, identifications, and behavior. In the case of groups who have experienced serious prejudice and discrimination, insularity may be especially pronounced. These groups may remain in ethnic neighborhoods and work and mingle socially almost entirely with others of similar background, fearful and often suspicious of the dominant culture. (Many families remain in ethnic neighborhoods, of course, simply because economics and racial barriers thwart their efforts at upward mobility.) Other families may attempt to deny or reject ethnic values and past identifications, eager to become a part of the dominant American value system, particularly as they move up in social class and into heterogeneous neighborhoods.

Clearly, just as an individual cannot be fully understood when viewed in isolation from his or her family context, so a comprehensive picture of a family requires a consideration of the cultural system of which the family is a part, its shared history and traditions. Rather than reinforce racial or ethnic stereotypes, we hope to alert counselors to the effect of cultural patterns on family lifestyle that they might otherwise fail to recognize or, worse, label as deviant or dysfunctional. For example, in working with African American clients over two decades ago, Thomas and Sillen (1974) commented that for white clinicians to be insistently "color blind" to racial differences is no virtue if it means denial of differences in experiences, history, and social existence between themselves and African American client families. This myth of sameness in effect denies the importance of color to the African American clients and closes off an opportunity for counselor and clients to deal with sensitive race-related issues. Although differences in skin color between counselor and client may be an uneasy topic to bring up, it would be folly to gloss over the subject, since how the client discloses information, how the client trusts the counselor, and how their relationship unfolds are likely to be influenced by such differences. As Williams (1996) observes, distinct differences may lead the client to be overcompliant, perhaps feeling a power differential, or ambivalent, struggling with internalized feelings of envy and oppression. Counselors in cross-racial situations, whether white or persons of color, may struggle with similar issues, refusing to deal with anything that calls attention to differences of color.

For most counselors, working with ethnic minority families represents a cross-cultural experience. As Ho (1987) points out, such clients are more likely than not to be relatively powerless, politically and economically; to receive unequal treatment in society; and to regard themselves as objects of discrimination. He argues that to treat their family problems using generalized white-middle-class American family standards is to be ethnically insensitive to their unique existence; that insensitivity may partially explain the frequent ineffectiveness of such services and their underuse by ethnic minority families. As Sue and Sue (1999) observe, half of all minority clients fail to return to counseling after only one visit. They contend that these dropouts are likely to have viewed the counseling as antagonistic and inappropriate to their life experiences, and as having been oppressive and discriminatory toward their minority group status.[2]

Discrimination in this context means more than refusing services to those who are ethnically different. The following also qualify as discrimination (Diller, 1999):

- Being unaware of one's own prejudices and how they are inadvertently communicated to clients
- Being unaware of differences in cultural style, interactive patterns, and values, leading to miscommunication
- Being unaware that many of the theories taught during training are culture-bound
- Being unaware of differences in cultural definitions of health and illness as well as the existence of traditional cultural healing methods
- Being unaware of the necessity of matching counseling modalities to the cultural style of clients or of adapting practices to the specific needs of clients

Counseling African American Families

African Americans, who make up approximately 12% of the population of the United States, together share a common heritage, but they are by no means a homogeneous group. The vast majority were involuntarily transported to the American continent as slaves as far back as the 1500s; Axelson (1999) estimates that by 1885, fully 10 million slaves were brought to the Americas from West African countries. Others (perhaps 1% of the total black population) migrated (as nonslaves) beginning in the early 1900s from the West Indies (for example, Haiti and Jamaica) and elsewhere, and represent different subcultural black groups.

---

[2] All three groups considered in this chapter tend to underuse mental health services (Cheung & Snowden, 1990). Poor African Americans have been historically wary of seeking out these services, frequently fearing that they will be stigmatized as crazy or perhaps that they will require hospitalization (Poussaint, 1990). Poor Hispanic and Asian/Pacific Americans often find that geographic isolation, language barriers, and perceived class differences between themselves and white counselors discourage access to mental health services (Homma-True, Greene, Lopez, & Trimble, 1993). Beyond the resistance of many members of these groups to counseling, Ridley (1995) notes the unintentional racism on the part of some counselors (and in some treatment centers) that may interfere with providing opportunities for needed counseling.

Despite some commonality, it is essential for the counselor to recognize that the various subgroups are characterized by different spiritual or religious backgrounds, socioeconomic status, educational level, skin color, family structure, and levels of acculturation, to say nothing of diverse sets of values and lifestyles (Boyd-Franklin, 1995). Regardless of specific differences between groups, however, *color* remains the predominant and distinguishing fact of life for all members of the black community. The counselor undertaking work with families of color must also take into account the social, economic, and political realities of living with racism in many aspects of this society. Understanding the realities that they face, and the culture developed in response to those conditions, is essential if the counselor hopes to help families cope with these realities. Shipler (1997), as well as Thernstrom and Thernstrom (1997), have offered informative discourses on racial stereotyping in black-white interactions.

The African American family must be understood as a social system in ongoing interaction with other systems; its family structure represents an adaptation to a unique set of historical, social, and political conditions that are an everyday part of African American life. They are represented among upper-, middle-, and lower-class families, with urban and rural backgrounds (overwhelmingly in metropolitan areas), in various parts of the United States (after a huge migration during the 1940s from the South to the North, the Midwest, and the West Coast). While an increasingly large number have been assimilated into middle-class society, at least one-fourth of black families continue to live below the poverty line (Thernstrom & Thernstrom, 1997). Acknowledging the stability of a black middle class able to attain an education and achieve socioeconomic mobility, Axelson (1999) also describes two other classes: *poor blacks* (working people with stable family structures and the potential for gaining an education and achieving greater mobility) and a *black underclass* (unstable families, weak or no job skills, many representing the third generation on welfare). He contends that this latter group has few role models or expectations of climbing out of poverty.

Powerlessness and the African American Experience

Despite the hardships and discrimination they have been exposed to and the condition of powerlessness that greeted their ancestors upon arrival in the United States as slaves, African American families have developed an amazing ability to survive. However, a sense of economic, social, and political powerlessness still characterizes much of their existence. Pinderhughes (1990) suggests that this sense of powerlessness is magnified by the vicious circle in which many African Americans find themselves: Denial of access to resources reduces the opportunity to develop self-esteem and function adequately in the family role; the consequent poverty and strain on family role cause problems in individual growth and development; problems in individual functioning further stress the community system, which is the expected source of support for individuals and families. The community that is under stress already has fewer resources (jobs, schools, housing), leading to increased disorganization and creating the conditions for crime and other

forms of social pathology. The ironic point here, as Pinderhughes (1990) emphasizes, is that the political, economic, and social forces to which the community
might expect to look for help are the same forces that cause the powerlessness.

Part of the social reality confronted by African American families is that, overall, a significant discrepancy between African American and white median family
income continues to exist. African Americans are overrepresented in low-paying
service jobs and underrepresented among professionals. As McAdoo (1988)
observes, African American families have historically been more vulnerable to
external economic conditions and have been affected by economic downturns
earlier than other groups ("last hired, first fired"). She believes improved circumstances for African Americans peaked and then deteriorated during the 1980s,
leading to a decline in their college enrollment, especially among males, and a
steady erosion in the proportion of African Americans employed by the traditional
professions. McAdoo (1988) suggests that the upwardly mobile patterns that have
occurred in African American families would have been impossible in many cases
without the help provided by their extended families. We'll return to the significant role of the extended family and kinship network in African American family
life later in this chapter.

Overall, although there is great diversity in economic level—African American
families may range from the inner-city single mother on public assistance to the
suburban dual-career professional couple—salaries typically lag behind whites',
even for the same work; their unemployment rates are the highest of any
American group. As Boyd-Franklin (1989) concludes, the reality of being African
American and underclass is doing without; coping with endless cycles of unemployment, with substandard housing and inadequate community services, and
with underfinanced inner-city schools from which the dropout rate is high; and living in fear of street crime and young family members' exposure to neighborhood
"crack houses." Often, domestic violence and child abuse erupt as despairing families struggle to survive. While the prevalence of domestic violence cuts across all
races and social classes, its rates are greatest among those, regardless of race, who
are poor, unemployed, and hold low-prestige jobs (Feldman & Ridley, 1995).

Racism, Discrimination, and the Victim System

No discussion of African American culture can overlook the effect of racism and
discrimination on overall functioning and identity formation. As Boyd-Franklin
(1989) points out, racism can be insidious, pervasive, and constant, having an
impact on the lives of all African Americans regardless of social class or attained
position. Racism is sometimes experienced externally as discrimination and sometimes internally as a sense of shame. Poor urban parents who attempt to motivate
their children to achieve, when evidence of discrimination and hopelessness is all
around them, are engaging in a struggle that often ends in defeat, as the children
lose hope and succumb to drugs, truancy, or other forms of destructive, antisocial
behavior. The more affluent, living in predominantly white suburbs, may experience forms of racism that are subtle (social isolation) or, in extreme cases, overt

(front-lawn cross burning). Regardless of where or how the discrimination occurs, the blow to self-esteem is real and powerful, and one of the counselor's tasks may be to help clients develop a positive racial and cultural identification ("black pride") and to gain a sense of empowerment in order to achieve some reasonable control over their own destinies.

Pinderhughes (1982) refers to the circular feedback process described earlier, which threatens self-esteem and reinforces problematic responses in communities, families, and individuals, as a **victim system.** She contends that victimization has exerted a pervasive effect on African American families throughout history, preventing the establishment of a unified culture and its integration with that of the American mainstream. In effect, she maintains, African American ethnic identity is likely to be influenced by three cultural sources: residuals from Africa, identification with mainstream America, and adaptation and responses to the victim system that results from poverty, racism, and oppression. African residual values stress collectivity, sharing, affiliation, belief in spirituality, and obedience to authority. Mainstream American values emphasize individualism, autonomy, planning, efficiency, and achievement. Victim-system values represent responses to oppression and characteristically stress cooperation to combat powerlessness, strict obedience to powerful authority, a toughness of character, the suppression of feelings, and a belief in luck, magic, and spirituality. Values and beliefs from all three systems are found in various combinations in African American families.

According to Pinderhughes (1982), the victim system of racism and oppression is akin to a societal projection process, in which victims are blamed and poor African American families are viewed as lazy and thus as having brought about their own poverty and other misfortunes. Similarly, many who are achieving are also made to feel inferior: It is suggested that their middle-class professional status was attained as a result of affirmative-action concessions rather than ability or hard work. Boyd-Franklin (1989) argues that whereas most ethnic groups experience some form of discrimination, particularly among first-generation immigrants, African Americans have had to endure this experience for 400 years.[3]

To break out of the victim system, to gain a sense of self-determination, to overcome despair—these can all be viewed as efforts to gain a sense of power and status. The counselor must look for ways to help African American individuals and families identify what they need in order to cope with their realities and then clarify the kind of functioning required to achieve those goals (Pinderhughes, 1990). *Empowerment* is a key theme here—mobilizing the strengths and the strong individuals in the family and extended family to work together to solve their problems

---

[3] A more optimistic, if controversial, view of the impact of white racism on people of color is offered by social scientists Thernstrom and Thernstrom (1997). While acknowledging that much remains to be done, they contend that life has improved considerably for most blacks since the civil rights movement. Rejecting the notion that blacks and whites live in separate and unequal worlds, they maintain that serious inequalities in opportunity remain but attribute the existing inequality between races less to white racism than to the continuing racial gap in levels of educational attainment, the structure of the black family, and the rise in black street crime.

(Boyd-Franklin, 1995). The danger is that the counselor may become over-whelmed by the magnitude of the task, begin to despair about reaching the goals, and finally succumb to his or her own sense of powerlessness. As a consequence, he or she may also give up hope and withdraw.

Family Structure and Kinship Networks

The family has always held a central place in the African American community despite efforts to obliterate African family heritage during slavery; nevertheless, such efforts did serve to loosen family boundaries, as family members were sepa-rated by slave sales and new slaves were thrust into existing family structures. Extended families and the role of "significant others" in African American families (Manns, 1988) have always been important, as individuals look to one another for help and support; this pattern has no doubt been intensified by the difficulty that African Americans experience in receiving validation from the larger society (McGoldrick, Garcia Preto, Hines, & Lee, 1991).

Extended families are commonly composed of relatives who have a variety of blood ties but are nevertheless absorbed into a coherent network of mutual sup-port—economically, emotionally, socially, and interpersonally. In such a loose arrangement, roles and boundaries among members of the kinship network are not rigidly defined, allowing for considerable role flexibility (and occasional boundary confusion). This fluid interchanging of roles within the African American nuclear-family structure, arising initially from the economic imperatives of an underclass life, often means that older children care for younger siblings and that fathers and mothers exchange roles, jobs, and family functions (caring for eco-nomic, expressive, emotional, or nurturant needs) depending on availability.

Beyond actual relatives (uncles, aunts, siblings, grandparents, cousins, even in-laws), other nonblood "relatives" (or fictive kin) may also be intimately involved in family matters. Often referred to as "play brothers and sisters" (Diller, 1999), they are likely to include neighbors, godparents, preachers, teachers, work col-leagues, baby-sitters, family friends, boarders, and sweethearts. Because of eco-nomic necessity, extended families, especially in low-income areas, may spill over into neighboring apartments; different family members may reside in different households, or two or more families (or parts of families) may live in one house-hold for periods of time. Whatever the arrangement, according to Boyd-Franklin (1989), extended families, regardless of social class, provide reciprocity—helping one another and sharing support along with goods and services. (This diffuse boundary arrangement may, of course, also lead to a lack of privacy, role confu-sion, jealousies, competitiveness, and perhaps a struggle for limited resources, thus leading to subsequent family conflict.) In the process, extended-family mem-bers may provide role models, offer nurturing and supplemental parenting, encourage achievement by the children, and together participate in rearing the African American child. Thus, counselors must be willing to expand their defini-tion of what constitutes a family and be flexible about whom to include in family counseling sessions. As Boyd-Franklin (1995) observes, counselors may insist on working with the "wrong" family or perhaps a small subsystem (such as a single mother and her children), overlooking powerful family members (biologically related or not); Boyd-Franklin contends that these members, if not involved, can undermine or sabotage the counseling process. Thus, family counselors need to remain open to bringing in other members as their presence is revealed by a cautious client.

Since three-generation African American households are commonplace (Hines & Boyd-Franklin, 1982), the culturally sensitive counselor would be wise to assume that one or more family members may have grown up in such a household, perhaps having been reared by a grandmother while one or both parents were away at work or school. The counselor should refrain from necessarily assuming that such an arrangement indicates a rejection of a child by a parent or that the child perceives it as such, since the practice represents a cultural norm. Furthermore, the counselor needs to explore some of the possible benefits of such practices. Similarly, a child may be cared for temporarily by a relative while a parent seeks employment, perhaps in another city. Again, the counselor should evaluate the circumstances and not automatically assume that rejection or neglect is involved.

Since living arrangements are flexible and changeable, depending on circumstances (loss of a job, temporary breakup of a relationship, a teenage pregnancy, someone down on his or her luck), it is useful for the counselor to view the resources commonly available in African American family life as typically involving permeable boundaries that are responsive to troubling situations and emergency circumstances. Elderly family members such as grandparents may be taken in, partly in recognition of the role that grandparents often play in parenting African American children. Family elders may be supported by the collective efforts of members both within and outside the nuclear family (Hines & Boyd-Franklin, 1982). Counselors often find it easier to get a comprehensive view of relationships between family participants by using a genogram to map out patterns over generations.

Informal adoption (Hill, 1977), practiced since slavery days, involves adult relatives or family friends caring for children whose parents, for a variety of circumstances, cannot do so themselves. Informal adoption may take the form of long-term foster care, day care for working parents, services for children born out of wedlock, or simply help for a friend or family member during a transitional period such as a new marriage or perhaps a period of loss or other crisis. Essentially, the informal adoption process functions as an unofficial social service network for African American families. For example, following divorce, children may be divided up among extended-family members for a brief period of time until the custodial parent, most likely the mother, gets back on her feet and is able to resume custody herself. A similar scenario may occur when a young parent is seriously ill or requires hospitalization. If a parent dies, a relative may be asked to keep and raise one or more of the children for an indefinite period of time.

For the most part, there are few problems over informal adoptions. Occasionally, disputes may arise over the duration of adoption, if the adoptive family believes the child will be theirs permanently but the biological parent chooses, after a lengthy period of time, to reclaim the child; serious allegiance problems may need to be resolved at this point. Note that the length of an informal adoption arrangement may not be predetermined, so in many cases it may end up as permanent if long-term emotional ties are established.

In the following case, an unmarried African American teenager becomes depressed and can no longer care for her children, provoking a family crisis and decisions about informal adoption.

Wynona, 16, was the only child in an intact low-income family in which the father, Andre, worked at an automobile assembly line and the mother, Bernice, helped out in a local cafe as a part-time cashier. Doing reasonably well in her studies, Wynona was nevertheless socially shy and tended to be with girlfriends rather than go out with boys. Although many of her girlfriends talked about having had sexual experiences with boys, Wynona was hesitant and scared until she met George, with whom she fell in love. When he pressed her for sexual intercourse, she acquiesced and, having little concern for birth control measures, soon found herself pregnant.

Although her parents were upset, Wynona's mother agreed to care for the child, Jamal, so that her daughter could finish high school. Unfortunately, Andre was laid off from work, finances became tight, Bernice took a full-time job, and Wynona was forced to drop out of school and care for Jamal on her own. Living with her parents, she did manage his care but soon felt lonely and isolated from her high school friends. Money, too, was a problem; what money she did receive from public assistance programs she paid to her parents to help out during their hard times. When she met Ellis, a 23-year-old, at the supermarket one day, she was attracted to him, and soon they began what Wynona hoped would be a long relationship. Because Ellis resisted the idea of using any kind of contraception, she became pregnant for the second time. Ellis, unemployed, decided to join the Army before Althea, their daughter, was born. He offered no financial support beyond the vague promise that he would send her money when he could—a promise, it turned out, that he never kept.

Now with the full responsibility of caring for two children by herself, Wynona became depressed. Her father, home without work and himself depressed and drinking, and her mother, tired and angry at all the responsibilities that awaited her at home after a hard day's work, added to the overall gloom in the house. Feeling isolated and seeing her young life slip by with nothing to look forward to, Wynona began neglecting her two children. Despite the scolding from her mother, Wynona found herself less and less able to function, some days forgetting to eat or comb her hair.

Uncertain about what to do to help, Wynona's parents took her to a local community mental health clinic, where she was seen for counseling by an African American female social worker. After several sessions, the counselor decided on a three-pronged set of interventions—getting Wynona evaluated for antidepressant medication, helping empower her to develop a stronger sense of herself as an individual, and enlisting her family to provide whatever support they could muster. As the counselor explored the possibility of help from the grandparents, Wynona mentioned that she had remained friendly with Harriette, George's mother and Jamal's grandmother.

Although 60 years of age, Harriette agreed to care for both Jamal and Althea while Wynona returned to finish high school. Under the arrangement, the children stayed with Harriette during weekdays but were taken home on weekends by Wynona.

Harriette's child-care role was not without its problems. She was not in good health, it had been a long time since she had cared for young children, and her child-rearing attitudes were stricter than Wynona thought desirable. However, the counselor was able to arrange for Harriette and her second husband to get some parent training, which they enjoyed and looked forward to each week. They especially needed help with Jamal, who was showing signs of hyperactivity and an attention deficit disorder; the grandparents initially took this to mean he was a bad child, but became aware through the classes that it reflected his psychological problems.

A multiproblem family, they needed extensive, coordinated social services, including weekly family counseling sessions attended by Wynona, her parents, Harriette and her husband, William, and occasionally the children. During family sessions, the counselor attempted to help them construct the best family arrangement possible, offering them a great deal of support as they struggled to work together as a unit. George, Jamal's father, had become a heavy drug user, and although he saw his son from time to time and was not disruptive, Wynona believed she could not depend on him for help, which he did not offer. She lost contact with Ellis, who remained in the Army but never contacted Wynona or his daughter, Althea. On her own, Wynona, with the counselor's help, was encouraged to develop a social group of which she could feel a part and to return to school for training that would help her develop a stronger sense of competence. When last seen by the counselor, she had started in an office computer training class, was working part time, had begun dating again, and was preparing for her children to move back home with her.

Socialization Experiences and Male-Female Relationships

The social rift between African American males and females begins early, according to Chapman (1988), as females are encouraged to seek scholastic achievement while their male counterparts are often discouraged from attaining such a goal. Young males, for a variety of reasons, frequently drop out of school before developing competitive job skills; this furthers their distance from females in the economic strata. Frustrated by lack of opportunity and without the skills needed to transcend their circumstances, many young men during adolescence drop out of school and drift into drugs, homicide, and, ultimately, incarceration (Boyd-Franklin & Franklin, 2000). Over a decade ago, Chapman (1988) estimated that 40% of the African American male population is functionally illiterate; that figure may be slightly less today. As a consequence, African American females have had greater access to economic opportunities in our society and in times of high unemployment have worked outside the home, often as the sole wage earner (Ho, 1987). The shift in recent years from an industrial to a high-tech economy has pushed ever larger numbers of unskilled African American males into unemployment.

Male-female relationships are thus often shaped by economic factors, and because of limited job options and the dismal odds of fulfilling the functions our society expects of adult men, the roles of African American males as husbands and fathers are further undermined (McGoldrick, Garcia Preto, Hines, & Lee, 1991). Since jobs have been more available to women, particularly during times of high employment, an African American family's economic survival very often depends primarily (if not solely) on the female head of household, thus accounting in part for the large number of female-headed households, married or unmarried. Some men, unable to provide for their families, may leave their homes in order to ensure that their family members will receive government assistance. However, the counselor should not assume that all contact between father and children or between marital partners has ceased, despite appearances.

African American men, particularly in urban, inner-city settings, are socialized to play a "macho" role—in Boyd-Franklin's (1989) words, to "act bad even if you're scared." That is, they learn to survive by never showing weakness, often using the sexual area to show their prowess and strength. Women, on the other hand, grow up observing and emulating the women in the family, who are often strong, competent, and self-reliant, learning to further their own education, get a job, and prepare to provide for themselves. Growing up in female-led families, with fathers frequently absent, African American females have likely seen their mothers rearing children, working outside the home, attending church, and engaging in transitory, if any, relationships with men—all of which reinforces the myths that "black men are no good" and "they won't be there for you when you need them" (Boyd-Franklin, 1989). It is hardly any wonder that many African American men and women grow up perpetuating powerful and controlling myths—that African American men are shiftless and lazy and can't be counted on for support, that African American women are domineering, hostile, and controlling (Chapman, 1988). As a result, male-female struggles are common, divorce rates are high, and the chasm between men and women is often great.

Adding to the imbalance, African American men are often viewed by African American women as powerless, economically and politically; this view may lead to estrangement or may be acted out angrily in their intimate relations. The high mortality rate among men—many are incarcerated, are substance abusers, delay seeking health care, are in the military, or die as a result of homicide—means that fewer are available for marriage or stable long-term relationships. Chapman (1988) described a mate-sharing arrangement in which two or more women share a man, with or without knowledge of one another. According to Staples (1985), African American women from both poor and middle-class backgrounds may opt for children without benefit of marriage, more because of the shortage of marriageable males than because of any devaluation of the institution of marriage.

Clients, whether African American or white, grow up in different households: some in traditional two-parent families and others in divorced, widowed, or never-married ones; some in poor, working-class families and others in middle-class surroundings; some with strong fathers who are good providers and good role models and others with no fathers or a series of father substitutes; some in abusive homes and others in more loving and egalitarian surroundings. It is imperative that the counselor explore the family histories of both partners to better understand their choices, expectations, and senses of entitlement from male-female relationships. In the case of African American clients, Hines and Boyd-Franklin (1982) caution that the counselor should proceed slowly, since many families are suspicious of white counselors, whom they view as prying, and are likely to be reluctant to discuss openly such family secrets as out-of-wedlock births, the couple's unmarried status, or the true paternity of the children. Here again the counselor must take care not to impose on African American couples a set of gender-role expectations based on a white, middle-class orientation (Boyd-Franklin, 1995).

Special Aspects of African American Family Life

Many African Americans grow up regularly attending church, most frequently Baptist or African Methodist, and the church plays a central role, sometimes nightly, in their family and community life. A wide variety of activities—trips, dinners, church socials, choir participation, Sunday school classes—take place in connection with the church, which serves as an available support system for its congregants, especially during troubled times. Hines and Boyd-Franklin (1982) contend that the church is frequently the most important institution in this community, providing an outlet for leadership and creative talents, and a forum for their expression. As examples, they cite a father who might be a porter during the week but takes on the responsible role of deacon or trustee in his church, or a mother or grandmother, overwhelmed by family responsibilities during the week but who finds her outlet in a church choir singing on Sunday. Particularly for the nonreligious counselor, an understanding of the role that religion and spirituality play in the lives of disenfranchised African American clients—providing respect for their abilities or mere escape from daily painful experiences—is essential.

Beyond providing a social network and an opportunity to be somebody significant, the church offers hope (frequently in short supply among these families) and a belief that adversity can be overcome. The numerous functions provided by the African American church may offer a refuge in a hostile white world. Indeed, the church is often the epicenter of African American life, socially, politically, culturally, educationally, and interpersonally. Much like the extended family, the church offers help, counsel, child care, food, role models, and schooling, to say nothing of the emotional outlet evoked by provocative preachers. Although many African Americans proclaim that "black is beautiful," they may nevertheless harbor many negative and self-deprecating feelings and attitudes about their racial identity (Acosta, Yamamoto, & Evans, 1982). Nowhere is this more evident than in mind-sets toward skin color, a remnant of slavery days, when "mulatto" or light-skinned children of white masters and African female slaves were given greater privileges than their darker-skinned counterparts. Thus, class distinctions within the African American community began in slavery, when lighter skin meant special treatment in the plantation system—living in the master's house (house slaves) and receiving some education, benefits not accorded field slaves. Grier and Cobbs (1968) suggest that the mark of slavery has never fully disappeared from the consciousness of African American people, despite the end of slavery, and a class system based on skin color persists in many communities. In this sense, African Americans collude with the dominant white culture in rejecting dark-skinned people.

Bass (1982) contends that such differential treatment historically led to discrimination and intraracial conflict based on skin color alone, and that skin color, along with hair texture, became a preoccupation among many African Americans, who tried to become as much like white people as possible. She argues that in the case of hairstyle, wearing a "natural" or African style, beginning with the black pride movement of the late 1960s, represents an attempt at liberation from the notion that only straight hair is attractive. Skin color, on the other hand, has remained a factor leading to discrimination: It is usually easier for a light-skinned person to get a job or education than an equally qualified dark-skinned African American. Although the exact number is unclear, some light-skinned members in each generation have denied their blackness and passed for white.

Boyd-Franklin (1989) observes that because skin color is such a toxic issue in our society, the darkest or perhaps lightest child in a family may be singled out as different and thus scapegoated at an early age with constant reminders about the color of his or her skin. In her experience, in some families dark-skinned people are preferred, and light skin color is viewed negatively, as a constant reminder of abuse of African American women by white men. In either case, being different from others in the family can lead to feelings of self-hatred, rejection, and ostracism.

Box 11.1 lists issues commonly faced by African American clients and of which the counselor should be aware.

Some Counseling Guidelines

Counseling as typically practiced by majority-culture (white) counselors has not usually been a source of help or comfort to African American families in times of crisis, and so it is not surprising that they typically look elsewhere: first to family

---

Box 11.1 A problem-appraisal checklist for African American families

African American families may experience problems in the following areas:

- Effects of poverty (poor housing, health care, unemployment, etc.)
- Lack of kinship and community support
- Skin-color–related problems
- Religion and spirituality issues
- Suspicion of institutions
- Feelings of powerlessness
- Problems with self-esteem
- Feelings of hopelessness and rage

and kinship network members, then to ministers and other respected "church family" members—elders, deacons, deaconesses, and on occasion close, trusted friends (Franklin & Boyd-Franklin, 1990). Grier and Cobbs (1968) describe a legacy of suspicion and mistrust of many of society's institutions among this population; this legacy, developed over generations, is more self-protective than pathological and is manifested as a "healthy cultural paranoia" about efforts by white professionals (and African American professionals in "white institutions") to engage them in counseling. As indicated earlier, the counselor must proceed carefully and sensitively, and trust must be built slowly, lest well-intentioned interventions be perceived as prying into family secrets (unwed pregnancies, true paternity, welfare entitlements) whose disclosure may be dangerous, as families' previous experiences with social agencies have taught them.

An understanding of the broader social and political context in which many poor African American families live is essential to working with this group. For example, Aponte (1987) depicts poor, underorganized families[4] as learning to view as normal their own impotence and their dependence on the community's network of institutions. He insists that any therapeutic intervention not only address the problems facing all families, but also help African American families develop a structure for effectively dealing with the institutional resources of their own community. Because their clients are likely to live with low self-esteem and little hope, counselors need to take an active, positive approach that builds on the clients' abilities, offering support and direction as they strive to achieve immediate, perceptible, concrete solutions to real-life problems. Grievous (1989) observes that counselors working with low-income families are often called upon to assume a variety of roles—educator, director advocate, problem solver, and role model.

Dealing with the complex issues typically facing these multiproblem families, Boyd-Franklin (1995) proposes a multisystem intervention model in which the counselor must take the following systems levels into account: the individual, family and extended family, nonblood kin and friend supports, church and community service agencies, and outside systems (schools, employers, courts, hospitals, police, welfare agencies). One major way in which the counselor can help is to aid the family in prioritizing each problem and furthering their restructuring efforts to take charge of their own problem resolution.

Such help is likely to be time-limited, highly focused, and aimed at solving specific problems. Because the experience may be viewed as suspect or perhaps threatening and dangerous, especially by poor clients, considerable time may have to be spent initially in overcoming distrust, and the counselor may be scruti-

---

[4] Although we have chosen to emphasize working with poor, underorganized, and dysfunctional families, often led by female single parents, we need to note that there also exist well-functioning poor families, as well as an increasing number of middle-income African American families. In the latter case, high achievers may feel isolated from other African Americans in their jobs or as a result of living in predominantly white neighborhoods, may have run up against a "glass ceiling" limiting their advancement at work, or may sometimes experience guilt over the other African American people they have left behind (Davis & Watson, 1982).

nized for signs of prejudice, condescension, or disrespect. Solomon (1982) cautions that the counselor may well be asked many personal questions—whether married, how many children, and so on—as the clients deliberate whether to trust the counselor, not as a counselor per se but as a person.

African American men may present a special problem to the counselor, often expressing resistance, distrust, suspicion, and frequently rage at efforts to involve them in couples or family counseling. The counselor may need to pursue them by telephone in order to engage them in the counseling process, and in some cases may opt to proceed with the woman alone until the man can be brought into the process—if he ever can. Should the counselor need to proceed with the woman alone, Boyd-Franklin (1989) urges that the counselor remain committed to working with a dyadic relationship, even in the absence of a key player. Should the man become available, he must learn to trust the counselor before being encouraged to express his feelings, something he has seen in the past as a sign of weakness and as unmasculine.

As with all families, African American clients must learn strategies for strengthening relationships. This is particularly true with those families that have little history of positive male-female communication patterns or few appropriate role models. Thus, counseling includes an psychoeducational component, in which family members learn techniques for the direct communication of feelings, whether positive or negative. For many African Americans, directness, expressiveness, and open communication between equals represent a new experience, and they must be convinced that it pays off in greater intimacy and ultimate satisfaction. Resistance can be expected, especially from men who fear that by urging the expression of feelings, the counselor is aligning with the woman (compounded if the counselor is a woman).

The issue of empowerment is likely to become a central element in the counseling process with any minority family. Within the constraints of the social, political, and economic realities of their lives, families must learn to use power appropriately within the family system and when dealing with external systems within the community. Given the legacy of racism and discrimination, this is especially true when attempting to engage African American families, who come with a multigenerational history of oppression and powerlessness, and must learn, to the extent possible, to strengthen the family's ability to become effective problem solvers and take greater control of their own lives. In practice, according to McGoldrick, Garcia Preto, Hines, and Lee (1991), the goal of empowerment should be interwoven with every intervention made by the counselor.

Wilson (1971) offers the following guidelines, appropriate for all clients considered in this chapter:

> Counselors should relate to clients with cultural differences in ways that will enhance the cultural identities of their clients. Counselors should relate to clients in ways which will permit the cultural identities of their clients to become positive sources of pride and major motivators of behavior. To do less is to ask a client to give up his values in order to participate in the dominant culture. To do less is to contribute to the destruction of life; and our mission is not to destroy life but to enhance life. (p. 424)

Counseling Hispanic American Families

The term *Hispanic* is generic, referring to Spanish roots, and has gained prominence, if not complete acceptance, in recent years as an overall way of alluding to all Spanish-speaking or Spanish-surnamed people residing in the United States. Although Hispanic Americans may have originally migrated from any number of places (Spain, Central or South America, the Caribbean), the four major subgroups, in order of population size, are Mexican Americans (63% of all Hispanics), Puerto Ricans living on the mainland (12%), Cuban Americans (6%), and others from Central and South America (19%). Together, Hispanic Americans make up close to 10% of the American population (U.S. Bureau of the Census, 1993), are the most rapidly growing segment of the U.S. population, and will likely surpass African Americans as America's largest minority group in the first decade of the 21st century (Crispell, 1991). The Hispanic population's immigration rate and birth rate today exceed that of any other U.S. ethnic group (Mezzich, Ruiz, & Munoz, 1999). Many regions of the United States have become increasingly bilingual, especially California, New York, Texas, and Florida. Axelson (1999) estimates that the burgeoning Hispanic population will be 39 million by 2025 and will have an increasingly powerful influence on mainstream American culture.

Because each country of origin has its own history, complex culture, traditions, mores, value systems, and migration patterns, and because members of each group may be intensely nationalistic, it would be naive to assume a homogeneity among members of this overall group. Some with Latin American backgrounds do not consider themselves Hispanic, because Spanish for them connotes white European colonists with racist policies; they may refer to themselves as *Latinos,* or people of Latin American origin, reflecting a biculturality without specifying racial or linguistic characteristics (Falicov, 1998). First- and second-generation people of Mexican ancestry living in the United States may consider themselves *Chicanos,* a term that was once considered a slur but now has taken on a connotation of raised consciousness committed to a full share of rights as American citizens. *La Raza* (literally, "the race") has an even more militant and political connotation; people so self-identified refer to themselves as a new ethnic group, a western hemispheric mixture of European (largely Spanish) and Indian (indigenous American) descent, thus sharing a social and cultural legacy of Spanish colonists and Native American peoples. With these caveats made clear, recognizing that no single term is acceptable to all groups and having alerted the counselor to carefully determine how the client family identifies itself, we have chosen to call these clients Hispanic Americans, the term still most frequently used in the growing literature on such families.

Socioeconomic, regional, and demographic characteristics vary among Hispanic American groups, making cultural generalizations risky. Within groups, the counselor needs to be alert to the client's generation level, acculturation level, languages spoken, educational background, socioeconomic status, rural or urban residence, adherence to cultural values, and religiosity or spirituality (Homma-True, Greene, Lopez, & Trimble, 1993). Younger Hispanics, for example, even those living in Cuban enclaves such as the Little Havana section of Miami, are likely to be influenced not only by the family's culture of origin, which exists in the living memories and also the values and behaviors of older members of the family, but also by the hybrid culture in which the children are immersed at school and through contact with acculturating peers (Szapocznik, Scopetta, Ceballos, & Santiseban, 1994). We mention such issues as clashing cultural influences to help the counselor avoid unwarranted generalizations and to reiterate that before undertaking counseling, it is imperative to learn as much as possible about the characteristics both of the specific Hispanic American group and of the particular family seeking help.

Family Structure: The Role of the Extended Family

No better introduction to the social and cultural environment of Hispanic Americans is available than some insight into the role of family and extended family in their lives. Language, culture, and ethnicity are interrelated influences not only in forging individual self-concepts but also in strengthening family bonds and carrying on family traditions. Family loyalty, unity, and honor, as well as family commitment, obligation, and responsibility, characterize most Hispanic American families, so much so that sacrifices of family members' own needs or pleasures for the sake of the family group are often encouraged if not expected. Family members struggling to rise out of poverty may at the same time feel an obligation to provide a similar opportunity for other family members.

In Puerto Rican families, for example, family ties are strong and relationships intense; separations are cause for extreme grief, and reunions bring extreme joy, so one who leaves the family does so only at extreme risk (McGoldrick, Garcia Preto, Hines, & Lee, 1991). In this patriarchal pattern, husbands as heads of the family are expected to be dignified and hard-working, to protect and provide for the family, and traditionally to feel free to make decisions without consulting their wives. This form of *machismo,* or maleness, in the self-perception of the Puerto Rican man, is not seen as negative, but rather as representing a desirable combination of virtue, courage, romanticism, and fearlessness. Because *respeto* (respect) plays such an important role—raising respectful children is a source of pride for Hispanic parents—family arrangements are such that although a wife may assume power behind the scenes, she and the children nevertheless overtly support and acknowledge the father's authority and do not openly challenge his rules. Participation in Catholic religious sacraments is common in these families, in some cases blended to African religious rituals (Diller, 1999).

In Mexican American families, too, especially among poor and working-class people (but also to a large extent with middle-class families), the family structure is typically hierarchical, with authority given the husband and father. Machismo also operates here, but beyond the popular stereotype of a swaggering or autocratic man, it pertains to the way a self-respecting Chicano man sees himself and his sex role, not simply how he dominates women. (Young boys may be taught, "Be macho. Respect and protect your mother and sisters. Don't be weak and feminine.

Don't cry.") Among traditional families, the female role is to be nurturing and emotionally supportive, with younger family members expected to be subordinate to and respectful of their elders; older children have authority over younger ones, and brothers are expected to protect sisters (Axelson, 1999). Middle-class families, especially those who are beyond first- or second-generation Americans, tend to be more egalitarian.

The maintenance of strong gender roles (for example, "macho" for men), so much a part of traditional family life, may prove to be an obstacle in counseling, as the Hispanic man may deny feelings or pain, remain silent, or divert feelings should they surge to the surface. Crying in front of the counselor means a loss of self-respect or the respect of other family members, and telling the counselor too many personal details may be perceived as giving power to another and assuming a one-down position. The counselor needs to recognize that feelings are being experienced and not expect to evoke an Americanized form of their expression. In some cases, the culturally aware counselor may need to give explicit permission, early in the counseling process, for all participants to express feelings, or may simply observe aloud, "I see that your father feels sad about this problem."

Along with the other Hispanic groups, Cuban Americans tend to value a community rather than an individual orientation and to show strong loyalty to the nuclear and extended family (Marin & Marin, 1991). Once again, the man's self-esteem rests on his ability to care for and protect his family, and should he lose his job or be unable to find work, he fears the loss of face and possibly the respect of his wife and family. Most Cubans who left their native country after the Castro revolution in 1959 were middle-class and upper-class professionals and businesspeople. Later migrations, especially during the 1980s, brought skilled and semiskilled workers, along with a group of political refugees and prison inmates released by Castro. Most Cuban Americans live in the south Florida area, and having emigrated here recently, are first-generation Americans. As a group, Cuban Americans today have higher incomes and smaller households and are better educated (1 in 5 has 4 years or more of college) than other Hispanic subgroups (Saxton, 1996). When working with Cuban Americans, then, the counselor should be aware that the specific phase of the family migration often provides important clues about the family's original socioeconomic status, political orientation, and educational level.

Extended-family life among all Hispanic Americans tends to be tightly knit; family membership and belonging are a source of great pride, and the collective needs of the family supersede those of the individual member. Ho (1987) even suggests that an individual's self-confidence, worth, security, and identity are determined by his or her relationships with other family members. Grandparents, uncles, aunts, cousins, lifelong friends, and even godparents created through a Catholic baptism custom may share responsibilities for the family's welfare and form coparenting bonds with parents. During times of crisis, for example, children may be transferred from one nuclear family to another within the extended-family system; as in the African American family, this should not necessarily be viewed by the counselor as rejection or neglect (although some children may, of course, be adversely affected).

Given the disadvantaged socioeconomic conditions under which most Hispanic (particularly Puerto Rican and Chicano) families live, a major function of this close-fitting family life is often economic survival (Bernal, Bernal, Martinez, Olmedo, & Santisteban, 1983). Low income, unemployment, undereducation, poor housing, prejudice, and discrimination—to say nothing of cultural-linguistic barriers or perhaps a traumatizing experience after having sought political refuge in this country—make life a struggle for most Hispanic Americans, and extended-family life helps provide an essential resource to buffer the stresses that result from these conditions. In addition, documented or undocumented Mexican Americans or Cuban Americans (Puerto Ricans are American citizens and need no documentation) typically look to a surrogate extended-family network or to priests for direction regarding the process of acculturation.

This point should not be lost on the counselor, who needs to be aware that when a strong extended-family system is operating, as it does in Hispanic American families, members are more likely to seek out the advice and support of other family members or close family acquaintances than to seek help from professional counselors (Carrillo, 1982). To do otherwise would be insulting to the family. Although this attitude may be changing as more Hispanics live in the United States longer and become more acculturated, it is essential that the counselor respect this tradition and recognize the effort it represents to clients to seek help outside the extended-family circle.

A great deal of personal strength may result from the safety net of close family ties (Falicov, 1998), but these ties may also lead to problems. For example, young adults may experience considerable difficulty and in some cases may be overwhelmed with anxiety and guilt when attempting to separate, geographically as well as psychologically, from the family. Younger women, especially more assimilated ones, may find traditional gender-assigned roles unacceptable in their new culture, provoking family conflict. Finally, cultural differences between children born in this country and parents from the old country are frequently associated with intergenerational conflict. Because the issues are complex and often go to the heart of cultural tradition, whenever possible the counselor should encourage inclusion of as many family members as feasible in the counseling process.

Acculturation and Ethnic Identity

The acculturation process of most immigrant groups is usually accompanied by considerable stress and value-system clashes. Especially for recent immigrants, integrating their own ethnic identity with the majority culture is often hazardous, slow, and conflict-laden, as participants strive to develop a sense of self and define a place for themselves in the new society. In the case of Hispanic Americans, the retention of Spanish surnames, the continued preference for, and use of, the Spanish language, and the predominantly brown skin color help set the group apart and leave them open to stereotyping and discrimination. Since most new arrivals are poor and without skills, their chances for adaptation and advancement in the new country are often minimal, and in many cases they can find affordable housing and a sense of community only in ghetto areas. Because they are then unable to make contact with members of the dominant culture, any assimilation is further retarded.

The Hispanic American is often caught in a dilemma between collectivism and individualism, according to Bernal, Bernal, Martinez, Olmedo, and Santisteban (1983). To assume American values that stress individualism, he or she must adopt behavior patterns that tend to disrupt the close-knit family ties from which that individual derives a sense of self, or risk becoming a socially marginal person. In the view of these authors, culture conflict arises because American cultural values are based on a pragmatic approach, effectiveness, and efficiency, while Hispanics are more attuned to a personal approach, idealism, and informality. To be respectful runs the risk of seeming obsequious; to passively avoid offending others may be viewed as weak and servile or insufficiently assertive by Anglo standards. Such value clashes often lead to conflict and loss of self-esteem. Thus, counselors must gauge the degree of acculturation of clients in order to have a better framework for evaluating their possible conflict over abandoning characteristics of the culture of origin and accommodating to the host culture.

Retaining the Spanish language serves as a link to cultural roots as well as a way of perpetuating group values. Unfortunately, its use often effectively cuts off potential clients from using counseling services, especially for non-English-speaking clients. Even in well-staffed clinics that use the services of bilingual interpreters (when Spanish-speaking counselors are unavailable), the overall results are frequently unsatisfactory to counselor and client alike, and much nuance in communication may be missed. Ruiz (1982) reports studies indicating that when psychiatric evaluations of Hispanic patients are carried out in English, even by experienced clinicians, the clients are judged to show greater psychopathology than when interviewed in their native language. Laval, Gomez, and Ruiz (1989) contend that language barriers have a significant effect on both the evaluation of psychopathology and the counseling or therapeutic process. In the latter case, they argue that counselors may misinterpret client verbalizations and may not be able to use the client's potential resources for therapeutic gain. Sue, Ivey, and Pedersen (1996) go further, attributing many interventions offered by counselors in such situations as reflecting racism, sexism, and prejudice in general.

As we noted at the beginning of this chapter, clinicians and clients alike are affected by their own cultural background, and problems arise when they come from different ethnic heritages or hold differing social-class membership.[5] In this

---

[5] The American Psychological Association has attempted to make its members who are service providers more sensitive to how their own cultural backgrounds and life experiences influence their attitudes and possible biases when working with clients from cultures different than their own. Its *Guidelines for Providers of Psychological Services to Ethnic, Linguistical, and Culturally Diverse Populations* (APA, 1993) emphasizes respect for unfamiliar community structures, values, beliefs, and

regard, counselors must be especially vigilant not to impose culturally specific standards or American middle-class values regarding such issues as child-rearing, male-female relationships, and assigned sex roles on others, especially clients from poor working-class environments. Similarly, nonreligious counselors should take care not to dismiss the use of religious behavior, such as prayer, as a therapeutic agent. Catholicism is a powerful force in most Spanish-speaking countries. Care must also be taken not to denigrate attitudes of suffering and self-denial or to underestimate the importance of an Hispanic person's idealism regarding service to God and fellow man, since these religious beliefs are a socially and culturally stabilizing factor and represent an affirmation of traditional Catholic values (Bach-y-Rita, 1982).

Families in cultural transition may develop multiple situational-stress problems that impair their ability to cope with the demands of the existing society. In the case of Mexican Americans, Falicov (1982) cites such issues as problems over social isolation, lack of knowledge regarding social or community resources, or perhaps the experience of dissonance between the normative expectations of the home and of the school, peer group, and other institutions.

In many cases, it may be difficult to distinguish the problems created by poverty from those caused by the family's migration. In the following case, what appears to be a problem of school truancy can be seen in broader social context as a sociocultural problem.

The Ortiz family, consisting of Roberto, 47, the father, Margarita, 44, the mother, and two daughters, Magdelena, 12, and Rosina, 10, had never been to a counselor before, and arrived together at the school counseling office for their early evening appointment with little prior understanding of what the process entailed. Unaware that they could talk to a counselor at school about child-related problems at home, they were summoned by the school authorities as a result of poor and sporadic school attendance by the children during the previous 6 months. Magdelena had actually stopped attending, and her younger sister, Rosina, had recently begun to copy her sister's behavior, although she did go to class some days.

Arranging for the Ortiz family to come to counseling presented several problems. Although Mrs. Ortiz had been in this country for two decades, having arrived from El Salvador by illegally crossing the border at Tijuana, Mexico, with an older brother when she was 25, Mrs. Ortiz spoke English poorly, and she felt self-conscious about her speech in front of the school authorities. Mr. Ortiz, himself an undocumented immigrant from rural Mexico, had been in this country longer and had taken classes in English soon after he arrived. He, too, had to be persuaded that all the family members needed to be present. Both parents had recently been granted amnesty under federal immigration regulations and had looked forward to their children having better

family role relationships among members of culturally diverse groups. Counselors are urged to identify and use resources within both the family and the community in delivering their services. Similarly, the National Association of Social Workers (1996) *Code of Ethics* calls for an understanding of cultural diversity in order to provide services relevant to the needs of clients from different ethnic and cultural groups.

lives in the United States. Needless to say, both parents were very upset upon learning that their children were school truants.

The school counseling office arranged for Augusto Diaz, one of the counselors, to see the Ortiz family. Of Mexican heritage, Mr. Diaz was a third-generation Hispanic American who had learned Spanish in high school, never having heard it spoken at home growing up. He was sensitive to what each of the Ortiz family members was feeling and to the proper protocol for reaching this family. He began respectfully by addressing the father as the head of the house, thanking him for allowing his family to attend, but indicating that the children could not be allowed to skip school and that there were legal consequences if they continued to do so. Aware that Mrs. Ortiz seemed to be having trouble following his English, he enlisted Magdalena as translator. From time to time, he used Spanish words or idioms when appropriate, although he himself was quite self-conscious about his Americanized Spanish, and he, too, turned to Magdalena when uncertain of whether he had said in Spanish exactly what he had intended.

The first session was essentially designed to familiarize the family with what they could expect from counseling, to build trust in the counselor, and to show them that he was interested in their situation and would try to help. Mr. Diaz encouraged all family members to participate and commented several times on the father's strength in bringing his family in to discuss these issues. They arranged another evening appointment for the following week, at a time that would not interfere with Mr. Ortiz's daytime gardening job or Mrs. Ortiz's daytime work as a domestic worker.

When Mr. Ortiz finally felt comfortable enough to share his thoughts, he said that girls did not need education, that they already knew how to read and write, and that had he had boys it would have been different. However, he was upset that they were disobedient and disrespectful in not telling the parents that they were not attending school, but lying instead about how they spent their days. Although Mrs. Ortiz seemed to agree, she also revealed that she was suspicious of the school as well as most of what transpired in her adopted country. She hinted that she knew about the truancy, adding that she was afraid for her children in the mixed Hispanic/African American neighborhood in which they lived, and was just as happy that they stayed home rather than be influenced by their rougher classmates. She saw their being home as an opportunity for some help for her after a long day and as good training for their eventual marriages.

Both Magdalena and Rosina, mute unless asked direct questions in the first two sessions, began to open up in the middle of the third family meeting. They admitted feeling isolated at school, especially because their parents would not allow them to bring classmates home or to visit others after dark. They confessed to being intimidated by gangs, something they had been afraid to reveal to their parents, who, they felt, would not understand. Staying away from school had started as a result of Magdalena's being attacked by an older girl on the school playground, after which the girl warned her to stay away or she would be seriously hurt. Rosina usually followed her older sister's lead and was certain that if her sister was afraid, then the danger was real.

By the fifth session, the counselor, having gained the respect of the family members, had succeeded in opening up family communication. Mrs. Ortiz expressed an interest in learning English better, and the counselor guided her to a class in English as a second language (ESL) at the high school at night. Mr. Ortiz was persuaded to allow her to go out in the evening to attend class with one of their neighbors, another woman from El Salvador. He was pleased that she was trying to improve her English, which would lead eventually to gaining citizenship and thus to greater security for the family. Learning English would also free Magdalena from her pivotal role as translator and pseudo-adult in the family. As the counselor learned of the family's need for other special services, such as filling out various insurance forms and income tax returns, he directed them to the local Catholic church, where some volunteers were helping parishioners with these problems.

The children were given added support by their mother, who walked them to school every day before she left for work. The school looked into the situation of the girl who had threatened Magdalena, at the counselor's request. That older girl still looked menacing, but as Magdalena and Rosina joined other children in the playground rather than being social isolates, they felt safer, and soon the terrorizing stopped. Magdalena joined the school drill team, and Rosina expressed an interest in learning to play an instrument and joining the school band.

The counselor, in an active, problem-solving fashion, was able to act successfully as a social intermediary among the family, the school, and the church, mobilizing the family to make better use of neighborhood and institutional resources and feel more a part of the overall community, thereby helping the family to solve the presenting truancy problem.

Sex-Role Issues in Hispanic Cultures

We are aware that in emphasizing traditional family structures in Hispanic American families, we run the risk of reinforcing the stereotype that all such families adhere to such a pattern. Certainly this is not the case, and clearly with increased acculturation such strict gender-defined roles diminish. Generational differences, differences in socioeconomic status, the greater incidence of single-parent families, working wives, the Chicano movement, and the feminist movement all may contribute to making many younger Hispanic families less like the traditional families we have been describing. As Carrillo (1982) observes, norms for Hispanic families are indeed changing, if slowly, leading to intrafamilial stresses and personal conflicts for family members. She adds, however, that despite these changes, the counselor can still expect a greater adherence to sex-role behavior within the Hispanic culture than among non-Hispanic groups.

Virility and male supremacy are taught to young Hispanic males from childhood; acts of courage, aggressiveness, and honor are especially rewarded. To be a man is never to run from a fight and always to honor one's word. From adolescence on, virility is measured primarily by sexual conquest and secondarily by showing physical prowess in relation to other men (Carrillo, 1982). Traditionally, the man has been the undisputed authority at home and in all other functions in relation to women. Older boys are expected to protect their sisters, and it is still commonplace for girls to assist mothers in serving their father and brothers. Especially in traditional families, the female role is expected to be nurturing and emotionally supportive (Axelson, 1999).

Both boys and girls learn sex-role-determined behaviors from an early age. Thus, in traditional homes, boys do not do tasks that are regarded as feminine, such as helping with the dishes or household chores. Instead, they can come and go as they please, something their female siblings have less freedom to do. Both boys and girls are raised to respect their parents, who are esteemed and accorded high status while children have low status. If the father is authoritarian and feared as a disciplinarian, the mother is usually submissive, self-sacrificing, and dependent, but is assured an honored place in the family nonetheless. Fathers are unlikely to involve themselves in the caretaking of children, but they will protect the mother and insist that the children obey her. If men need to prove their virility through sexual conquest, women are expected to remain pure—sexually naive and faithful to men (Canino, 1982). In addition, women are expected to be tender, affectionate, sentimental, and overprotective mothers—all characteristics that give women status within the Hispanic community.

Young girls growing up in traditional Hispanic families emulate their mother's role. They learn from observing their parents that the man is the final authority; he ultimately determines whether the daughter will be permitted to realize her plans, and it is he who must be pleased. More likely than not, her father will expect her to live a chaste life, far more sheltered than her brothers. Mate selection in traditional families requires the young man to speak to the young woman's parents about his intentions, and it is the father's permission that is particularly important. Once a couple is married, the hierarchical role of male dominance and female submissiveness tends to be followed. This discrepancy in power may be more façade or social fiction than actuality. Canino (1982) suggests that many Hispanic women develop covert manipulative strategies, exerting power and influence in the family but in a socially acceptable manner. (This tactic is frequently practiced by oppressed or lower-status people in all cultures and should not be considered necessarily Hispanic.) Especially as Hispanic Americans become upwardly mobile and assimilate Anglo lifestyles, traditional husband-wife sex-role delineations become less strict (Ho, 1987).

Box 11.2, on page 335, lists issues commonly faced by Hispanic American clients and of which the counselor should be aware.

Some Counseling Guidelines

Despite the myriad problems that would seem to put them at risk—immigration, low income, unemployment, undereducation, oppression and discrimination, as well as various cultural and language barriers, and in some cases the traumatic aftermath of political persecution—Hispanic Americans as a group tend to under-

---

Box 11.2   A problem-appraisal checklist for Hispanic American families

---

The counselor must take the following circumstances into account in appraising the problems of Hispanic American families:

- Country of origin
- Circumstances of immigration
- Degree of acculturation
- Generation in the United States
- English fluency
- Sex-role assignments
- Socioeconomic status
- Devotion to church
- Machismo
- Male-female relationships

---

use counseling and other mental health services (Padilla, Ruiz, & Alvarez, 1989).[6] In part, this underuse is due to the shortage of trained bilingual and bicultural counselors, in part, perhaps, to a low level of cultural sensitivity among clinicians to this group's special needs, and in part, to the geographic or financial inaccessibility of many programs to Hispanic populations (Bernal, Bernal, Martinez, Olmedo, & Santisteban, 1983). Resources in Hispanic communities are typically inadequate in number to meet needs, and when services are offered they are likely to be carried out by paraprofessionals with limited training (Carrillo, 1982). Padilla, Ruiz, and Alvarez (1989) contend that even where services are available, Hispanic Americans by and large will not refer themselves to agencies when they perceive them as alien institutions intruding into their community and when such agencies are staffed by non-Spanish-speaking personnel. As the result of a recent survey of mental health care for Hispanic Americans, Mezzich, Ruiz, and Munoz (1999) conclude that the availability of *culturally congruent services* (including the use of Spanish-speaking counselors) is the most important factor associated with increased use of mental health services by this group, and the most likely way to lower the dropout rate once the services are undertaken.

Acosta and Evans (1982) suggest that Mexican Americans, whether faithful churchgoers or not, are likely to turn to the Catholic church in times of stress— using prayer or seeing a priest for the sacrament of confession and immediate absolution—rather than enter a more prolonged professional counseling arrangement. Similarly, Puerto Ricans are likely to wait until there is a crisis and then expect the same help they are accustomed to in a hospital emergency room—brief, immediate, concrete, direct, problem-oriented, and offered by an authority (McGoldrick, Garcia

---

[6]One noteworthy exception is the Hispanic community's response to the Roberto Clemente Family Center, the first family-oriented public mental health center in New York City. Founded and directed by Puerto Rico-born psychologist Jaime Inchan, this unique training and service facility has offered culturally attuned family counseling services since 1983, with an excellent response from the community.

Preto, Hines, & Lee, 1991). Bernal (1982) agrees that to involve Cubans in any ongoing counseling situation calls for Spanish-language skills as well as sensitivity to cultural issues. As noted earlier, how long the Cuban family has resided in the United States, why they moved and who initiated the move, and what family members remain behind in Cuba are all important questions that will help the counselor determine the family's migration phase, its level of acculturation, and any invisible obligations to those left behind—whom they never expect to see again—that may affect current family functioning.

Establishing a warm, personal, and respectful relationship, rather than a distant and professional one, is crucial if counseling with Hispanic American families is to proceed and be successful. Trust must be built up slowly, attention paid to nuances in language, and community resources enlisted whenever feasible. A plan for treatment may need to be explained early on: what the counselor will be doing, what will be expected of the family members, and approximately how long all this will take, with some specific statement regarding ultimate goals. Clients view the counselor as an authority and expect him or her to take an active, informative role (Diller, 1999). Since Hispanics consider the family their primary source of support, the counselor must remain aware that the integrity of the family must be protected. To suggest that the father has failed to provide proper family leadership, that the mother is less than loving or sacrificing, or that the children no longer respect their parents is to strike a shattering blow; great sensitivity is demanded when the counselor explores these areas.

Especially for newly arrived or unacculturated groups, counseling seems more familiar and more palatable if regarded as a form of medical treatment: A person going to a family physician is simply ill and does not carry the stigma—particularly among uneducated and unsophisticated families—of being crazy. Before beginning to counsel family members, it is wise to secure the permission of the husband or father; this aids the process and helps guard against abrupt termination, even if he only participates sporadically.

Clinical interventions with Hispanics are greatly enhanced if extended-family members, such as grandparents, are included in the process. Because of their close-knit family ties and their sense of being responsible to one another, Hispanic Americans are apt to respond more readily to a family counseling approach than to individual counseling. Padilla and Salgado de Snyder (1985) suggest that Minuchin's (1974) structural approach is particularly applicable, specifically because it emphasizes the role of socioeconomic and cultural factors as individual subsystems in the formation of the problem as well as in its solution. To function successfully, the Anglo American counselor must be sensitized to the subtleties of Hispanic American family structure and lifestyle patterns, able to refrain from imposing value judgments based on majority cultural standards, and respectful of the special strengths and expectations of culturally distinct Hispanic families. Falicov (1998) offers a guide to multicultural practice, helping counselors move beyond cultural stereotypes when working with Mexican, Puerto Rican, and Cuban families. In particular, she emphasizes each group's migration experiences and subsequent adaptation to American life. Counseling is viewed as an encounter between the counselor's and the family's cultural and personal constructions of family life.

Szapocznik and Kurtines (1993) describe a psychoeducational program aimed at troubled Cuban youth, whose behavior they view as embedded within a family that is itself exposed to both mainstream and Hispanic values and customs. In families caught up in such a culturally pluralistic milieu, young members, typically around the time of adolescence, struggle for autonomy while their elders seek family connectedness. Added to the intergenerational conflicts common to all families with adolescents are these compounding intercultural conflicts, in which the teenagers no longer accept their parents' Cuban ways. Together, these conflicts may give rise to behavioral problems (oppositional and defiant behavior, drug use, and so on) in the young people. These authors have developed an effective bicultural approach, conducted in 12 conjoint family sessions, aimed at achieving structural family changes. Through a series of carefully designed exercises, parents are encouraged to understand and accept the value of certain aspects of American culture represented by their children at the same time that the young people are encouraged to do the same for their parents' Hispanic cultural positions. The result, if successful, is the reduction of intergenerational conflict and the building of firmer but flexible boundaries around the family as a whole, as alliances between parents, adolescents, and both cultures are established.

Counseling Asian/Pacific American Families

Although we group them together for classification purposes, we hasten to point out at the outset of our discussion that immigrants from Asia and the Pacific Islands and their descendants do not represent a homogeneous, monolithic group. Rather, these communities represent a heterogeneity of history, religion, language, culture, and appearance, to say nothing of differential patterns of immigration and acculturation. Counselors should be careful to avoid categorizing all clients from this area as the same or interchangeable, any more than it would make sense to aggregate the Irish, Poles, Swedes, and Italians into one group—European—ignoring their vast language and cultural differences (Morishima, 1978).

Instead, counselors might take heed of the observation made by Kuramoto, Morales, Munoz, and Murase (1983) that vast differences exist among Asian and Pacific families; as an example, they cite the obvious gulf between an affluent, fourth-generation Japanese American family and the impoverished, non-English-speaking, illiterate family of a fisherman who fled Vietnam in their fishing boat. The recent influx of refugees from Southeast Asia has made for an even more diverse and heterogeneous Asian/Pacific American population. Once in this country, according to Axelson (1999), the great majority of Chinese, Japanese, Korean, and Filipino immigrants settle in urban population centers, while the Vietnamese tend to be scattered across the United States. Over half the total Asian and Pacific American population resides in the states of California, New York, and Hawaii.

Asian and Pacific Americans come from such disparate places as East Asia (China, Japan, Korea), South Asia (India, Pakistan), Southeast Asia (the Philippines, Thailand, Vietnam, Cambodia, Laos, Indonesia), and the Pacific islands (Hawaii, Samoa, and Guam). While many Japanese Americans and some Chinese Americans have been in the United States for several generations, the vast majority of Chinese, Koreans, Filipinos, Vietnamese, Cambodians, Indians, and Pakistanis living here are foreign born (Homma-True, Greene, Lopez, & Trimble, 1993). At present, together they represent perhaps 3% of the American population, although they are its fastest growing, most diverse, and most affluent minority (Saxton, 1996).

The Asian/Pacific American population is expected to increase sharply within the next few decades as new immigrant groups continue to arrive, especially from Hong Kong, Korea, the Philippines, and Southeast Asia. Each national group not only has a distinctive cultural heritage but also a different history and, equally important, a different reason for immigration (Takaki, 1990). Currently, the Chinese, the Filipinos, and the Japanese represent the three largest groups.

Cultural Transitions

The immigration patterns of Asian and Pacific Americans reflect legal restrictions imposed by U.S. immigration policy. Earliest to arrive, in the mid-1800s, were the Chinese, induced to come here as laborers for the transcontinental railroads in the process of developing the West. They were initially welcomed as cheap labor, but when a diminishing labor market and xenophobic fear of what was labeled the "yellow peril" made their immigration no longer welcome, laws were enacted in the United States to deny them the rights of citizenship, ownership of land, and marriage (Sue, 1989). Prohibited by early exclusionary immigration legislation— the federal Chinese Exclusion Act of 1882—suspending further immigration and making Chinese born in China ineligible for U.S. citizenship, those Chinese already in this country remained living in essentially Chinatown ghettos on the West Coast of the United States when the railroad work was completed. It was only with the end of World War II and, two decades later, the 1965 Immigration and Nationality Act repeal of these discriminatory provisions of citizenship based on national origin that the Chinese renewed their high immigration rates. As recently as 1980, according to one estimate (Lee, 1982), fully 60% of all Chinese Americans were first-generation immigrants, many of them women and children who had been separated from the other generations of their families but were now members of surrogate extended families in Chinatown.

The Japanese, immigrating primarily between 1890 and 1924, experienced similar resistance (for example, the Gentleman's Agreement of 1907 limiting the immigration of Japanese). Because they came from rural agricultural and fishing villages, this first generation, called *Issei,* moved into similar areas in this country (Hawaii and later the West Coast) to provide cheap agricultural labor. Later, they were joined by Japanese females ("picture brides"), whom they brought to the

United States after an exchange of photographs (Kitano, 1982). Like many Asian Americans to follow, with modest expectations for themselves in terms of economic or social mobility, they placed their hopes and dreams on their U.S.-born children, the *Nisei,* or second generation. Both foreign- and U.S.-born Japanese Americans living on the West Coast suffered innumerable hardships when they were relocated and incarcerated, as potential enemies, after the Japanese attack on Pearl Harbor in World War II.

Filipino immigrants also arrived in the 1920s and, like the Chinese, were not allowed citizenship privileges. Koreans, arriving during the same period, were able to preserve family life by bringing wives and children. Pacific Islanders, such as Samoans, are more recent arrivals; as their predecessors had done, they came in search of a better life, but lacking language and work skills, they often lived in poverty. The most recent Southeast Asian immigrants, from Vietnam, Cambodia, and Laos, came here to escape political persecution, only to face prejudice and discrimination in this country. In general, the newer immigrants from Southeast Asia, Samoa, Korea, and the Philippines are currently much lower in socioeconomic status than those American-born descendants of earlier Chinese and Japanese immigrants.

Physical appearance and language are the most prominent features that immediately separate Asians from Westerners. Although it is difficult for Westerners to see beyond these primary physical and cultural distinctions, in actuality the countries of origin of Asian/Pacific peoples are themselves very different in historical, social, and economic development (Shon & Ja, 1982). In addition, each nation has its distinctive language, although some (Chinese, Japanese, Vietnamese) use common Chinese characters, which have been given different pronunciations as they became assimilated into separate native languages. Within groups, such as the Chinese, several dialects distinguish different parts of the country or, in some cases, different villages. Non-English-speaking Asians usually cannot communicate from one group to the other (Chien & Yamamoto, 1982).

Since cultural transitions play such significant roles in understanding Asian families, counselors must take care early on to identify problems in adapting to American society and assess the degree of acculturation exhibited by the family seeking help (Lee, 1997). To begin with, then, counselors must first assess where the client or family stands on the continuum of acculturation (Diller, 1999). Counselors will likely find differences between family members—certainly between children and their parents but also between husband and wife—that may require attention. Helping families adapt more smoothly to the new majority culture may help alleviate some stress, but counselors must take care that, in the process, the family is not forced abruptly to give up all remnants of the life left behind (Lappin & Scott, 1982). Here the counselor would do well to attend to Ho's (1987) distinction among three types of Asian/Pacific American families, since each is likely to show differing sets of socioeconomic levels, parenting styles, communication patterns, language skills, acculturation to American lifestyles, availability for counseling, and so on: (1) *recently arrived immigrant families,* (2) *immigrant American families,* and (3) *immigrant descendant families.*

The process of immigration inevitably causes a large number of life changes and adaptations over a short period of time. Immigrant families must simultaneously deal first with physical or material, economic, educational, and language transitions, and second with the cognitive, affective, and psychological transitions for individuals and the family as a whole. Migration involves being uprooted from a familiar environment—neighbors, streets, sounds, customs, a supportive extended-family structure, cultural guidelines—and is inevitably stressful; it requires adaptation in stages as cultural boundaries are crossed (Sluzki, 1979). Some immigrants plan to stay a short time before returning to their native country, whereas others—in some cases political refugees—see the new land as a haven, an opportunity for a new life for themselves and their children.

As has been true of most immigrant groups, language is a major obstacle in the acculturation process of Asian/Pacific families. Because the parents are usually unable to communicate effectively with landlords, store clerks, school officials, potential employers, and neighbors, family hierarchy is often (temporarily) reversed, and children, having learned the new language and customs more quickly, may become interpreters for parents, throwing the customary patriarchy off balance (Lappin & Scott, 1982).

Economic necessities may force the adult family members to begin employment immediately upon arrival in the United States. Those who lack professional skills or proficiency in the English language may have no choice but to work long hours, six or seven days per week, at subminimum pay, with few if any employee benefits. Even with both parents working, the family is apt to live in substandard housing. New arrivals may grieve over the loss of support from family members left behind in the home country, which may or may not be partially replaced by relatives in the adopted country.

For newly arriving immigrants, according to Shon and Ja (1982), the initial phase of cognitive reactions almost certainly involves cultural shock and disbelief at the disparity between what was expected and what actually exists. For some there is a loss of status (for example, from physician in the old country to laboratory technician in the new because of the lack of a medical license); others, escaping tyranny, must leave money and possessions behind, and thus must begin life in the new land with few tangible assets; still others, rural people, must adapt to American urban life without adequate preparation to do so. This transition is often followed by anger and resentment, and ultimately some accommodation and mobilization of family resources and energy. Because of cultural differences and language barriers, such families are not likely to seek psychological help from a counselor, although they may require referral for legal aid, information on educational opportunities to learn English, or overall advocacy.

Immigrant American families (foreign-born parents, American-born children), if they seek help from a counselor, probably do so as a result of ongoing culture clash within the family. Younger members, usually better assimilated, are likely to value more Americanized characteristics—individuality, independence, assertiveness—while their elders frown on their disrespectful behavior, perhaps express regret over coming to the United States, and may even threaten to return to the home country. (The case of the Singh family from India, in which intergenerational problems between parents and American-schooled adolescents threatened family unity, is presented in Chapter 1.) Counselors need to provide negotiating tools so that such families can resolve parent-child conflicts and communication difficulties, and gain some role clarification (Ho, 1987).

Immigrant descendant families, composed of second-, third-, or fourth-generation American-born families, are almost certainly highly acculturated to American values, speak English at home, probably live outside traditional Asian/Pacific neighborhoods, and seek help when required in the same manner and with the same degree of comfort or discomfort as most other assimilated Americans. However, they frequently retain certain strong cultural values (for example, fealty to parents, marrying within their ethnic group) despite their assimilation.

Family Structure and Responsibilities

In most Asian and Pacific Island cultures, the family—immediate and extended—is the central unit, and the individual is secondary. For example, Chinese culture stresses kinship from birth to death, and it is expected that the family will serve as a major resource in providing stability, a sense of self-esteem, and satisfaction. Even if the person leaves for another country and is permanently separated from his or her family of origin, it is expected that devotion to family values and adherence to family standards will be maintained. So, too, in Japanese households, where, unlike the tendency in most American families to relate in an intimate fashion, self-expression is subordinate to acting in accordance with role expectations (Sue & Morishima, 1982). Filipino families often draw a strong boundary between the members of their extended family (or clan) and outsiders; the clan becomes the locus of identity formation, social learning, support, and role development, and is turned to first when problem solving is required (Cimmarusti, 1996).

Counselors can expect a restraint of feeling and self-disclosure, perhaps even shame and stigma for leaving the community and seeking professional help (Diller, 1999). Those who do seek counseling are apt to expect that they are there for advice and guidance from an authority and not to engage in two-way communication. Since an individual's actions during this lifetime are traditionally believed to reflect on his or her ancestors and future generations, emotional problems and the need for counseling may take on a powerful stigma in many Asian/Pacific families, who may then not avail themselves of psychiatric or psychological services (Wong, Lu, Shon, & Gaw, 1983). The telling of private affairs to strangers is alien to Asian culture; to expose even minor problems may imply a criticism of how one's parents failed in child-rearing, and thus such self-examination and revelation may be avoided.

Investment in children, as we have indicated, has very high priority among Asian/Pacific populations. Young children are indulged long beyond what is considered standard among traditional American families. Toilet training is often delayed, according to Berg and Jaya (1993), until the child insists on it, and older children, even up to the age of 10 or 11, frequently sleep with their parents. Adolescents are not encouraged to learn self-care skills (cleaning their rooms, doing their own laundry, cooking their own meals) and are permitted to maintain a dependent position as long as they wish. What they are expected to do, however, is to be well behaved and obedient and, above all, to bring honor to the family. School achievement is a particularly visible way to do so, but so is earning praise from others in the community for being respectful, knowing good manners, and eventually marrying into a good family.

Heavily influenced by Confucian philosophy and ethics, Asian/Pacific family role definitions are traditionally hierarchical and patriarchal. Marriage represents a continuation of the male family line rather than the creation of a new family, and women are expected to show obedience toward their husbands (del Carmen, 1990). Although this disparity has shifted to a more egalitarian marital relationship among contemporary Asian/Pacific Americans, it remains true that loyalty and respect are emphasized within the family. Though some culture conflict may occur as a result of increased exposure to American norms, values, and behavior patterns, adaptations evidently can readily be made: Asians have the lowest divorce rate among American households, as well as the lowest proportion of households headed by women. It is not clear whether and to what extent these low rates represent successful marriages, as opposed to the importance of maintaining the appearance of success and avoiding the loss of face associated with bringing dishonor to the family.

In traditional Asian society, fathers are expected to be providers and to be responsible for educating and disciplining the children. Mothers in this arrangement are nurturing figures, protective of their offspring. Sons have traditionally been held in higher esteem than daughters; eldest sons are expected to be role models for the younger children and to take over family leadership after the death or incapacity of the father. By way of contrast, daughters are socialized as homemakers and expected to marry and be absorbed into their husbands' families (Shon & Ja, 1982). Although this pattern is less rigidly adhered to among younger and more assimilated Asian/Pacific families, the basic role assignments and expectations continue today.

Berg and Jaya (1993) describe the Asian mother as failing to maintain boundaries with her son's family and consequently appearing to meddle by maintaining a close relationship with him from which his wife is typically excluded. These authors view this behavior as a way of solidifying her position when the first-born son becomes head of the household, thus ensuring her security for her old age. They caution the counselor to take special note of this traditional arrangement as culturally appropriate and warn against any hasty attempt to restructure it—as too enmeshed, by American standards—before its importance in Asian family patterns has been understood.

Intermarriage (or cross-cultural marriage) between partners of diverse racial or ethnic backgrounds has become increasingly familiar as social tolerances increase,[7] but within such marriages the diverse outlooks and expectations of the spouses often produce strains and occasionally serious conflict. As Falicov (1995a) notes, the inevitable accommodations in a marriage may be longer and more complicated as the differences in background between the pair widens. Strains may arise from family disapproval; one family may consider the new spouse a cultural outsider at the same time that that person experiences culture shock or otherwise feels alienated from, or uncomfortable with, the attitudes and behavior patterns of the new in-law family. Although we are in no way suggesting that marital happiness or unhappiness can be reduced simply to degrees of cultural commonality, it is nevertheless true that the lack of a shared cultural code—interpersonal expectations, child-rearing values, anticipated boundary lines with extended family, styles of communicating—can lead to serious marital conflict, as in the following case:

Darryl Chang and his wife, Rebecca Wilson Chang, were a middle-class couple in their early thirties, married for 6 years, when they sought help from a private-practice counselor. Darryl was a third-generation Chinese American, an oldest son with three younger sisters, brought up in Hawaii by well-to-do parents who were large landowners. Sent to the mainland to study as an undergraduate at a prestigious private Midwest university, he met Rebecca during his freshman year, and they were inseparable thereafter throughout their college careers. Rebecca was the only child of white middle-class parents, New Englanders, both professionals who had to strain financially to send her to the university, but did so willingly because they wanted to encourage her to pursue a professional career. Darryl's goal, responding to family expectations, was to become a physician, while Rebecca had dreams of pursuing an academic career as an anthropologist.

Married upon graduation, they returned to Hawaii, where Darryl received his medical training while Rebecca studied for her master's degree; her studies were interrupted when she gave birth to Robby. They resided in the Chang compound and ate their meals together every night with Darryl's parents, forming the close bond that Darryl insisted was the way respectful children should behave. Darryl's mother occasionally intimated to him that she and her husband were disappointed that he had

---

[7] Interracial families, while still small in percentage terms of the total U.S. number of families, nevertheless represent an important developing social and demographic phenomenon. Three million Americans told the Census Bureau in 1990 that they were married to or living with someone of a different race. The rate of interracial marriage doubled from 1960 to 1970 and tripled from 1970 to 1980, at least in part because of the Supreme Court decision striking down those remaining state laws prohibiting such mixed marriages (Mathews, 1996). The degree to which marrying out occurs in any group affects the likelihood that a specific intermarriage will gain acceptance by the families or communities involved. For example, the *sansei* (third-generation Japanese Americans) have a very high rate of marrying out; more than half marry non-Asian partners (Kitano, 1982). This phenomenon reflects the degree of assimilation of Japanese Americans into U.S. society.

married "down," although she appeared cordial if somewhat distant with Rebecca. By way of contrast, Rebecca's parents accepted Darryl after some initial misgivings about the couple's differences in background, but did express some regrets that the young couple and their grandchild lived so far away that visiting was infrequent. While Rebecca was not happy about her mother-in-law's involvement in Robby's upbringing, she generally kept her feelings to herself, having learned that criticizing his parents only aroused Darryl's wrath.

An opportunity to gain intern and residency experience in dermatology brought Darryl, Rebecca, and Robby to California. Lack of sufficient income became a problem, and Rebecca especially resented her husband's parents' unwillingness to help them out when she knew they could well afford it. In addition, she became angry and depressed that Darryl not only was away for long periods of time but was fatigued and often irritable when they were together. He offered no help with Robby and seemed puzzled that she should expect him to participate in child-rearing activities.

Rebecca's insistence that they seek counseling was triggered when the elder Changs visited from Hawaii. Showing limited interest in Rebecca, Mrs. Chang spent a great deal of time with her son, lunching with him and shopping for clothes. Insisting that it was not proper for a doctor to dress poorly, she spent several thousand dollars on three suits and accessories for her son, but nothing comparable for her daughter-in-law or grandchild. Rebecca was furious, but Darryl argued that the behavior was appropriate, since his mother was apparently concerned that he would lose face if not properly attired. Rebecca was enraged at his lack of empathy with her feelings and burst forth with a recitation of all of the slights and other grievances she had felt over the years when she felt treated as an outsider. She was sick of being deferential, sick of meeting a stone wall when she tried to talk to him about her unhappiness, and sick of being made to feel unwelcome by his family.

The couple saw the counselor for four sessions. In contrast to Rebecca's intensity, Darryl was taciturn and had difficulty talking about family matters, which he finally acknowledged, but said belonged within the family and not in front of the counselor, an outsider. Careful not to give the appearance of taking sides, the counselor began by focusing on cultural differences and cultural expectations. She attempted as best she could to explain her perception of the cultural code each partner operated from, thus relabeling their differences as cultural (and thus fixable with increased understanding) rather than the result of irreconcilable personality differences. Her goal here was to help each partner start to understand underlying cultural issues, and in this way begin a dialogue with the goal of achieving better and more open communication.

The counselor next tried to get the couple to look at the structure of their relationship, stating that greater attention needed to be paid to Rebecca's sense that she was a second-class person in Darryl's eyes, and Darryl's view that Rebecca wanted too much, expecting him to do things—such as help with their child—that he found completely alien and for which he had no role model. Careful to keep them from blaming each other for their cultural blinders ("She's spoiled, like all American women"; "He's a Chinese eldest son and thinks he's a crown prince"), the counselor agreed that while cultural factors were operating, these factors did not make the situation unchangeable or exonerate either one from personal responsibility to improving their relationship. Despite differences in background, negotiations were nevertheless possible, and some of their culturally unique outlooks could be maintained but better integrated into new family traditions.

The couple made some progress, but Darryl in particular was minimally open to change. By the start of the fourth session, he said he thought they were ready to work out differences on their own, that they appreciated the help, and that they would contact the counselor if needed in the future—all, it seemed to the counselor, ways of exiting prematurely from counseling. Rebecca appeared reluctantly to go along with her husband's plans, and she also expressed relief that the crisis in their marriage was over, although she appeared to worry that it might just erupt again some day.

Values, Beliefs, Obligations

In Asian/Pacific culture, form—how things are done—often takes precedence over content—what is done. Proper protocol, procedures, and ways of addressing one another are all important, even before getting down to the business at hand. Berg and Jaya (1993) advise counselors to be sure to pay proper respect to procedural rules as the first step in achieving a positive alliance with the family. As examples, they point out several possible errors: addressing parents by their first names, encouraging a wife to complain for too long about her husband, or confronting parents directly about their mishandling of their children. In their experiences, the first session might profitably be spent establishing a social relationship, paying proper deference to age (the counselor's or the client's, whichever is greater), and establishing order, hierarchy, and social boundaries between the counselor and the family. As part of this process, the counselor can expect to be asked many personal questions.

Filial piety—loyalty, respect, and devotion of children to their parents—is of prime importance in traditional Asian/Pacific families. Children are expected to obey their parents in a deferential way and to respect and care for family elders as they age (del Carmen, 1990). Elders are afforded unquestioned respect. In Filipino families, for example, elders are greeted in culturally defined ceremonial ways and with kinship terms that denote their special rank; failure either to carry out the ritualized greeting or to use these terms would be considered disrespectful (Cimmarusti, 1996). Although some modification takes place with longer residence in the United States, many such traditions and values continue.

Spiritual and religious issues are likely to play a central role in the lives of many Asians (Lee, 1997). Many such traditions are dictated by adherence to Confucianism and Buddhism, which specify more rules of behavior and conduct for family members than is usual in most cultures (Shon & Ja, 1982). As we have indicated, an individual's adherence to an established code of conduct becomes more than a reflection of that person's standards; it reflects the standards of the family and kinship network to which he or she belongs. Deeply rooted in the lives of most Asians, the philosophy of Confucianism, in particular, strongly emphasizes respect for elders, obedience, and close family ties. In the case of Filipinos, duty and obligation help maintain family roles, particularly important in large extended families, and are consistent with that culture's strong Catholic belief system.

Duties and obligations, largely unspoken but understood by all, govern much of the lives of Asian family members. Whatever a parent does, Ho (1987) reports, the child is still obligated to show respect and obedience. Parents are considered to deserve the highest obligation because it was they who brought children into the world and cared for them when they were helpless. Obligation can be incurred in two ways: through the playing out of ascribed roles (parent/child, teacher/pupil) emphasizing status differences and the hierarchical or vertical nature of relationships, and through actions that incur obligation because of their kindness and helpfulness (Shon & Ja, 1982).

Closely related to obligation is the concept of shame and loss of face, which is frequently used to reinforce adherence to a prescribed set of obligations. In contrast to American ideals regarding self-sufficiency and self-reliance, Asian/Pacific people believe they are the product of their relationships and consequently value the maintenance of harmony through proper conduct and attitudes. Shaming someone is a way of getting that person to adhere to societal expectations of proper behavior. To act in a shameful way not only leads to loss of face through exposure of errant action for all to see, but also leads to withdrawal of support and confidence in the person by family and community. In a communal society where interdependence is crucial, actual or threatened withdrawal of support is a powerful weapon to force conformity to family and societal expectations (Shon & Ja, 1982).

Counselors need to assess the role of obligation and fear of being shamed if they are to fully understand and evaluate what information is being given by client families and what is being withheld. Direct confrontation, which some counselors question for any clients, is likely to be especially unsuccessful with Asian/Pacific clients because it runs the risk of forcing them to expose previously unacknowledged feelings and/or making them fearful of committing a social error and thus facing the dread of losing face. Nevertheless, Root (1989) reports that most Asian/Pacific families will come in together with a distressed family member and at least give the outward appearance of support for the counseling process. However, the identified patient is likely to believe that his or her recovery rests on the exercise of willpower and, despite the need for support, may not want family members involved.

Box 11.3 on page 347 lists issues commonly faced by Asian/Pacific clients and of which the counselor should be aware.

Some Counseling Guidelines

A useful starting point for counselors working with any ethnic family is to gain some awareness of the ethnic and cultural traditions of their own family (Pedersen, 1994). They may discover that particular beliefs or behavior patterns

---

Box 11.3   A problem-appraisal checklist for Asian/Pacific families

---

The counselor must take the following circumstances into account in appraising
the problems of Asian/Pacific families:

- Country of origin
- Generation in the United States
- Social class (in country of origin and in the United States)
- Degree of identification with home country
- Language barriers
- Culture shock and degree of assimilation
- Prejudice and discrimination
- Role and status reversal
- Intergenerational family conflicts
- Lack of community support systems
- Expectations of temporary or permanent residence

---

previously attributed to idiosyncracies in their family may actually be more accurately linked to the counselor's ethnic background. Further investigation may lead
to the surprising discovery of the commonality of much of the behavior in their
family with their larger ethnic community (Preli & Bernard, 1993).
Multiculturalism is likely to become a more meaningful and relevant construct to
a counselor once the counselor becomes sensitized to his or her own ethnic and
cultural roots. A dividend of such increased self-awareness might be not simply a
raised consciousness regarding the experiences of ethnic minorities but also a
greater awareness of one's own cultural blindness.

As we have indicated, the beginning phase of counseling, always important in
establishing a relationship and helping clients learn what to expect, takes on special significance for Asian/Pacific American clients, particularly those who are less
acculturated. According to Ho (1987), the first interview, if not conducted sensitively, may also be the last. He suggests that from the start the counselor confidently assume the role of authority figure and actively direct the counseling
process. When asked, even in a subtle or indirect manner, the counselor must be
willing to disclose his or her educational background and work experience, and
even to respond openly to more personal questions about marriage or children;
all this is the family's way of assessing the counselor's credentials to help them.
Only after the family has developed a sense of trust in the counselor and in the
leadership they expect that person to provide will they be able to begin to form a
closer relationship with the counselor—a task that usually proceeds deliberately
among Asian/Pacific peoples.

Especially when working with first-generation families, Sluzki (1979) attempts
early in the counseling process to determine what phase of the migration process
best characterizes their situation. He contends that the migration process follows a
predictable pattern, occurring in phases, each with corresponding manifestations

of family conflict. Contrary to expectations, he believes migratory stress is not greatest in the weeks and months following the move, but rather that families overcompensate as they attempt to deal with the adaptational tasks needed for survival. In Sluzki's experience, although family disorganization may occur under extreme circumstances or when effective coping skills are lacking, the majority of families show no symptoms during this phase of their acculturation, although conflicts may remain dormant. Several months later, however, a major crisis may develop; it is typically at this phase—which Sluzki labeled *decompensation*—that counselors are likely to see such families, who are now struggling to come to terms with maximizing the family's continuity and its compatibility with the new environment. Later, especially if there is a long-term delay in the family's adaptive process, conflict will likely break out into the open, perhaps in the form of intergenerational conflicts between parents and children raised in the adopted country.

In many cases, families may fail to perceive any correlation between the move and their conflicts, seeing their migration in historical perspective but not as any longer impinging on their adaptive capabilities. Sluzki (1979) urges the counselor to convey to the family the counselor's recognition that the migratory process is stressful and that any presenting symptoms are an understandable and frequent by-product of the migration experience. This is an attempt to depathologize the presenting complaint and set it in its larger, overall context. He advises a future orientation and planning as part of any counseling process, especially for those families still stunned and confused by the migratory experience and not yet anchored to their new community.

Sufficiently detailed knowledge about the family's ethnic, cultural, and religious background is the key to effectively assessing the content of the material introduced by family members (Lau, 1986). In the same vein, it is helpful to be aware of the political and economic stresses—both present and historical—experienced by the particular ethnic group of which the client family is a member. Client language skills, years in the United States, age at time of arrival, and immigration and relocation history all need to be evaluated as the counselor attempts to assess family adaptation.

Mobilizing the family to work together on a specific problem, the counselor must take care not to usurp parental authority or, by his or her leadership, cause the parents to lose face in front of their children. Since shame is so much a part of Asian life, the non-Asian counselor must be especially sensitive about not embarrassing family members in front of one another and the counselor. To encourage the open expression of negative feelings by children toward their parents might be viewed as disrespectful, shaming the parents, and is likely in the long run to be countertherapeutic. One tactic recommended by Ho (1987), when there is an impasse between counselor and family or perhaps an impenetrable language barrier, is to enlist the aid of an extended-family member or trusted friend, normally an older male, who might attend family sessions and help negotiate conflict resolution, as between generations.

Counseling is likely to be brief, concrete, highly focused, and directed at achievable goals. Leong (1986) suggests that Asian/Pacific American clients tend to prefer structured situations and practical, immediate solutions to problems. Because they tend to view counseling as a directive, paternalistic, and authoritarian process, they are likely to expect the counselor, as an experienced person, to provide advice and recommend a specific course of action. Accustomed to medical visits in which symptomatic relief is offered and treatment is short term, Asian/Pacific families may focus on the improvement of symptoms or problems rather than seek long-term understanding or insight (Chien & Yamamoto, 1982).

Most authorities (Berg & Jaya, 1993; Homma-True, Greene, Lopez, & Trimble, 1993) suggest that the counselor be active and offer pragmatic "how-to" suggestions designed more to solve problems than to emphasize feelings or provide insights. Reasonable, practical, result-oriented solutions are more effective than cause-and-effect explanations regarding the origins of the presenting problem. Helping the family achieve a consensus and discover what will help them achieve family harmony is more consistent with Asian/Pacific philosophy than any attempts to place the needs and desires of individuals above family considerations. It is essential that the counselor not attempt to disengage family members from one another, even if in his or her non-Asian view the family lacks clear boundaries. Since the expression of anger and hostility is often discouraged in these families, counselor confrontational techniques are not likely to be effective and will more probably alienate the family.

Asian/Pacific Americans as a group underuse counseling services (Root, 1989) and, according to Shon and Ja (1982), generally seek psychological help only when all else has failed. For many poor and marginally acculturated Asian Americans, learning how to access counseling as well as other medical and social services may itself be a barrier to receiving help (Aponte & Barnes, 1995). Particularly among older or less assimilated people, in addition to the social stigma, there exists a lack of familiarity with Western mental health concepts. Problem solving is supposed to take place at home and within the family context; seeking help from a counselor is often seen as shameful public exposure that the parents have failed the family by not fulfilling what was expected of them. Kitano (1982) suggests that the inability to use community resources may be a symptom of a group that remains apart from the mainstream and as a consequence is relatively disadvantaged and deprived of what the community has to offer.

Summary

The United States, increasingly, is a pluralistic society, which represents a gain in diversity and vitality, but also creates the conditions for intergroup misunderstanding and strife. Assimilation, if too rapid, runs the risk of separating people from their ethnic and cultural roots. Counselors need to cultivate sensitivities to various minority families—African Americans, Hispanic Americans, and Asian/Pacific Americans serve as examples—in order to broaden the counseling focus and develop an understanding of the sociocultural contexts that influence family behavior. Knowledge of a family's cultural background helps the counselor differentiate cultural from idiosyncratic family attitudes and behavioral patterns.

African American families are not a homogeneous group, although color remains the predominant and distinguishing fact of life for most members of the community. Counselors must take into account the realities of African American life in our society in order to understand the culture developed in response to the prejudice and racial discrimination experienced on an ongoing basis. Economic, social, and political powerlessness characterize the existence of most African Americans; although a middle class has emerged in recent years, the proportion in poverty continues to increase. All classes reflect attitudes that combine residual values from Africa, American mainstream values, and a set of attitudes, values, and behavior that is the result of living as part of a victim system.

African American family life relies heavily on a kinship network in which boundaries are loose and help and support are exchanged with a large extended family as well as with nonblood "relatives." Informal adoptions of children by adult relatives or family friends provide an unofficial social service network. Females are likely to have more economic opportunities than their male counterparts, whose roles as husbands and fathers are frequently undermined by a dismal future outlook. Female-led families are common, and divorce rates are high among African Americans. Skin color further divides the community, with lighter skin often accorded greater status. The church often serves as the epicenter of African American life. In stressful times, members of this community are more likely to reach out to relatives or the church than to counselors, of whom they are suspicious. Effective counseling with African Americans demands an active, positive approach, in which trust is built slowly and the counselor may need to intervene simultaneously on several levels—individual, family, and community—to strengthen the family's problem-solving abilities.

Hispanic Americans, too, are a heterogeneous population; immigrants from Mexico, Cuba, and Puerto Rico form the largest groups. Language, cultural ties, and ethnicity all play a part in strengthening family bonds and continuing family traditions in each group. Families tend to be patriarchal, with a hierarchical structure in which most overt authority resides with the father. *Machismo* is highly valued, and males, who typically have more privileges than females, are raised to be strong, courageous, and protective of their mothers and sisters. Respect for parents is considered essential, and open challenge to paternal authority is rare. Extended-family life is usually tightly knit, family membership is a source of pride, and the collective needs of the family are believed to supersede those of individual members. Economic survival often requires reliance on extended family; undocumented aliens largely turn to surrogate family members for direction in the acculturation process. Although personal strength may be reinforced by family ties, separation from family may be difficult and family conflict may result from women's resistance to playing out traditional sex-assigned roles.

Many Hispanic American families find the acculturation process extremely stressful as they attempt to assume American values that, with their emphasis on individualism, may disrupt the close family ties of their cultural heritage. Non-

Hispanic counselors need to be especially careful not to impose culturally specific Anglo American standards on those whose cultural background has led them to live by other standards, unless that adoption has led to problematic behavior. Hispanics tend to underuse counseling services, often turning to the Catholic church rather than professional counselors, with whom there is likely to be a language barrier as well as fear of a lack of cultural sensitivity. However, traditional Hispanic Americans who do seek counseling are more likely to regard the experience as akin to a medical service and to go as a family rather than individually.

Asian/Pacific Americans encompass immigrants from East Asia (China, Japan), South Asia (India, Pakistan), Southeast Asia (Thailand, Vietnam), and the Pacific islands (Hawaii, Samoa), and thus are not a homogeneous or monolithic group. Different groups arrived in the United States during different periods over the last century and were greeted with various forms of discrimination, including a series of exclusionary immigration laws. As such restrictions have lifted, and as a result of groups seeking political refuge, the influx has increased in recent years, and many current Asian/Pacific Americans are first-generation immigrants. Physical appearance and language immediately separate Asians from Westerners and may give the erroneous impression that their differences from one another are minimal. In reality, their histories, languages, and social and economic backgrounds are markedly different, and the counselor must take care to understand the specific country of origin and its distinctive features before commencing counseling with an Asian/Pacific American family. The culturally sensitive counselor also needs to pay attention to whether they are recent arrivals, immigrant American families (foreign-born parents, American-born children), or descendants of immigrants, since each group is likely to present a unique set of problems.

The family is of prime importance in Asian/Pacific American families, and family members are required to behave with loyalty and devotion to its values. Role expectations are carefully followed, especially in less acculturated families; even in more assimilated populations, hierarchical and patriarchal patterns are likely to be continued in a somewhat abated fashion. Marriage represents a continuation of the male family line. Filial piety and obeying parents in a deferential manner follow from the dictates of Confucianism. Family obligation and fear of being shamed and losing face are strong motivational forces. Counseling is more likely to succeed, particularly with less acculturated clients, if the counselor acts confidently and with authority and actively directs the process, mobilizing the family to work together on a problem but taking care not to arouse disrespect within the family or to cause someone to lose face.

Glossary

AIDS Acquired immune deficiency syndrome, an infectious disease in which the body's immune system is damaged, often in progressive degrees, making the person vulnerable to fatal opportunistic infections and malignancies—gay men and drug abusers are at greatest risk.

anorexia nervosa Prolonged, severe diminution of appetite, particularly although not exclusively in adolescent females, to the point of becoming life-threatening.

behavioral The viewpoint that objective and experimentally verified procedures should be the basis for modifying maladaptive, undesired, or problematic behavior.

binuclear family A postdivorce family structure in which the ex-spouses reside in separate but interrelated households—the maternal and paternal households thus form one family system.

bisexual An individual sexually attracted to both males and females.

boundaries Abstract delineations between parts of a system or between systems, typically defined by implicit or explicit rules regarding who may participate and in what manner.

centrifugal Tending to move outward or away from the center—within a family, forces that push the members apart, especially when the family organization lacks cohesiveness.

352

centripetal   Tending to move toward the center—within a family, forces that bind or otherwise keep the members together so that they seek fulfillment from intrafamilial rather than outside relationships.

circular causality   The view that causality is nonlinear, occurring instead within a relationship context and by means of a network of interacting loops—any cause is thus seen as an effect of a prior cause, as in the interactions within a family.

circular questioning   An interviewing technique, first formulated by the Milan group, aimed at eliciting differences in perceptions about events or relationships from different family members, particularly in regard to points in the family life cycle when significant coalition shifts and adaptations occurred.

cohabitation   The living arrangement of an unmarried heterosexual couple as an alternative to marriage.

commuter marriage   An intact marriage in which the partners maintain separate households, usually in distant cities, typically to pursue dual careers simultaneously.

constructivist   An advocate of the view that emphasizes the subjective ways in which each individual creates a perception of reality.

contextual   Pertaining to circumstances or situations in which an event took place—as a therapeutic approach, an emphasis on relational determinants, entitlements, and indebtedness across generations that bind families together.

countertransference   A counselor's unconscious emotional response to a client or couple that may interfere with objectivity.

custody   The assignment of children to one or both parents in a postdivorce family system, as well as the determination of the children's living arrangements (see also *joint legal custody, joint physical custody, sole custody,* and *split custody*).

cybernetics   The study of methods of feedback control within a system, especially the flow of information through feedback loops.

differentiation of self   In Bowen's formulation, the separation of one's intellectual and emotional functioning—the greater the differentiation, the better the person is able to resist being overwhelmed by his or her family's emotional reactivity, and the less prone to dysfunction the person therefore is.

disengagement   A family process in which members become psychologically isolated from one another because of overly rigid boundaries among the participants.

divorce mediation   A form of divorce arbitration in which the couple voluntarily learns to negotiate a mutually satisfying settlement through brief nonadversarial contact with a team knowledgeable in counseling and the law.

donor insemination   A technique for becoming pregnant outside of sexual intercourse in which sperm from sperm banks or family planning centers is used to fertilize a woman's egg.

ecomaps   An appraisal tool designed to depict graphically a family's connections with outside organizations and institutions, enabling the counselor to examine pictorially those relationship bonds that connect the family to these systems.

enmeshment   A family process in which boundaries become blurred and members become overconcerned and overinvolved in one another's lives, limiting the autonomy of individual family members.

entropy   The tendency of a system to go into disorder—that is, to reach a disorganized and undifferentiated state.

epistemology   The study of the origin, nature, and methods, as well as the limits, of knowledge—thus, a framework for describing and conceptualizing what is being observed and experienced.

equifinality   In contrast to simple cause-and-effect explanations, the principle that similar outcomes may result from different origins.

ethnicity   The defining characteristics of a cultural subgroup, transmitted over generations and reinforced by the expectations of the subgroup in which the individual or family maintains membership.

experiential   The approach by which the counselor reveals himself or herself as a real person and uses that self in interacting with the family being counseled.

family mapping   A symbolic representation of a family's organizational structure, particularly its boundaries and coalitions, used by structural counselors to plan their interventions.

family systems model   As proposed by Bowen, the theoretical model that emphasizes the family as an emotional unit or network of interlocking relationships best understood from a historical or transgenerational perspective.

feedback   The reinsertion into a system of the results of its past performance as a method of controlling the system.

feedback loops   Those circular mechanisms by which information about a system's output is continuously reintroduced into the system, initiating a chain of subsequent events.

first-order cybernetics   A view from outside the family system of the feedback loops and homeostatic mechanisms that transpire within the system.

forensic   Pertaining to legal matters, usually involving a courtroom or judicial procedure.

fusion   The merging of the intellectual and emotional aspects of a family member, paralleling the degree to which that person is caught up in, and loses a separate sense of self in, family relationships.

gay   A male engaged with another male in a sexual relationship.

general systems theory   As proposed by Bertalanffy in regard to all living systems, the study of the relationship of interactional parts in context, emphasizing their unity and organizational hierarchy.

genogram   A schematic device of a family's relationship system in the form of a genetic tree, usually including at least three generations, often used by the counselor to trace recurring behavior patterns within the family.

glass ceiling   An invisible and unacknowledged barrier to work or career advancement beyond a certain level.

homeostasis   A dynamic state of balance or equilibrium in a system, or a tendency toward achieving and maintaining such a state in an effort to ensure a stable environment.

homophobic   Excessively fearful of being homosexual oneself or of associating with homosexuals.

human validation model   Satir's therapeutic model, based on a humanistic or experiential outlook, in which the counselor and family join forces to stimulate an inherent health-promoting process in the family.

identified patient   The family member with the presenting symptom or problem—thus, the person who initially seeks counseling or for whom counseling is sought.

intrapsychic   Within the mind or psyche—used especially in regard to conflicting forces.

joint legal custody   A term used in the law to denote the rights of both parents to share in certain major decisions (for example, religious upbringing and choice of schools) regarding their children.

joint physical custody   A shared legal arrangement between ex-spouses in which their children spend time on a regular basis with one and then the other parent.

lesbian   A female engaged with another female in a sexual relationship.

linear causality   The view that a nonreciprocal relationship exists between events in a sequence so that one event causes the next event, but not vice versa.

managed care   A system by which third-party payers regulate and control the cost, quality, and terms of treatment of medical (including mental health) services.

modernist   Someone who contends that there exists an objectively knowable universe, able to be discovered and measured by impartial scientific methods.

morphogenesis   A process by which a system changes its basic structure, typically in response to positive feedback, in order to adapt to changing environmental demands or conditions.

morphostasis   A process by which a system maintains constancy in its structure or organization, usually in response to negative feedback in the face of environmental changes.

multigenerational transmission process   The process, occurring over several generations, in which poorly differentiated persons marry similar differentiated mates, ultimately resulting in offspring suffering from severe mental disorders.

narratives   Stories that families tell about themselves to explain their circumstances or particular set of problems.

negative feedback   The flow of corrective information from the output of a system back into the system in order to attenuate deviation and keep the system functioning within prescribed limits.

negentropy The tendency of a system to remain flexible and open to new input that is necessary for change and survival of the system.

no-fault divorce A legal dissolution of a marriage in which neither spouse is held to be at blame.

nuclear family A family composed of a husband, wife, and their offspring living together as a family unit.

paradigm A set of assumptions delimiting an area to be investigated scientifically and specifying the methods to be used to collect and interpret the forthcoming data.

paradoxical intervention A therapeutic technique whereby the counselor gives a client or family a directive he or she wants resisted—a change takes place as a result of defying the directive.

parentified child A child forced by his or her parents into a caretaking or nurturing parental role within the family—in extreme cases, the parents may abdicate the position of authority and assign the adult role to the child.

positive connotation A reframing technique whereby positive motives are ascribed to family behavior patterns because these patterns help maintain family balance and cohesion—as a result, family members are helped to view one another's motives more positively.

positive feedback The flow of information from the output of a system back into the system in order to amplify deviation from the state of equilibrium, thus leading to instability and change.

postmodern A philosophical outlook that rejects the notion that there exists an objectively knowable universe discoverable by impartial science, and instead argues that there are multiple views of reality ungovernable by universal laws.

prenuptial agreement A contract made by a couple prior to marriage in which they agree about the disposition of monies or property so as to avoid or modify legal repercussions regarding these matters that would ordinarily occur in the event of the dissolution of their marriage.

process A series of linked behavioral transactions among individuals occurring over a period of time and focused on *how* events are taking place rather than *what* is happening.

psychoanalytic A viewpoint reflecting the theory of personality formation as well as the therapeutic approach developed by Sigmund Freud.

psychoeducational A view emphasizing educating the family so that they might better understand and cope with a symptomatic family member.

psychopathology Severe problematic, maladaptive, or dysfunctional behavior.

reframing Relabeling behavior by putting it into a new, more positive perspective ("Mother is trying to help" in place of "She's intrusive"), thus altering the context in which it is perceived and inviting new responses to the same behavior.

relational ethics   In contextual counseling, the overall, long-term preservation of fairness within a family, ensuring that each member's basic interests are taken into account by other family members.

resilience   The ability to rebound from adversity or a crisis situation.

role overload   Stress that occurs in a family when members, most likely one or both parents, attempt to fulfill a greater variety of roles than their energies or time will permit.

second-order cybernetics   A view of an observing system in which the counselor is part of what is being observed rather than attempting to describe the system by being an outside observer.

single parent   A divorced person of either sex with whom the children of the marriage reside.

social construction   The postmodern view that there is no objective "truth," only versions of "reality" constructed from social interaction, including conversation, with others.

sole custody   The award by the court of total physical and legal responsibilities for the children to one of the parents in a divorcing couple.

solution-focused model   A postmodern approach in which the conversation with clients is focused on ways to construct positive changes in attitude and behavior rather than on searching for explanations regarding the origins of the presenting problem.

split custody   The award by the court of custody of one or more of the children to each of the parents in a divorcing couple.

stepfamily   A linked family system created by the marriage of two people, one or both of whom has been previously married, in which one or more children from the earlier marriages lives with the remarried couple.

strategic   A therapeutic approach in which the counselor develops a plan or strategy and designs interventions aimed at solving a specific presenting problem.

structural   A therapeutic approach directed at changing or realigning the family organization or structure in order to alter dysfunctional transactions and clarify subsystem boundaries.

structuralist   An advocate of the theory and techniques of the structural approach to counseling (see *structural*).

subsystems   Organized, coexisting components within an overall system, each having its own autonomous functions as well as a specific role in the operation of the larger system—within families, a member can belong to a number of such units.

suprasystem   A higher-level system in which other systems represent component parts and play subsystem roles—within a remarried family, a network of people (the former couple and their current family members, grandparents, aunts and uncles, cousins, and so on) who influence the remarried system.

symbolic-experiential model   Whitaker's therapeutic model emphasizing the covert, nonverbal, symbolic processes that occur within a family and that contain a powerful potential force for change.

system   A set of interacting units or component parts that together make up a whole arrangement or organization.

transgenerational   Involving patterns and influences occurring over two or more generations.

victim system   A circular-feedback process, most noticeable among African Americans, whereby regularly experiencing poverty, racism, and discrimination lowers self-esteem and produces problematic antisocial behaviors. These in turn impede the integration of African American culture with that of the American mainstream and lead to despair.

References

ABE-KIM, J. S., & TAKEUCHI, D. T. (1996). Cultural competence and quality of care: Issues for mental health service delivery in managed care. *Clinical Psychology, Science and Practice, 3,* 273–295.

ABRAHAMSE, A. E., MORRISON, P. A., & WAITE, L. J. (1988). *Beyond stereotypes: Who becomes a single teenage mother?* Santa Monica, CA: Rand.

ACOSTA, F. X., & EVANS, L. A. (1982). The Hispanic-American patient. In F. X. Acosta, J. Yamamoto, & L. A. Evans (Eds.), *Effective psychotherapy for low-income and minority patients.* New York: Plenum.

ACOSTA, F. X., YAMAMOTO, J., & EVANS, L. A. (Eds.). (1982). *Effective psychotherapy for low-income and minority patients.* New York: Plenum.

ADDIS, M. E. (1997). Evaluating the treatment manual as a means of disseminating empirically validated psychotherapies. *Clinical Psychology: Science and Practice, 4,* 1–11.

ADDIS, M. E., WADE, W. A., & HATGIS, C. (1999). Barriers to dissemination of evidence-based practices: Addressing practitioners' concerns about manual-based psychotherapies. *Clinical Psychology: Science and Practice, 6,* 430–441.

AHRONS, C. R. (1994). *The good divorce: Keeping the family together while your marriage comes apart.* New York: HarperCollins.

AHRONS, C. R., & RODGERS, R. H. (1987). *Divorced families: A multidisciplinary view.* New York: Norton.

ALAN GUTTMACHER INSTITUTE. (1994). *Sex and America's teenagers.* New York: Author.

ALBA, R. D. (1990). *Ethnic identity.* New Haven, CT: Yale University Press.

AMATO, P. R. (1993). Children's adjustment to divorce: Theories, hypotheses, and empirical support. *Journal of Marriage and the Family, 55,* 23–38.

AMERICAN PSYCHOLOGICAL ASSOCIATION. (1993). Guidelines for providers of psychological services to ethnic, linguistical, and culturally diverse populations. *American Psychologist, 48,* 45–48.

AMERICAN PSYCHOLOGICAL ASSOCIATION. (1994). Guidelines for child custody evaluations in divorce proceedings. *American Psychologist, 49,* 677–670.

AMERICAN PSYCHOLOGICAL ASSOCIATION TASK FORCE. (1995). *Template for developing guidelines: Interventions for mental disorders and psychosocial aspects of physical disorders.* Washington, DC: American Psychological Association.

ANDERSON, H. D. (1995). Collaborative language systems: Toward postmodern therapy. In R. H. Mikesell, D.-D. Lusterman, & S. H. McDaniel (Eds.), *Integrating family therapy: Handbook of family psychology and systems theory.* Washington, DC: American Psychological Association.

ANDERSON, H. D., & GOOLISHIAN, H. A. (1988). Human systems as linguistic systems: Preliminary and evolving ideas about the implications for clinical theories. *Family Process, 27,* 371–393.

APONTE, H. J. (1987). The treatment of society's poor: An ecological perspective on the underorganized family. *Family Therapy Today, 2*(1), 1–7.

APONTE, H. J. (1994). *Bread and spirit: Therapy with the new poor.* New York: Norton.

APONTE, J. F., & BARNES, J. M. (1995). Impact of acculturation and moderator variables on the intervention and treatment of ethnic groups. In J. F. Aponte, R. Y. Rivers, & J. Wohl (Eds.), *Psychological interventions and cultural diversity.* Needham Heights, MA: Allyn & Bacon.

APONTE, J. F., & WOHL, J. (2000). *Psychological intervention and cultural diversity* (2nd ed.). Des Moines, IA: Allyn & Bacon.

APPLEBY, G. A., & ANASTAS, J. W. (1995). Social work practice with lesbians and gays. In A. Morales (Ed.), *Social work: A profession of many faces* (7th ed.). Boston: Allyn & Bacon.

ARDITTI, J. A., & KELLY, M. (1994). Fathers' perspectives of their co-parental relationships postdivorce. *Family Relations, 43,* 61–67.

ATKINSON, D. R., MORTEN, G., & SUE, D. W. (Eds.). (1989). *Counseling American minorities: A cross-cultural perspective* (3rd ed.). Dubuque, IA: Brown.

AULETTE, J. R. (1994). *Changing families.* Belmont, CA: Wadsworth.

AXELSON, J. A. (1999). *Counseling and development in a multicultural society* (3rd ed.). Pacific Grove, CA: Brooks/Cole.

AXINN, W. G., & THORNTON, A. (1992). The relationship between cohabitation and divorce: Selectivity or causal influence? *Demography, 29*(3), 357–374.

BACHMAN, J. G., JOHNSTON, L. D., & O'MALLEY, P. M. (1997). *Monitoring the future: Questionnaire responses from the nation's high school seniors, 1995.* Ann Arbor: Survey Research Center of the University of Michigan.

BACH-Y-RITA, G. (1982). The Mexican American religious and cultural influences. In R. M. Becerra, M. Karno, & J. I. Escobar (Eds.), *Mental health and Hispanic Americans: Clinical perspectives.* New York: Grune & Stratton.

BAGAROZZI, D. A. (1985). *Dimensions of family evaluation*. In L. L. L'Abate (Ed.), *The handbook of family psychology and therapy* (Vol. II). Pacific Grove, CA: Brooks/Cole.

BASS, B. A. (1982). The validity of sociocultural factors in the assessment and treatment of Afro-Americans. In B. A. Bass, G. E. Wyatt, & G. J. Powell (Eds.), *The Afro-American family: Assessment, treatment, and research issues*. New York: Grune & Stratton.

BATESON, G. (1979). *Mind and nature*. New York: Dutton.

BEAVERS, W. R. (1981). A systems model of family for family therapists. *Journal of Marriage and Family Therapy, 7,* 299–307.

BEAVERS, W. R. (1982). Healthy, midrange, and severely dysfunctional families. In F. Walsh (Ed.), *Normal family processes*. New York: Guilford.

BEAVERS, W. R., & VOELLER, M. N. (1983). Family models: Comparing and contrasting the Olson circumplex with the Beavers model. *Family Process, 22,* 85–98.

BECK, A., RUSH, J., SHAW, B., & EMERY, G. (1979). *Cognitive therapy of depression*. New York: Guilford.

BEM, D. (1996). Exotic becomes erotic: A developmental theory of sexual orientation. *Psychological Review, 103,* 320–335.

BEM, S. L. (1998). *An unconventional family*. New Haven, CT: Yale University Press.

BENNETT, N. G., BLANC, A. K., & BLOOM, D. E. (1988). Commitment and the modern union: Assessing the link between premarital cohabitation and subsequent marital stability. *American Sociological Review, 53*(1), 127–138.

BERG, I. K., & JAYA, K. P. (1993). Different and same: Family therapy with Asian-American families. *Journal of Marital and Family Therapy, 19*(1), 31–38.

BERMAN, E. M., & GOLDBERG, M. (1986). Therapy with unmarried couples. In N. S. Jacobson & A. S. Gurman (Eds.), *Clinical handbook of marital therapy*. New York: Guilford.

BERNAL, G. (1982). Cuban families. In M. McGoldrick, J. K. Pearce, & J. Giordano (Eds.), *Ethnicity and family therapy*. New York: Guilford.

BERNAL, G., BERNAL, M., MARTINEZ, A. C., OLMEDO, E. L., & SANTISTEBAN, D. (1983). Hispanic mental health curriculum for psychology. In J. C. Chunn II, P. J. Dunston, & E. Ross-Sheriff (Eds.), *Mental health and people of color: Curriculum development and change*. Washington, DC: Howard University Press.

BERNSTEIN, A. C. (1999). Reconstructing the Brothers Grimm: New tales for stepfamily life. *Family Process, 38,* 415–429.

BERRILL, K. T. (1990). Anti-gay violence and victimization in the United States: An overview. *Journal of Interpersonal Violence, 5,* 274–294.

BERTALANFFY, L. Von. (1968). *General systems theory: Foundation, development, applications*. New York: Braziller.

BERZON, B. (1979). *Positively gay*. Los Angeles: Mediamix.

BLASBAND, D., & PEPLAU, L. A. (1985). Sexual exclusivity versus openness in gay male couples. *Archives of Sexual Behavior, 14,* 395–412.

BLUMENFELD, W. J. (1992). *How we all pay the price*. Boston: Beacon.

BLUMSTEIN, P., & SCHWARTZ, P. (1983). *American couples*. New York: Morrow.

BOHANNAN, P. (1970). *Divorce and after*. Garden City, NY: Doubleday.

BOHANNAN, P. (1984). *All the happy families: Exploring the varieties of family life.* New York: McGraw-Hill.

BOOTH, A., & CROUTER, A. C. (Eds.). (1998). *Understanding men in the family: Contemporary research studies.* Mahwah, NJ: Erlbaum.

BOOTH, A., & DUNN, J. (Eds.). (1994). *Stepfamilies: Who benefits? Who does not?* Hillsdale, NJ: Erlbaum.

BOOTH, A., & JOHNSON, D. (1988). Premarital cohabitation and marital success. *Journal of Family Issues, 9,* 255–272.

BOSCOLO, L., CECCHIN, G., HOFFMAN, L., & PENN, P. (1987). *Milan systemic family therapy: Conversations in theory and practice.* New York: Basic.

BOSZORMENYI-NAGY, I. (1987). *Foundations of contextual therapy: Collected papers of Ivan Boszormenyi-Nagy.* New York: Brunner/Mazel.

BOUGHNER, S. R., HAYES, S. F., BUBENZER, D. L., & WEST, J. D. (1994). Use of standardized assessment instruments by marital and family therapists: A survey. *Journal of Marital and Family Therapy, 20,* 69–75.

BOWEN, M. (1978). *Family therapy in clinical practice.* New York: Aronson.

BOYD, H. (1998). *The step-parent's survival guide.* New York: Sterling.

BOYD-FRANKLIN, N. (1989). *Black families in therapy: A multisystems approach.* New York: Guilford.

BOYD-FRANKLIN, N. (1995). Therapy with African-American inner-city families. In R. H. Mikesell, D.-D. Lusterman, & S. H. McDaniel (Eds.), *Integrating family therapy: Handbook of family psychology and systems theory.* Washington, DC: American Psychological Association.

BOYD-FRANKLIN, N., & FRANKLIN, A. J. (2000). *Boys into men: Raising our African American teenage sons.* New York: Dutton.

BOYD-FRANKLIN, N., STEINER, G., & BOLAND, M. (1995). *Children, families, and AIDS/HIV: Psychosocial and psychotherapeutic issues.* New York: Guilford.

BOZETT, F. W. (1982). Heterogeneous couples in heterosexual marriages: Gay men and straight women. *Journal of Marital and Family Therapy, 8,* 81–89.

BOZETT, F. W. (1985). Gay men as fathers. In S. M. Hanson & E. W. Bozett (Eds.), *Dimensions of fatherhood.* Newbury Park, CA: Sage.

BRADT, J. O., & BRADT, C. M. (1986). Resources in remarried families. In M. Karpel (Ed.), *Family resources: The hidden partner in family therapy.* New York: Guilford.

BRAVER, S. L., WOLCHIK, S. A., SANDLER, I. N., SHEETS, V. L., FOGAS, B., & BAY, R. C. (1993). A longitudinal study of noncustodial parents: Parents without children. *Journal of Family Psychology, 7*(1), 9–23.

BRAY, J. H. (1988). *What's in the best interest of the child? Custodial arrangements and visitation issues.* Unpublished manuscript.

BRAY, J. H. (1992). Family relationships and children's adjustment in clinical and nonclinical stepfather families. *Journal of Family Psychology, 6,* 60–68.

BRAY, J. H. (1995). Systems-oriented therapy with stepfamilies. In R. H. Mikesell, D. D. Lusterman, & S. H. McDaniel (Eds.), *Integrating family therapy: Handbook of family psychology and systems theory.* Washington, DC: American Psychological Association.

BRAY, J. H., & ANDERSON, H. (1984). Strategic interventions with single-parent families. *Psychotherapy, 21,* 101–109.

BROSS, A. (1982). *Family therapy: Principles of strategic practice.* New York: Guilford.

BROWN, E. M. (1985). The comprehensive divorce treatment center: The divorce and marital stress clinic model. In D. H. Sprenkle (Ed.), *Divorce therapy.* Binghampton, NY: Haworth.

BROWN, L. S. (1995). Therapy with same-sex couples. In N. S. Jacobson & A. S. Gurman (Eds.), *Clinical handbook of couple therapy.* New York: Guilford.

BRUCE, W. M., & REED, C. M. (1991). *Dual-career couples in the public sector: A management guide for human resource professionals.* New York: Quorum.

BRUNER, J. (1986). *Actual minds, possible worlds.* Cambridge, MA: Harvard University Press.

BUMPASS, L. L., RALEY, R. K., & SWEET, J. A. (1995). The changing character of stepfamilies: Implications of cohabitation and nonmarital childbearing. *Demography, 32,* 425–436.

BUMPASS, L. L., & SWEET, J. A. (1989). National estimates of cohabitation. *Demography, 26*(4), 615–625.

BUMPASS, L. L., SWEET, J. A., & CHERLIN, A. (1991). The role of cohabitation in declining rates of marriage. *Journal of Marriage and the Family, 53,* 913–927.

BUMPASS, L. L., SWEET, J. A., & MARTIN, T. C. (1990). Changing patterns of remarriage. *Journal of Marriage and the Family, 52,* 747–756.

BURDEN, D. (1986). Single parents and the work setting: The impact of multiple job and homelife responsibilities. *Family Relations, 35,* 37–43.

BURDEN, D., & KLERMAN, L. (1984). Teenage parenthood: Factors that lessen economic dependence. *Social Work, 29*(1), 11–16.

BURT, M. S., & BURT, R. B. (1996). *Stepfamilies: The step by step model of brief therapy.* New York: Brunner/Mazel.

BUUNK, B. M., & VAN DRIEL, B. (1989). *Variant lifestyles and relationships.* Newbury Park, CA: Sage.

BUXTON, A. (1994). *The other side of the closet: The coming out crisis for straight spouses and families.* New York: Wiley.

CAILLE, P. (1982). The evaluation phase of systemic family therapy. *Journal of Marital and Family Therapy, 8,* 29–39.

CAMPOS, L. P. (1996, September). Cultural competence in the courtroom. *California Psychologist,* p. 32.

CANINO, G. (1982). The Hispanic woman: Sociocultural influences on diagnoses and treatment. In R. M. Becerra, M. Karno, & J. I. Escobar (Eds.), *Mental health and Hispanic Americans: Clinical perspectives.* New York: Grune & Stratton.

CARL, D. (1990). Parenting/blended family issues. In D. Carl (Ed.), *Counseling same sex couples.* New York: Norton.

CARLSON, J., SPERRY, L., & LEWIS, J. A. (1997). *Family therapy: Ensuring treatment efficacy.* Pacific Grove, CA: Brooks/Cole.

CARRILLO, C. (1982). Changing norms of Hispanic families: Implications for treatment. In E. E. Jones & S. J. Korchin (Eds.), *Minority mental health.* New York: Praeger.

CARTER, E. A., & McGOLDRICK, M. (Eds.). (1980). *The family life cycle.* New York: Gardner.

CARTER, E. A., & McGOLDRICK, M. (1988). Overview: The changing family life cycle. In E. A. Carter & M. McGoldrick (Eds.), *The changing family life cycle: A framework for family therapy* (2nd ed.). New York: Gardner.

CASHON, B. (1982). Female-headed families: Effects on children and clinical implications. *Journal of Marital and Family Therapy, 8,* 77–85.

CATTON, T. (1991, October). Child-care problems: An obstacle to work. *Monthly Labor Review.* Washington, DC: U.S. Department of Labor.

CAZENAVE, N. A. (1980). Alternative intimacy, marriage, and family lifestyle among low-income Black-Americans. *Alternative Lifestyles, 4*(4), 425–444.

CHAMBLESS, D. L., & HOLLON, S. D. (1998). Defining empirically supported therapies. *Journal of Consulting and Clinical Psychology, 66,* 7–18.

CHAPMAN, A. B. (1988). Male-female relations: How the past affects the present. In H. P. McAdoo (Ed.), *Black families* (2nd ed.). Newbury Park, CA: Sage.

CHERLIN, A. J. (1992). *Marriage, divorce, remarriage* (rev. ed.). Cambridge, MA: Harvard University Press.

CHEUNG, F. K., & SNOWDEN, L. R. (1990). Community mental health and ethnic minority populations. *Community Mental Health Journal, 26,* 277–291.

CHEVAL, A. (1996). As cheaply as one: Cohabitation in the older population. *Journal of Marriage and the Family, 58,* 656–667.

CHIEN, C., & YAMAMOTO, J. (1982). Asian-American and Pacific-Islander patients. In F. X. Acosta, J. Yamamoto, & L. A. Evans (Eds.), *Effective psychotherapy with low-income and minority patients.* New York: Plenum.

CIMMARUSTI, R. A. (1996). Exploring aspects of Filipino-American families. *Journal of Marital and Family Therapy, 22,* 205–217.

CLARKE-STEWART, K. A., & HAYWARD, C. (1996). Advantages of father custody and contact for the psychological well-being of the school-age children. *Journal of Applied Developmental Psychology, 17,* 239–270.

CLINGEMPEEL, A. J., BRAND, E., & IEVOLI, R. (1984). Stepparent-stepchild relationships in stepmother and stepfather families: A multimethod study. *Family Relations, 33,* 465–473.

COLE, C. L. (1988). Family and couples therapy with nonmarital cohabiting couples: Treatment issues and case studies. In C. S. Chilman, E. W. Nunnally, & E. M. Cox (Eds.), *Variant family forms.* Newbury Park, CA: Sage.

COLEY, R. L., & CHASE-LANSDALE, P. L. (1998). Adolescent pregnancy and parenthood: Recent evidence and future directions. *American Psychologist, 53,* 152–166.

COMPTON, B. R., & GALAWAY, B. (1999). *Social work processes* (6th ed.). Pacific Grove, CA: Brooks/Cole.

CONGER, J. J. (1981). Freedom and commitment: Families, youth, and social change. *American Psychologist, 36,* 1475–1484.

CONSTANTINE, L. L. (1986). *Family paradigms: The practice of theory in family therapy.* New York: Guilford.

COONTZ, S. (1992). *The way we never were: American families and the nostalgia trap.* New York: HarperCollins.

COWAN, P., & HETHERINGTON, M. (Eds.). (1990). *Family transitions*. Hillsdale, NJ: Erlbaum.

COX, F. D. (1996). *Human intimacy: Marriage, the family, and its meaning*. Minneapolis: West.

CRAWFORD, S. (1987). Lesbian families: Psychosocial stress and the family-building process. In Boston Lesbian Psychologies Collective (Eds.), *Lesbian psychologies: Explorations and challenges*. Urbana: University of Illinois Press.

CRISPELL, D. (1991). How to avoid big mistakes. *American Demographics, 15,* 1.

CROHN, H., SAGER, C. J., BROWN, H., RODSTEIN, E., & WALKER, L. (1982). A basis for understanding and treating the remarried family. In J. C. Hansen & L. Messinger (Eds.), *Therapy with remarried families*. Rockville, MD: Aspen.

CROSBIE-BURNETT, M., & LEWIS, E. A. (1993). Use of African-American family structures and functioning to address the challenges of European-American postdivorce families. *Family Relations, 42,* 243–248.

CROUTER, A. C., & MANKE, B. (1997). Development of a typology of dual-earner families: A window into differences between and within families in relationships, roles, and activities. *Journal of Family Psychology, 11,* 62–75.

DAVIS, G., & WATSON, G. (1982). *Black life in corporate America*. New York: Doubleday.

DAY, R. D., & BAHR, S. J. (1986). Income changes following divorce and remarriage. *Journal of Divorce, 9,* 75–88.

DeCECCHO, J. P., & ELIA, J. P. (Eds.). (1993). *If you seduce a straight person, can you make them gay? Issues in biological essentialism versus social constructionism in gay and lesbian identities*. New York: Harrington Park.

DEL CARMEN, R. (1990). Assessment of Asian-Americans for family therapy. In E. C. Serafica, A. I. Schwebel, R. K. Russell, P. D. Isaac, & L. B. Myers (Eds.), *Mental health of ethnic minorities*. New York: Praeger.

DeMARIS, A., & MACDONALD, W. (1993). Premarital cohabitation and marital instability: A test of unconventionality. *Journal of Marriage and the Family, 7,* 399–407.

deSHAZER, S. (1983). Diagnosing + researching + doing therapy. In B. Keeney (Ed.), *Diagnosis and assessment in family therapy*. Rockville, MD: Aspen.

deSHAZER, S. (1991). *Putting differences to work*. New York: Norton.

DILLER, J. V. (1999). *Cultural diversity: A primer for the human services*. Belmont, CA: Brooks/Cole–Wadsworth.

DOHERTY, W. J., & BAIRD, M. A. (1983). *Family therapy and family medicine: Toward the primary care of families*. New York: Guilford.

DUBERMAN, L. (1975). *The reconstituted family: A study of remarried couples and their children*. Chicago: Nelson-Hall.

EIDELSON, R. J. (1983). Affiliation and independence issues in marriage. *Journal of Marriage and the Family, 45,* 683–688.

EINSTEIN, E. (1982). *The stepfamily: Living, loving and learning*. Boston: Shambhala.

EMERY, R. E. (1994). *Renegotiating family relationships: Divorce, child custody, and mediation*. New York: Guilford.

EMERY, R. E. (1999). *Marriage, divorce, and children's adjustment* (2nd ed.). Newbury Park, CA: Sage.

EMERY, R. E., & FOREHAND, R. (1994). Parental divorce and children's well-being: A focus on resilience. In R. J. Haggerty, L. R. Sherrod, N. Garmezy, & M. Rutter (Eds.), *Stress, risk, and resilience in children and adolescents.* Cambridge, England: Cambridge University Press.

EPSTEIN, N. B., BALDWIN, L. M., & BISHOP, D. S. (1983). The McMaster family assessment device. *Journal of Marital and Family Therapy, 9,* 171–180.

EPSTEIN, N. B., BISHOP, D. S., & BALDWIN, L. M. (1982). McMaster model of family functioning: A view of the normal family. In E. Walsh (Ed.), *Normal family processes.* New York: Guilford.

ERIKSON, E. H. (1963). *Childhood and society.* New York: Norton.

EVERETT, C. A. (1987). *The divorce process: A handbook for clinicians.* New York: Haworth.

EVERETT, C. A., & VOLGY, S. S. (1991). Treating divorce in family therapy practice. In A. S. Gurman & D. P. Kniskern (Eds.), *Handbook of family therapy* (Vol. II). New York: Brunner/Mazel.

EVERETT, C. A., & VOLGY EVERETT, S. S. (1994). *Healthy divorce.* San Francisco: Jossey-Bass.

FALICOV, C. J. (1982). Mexican families. In M. McGoldrick, J. Pearce, & J. Giordano (Eds.), *Ethnicity and family therapy.* New York: Guilford.

FALICOV, C. J. (1988). Learning to think culturally. In H. A. Liddle, D. C. Breunlin, & R. C. Schwartz (Eds.), *Handbook of family therapy training and supervision.* New York: Guilford.

FALICOV, C. J. (1995a). Cross-cultural marriages. In N. S. Jacobson & A. S. Gurman (Eds.), *Clinical handbook of couple therapy.* New York: Guilford.

FALICOV, C. J. (1995b). Training to think culturally: A multidimensional comparative framework. *Family Process, 34,* 373–388.

FALICOV, C. J. (1998). *Latino families in therapy: A guide to multicultural practice.* New York: Guilford.

FARBER, R. S. (1988). Integrated treatment of the dual-career couple. *Journal of Family Therapy, 16,* 46–57.

FASSINGER, R. (1991). Counseling lesbian women and gay men. *Counseling Psychologist, 19,* 157–176.

FELDMAN, C. M., & RIDLEY, C. A. (1995). The etiology and treatment of domestic violence between adult partners. *Clinical Psychology: Science and Practice, 2,* 317–348.

FINE, M. A., McKENRY, P. C., DONNELLY, B. W., & VOYDANOFF, P. (1992). Perceived adjustment of parents and children: Variations by family structure, race, and gender. *Journal of Marriage and the Family, 54,* 118–127.

FISHMAN, H. C. (1985). Diagnosis and context: An Alexandrian quartet. In R. L. Ziffer (Ed.), *Adjunctive techniques in family therapy.* New York: Grune & Stratton.

FLOYD, F. J., MARKMAN, H. J., KELLY, S., BLUMBERG, S. L., & STANLEY, S. M. (1995). Preventive intervention and relationship enhancement. In N. J. Jacobson & A. S. Gurman (Eds.), *Clinical handbook of couple therapy.* New York: Guilford.

FOLBERG, J., & MILNE, A. (Eds.). (1988). *Divorce mediation: Theory and practice.* New York: Guilford.

FOLK, K., & YI, Y. (1994). Piecing together child care with multiple arrangements: Crazy quilts or preferred patterns for employed parents or preschool children? *Journal of Marriage and the Family, 56,* 669–680.

FOWERS, B. J., MONTEL, K. H., & OLSON, D. H. (1996). Predicting marital success for premarital couple types based on PREPARE. *Journal of Marital and Family Therapy, 22,* 102–119.

FOWERS, B. J., & OLSON, D. H. (1992). Four types of premarital couples: An empirical typology based on PREPARE. *Journal of Family Psychology, 6*(1), 10–21.

FRANCES, A., CLARKIN, J. E, & PERRY, S. (1984). *Differential therapeutics in psychiatry: The art and science of treatment selection.* New York: Brunner/Mazel.

FRANKLIN, A. J., & BOYD-FRANKLIN, N. (1990). Psychotherapy with African-American clients. *Register Reports, 16*(3), 20–22.

FRIESEN, J. D. (1985). *Structural-strategic marriage and family therapy.* New York: Gardner.

FULMER, R. H. (1983). A structural approach to unresolved mourning in single-parent family systems. *Journal of Marital and Family Therapy, 9,* 259–269.

FURSTENBERG, E. E., JR. (1987). The new extended family: The experience of parents and children after remarriage. In K. Pasley & M. Ihinger-Tallman (Eds.), *Remarriage and stepparenting: Current research and theory.* New York: Guilford.

FURSTENBERG, E. E. (1988). Child care after divorce and remarriage. In E. M. Hetherington & J. D. Arasteh (Eds.), *Impact of divorce: Single parenting, and stepparenting on children.* Hillsdale, NJ: Erlbaum.

FURSTENBERG, E. E., JR., BROOKS-GUNN, J., & CHASE-LANSDALE, L. (1989). Teenage pregnancy and childbearing. *American Psychologist, 44,* 313–320.

FURSTENBERG, E. E., JR., & CHERLIN, A. J. (1991). *Divided families: What happens to children when parents part.* Cambridge, MA: Harvard University Press.

GANONG, L. H., & COLEMAN, M. (1994). *Remarried family relationships.* Thousand Oaks, CA: Sage.

GANONG, L. H., & COLEMAN, M. (1999). *Changing families, changing responsibilities: Family obligations following divorce and remarriage.* Mahwah, NJ: Erlbaum.

GANONG, L. H., COLEMAN, M., & FINE, M. (1995). Remarriage and stepfamilies. In R. D. Day, K. R. Gilbert, B. H. Settles, & W. E. Burr (Eds.), *Research and theory in family science.* Pacific Grove, CA: Brooks/Cole.

GARFIELD, S. L. (1996). Some problems associated with "validated" forms of psychotherapy. *Clinical Psychology: Science and Practice, 3,* 218–229.

GARTRELL, N. (1983). Gay patients in the medical setting. In C. C. Nadelson & D. B. Marcotte (Eds.), *Treatment interventions in human sexuality.* New York: Plenum.

GARTRELL, N., HAMILTON, M. D., BANKS, A., MOSBACHER, D., REED, N., SPARKS, C. H., & BISHOP, H. (1996). The national lesbian family study: 1. Interviews with prospective mothers. *American Journal of Orthopsychiatry, 66,* 272–281.

GARTRELL, N., BANKS, A., HAMILTON, J., REED, N., BISHOP, H., & RODAS, C. (1999). The national lesbian family study: 2. Interviews with mothers of toddlers. *American Journal of Orthopsychiatry, 69,* 362–369.

GELFAND, D., & YEE, B. W. K. (1991). Trends and forces: Influence of immigration, migration, and acculturation on the fabric of aging in America. *Generations, 15,* 7–10.

References

GERGEN, K. J. (1985). The social construction movement in modern psychology. *American Psychologist, 40,* 266–275.

GERGEN, K. J. (1993). Foreword. In S. Friedman (Ed.), *The new language of change: Constructive collaboration in psychotherapy.* New York: Guilford.

GERSTEL, N., & GROSS, H. (1984). *Commuter marriage.* New York: Guilford.

GETTY, C. (1981). Considerations for working with single-parent families. In C. Getty & D. B. Marcotte (Eds.), *Understanding the family: Stress and change in American family life.* New York: Appleton-Century-Crofts.

GILBERT, L. A. (1985). *Men in dual-career families: Current realities and future prospects.* Hillsdale, NJ: Erlbaum.

GILBERT, L. A. (1988). *Sharing it all: The rewards and struggles of two-career families.* New York: Plenum.

GILGUN, J. F. (1999). An ecosystemic approach to assessment. In B. R. Compton & B. Galaway (Eds.), *Social work processes* (6th ed.). Pacific Grove, CA: Brooks/Cole.

GINN, C. W. (1995). *Families: Using types to enhance mutual understanding.* Gainesville, FL: Center for Application of Psychological Type.

GIORDANO, J., & CARINI-GIORDANO, M. A. (1995). Ethnic dimensions in family treatment. In R. H. Mikesell, D.-D. Lusterman, & S. H. McDaniel (Eds.), *Integrating family therapy: Handbook of family psychology and systems theory.* Washington, DC: American Psychological Association.

GLICK, P. C. (1984a). American household structure in transition. *Family Planning Perspectives, 16,* 205–211.

GLICK, P. C. (1984b). How American families are changing. *American Demographics, 5,* 21–25.

GLICK, P. C. (1984c). Marriage, divorce, and living arrangements: Prospective changes. *Journal of Family Issues, 5,* 7–26.

GLICK, P. C. (1989). Remarried families, stepfamilies, and stepchildren: A brief demographic analysis. *Family Relations, 38,* 24–27.

GLICKAUF-HUGHES, C. L., HUGHES, G. B., & WELLS, M. C. (1986). A developmental approach to treating dual-career couples. *American Journal of Family Therapy, 14,* 254–263.

GOLD, R., & SKINNER, M. (1992). Situational factors and thought processes associated with unprotected intercourse in young gay men. *AIDS, 6,* 1021–1030.

GOLDENBERG, H. (1977). *Abnormal psychology: A social/community approach.* Pacific Grove, CA: Brooks/Cole.

GOLDENBERG, H. (1986). Treating contemporary couples in dual-career relationships. *Family Therapy Today, 1*(1), 1–7.

GOLDENBERG, I., & GOLDENBERG, H. (1984). Treating the dual-career couple. *American Journal of Family Therapy, 12,* 29–37.

GOLDENBERG, I., & GOLDENBERG, H. (2000). *Family therapy: An overview* (5th ed.). Pacific Grove, CA: Brooks/Cole.

GOLDFRIED, M. R., & WOLFE, B. (1996). Psychotherapy practice and research: Repairing a strained relationship. *American Psychologist, 51,* 1007–1016.

GOLDSTEIN, M. J., & MIKLOWITZ, D. J. (1995). The effectiveness of psychoeducational family therapy in the treatment of schizophrenic disorders. *Journal of Marital and Family Therapy, 21,* 361–376.

GOOGINS, B. (1991). *Work/family conflicts: Private lives—public responses.* New York: Auburn House.

GORALL, D. M., & OLSON, D. H. (1995). Circumplex model of family systems: Integrating ethnic diversity and other social systems. In R. H. Mikesell, D.-D. Lusterman, & S. H. McDaniel (Eds.), *Integrating family therapy: Handbook of family psychology and systems theory.* Washington, DC: American Psychological Association.

GOTTMAN, J. M. (1993). A theory of marital dissolution and stability. *Journal of Family Psychology, 7,* 57–75.

GOTTMAN, J. M. (1994). *What predicts divorce?* Hillsdale, NJ: Erlbaum.

GOTTMAN, J. M., COAN, J., CARRÈRE, S., & SWANSON, C. (1998). Predicting marital happiness and stability from newlywed interactions. *Journal of Marriage and the Family, 60,* 5–22.

GRANVOLD, D. K. (1983). Structured separation for marital treatment and decision-making. *Journal of Marital and Family Therapy, 9,* 403–412.

GREEN, J. (1989). Post-test counselling. In J. Green & A. McCreaner (Eds.), *Counselling in HIV infection and AIDS.* Oxford, England: Blackwell Scientific Publications.

GREEN, R. G., KOLEVZON, M. S., & VOSLER, N. R. (1985). The Beavers-Timberlawn model of family competence and the circumplex model of family adaptability and coherence: Separate, but equal? *Family Process, 24,* 385–398.

GREENE, B. (1994). Ethnic minority lesbians and gay men mental health and treatment issues. *Journal of Consulting and Clinical Psychology, 62,* 243–251.

GREEN, R. J. (1998). Race and the field of family therapy. In M. McGoldrick (Ed.), *Revisioning family therapy: Race, culture, and gender in clinical practice.* New York: Norton.

GREIF, G. L. (1995). Single fathers with custody following separation and divorce. In S. M. H. Hanson, M. L. Heims, D. J. Julian, & M. B. Sussman (Eds.), *Single parent families: Diversity, myths, and realities.* New York: Haworth.

GRIER, W. H., & COBBS, P. M. (1968). *Black rage.* New York: Basic.

GRIEVOUS, C. (1989). The role of the family therapist with low-income black families. In D. R. Atkinson, G. Morten, & D. W. Sue (Eds.), *Counseling American minorities: A cross-cultural perspective.* Dubuque, IA: Brown.

GROTEVANT, H. D., & CARLSON, C. I. (1999). *Family assessment: A guide to methods and measures* (2nd ed.). New York: Guilford.

GUERIN, P., FAY, L., BURDEN, S., & KAUTTO, J. (1987). *The evaluation and treatment of marital conflict.* New York: Basic.

GUILBORD, G. M. (1999, November/December). The religious and spiritual struggle surrounding G/L/B/T people. *Los Angeles Psychologist,* pp. 4, 16.

GULLOTTA, T. P., ADAMS, G. R., & ALEXANDER, S. J. (1986). *Today's marriages and families: A wellness approach.* Pacific Grove, CA: Brooks/Cole.

GUTIERREZ, M. J. (1987). Teenage pregnancy and the Puerto Rican family. In M. Lindblad-Goldberg (Ed.), *Clinical issues in single-parent households*. Rockville, MD: Aspen.

GUTTMAN, H. A. (1991). Systems theory, cybernetics, and epistemology. In A. S. Gurman & D. P. Kniskern (Eds.), *Handbook of family therapy* (Vol. II). New York: Brunner/Mazel.

HALDERMAN, D. C. (1994). The practice and ethics of sexual orientation conversion therapy. *Journal of Consulting and Clinical Psychology, 62*, 221–227.

HALEY, J. (Ed.). (1976). *Problem-solving therapy*. San Francisco: Jossey-Bass.

HALEY, J. (1984). *Ordeal therapy: Unusual ways to change behavior*. San Francisco: Jossey-Bass.

HALL, A. S., PULVER, C. A., & COOLEY, M. J. (1996). Psychology of best interests standard: Fifty state statutes and their theoretical antecedents. *American Journal of Family Therapy, 24*, 171–180.

HALL, E. S., & HALL, D. T. (1979). *The two-career couple*. Reading, MA: Addison-Wesley.

HAMPSON, R. B., & BEAVERS, W. R. (1996). Measuring family therapy outcomes in a clinical setting: Families that do better or do worse in therapy. *Family Process, 35*, 347–361.

HANSEN, J. C. (Ed.). (1983). *Clinical implications of the family life cycle*. Rockville, MD: Aspen.

HAREVEN, T. K. (1982). American families in transition: Historical perspective on change. In F. Walsh (Ed.), *Normal family processes*. New York: Guilford.

HARRISON, J. (1987). Counseling gay men. In M. Scher, M. Stevens, G. Good, & G. A. Eichenfield (Eds.), *Handbook of counseling and psychotherapy with men*. Newbury Park, CA: Sage.

HARRY, J. (1983). Gay male and lesbian relationships. In E. D. Macklin & R. H. Rubin (Eds.), *Contemporary families and alternative lifestyles*. Newbury Park, CA: Sage.

HARRY, J. (1988). Some problems of gay/lesbian families. In C. S. Chilman, E. W. Nunnally, & E. M. Fox (Eds.), *Variant family forms*. Newbury Park, CA: Sage.

HATCH, R. G. (1995). *Aging and cohabitation*. New York: Garland.

HAWKINS, A. J., MARSHALL, C. M., & ALLEN, S. M. (1998). The orientation toward domestic labor questionnaire: Exploring dual-earner wives' sense of fairness about family work. *Journal of Family Psychology, 12*, 244–258.

HAWLEY, D. R., & de HAAN, L. (1996). Toward a definition of family resilience: Integrating life-span and family perspectives. *Family Process, 35*, 283–298.

HELD, B. S. (1998). The antisystematic impact of postmodern philosophy. *Clinical Psychology, 5*, 264–273.

HENGGELER, S. W., & BORDUIN, C. M. (1990). *Family therapy and beyond: A multisystemic approach to treating the behavior problems of children and adolescents*. Pacific Grove, CA: Brooks/Cole.

HEREK, G. (1994). Assessing heterosexuals' attitudes toward lesbians and gay men: A review of empirical research with the ATLG Scale. In B. Greene & G. Herek (Eds.), *Lesbian and gay psychology: Theory, research, and clinical application*. Thousand Oaks, CA: Sage.

HETHERINGTON, E. M. (1993). An overview of the Virginia Longitudinal Study of Divorce and Remarriage with a focus on early adolescence. *Journal of Family Psychology, 7*(1), 39–56.

HETHERINGTON, E. M. (Ed.). (1999). *Coping with divorce, single parenting, and remarriage: A risk and resiliency perspective.* Mahwah, NJ: Erlbaum.

HETHERINGTON, E. M., BRIDGES, M., & INSABELLA, G. M. (1998). What matters? What does not? Five perspectives on the association between marital transitions and children's adjustments. *American Psychologist, 53,* 167–184.

HETHERINGTON, E. M., & STANLEY-HAGAN, M. S. (1997). The effects of divorce on fathers and their children. In M. Bornstein (Ed.), *The role of the father in child development.* New York: Wiley.

HETHERINGTON, E. M., STANLEY-HAGAN, M., & ANDERSON, E. R. (1989). Marital transitions: A child's perspective. *American Psychologist, 44,* 303–312.

HILL, R. (1977). *Informal adoption among black families.* Washington, DC: Urban League Research Department.

HINES, P. M., & BOYD-FRANKLIN, N. (1982). Black families. In M. McGoldrick, J. K. Pearce, & J. Giordano (Eds.), *Ethnicity and family therapy.* New York: Guilford.

HO, M. K. (1987). *Family therapy with ethnic minorities.* Newbury Park, CA: Sage.

HOCHSCHILD, A. (1989). *The second shift: Working parents and the revolution at home.* New York: Viking.

HOCHSCHILD, A. (1997). *The second shift.* New York: Avon.

HODGES, W. E. (1991). *Intervention for children of divorce: Custody, access, and psychotherapy* (2nd ed.). New York: Wiley.

HOFFMAN, L. (1985). Beyond power and control: Toward a second-order family systems therapy. *Family Systems, 3,* 381–396.

HOFFMAN, L. (1990). Constructing realities: An art of lenses. *Family Process, 29,* 1–12.

HOFFMAN, L. W. (1989). Effects of maternal employment in the two-parent family. *American Psychologist, 44,* 283–292.

HOMMA-TRUE, R., GREENE, B., LOPEZ, S. R., & TRIMBLE, J. E. (1993). Ethnocultural diversity in clinical psychology. *Clinical Psychologist, 46,* 50–63.

HOOKER, E. (1957). The adjustment of the male homosexual. *Journal of Projective Techniques, 21,* 18–31.

HUBER, C. H., & BARUTH, L. G. (1987). *Ethical, legal, and professional issues in the practice of marriage and family therapy.* Columbus, OH: Merrill.

HUDSON INSTITUTE. (1988). *Opportunities 2000: Creative affirmative action strategies for a changing workforce.* Washington, DC: U.S. Department of Labor.

HUMPHREYS, L., & MILLER, B. (1980). Identities and the emerging gay culture. In J. Marmor (Ed.), *Homosexual behavior: A modern reappraisal.* New York: Basic.

HUNT, J. G., & HUNT, L. L. (1977). Dilemmas and contradictions of status: The case of the dual-career family. *Social Problems, 24,* 407–416.

HUNT, J. G., & HUNT, L. L. (1982). Dual-career families: Vanguards of the future or residue of the past? In J. Aldous (Ed.), *Two paychecks: Life in dual-earner families.* Newbury Park, CA: Sage.

HUSTON, T. L., & ROBINS, E. (1982). Conceptual and methodological issues in studying close relationships. In L. H. Brown & J. S. Kidwell (Eds.), Methodology: The
other side of caring. *Journal of Marriage and the Family, 44*(4), 901–925.

IHINGER-TALLMAN, M. (1987). Sibling and stepsibling bonding in stepfamilies. In K.
Pasley and M. Ihinger-Tallman (Eds.), *Remarriage and stepparenting: Current
research and theory.* New York: Guilford.

IHINGER-TALLMAN, M., & PASLEY, K. (1987). Divorce and remarriage in the American
family: A historical review. In K. Pasley & M. Ihinger-Tallman (Eds.), *Remarriage
and stepparenting: Current research and theory.* New York: Guilford.

IMBER-BLACK, E. (1988). *Families and larger systems: A family therapist's guide
through the labyrinth.* New York: Guilford.

IMBER-BLACK, E. (1990). Multiple embedded systems. In M. P. Mirkin (Ed.), *The
social and political contexts of family therapy.* Boston: Allyn & Bacon.

ISAACS, M. B. (1982). Facilitating family restructuring and relinkage. In J. C. Hansen
& L. Messinger (Eds.), *Therapy with remarried families.* Rockville, MD: Aspen.

ISAACS, M. B., MONTALVO, B., & ABELSOHN, D. (1986). *The difficult divorce:
Therapy for children and families.* New York: Basic.

ISENSEE, R. (1991). *Growing up gay in a dysfunctional family: A guide for gay men
reclaiming their lives.* New York: Simon & Schuster.

JACKSON, J. (1973). Family organization and ideology. In D. Miller (Ed.), *Comparative
studies of blacks and whites in the United States.* New York: Seminar.

JACOBSON, D. S. (1987). Family type, visiting patterns, and children's behavior in the
stepfamily: A linked family system. In K. Pasley & M. Ihinger-Tallman (Eds.),
Remarriage and stepparenting: Current research and theory. New York: Guilford.

JEMAIL, J. A., & NATHANSON, M. (1987). Adolescent single-parent families. In M.
Lindblad-Goldberg (Ed.), *Clinical issues in single-parent households.* Rockville, MD:
Aspen.

JONES, J. M. (1991). Psychological models of race: What have they been and what
should they be? In J. D. Goodchilds (Ed.), *Psychological perspectives on human
diversity in America.* Washington, DC: American Psychological Association.

JUNG, C. G. (1926). *Psychological types or the psychology of individuation.* New York:
Harcourt, Brace.

KALICHMAN, S. C. (1998). *Understanding AIDS: Advances in research and treatment*
(2nd ed.). Washington, DC: American Psychological Association.

KARPEL, M. A., & STRAUSS, E. S. (1983). *Family evaluation.* New York: Gardner.

KASLOW, F. W. (1988). The psychological dimensions of divorce mediation. In J.
Folberg & A. Milne (Eds.), *Divorce mediation: Theory and practice.* New York:
Guilford.

KASLOW, F. W. (1994). Painful partings: Providing therapeutic guidance. In L. L.
Schwartz (Ed.), *Mid-life counseling.* Alexandria, VA: American Counseling
Association.

KASLOW, F. W. (1995). The dynamics of divorce therapy. In R. H. Mikesell, D.-D.
Lusterman, & S. H. McDaniel (Eds.), *Integrating family therapy: Handbook of fam-
ily psychology and systems theory.* Washington, DC: American Psychological
Association.

KASLOW, F. W. (1996). *Handbook of relational diagnosis and dysfunctional family patterns.* New York: Wiley.

KASLOW, F. W., & SCHWARTZ, L. L. (1987). *The dynamics of divorce: A life cycle perspective.* New York: Brunner/Mazel.

KAVANAGH, K. (1995). Don't ask, don't tell: Deception required, disclosure denied. *Psychology, Public Policy, and Law, 1,* 142–160.

KEIM, J. (1999). Strategic therapy. In D. M. Lawson & F. F. Prevatt (Eds.), *Casebook in family therapy.* Belmont, CA: Brooks/Cole–Wadsworth.

KELLEY, P. (1995). *Developing healthy stepfamilies: Twenty families tell their stories.* New York: Haworth.

KELLY, J. (1993). Current research on children's postdivorce adjustment: No simple answers. *Family and Conciliatory Courts Review, 31,* 29–49.

KEMENOFF, S., JACHIMCZYK, J., & FUSSNER, A. (1999). Structural family therapy. In D. M. Lawson & F. F. Prevatt (Eds.), *Casebook in family therapy.* Belmont, CA: Brooks/Cole–Wadsworth.

KESHET, J. K., & MIRKIN, M. P. (1985). Troubled adolescents in divorced and remarried families. In M. P. Mirkin & S. L. Koman (Eds.), *Handbook of adolescents and family therapy.* New York: Gardner.

KESSLER, S. (1975). *The American way of divorce: Prescriptions for change.* Chicago: Nelson-Hall.

KIRKPATRICK, M. (1987). Clinical implications of lesbian mothers studies. *Journal of Homosexuality, 13,* 201–211.

KIRSCHNER, B., & WALLUM, L. (1978, November). Two-location families: Married singles. *Alternative Lifestyles, 1,* 513–525.

KITANO, H. H. (1982). Mental health in the Japanese-American community. In E. E. Jones & S. J. Korchin (Eds.), *Minority mental health.* New York: Praeger.

KLEIN, D. P. (1975, November). Women in the work force: The middle years. *Monthly Labor Review,* pp. 10–16.

KOMAN, S. L., & STECHLER, G. (1985). Making the jump to systems. In M. P. Mirkin & S. L. Koman (Eds.), *Handbook of adolescents and family therapy.* New York: Gardner.

KRESTAN, J., & BEPKO, C. (1980). The problem of fusion in the lesbian relationship. *Family Process, 19*(3), 277–290.

KURAMOTO, E. H., MORALES, R. F., MUNOZ, F. U., & MURASE, K. (1983). Education for social work practice in Asian and Pacific American communities. In J. C. Chunn II, P. J. Dunston, & F. Ross-Sheriff (Eds.), *Mental health and people of color: Curriculum development and change.* Washington, DC: Howard University Press.

KURDEK, L. A. (1995). Lesbian and gay close relationships. In A. R. D'Augelli & C. J. Patterson (Eds.), *Lesbian and gay identities over a lifespan: Psychological perspectives on personal, relational, and community processes.* New York: Oxford University Press.

LAIRD, L., & GREEN, R.-J. (Eds.). (1996). *Lesbians and gays in couples and families: A handbook for therapists.* San Francisco: Jossey-Bass.

LANDAU-STANTON, J. (1993). *AIDS, health, and mental health: A primary sourcebook.* New York: Brunner/Mazel.

LANG, D. (1988). *The phantom spouse: Helping you and your family survive business travel and relocation.* New York: Dodd, Mead.

LAPPIN, J., & SCOTT, S. (1982). Intervention in a Vietnamese refugee family. In M. McGoldrick, J. K. Pearce, & J. Giordano (Eds.), *Ethnicity and family therapy.* New York: Guilford.

LARSON, J. (1992, January). Understanding stepfamilies. *American Demographics, 36–40.*

LaSALA, M. C. (2000). Lesbians, gay men, and their parents: Family therapy for the coming-out crisis. *Family Process, 39,* 67–81.

LASSWELL, M., & LASSWELL, T. (1991). *Marriage and the family* (3rd ed.). Belmont, CA: Wadsworth.

LAU, A. (1986). Family therapy across cultures. In J. L. Cox (Ed.), *Transcultural psychiatry.* London: Croom Helm.

LAVAL, R. A., GOMEZ, E. A., & RUIZ, P. (1989). A language minority: Hispanic Americans and mental health care. In D. R. Atkinson, G. Morten, & D. W. Sue (Eds.), *Counseling American minorities: A cross-cultural perspective.* Dubuque, IA: Brown.

LAWRENCE, E. C. (1999). The humanistic approach of Virginia Satir. In D. M. Lawson & F. F. Prevatt (Eds.), *Casebook in family therapy.* Belmont, CA: Brooks/Cole–Wadsworth.

LEE, E. (1982). A social systems approach to assessment and treatment for Chinese American families. In M. McGoldrick, J. K. Pearce, & J. Giordano (Eds.), *Ethnicity and family therapy.* New York: Guilford.

LEE, E. (Ed.). (1997). *Working with Asian Americans: A guide for clinicians.* New York: Guilford.

LENNON, M. C., & ROSENFIELD, S. (1994). Relative fairness and the division of housework: The importance of options. *American Journal of Sociology, 100,* 506–531.

LEONG, E. T. L. (1986). Counseling and psychotherapy with Asian-Americans: Review of the literature. *Journal of Counseling Psychology, 33,* 196–206.

LERMAN, R. I. (1993). A national survey of young unwed fathers. In R. I. Lerman & T. J. Ooms (Eds.), *Young unwed fathers.* Philadelphia: Temple University Press.

LEVANT, R. E. (1988). Facilitating fathering skills through psychoeducational programs. *Family Therapy Today, 3*(12), 1–5.

LEWIS, J. M., BEAVERS, W. R., GOSSETT, J. T., & PHILLIPS, V. A. (1976). *No single thread: Psychological health in family systems.* New York: Brunner/Mazel.

LINDBLAD-GOLDBERG, M. (1989). Successful minority single-parent families. In L. Combrinck-Graham (Ed.), *Children in family context: Perspectives on treatment.* New York: Guilford.

LUBORSKY, L., & DeRubeis, R. J. (1984). The use of psychotherapy treatment manuals: A small revolution in psychotherapy research style. *Clinical Psychology Review, 4,* 5–16.

LUNDBERG, U., & FRANKENHAEUSER, M. (1999). Stress and workload of men and women in high-ranking positions. *Journal of Occupational Health Psychology, 4,* 142–151.

MACKLIN, E. D. (1983). Nonmarital heterosexual cohabitation: An overview. In E. D. Macklin & R. H. Rubin (Eds.), *Contemporary families and alternative lifestyles.* Newbury Park, CA: Sage.

MADANES, C. (1991). Strategic family therapy. In A. S. Gurman & D. P. Kniskern (Eds.), *Handbook of family therapy* (Vol. II). New York: Brunner/Mazel.

MALYON, A. K. (1982). Psychotherapeutic implications of internalized homophobia in gay men. In J. C. Gonsiorek (Ed.), *Homosexuality and psychotherapy: A practitioner's handbook of affirmative models.* New York: Haworth.

MANKE, B., SEERY, B., CROUTER, A., & MCHALE, S. (1994). The three corners of the domestic labor: Mother's, father's and children's weekly and weekend housework. *Journal of Marriage and the Family, 56,* 657–669.

MANNS, W. (1988). Supportive roles of significant others in black families. In H. R. McAdoo (Ed.), *Black families* (2nd ed.). Newbury Park, CA: Sage.

MARIN, G., & MARIN, B. V. (1991). *Research with Hispanic populations.* Newbury Park, CA: Sage.

MARKS, R., & GOLDBLUM, P. B. (1989). The decision to test: A personal choice. In J. W. Dilley, C. Pies, & M. Helquist (Eds.), *Face to face: A guide to AIDS counseling.* Berkeley, CA: Celestial Arts.

MARMOR, J. (1980). Overview: The multiple roots of homosexual behavior. In J. Marmor (Ed.), *Homosexual behavior: A modern reappraisal.* New York: Basic.

MARTIN, A. (1993). *The lesbian and gay parenting handbook.* New York: HarperCollins.

MASON, M. A. (1994). *From father's property to children's rights: The history of child custody in the United States.* New York: Columbia University Press.

MASON, M. A., SKOLNICK, A., & SUGARMAN, S. D. (Eds.). (1998). *All our families: New policies for a new century.* New York: Oxford University Press.

MATHEWS, L. (1996, July 6). More than identity rides on a new racial category. *New York Times,* pp. 1, 7.

McADOO, H. P. (1977). Family therapy in the black community. *American Journal of Orthopsychiatry, 47,* 74–79.

McADOO, H. P. (1988). Transgenerational patterns of upward mobility in African-American families. In H. P. McAdoo (Ed.), *Black families* (2nd ed.). Newbury Park, CA: Sage.

McCREANER, A. (1989). Pre-test counselling. In J. Green & A. McCreaner (Eds.), *Counselling in HIV infection and AIDS.* Oxford, England: Blackwell Scientific Publications.

McCUBBIN, H. I., McCUBBIN, M. A., & THOMPSON, A. I. (1993). Resiliency in families: The role of family schema and appraisal in family adaptation to crises. In T. H. Brubaker (Ed.), *Family relations: Challenges for the future.* Newbury Park, CA: Sage.

McGOLDRICK, M. (1982). Ethnicity and family therapy: An overview. In M. McGoldrick, J. K. Pearce, & J. Giordano (Eds.), *Ethnicity and family therapy.* New York: Guilford.

McGOLDRICK, M. (1998). *Re-visioning family therapy: Race, culture, and gender in clinical practice.* New York: Guilford.

McGOLDRICK, M., & CARTER, E. A. (1988). Forming a remarried family. In E. A. Carter & M. McGoldrick (Eds.), *The changing family life cycle: A framework for family therapy* (2nd ed.). New York: Gardner.

McGOLDRICK, M., GARCIA PRETO, N., HINES, P. M., & LEE, E. (1991). Ethnicity and family therapy. In A. S. Gurman & D. P. Kniskern (Eds.), *Handbook of family therapy* (Vol. II). New York: Brunner/Mazel.

McGOLDRICK, M., & GERSON, R. (1985). *Genograms in family assessment.* New York: Norton.

McGOLDRICK, M., GIORDANO, J., & PEARCE, J. K. (1996). *Ethnicity and family therapy* (2nd ed.). New York: Guilford.

McLANAHAN, S. S., & SANDEFUR, G. (1994). *Growing up with a single parent: What hurts, what helps?* Cambridge, MA: Harvard University Press.

McNAUGHT, B. (1979). Gay and Catholic. In B. Berzon (Ed.), *Positively gay.* Los Angeles: Mediamix.

McRAE, S. (1997). Cohabitation: A trial run for marriage? *Sexual and Marital Therapy, 12,* 259–273.

McWHIRTER, D. R., & MATTISON, A. M. (1982). Psychotherapy for gay couples. In J. C. Gonsiorek (Ed.), *Homosexuality and psychotherapy.* New York: Haworth.

MEDNICK, M. T. (1987). Single mothers: A review and critique of current research. In S. Oskamp (Ed.), *Family processes and problems: Social psychological aspects.* Newbury Park, CA: Sage.

MEYER, D. R., & GARASKY, S. (1991). Custodial fathers: Myths, realities, and child support policies. *Journal of Marriage and the Family, 55,* 73–89.

MEZZICH, J. E., RUIZ, P., & MUNOZ, R. A. (1999). Mental health care for Hispanic Americans: A current perspective. *Cultural Diversity and Ethnic Minority Psychology, 5,* 91–102.

MICHAEL, R. T., GAGNON, J. H., LAUMANN, E. O., & KOLATA, G. (1984). *Sex in America: A definitive survey.* Boston: Little, Brown.

MICHAELS, M. L. (2000). The stepfamily enrichment program: A preliminary evaluation using focus groups. *American Journal of Family Therapy, 28,* 61–73.

MIKESELL, R. H., LUSTERMAN, D.-D., & McDANIEL, S. H. (Eds.). (1995). *Integrating family therapy: Handbook of family psychology and systems theory.* Washington, DC: American Psychological Association.

MILLER, I. W., KABACOFF, R. I., EPSTEIN, N. B., BISHOP, D. S., KEITER, G. I., BALDWIN, L. M., & VAN DER SPUY, H. I. J. (1994). The development of a clinical rating scale for the McMaster Model of family functioning. *Family Process, 33,* 53–69.

MILLER, N. (1992). *Single parents by choice.* New York: Plenum.

MILNE, A. (1988). The nature of divorce disputes. In J. Folberg & A. Milne (Eds.), *Divorce mediation: Theory and practice.* New York: Guilford.

MINUCHIN, S. (1974). *Families and family therapy.* Cambridge, MA: Harvard University Press.

MORAWETZ, A., & WALKER, G. (1984). *Brief therapy with single-parent families.* New York: Brunner/Mazel.

MORISHIMA, J. K. (1978). The Asian American experience: 1850–1975. *Journal of the Society of Ethnic and Special Studies, 2,* 8–10.

MORRISON, A. M., & VON GLINOW, M. A. (1990). Women and minorities in management. *American Psychologist, 45,* 200–208.

MORRISON, P. A. (1992). *Testimony before the House Subcommittee on Census and Population.* Santa Monica, CA: Rand.

MYERS, I. B. (1962). *Manual: The Myers-Briggs Type Indicator.* Palo Alto, CA: Consulting Psychologists Press.

MYERS, I. B., Introduction to Type: *A guide to understanding your results on the Meyers-Briggs Type Indicator* (6th ed.). Palo Alto, CA: Consulting Psychologists Press.

MYERS, I. B., & McCAULLEY, M. H. (1985). *A guide to the development and use of the Myers-Briggs Type Indicator.* Palo Alto, CA: Consulting Psychologists Press.

MYERS, I. B., & MYERS, P. B. (1980). *Gifts differing.* Palo Alto, CA: Consulting Psychologists Press.

NATHAN, P. E. (1998). Practice guidelines: Not yet ideal. *American Psychologist, 53,* 290–299.

NATIONAL ASSOCIATION OF SOCIAL WORKERS. (1996). *Code of ethics.* Washington, DC: Author.

NEIMEYER, G. J. (Ed.). (1993). *Constructivist assessment: A casebook.* Thousand Oaks, CA: Sage.

NEVILLE, W. G. (1990). Mediation. In M. R. Textor (Ed.), *The divorce and divorce therapy handbook.* Northvale, NJ: Aronson.

NEWCOMB, M. D. (1987). Cohabitation and marriage: A quest for independence and relatedness. In S. Oskamp (Ed.), *Family processes and problems: Social psychological aspects.* Newbury Park, CA: Sage.

NICHOLS, M. P. (1987). *The self in the system: Expanding the limits of family therapy.* New York: Brunner/Mazel.

NICHOLS, S. E. (1986). Psychotherapy and AIDS. In T. S. Stein & C. J. Cohen (Eds.), *Contemporary perspectives on psychotherapy with lesbians and gay men.* New York: Plenum.

NICHOLS, W. C. (1988). *Marital therapy: An integrative approach.* New York: Guilford.

NICHOLS, W. C., & EVERETT, C. A. (1986). *Systemic family therapy: An integrative approach.* New York: Guilford.

NICOLOSI, J. (1991). *Reparative therapy of male homosexuality.* Northvale, NJ: Aronson.

NORD, C. W., & ZILL, N. (1996). *Non-custodial parents' participation in their children's lives: Evidence from the survey of income and program participation.* Washington, DC: U.S. Department of Health and Human Services.

NORTON, A. J., & MILLER, L. (1992). *Marriage, divorce, and remarriage in the 1990s.* Washington, DC: U.S. Bureau of the Census, Current Population Reports, Series P23-180.

NOT ALL PARENTS ARE STRAIGHT (television documentary). (1987, July). Los Angeles: KCET Television.

O'DONOHUE, W., & BRADLEY, A. R. (1999). Conceptual and empirical issues in child custody evaluations. *Clinical Psychology, 6,* 310–322.

OLSON, D. H. (1986). Circumplex model VII: Validation studies and FACES III. *Family Process, 26,* 337–351.

OLSON, D. H. (1996). *PREPARE-ENRICH counselor's manual.* Minneapolis: Life Innovations.

OLSON, D. H., FOURNIER, D. G., & DRUCKMAN, J. M. (1986). *PREPARE/Enrich counselor's manual.* Minneapolis: PREPARE/Enrich.

OLSON, D. H., RUSSELL, C. S., & SPRENKLE, D. H. (1983). Circumplex model of marital and family systems: VI. Theoretical update. *Family Process, 22,* 69–83.

OLSON, D. H., RUSSELL, C. S., & SPRENKLE, D. H. (1989). *Circumplex model: Systemic assessment and treatment of families.* New York: Haworth.

PADILLA, A. M., RUIZ, R. A., & ALVAREZ, R. (1989). Community mental health services for the Spanish-speaking/surname populations. In D. R. Atkinson, G. Morten, & D. W. Sue (Eds.), *Counseling American minorities: A cross-cultural perspective.* Dubuque, IA: Brown.

PADILLA, A. M., & SALGADO DE SNYDER, V. N. (1985). Counseling Hispanics: Strategies for effective intervention. In P. Pedersen (Ed.), *Handbook of cross-cultural counseling and therapy.* Westport, CT: Greenwood.

PAPP, P. (1983). *The process of change.* New York: Guilford.

PARKS, C. A. (1999). Lesbian identity development: An examination of differences across generations. *American Journal of Orthopsychiatry, 69,* 347–361.

PARNELL, M., & VANDERKLOOT, J. (1989). Ghetto children: Children growing up in poverty. In L. Combrinck-Graham (Ed.), *Children in family contexts: Perspectives on treatment.* New York: Guilford.

PASLEY, K. (1985). Stepfathers. In S. M. H. Hanson & E. W. Bozett (Eds.), *Dimensions of fatherhood.* Newbury Park, CA: Sage.

PASLEY, K., & IHINGER-TALLMAN, M. (Eds.). (1994). *Stepparenting: Issues in theory, research, and practice.* Westport, CT: Greenwood.

PATTERSON, C. J. (1995). *Lesbian and gay parenting: A resource for psychologists.* Washington, DC: American Psychological Association.

PAUL, G. L. (1967). Strategy of outcome research in psychotherapy. *Journal of Consulting Psychology, 31,* 109–118.

PAUL, J. P., HAYS, R. B., & COATES, T. J. (1995). The impact of the HIV epidemic on U.S. gay male communities. In A. R. D'Augelli & C. J. Patterson (Eds.), *Lesbian and gay identities across the lifespan: Psychological perspectives on personal, relational, and community processes.* New York: Oxford University Press.

PEDERSEN, P. (1994). *A handbook for developing multicultural awareness* (2nd ed.). Alexandria, VA: American Counseling Association.

PELAVIN, E. (1995). *Bringing women's voices to the organization: Experiences of working mothers of adolescents.* Unpublished doctoral dissertation. California School of Professional Psychology, Alameda, California.

PEPLAU, L. A. (1991). Lesbian and gay relationships. In J. C. Gonsiorek & J. D. Weinrich (Eds.), *Homosexuality: Research implications for public policy.* Newbury Park, CA: Sage.

PEREZ, R. M., DEBORD, K. A., & BIESCHKLE, K. J. (Eds.). (2000). *Handbook of counseling and psychotherapy with lesbian, gay, and bisexual clients.* Washington, DC: American Psychological Association.

PEREZ, S. M., & DUANY, L. A. (1992). *Reducing Hispanic teenage pregnancy and family poverty: A replication guide.* Washington, DC: National Council of La Raza.

PERRY, S., FRANCES, A., & CLARKIN, J. (1990). *A DSM-III casebook of treatment selection.* New York: Brunner/Mazel.

PIES, C. (1985). *Considering parenthood: A workbook for lesbians.* San Francisco: Spinsters/Aunt Lute.

PIES, C. (1990). Lesbians and the choice to parent. *Marriage and Family Review, 14,* 137–154.

PINDERHUGHES, E. (1982). Afro-American families and the victim system. In M. McGoldrick, J. K. Pearce, & J. Giordano (Eds.), *Ethnicity and family therapy.* New York: Guilford.

PINDERHUGHES, E. (1990). Legacy of slavery: The experience of black families in America. In M. P. Mirkin (Ed.), *The social and political contexts of family therapy.* Boston: Allyn & Bacon.

PINSOF, W. M., & WYNNE, L. C. (1995). The effectiveness and efficacy of marital and family therapy: Introduction to the special issue. *Journal of Marital and Family Therapy, 21,* 341–343.

PION, G. M., MEDNICK, M. T., ASTIN, H. S., HALL, C. C., KENKEL, M. B., KEITA, G. P., KOHOUT, J. L., & KELLEHER, J. C. (1996). The shifting gender composition of psychology: Trends and implications for the discipline. *American Psychologist, 51,* 509–528.

PLECK, J. H. (1985). *Working wives, working husbands.* Newbury Park, CA: Sage.

POLLACK, S., & VAUGHN, J. (Eds.). (1987). *Politics of the heart: A lesbian parenting anthology.* Ithaca, NY: Firebrand.

POLOMA, M. M., PENDLETON, B. E., & GARLAND, T. N. (1981). Reconsidering the dual-career marriage: A longitudinal approach. *Journal of Family Issues, 2,* 205–224.

POPENOE, D., & WHITEHEAD, B. D. (1999a). *Should we live together? What young adults need to know about cohabitation before marriage: A comprehensive review of recent research.* New Brunswick, NJ: National Marriage Project, Rutgers University.

POPENOE, D., & WHITEHEAD, B. D. (1999b). *The state of our unions: The social health of marriage in America.* New Brunswick, NJ: National Marriage Project, Rutgers University.

POUSSAINT, A. (1990). The mental health status of black Americans. In D. S. Ruiz (Ed.), *Handbook of mental health and mental disorder among black Americans.* New York: Greenwood.

PRELI, R., & BERNARD, J. M. (1993). Making multiculturalism relevant for majority culture graduate students. *Journal of Marital and Family Therapy, 19,* 5–15.

PREVATT, F. F. (1999). Milan systemic therapy. In D. M. Lawson & F. F. Prevatt (Eds.), *Casebook in family therapy.* Belmont, CA: Brooks/Cole–Wadsworth.

PRICE-BONHAM, S., & MURPHY, D. C. (1980). Dual-career marriages: Implications for the clinician. *Journal of Marital and Family Therapy, 6,* 181–188.

PROCHASKA, J. O., & NORCROSS, J. C. (1998). *Systems of psychotherapy: A transtheoretical analysis.* Pacific Grove, CA: Brooks/Cole.

PURDUM, T. S. (2000, July 4). Shift in mix alters the face of California. *New York Times,* pp. 1, 12.

RAMIREZ, M., III. (1991). *Psychotherapy and counseling with minorities: A cognitive approach to individual and cultural differences.* Boston: Allyn & Bacon.

RAPOPORT, R., & RAPOPORT, R. (1969). The dual-career family. *Human Relations, 22,* 3–30.

RAPOPORT, R., & RAPOPORT, R. (1976). *Dual-career families reexamined: New integration of work and family.* New York: Harper.

REAL, T. (1990). The therapeutic use of self in constructionist systematic therapy. *Family Process, 29,* 255–272.

REISS, D. (1980). Pathways to assessing the family: Some choice points and a sample route. In C. K. Hofling & J. M. Lewis (Eds.), *The family: Evaluation and treatment.* New York: Brunner/Mazel.

RICE, D. G. (1989). Marital therapy and the divorcing family. In M. R. Textor (Ed.), *The divorce and divorce therapy book.* Northvale, NJ: Aronson.

RICE, J. K., & RICE, D. G. (1986). *Living through divorce: A developmental approach to divorce therapy.* New York: Guilford.

RICE, S., & KELLY, J. (1988). Choosing a gay/lesbian lifestyle: Related issues of treatment services. In C. S. Chilman, E. W. Nunnally, & F. M. Cox (Eds.), *Variant family forms.* Newbury Park, CA: Sage.

RIDLEY, C. A. (1995). *Overcoming unintentional racism in counseling and therapy: A practitioner's guide to intentional intervention.* Thousand Oaks, CA: Sage.

RIDLEY, C. A., PETERMAN, D. J., & AVERY, A. W. (1978). Cohabitation: Does it make for a better marriage? *Family Coordinator, 27,* 129–137.

ROBERTO, L. G. (1998). Transgenerational family therapy. In F. M. Dattilio (Ed.), *Case studies in couple and family therapy: Systemic and cognitive perspectives.* New York: Guilford.

ROCHLIN, M. (1979). Becoming a gay professional. In B. Berzon (Ed.), *Positively gay.* Los Angeles: Mediamix.

ROOT, M. P. (1989). Guidelines for facilitating therapy with Asian American clients. In D. R. Atkinson, G. Morten, & D. W. Sue (Eds.), *Counseling American minorities: A cross-cultural perspective.* Dubuque, IA: Brown.

ROSENTHAL, J. M., BOYD-FRANKLIN, N., STEINER, G., & TUNNELL, G. (1996). Families with HIV illness. In M. Harway (Ed.), *Treating the changing family: Handling normative and unusual events.* New York: Wiley.

ROSS, C., & MIROWSKY, J. (1994). Women, work, and family: Changing gender roles and psychological well-being. In G. Handel & G. Whitchurch (Eds.), *The psychological interior of the family* (4th ed.). New York: Aldine De Gruyter.

RUIZ, P (1982). The Hispanic patient: Sociocultural perspectives. In R. M. Becerra, M. Karno, & J. I. Escobar (Eds.), *Mental health and Hispanic Americans: Clinical perspectives.* New York: Grune & Stratton.

SACHS, N. (1986). The pregnant lesbian therapist. In T. S. Stein & C. J. Cohen (Eds.), *Contemporary perspectives on psychotherapy with lesbians and gay men*. New York: Plenum.

SAGER, C. J., BROWN, H. S., CROHN, H., ENGEL, T., RODSTEIN, E., & WALKER, L. (1983). *Treating the remarried family*. New York: Brunner/Mazel.

SAGER, C. J., WALKER, L., BROWN, H. S., CROHN, H. M., & RODSTEIN, E. (1981). Improving functioning of the remarried family system. *Journal of Marital and Family Therapy, 7*, 3–13.

SAGHIR, M. T., & ROBINS, E. (1980). Clinical aspects of female homosexuality. In J. Marmor (Ed.), *Homosexual behavior: A modern reappraisal*. New York: Basic.

SALTS, C. J. (1985). Divorce stage theory and therapy: Therapeutic implications through the divorcing process. In D. H. Sprenkle (Ed.), *Divorce therapy*. New York: Haworth.

SALUTER, A. F. (1989). *Changes in American family life* (U.S. Bureau of the Census, CPR Series P-23, No. 163). Washington, DC: U.S. Government Printing Office.

SATIR, V., BANMEN, J., GERBER, J., & GOMORI, M. (1991). *The Satir model: Family therapy and beyond*. Palo Alto, CA: Science and Behavior Books.

SAUBER, S. R. (1983). *The human services delivery system*. New York: Columbia University Press.

SAUBER, S. R., BEINER, S. F., & MEDDOFF, G. S. (1995). Divorce mediation: A system for dealing with the family in transition. In R. H. Mikesell, D.-D. Lusterman, & S. H. McDaniel (Eds.), *Integrating family therapy: Handbook of family psychology and systems theory*. Washington, DC: American Psychological Association.

SAVIN-WILLIAMS, R. C. (1994). Verbal and physical abuse as stressors in the lives of lesbians, gay males, and bisexual youths: Associations with school problems, running away, substance abuse, prostitution, and suicide. *Journal of Consulting and Clinical Psychology, 62*, 261–269.

SAXTON, L. (1996). *The individual, marriage, and the family* (9th ed.). Belmont, CA: Wadsworth.

SCHWARTZ, F. (1989, January/February). Management, women, and the new facts of life. *Harvard Business Review, 67*, 65–76.

SCHWARTZ, F. (1992). *Breaking with tradition*. New York: Warner.

SCHWARTZ, R. C. (1999). Narrative therapy expands and contracts family therapy's horizons. *Journal of Marital and Family Therapy, 25*, 263–267.

SCRIVNER, R., & ELDRIDGE, N. S. (1995). Lesbian and gay family psychology. In R. H. Mikesell, D.-D. Lusterman, & S. H. McDaniel (Eds.), *Integrative family therapy: Handbook of family psychology and systems theory*. Washington, DC: American Psychological Association.

SEABURN, D., LANDAU-STANTON, J., & HORWITZ, S. (1995). Core techniques in family therapy. In R. H. Mikesell, D.-D. Lusterman, & S. H. McDaniel (Eds.), *Integrating family therapy: Handbook of family psychology and systems theory*. Washington, DC: American Psychological Association.

SEGAL, L. (1987). What is a problem? A brief therapist's view. *Family Therapy Today, 2*(7), 1–7.

SEGAL, L., & BAVELAS, J. B. (1983). Human systems and communication theory. In B. B. Wolman & G. Stricker (Eds.), *Handbook of family and marital therapy*. New York: Plenum.

SEKARAN, U. (1986). *Dual-career families: Contemporary organizational and counseling issues*. San Francisco: Jossey-Bass.

SELVINI-PALAZZOLI, M., BOSCOLO, L., CECCHIN, G., & PRATA, G. (1978). *Paradox and counterparadox: A new model in the therapy of the family in schizophrenic transaction*. New York: Aronson.

SELVINI-PALAZZOLI, M., CIRILLO, S., SELVINI, M., & SORRENTINO, A. M. (1989). *Family games: General models of psychotic processes in the family*. New York: Norton.

SEWARD, R. (1978). *The American family: A demographic history*. Newbury Park, CA: Sage.

SHAEVITZ, M. H., & SHAEVITZ, H. J. (1980). *Making it together as a two career couple*. Boston: Houghton Mifflin.

SHELLENBERGER, S., & HOFFMAN, S. S. (1995). The changing family-work system. In R. H. Mikesell, D.-D. Lusterman, & S. H. McDaniel (Eds.), *Integrating family therapy: Handbook of family psychology and systems theory*. Washington, DC: American Psychological Association.

SHERMAN, R., & FREDMAN, N. (1986). *Handbook of structured techniques in marriage and family therapy*. New York: Brunner/Mazel.

SHIPLER, D. K. (1997). *A country of strangers: Blacks and whites in America*. New York: Knopf.

SHON, S. P., & JA, D. Y. (1982). Asian families. In M. McGoldrick, J. K. Pearce, & J. Giordano (Eds.), *Ethnicity and family therapy*. New York: Guilford.

SHUSTER, R. (1987). Sexuality as a continuum: The bisexual identity. In Boston Lesbian Psychologies Collective (Eds.), *Lesbian psychologies: Explorations and challenges*. Urbana: University of Illinois Press.

SIEGEL, S., & WALKER, G. (1996). Connections: Conversations between a gay therapist and a straight therapist. In L. Laird & R.-J. Green (Eds.), *Lesbians and gays in couples and families: A handbook for therapists*. San Francisco: Jossey-Bass.

SILBERSTEIN, L. R. (1992). *Dual-career marriage: A system in transition*. Hillsdale, NJ: Erlbaum.

SILVERMAN, W. H. (1996). Cookbooks, manuals, and paint-by-numbers: Psychotherapy in the 90's. *Psychotherapy, 33*, 207–215.

SILVERSTEIN, C. (1981). *Man to man: Gay couples in America*. New York: Morrow.

SILVERSTEIN, C. (Ed.). (1991). *Gays, lesbians, and their therapies: Studies in psychotherapy*. New York: Norton.

SILVERSTEIN, L. B., & QUARTIRONI, B. (1996, Winter). Gay fathers. *Family Psychologist, 12*, 23–24.

SIMONS, R. L. (1996). The effect of divorce on adult and child adjustment. In R. L. Simons & associates (Eds.), *Understanding differences between divorced and intact families: Stress, interaction, and child outcome*. Thousand Oaks, CA: Sage.

SKOLNICK, A. (1991). *Embattled paradise: The American family in an age of uncertainty*. New York: Basic.

SLUZKI, C. (1979). Migration and family conflict. *Family Process, 18*(4), 379–390.

SNYDER, D. K., CAVELL, T. A., HEFFER, R. W., & MANGRUM, L. F. (1995). Marital and family assessment: A multifaceted, multilevel approach. In R. H. Mikesell, D.-D. Lusterman, & S. H. McDaniel (Eds.), *Integrating family therapy: Handbook of family psychology and systems theory.* Washington, DC: American Psychological Association.

SNYDER, T. D., & HOFFMAN, C. M. (1994). *Digest of education statistics: 1994.* NCES 94-115. Washington, DC: U.S. Department of Education, Office of Educational Research and Improvement.

SOBOL, M. P., & DALY, K. J. (1992). The adoption alternative for pregnant adolescents: Decision making, consequences, and policy implications. *Journal of Social Issues, 48*(3), 143–161.

SOLOMON, B. B. (1982). The delivery of mental health services to Afro-Americans and their families: Translating theory into practice. In B. A. Bass, G. E. Wyatt, & G. J. Powell (Eds.), *The Afro-American family: Assessment, treatment, and research issues.* New York: Grune & Stratton.

SPARKS, C., & HAMILTON, J. A. (1991). Psychological issues related to alternative insemination. *Professional Psychology, 22,* 308–314.

SPERRY, L. (1992). Tailoring treatment with couples and families: Resistances, prospects, and perspectives. *Topics in Family Psychology and Counseling, 1*(3), 1–6.

SPRAGUE, L. (1999, November/December). A caution for psychologists: The larger view of gay and lesbian people. *Los Angeles Psychologist,* p. 8.

SPRENKLE, D. H. (Ed.). (1985). *Divorce therapy.* New York: Haworth.

SPRENKLE, D. H. (1990). The clinical practice of divorce therapy. In M. R. Textor (Ed.), *The divorce and divorce therapy book.* Northvale, NJ: Aronson.

SPRENKLE, D. H., & GONZALEZ-DOUPE, P. (1996). Divorce therapy. In F. P. Piercy, D. H. Sprenkle, J. L. Wetchler, & associates (Eds.), *Family therapy sourcebook* (2nd ed.). New York: Guilford.

STAHMANN, R. F., & HIEBERT, W. J. (1987). *Premarital counseling: The professional's handbook.* Lexington, MA: Lexington.

STAHMANN, R. F., & HIEBERT, W. J. (1997). *Premarital and remarital counseling: The professional's handbook.* San Francisco: Jossey-Bass.

STAPLES, R. (1985). Changes in black family structures: The conflict between family ideology and structural conditions. *Journal of Marriage and the Family, 47,* 1005–1013.

STIER, S. (1986). Divorce mediation. *Family Therapy Today, 1*(3), 1–7.

STOLTZ-LOIKE, M. (1992). *Dual-career couples: New perspectives in counseling.* Alexandria, VA: American Association for Counseling and Development.

STORMS, M. (1986). *The development of sexual orientation.* Washington, DC: American Psychological Association.

STROM, K. (1992). Reimbursement demands and treatment decisions: A growing dilemma for social workers. *Social Work, 37,* 398–403.

SUE, D. (1994). Incorporating cultural diversity in family therapy. *Family Psychologist, 10,* 19–21.

SUE, D. W. (1989). Ethnic identity: The impact of two cultures on the psychological development of Asians in America. In D. R. Atkinson, G. Morten, & D. W. Sue (Eds.), *Counseling American minorities: A cross-cultural perspective*. Dubuque, IA: Brown.

SUE, D. W., IVEY, A. E., & PEDERSEN, P. B. (1996). *A theory of multicultural counseling and therapy*. Pacific Grove, CA: Brooks/Cole.

SUE, D. W., & SUE, D. (1999). *Counseling the culturally different: Theory and practice* (3rd ed.). New York: Wiley.

SUE, S. (1999). Science, ethnicity, and bias: Where have we gone wrong? *American Psychologist, 54,* 1070–1077.

SUE, S., & MORISHIMA, J. K. (1982). *The mental health of Asian-Americans*. San Francisco: Jossey-Bass.

SZAPOCZNIK, J., & KURTINES, W. M. (1993). Family psychology and cultural diversity: Opportunities for theory, research, and application. *American Psychologist, 48,* 400–407.

SZAPOCZNIK, J., SCOPETTA, M. A., CEBALLOS, A., & SANTISEBAN, D. (1994). Understanding, supporting, and empowering families: From microanalysis to macrointervention. *Family Psychologist, 10*(2), 23–26.

TAKAKI, R. (1990). *Strangers from a different shore: A history of Asian Americans*. Boston: Little, Brown.

TASKER, F., & GOLOMBOK, S. (1997). *Growing up in a lesbian family: Effects on child development*. New York: Guilford.

TAYLOR, A. (1988). A general theory of divorce mediation. In J. Folberg & A. Milne (Eds.), *Divorce mediation: Theory and practice*. New York: Guilford.

TEXTOR, M. R. (Ed.). (1989). *The divorce and divorce therapy book*. Northvale, NJ: Aronson.

THERNSTROM, S., & THERNSTROM, A. (1997). *America in black and white: One nation, indivisible*. New York: Simon & Schuster.

THOMAS, A., & SILLEN, S. (1974). *Racism and psychiatry*. Secaucas, NJ: Citadel.

THOMPSON, E. H., JR., & GONGLA, P. A. (1983). Single parent families: In the mainstream of American society. In E. D. Macklin & R. H. Rubin (Eds.), *Contemporary families and alternative lifestyles*. Newbury Park, CA: Sage.

TODER, N. (1979). Lesbian couples: Special issues. In B. Berzon (Ed.), *Positively gay*. Los Angeles: Mediamix.

TOULIATOS, J., PERLMUTTER, B. F., & STRAUS, M. A. (Eds.). (1990). *Handbook of family measurement techniques*. Newbury Park, CA: Sage.

TURNER, N. W. (1985). Divorce: Dynamics of decision therapy. In D. H. Sprenkle (Ed.), *Divorce therapy*. New York: Haworth.

TURNER, P. H., SCADDEN, L., & HARRIS, M. B. (1990). Parenting in gay and lesbian families. *Journal of Gay and Lesbian Psychotherapy, 1*(3), 55–66.

ULRICH, D. N. (1998). Contextual family therapy. In F. M. Dattilio (Ed.), *Case studies in couple and family therapy: Systemic and cognitive perspectives*. New York: Guilford.

UMBARGER, C. C. (1983). *Structural family therapy*. New York: Grune & Stratton.

UPCHURCH, D. M., & McCARTHY, J. (1990). The timing of first birth and high school completion. *American Sociological Review, 55,* 224–234.

U.S. BUREAU OF THE CENSUS. (1993). Resident population, by race and Hispanic origin: 1980 and 1990. *Statistical Abstracts of the United States* (113th ed.). Washington, DC: U.S. Government Printing Office.

U.S. BUREAU OF THE CENSUS. (1994). Marital status and living arrangements: March 1993. *Current Population Reports,* Series P20-188. Washington, DC: U.S. Government Printing Office.

U.S. BUREAU OF THE CENSUS. (1995). Child support for custodial mothers and fathers: 1991. *Current Population Reports,* Series P60-187. Washington, DC: U.S. Government Printing Office.

U.S. BUREAU OF THE CENSUS. (1998). Marital status and living arrangements. *Current Population Reports,* Series P20-514. Washington, DC: U.S. Government Printing Office.

U.S. BUREAU OF LABOR STATISTICS. (1999a). *Current population survey: Employment characteristics of families in 1998.* Washington, DC: U.S. Government Printing Office.

U.S. BUREAU OF LABOR STATISTICS. (1999b). *Current population survey: Report on the American workforce 1999.* Washington, DC: U.S. Government Printing Office.

VANNOY-HILLER, D., & PHILLIBER, W. W. (1989). *Equal partners: Successful women in marriage.* Newbury Park, CA: Sage.

VISHER, E. B., & VISHER, J. S. (1979). *Stepfamilies: A guide to working with stepparents and stepchildren.* New York: Brunner/Mazel.

VISHER, E. B., & VISHER, J. S. (1986). *Stepfamily workbook manual.* Baltimore: Stepfamily Association of America.

VISHER, E. B., & VISHER, J. S. (1988a). *Old loyalties, new ties: Therapeutic strategies with stepfamilies.* New York: Brunner/Mazel.

VISHER, E. B., & VISHER, J. S. (1988b). Treating families with problems associated with remarriage and step relationships. In C. S. Chilman, E. W. Nunnally, & E. M. Cox (Eds.), *Variant family forms.* Newbury Park, CA: Sage.

VISHER, E. B., & VISHER, J. S. (1996). *Therapy with stepfamilies.* New York: Brunner/Mazel.

WALKER, G. (1987, April and June). AIDS and family therapy. *Family Therapy Today, 2*(4), 1–7; *2*(6), 1–7.

WALKER, L. S., & WALLSTON, B. S. (1985). Social adaptation: A review of dual-earner family literature. In L. L'Abate (Ed.), *The handbook of family psychology and therapy.* Pacific Grove, CA: Brooks/Cole.

WALLERSTEIN, J. S., & BLAKESLEE, S. (1989). *Second chances: Men, women, and children a decade after divorce.* New York: Ticknor & Fields.

WALLERSTEIN, J. S., CORBIN, S. B., & LEWIS, J. M. (1988). Children of divorce: Report of a ten-year follow-up of early latency-age children. In E. M. Hetherington & J. D. Arasteh (Eds.), *Impact of divorce, single parenting, and stepparenting on children.* Hillsdale, NJ: Erlbaum.

WALLERSTEIN, J. S., & KELLY, J. B. (1974). The effects of parental divorce: The adolescent experience. In E. J. Anthony & C. Koupernik (Eds.), *The child in his family: Children at psychiatric risk.* New York: Wiley.

WALLERSTEIN, J. S., & KELLY, J. B. (1975). The effects of parental divorce: Experiences of the preschool child. *Journal of the American Academy of Child Psychiatry, 14,* 600–616.

WALLERSTEIN, J. S., & KELLY, J. B. (1976). The effects of parental divorce: Experiences of the child in later latency. *American Journal of Orthopsychiatry, 46,* 256–269.

WALLERSTEIN, J. S., & KELLY, J. B. (1980a). Effects of divorce on the visiting father-child relationship. *American Journal of Psychiatry, 137,* 1534–1539.

WALLERSTEIN, J. S., & KELLY, J. B. (1980b). *Surviving the breakup: How parents and children cope with divorce.* New York: Basic.

WALSH, F. (1983). The timing of symptoms and critical events in the family life cycle. In J. C. Hanson (Ed.), *Clinical implications of the family life cycle.* Rockville, MD: Aspen.

WALSH, F. (1995). From family damage to family challenge. In R. H. Mikesell, D.-D. Lusterman, & S. H. McDaniel (Eds.), *Integrating family therapy: Handbook of family psychology and systems theory.* Washington, DC: American Psychological Association.

WALSH, F. (1996). The concept of family resilience: Crisis and challenge. *Family Process, 35,* 261–281.

WALSH, F. (1998). *Strengthening family resilience.* New York: Guilford.

WARREN, C. (1980). Homosexuality and stigma. In J. Marmor (Ed.), *Homosexual behavior: A modern reappraisal.* New York: Basic.

WATT-JONES, D. (1997). Toward an African American genogram. *Family Process, 36,* 375–383.

WATZLAWICK, P., WEAKLAND, J. H., & FISCH, R. (1974). *Change: Principles of problem formation and problem resolution.* New York: Norton.

WEATHERLEY, R. A., & CARTOOF, V. G. (1988). Helping single adolescent parents. In C. S. Chilman, E. W. Nunnally, & E. M. Cox (Eds.), *Variant family forms.* Newbury Park, CA: Sage.

WEBER, T., & LEVINE, F. (1995). Engaging the family: An integrative approach. In R. H. Mikesell, D.-D. Lusterman, & S. H. McDaniel (Eds.), *Integrative family therapy: Handbook of family psychology and systems theory.* Washington, DC: American Psychological Association.

WEBER, T., McKEEVER, J. E., & McDANIEL, S. H. (1985). A beginner's guide to the problem-oriented first family interview. *Family Process, 24,* 356–364.

WEINGARTEN, K. (1998). The small and the ordinary: The daily practice of a postmodern narrative therapy. *Family Process, 37,* 3–15.

WEISS, R. S. (1975). *Marital separation.* New York: Basic.

WEISS, R. S. (1979). *Going it alone: The family life and social situation of the single parent.* New York: Basic.

WEITZMAN, L. (1985). *The divorce revolution: The unexpected social and economic consequences for women and children in America.* New York: Free Press.

WELTNER, J. S. (1982). A structuralist approach to the single-parent family. *Family Process, 21,* 203–210.

WELTNER, J. S. (1992). Matchmaking: Therapist, client, and therapy. *Topics in Family Psychology and Counseling, 1*(3), 37–52.

WHITAKER, C. A. (1977). Process techniques of family therapy. *Interaction, 1,* 4–19.

WHITAKER, C. A., & BUMBERRY, W. M. (1988). *Dancing with the family: A symbolic-experiential approach.* New York: Brunner/Mazel.

WHITE, M. (1989). *Selected papers.* Adelaide, Australia: Dulwich Centre Publications.

WHITE, M. (1995). *Re-authoring lives: Interviews and essays.* Adelaide, Australia: Dulwich Centre Publications.

WHITE, M., & EPSTON, D. (1990). *Narrative means to therapeutic ends.* New York: Norton.

WHITE, S. L. (1978). Family therapy according to the Cambridge Model. *Journal of Marriage and Family Counseling, 4,* 91–100.

WHITESIDE, M. F. (1982). Remarriage: A family developmental process. *Journal of Marital and Family Therapy, 8*(2), 59–68.

WHITESIDE, M. F. (1989). Remarried systems. In L. Combrinck-Graham (Ed.), *Children in family contexts: Perspectives on treatment.* New York: Guilford.

WHITESIDE, M. F., & BECKER, B. J. (2000). Parental factors and the young child's postdivorce adjustment: A meta-analysis with implications for parenting arrangements. *Journal of Family Psychology, 14,* 5–26.

WIENER, N. (1948). *Cybernetics or control and communication in the animal and the machine.* Cambridge, MA: MIT Press.

WILLIAMS, A. L. (1996). Skin color in psychotherapy. In R. Perez Foster, M. Moskowitz, & R. Javier (Eds.), *Reaching across boundaries of culture and class: Widening the scope of psychotherapy.* New York: Aronson.

WILSON, B. F., & CLARKE, S. C. (1992). Remarriages: A demographic profile. *Journal of Family Issues, 13,* 123–141.

WILSON, M. E. (1971). The significance of communication in counseling the culturally disadvantaged. In R. Wilcox (Ed.), *The psychological consequences of being a black American.* New York: Wiley.

WINFIELD, E. E. (1985). *Commuter marriage: Living apart together.* New York: Columbia University Press.

WONG, N., LU, E. G., SHON, S. P., & GAW, A. C. (1983). Asian and Pacific American issues in psychiatric residency training programs. In J. C. Chunn, II, P. J. Dunston, & E. Ross-Sheriff (Eds.), *Mental health and people of color: Curriculum development and change.* Washington, DC: Howard University Press.

WOODY, J. D. (1983). Sexuality in divorce and remarriage. In J. C. Hansen, J. D. Woody, & R. H. Woody (Eds.), *Sexual issues in family therapy.* Rockville, MD: Aspen.

WORDEN, M. (1994). *Family therapy basics.* Pacific Grove, CA: Brooks/Cole.

WORTHINGTON, E. (1992). Strategic matching and tailoring of treatment to couples and families. *Topics in Family Psychology and Counseling, 1*(3), 21–32.

WYATT, E. (1999, November 4). Women gain in the doctoral chase. *New York Times,* p. 7.

Name Index

Subject Index

Credits

This page constitutes an extension of the copyright page. We have made every effort to trace the ownership of all copyrighted material and to secure permission from copyright holders. In the event of any question arising as to the use of any material, we will be pleased to make the necessary corrections in future printings. Thanks are due to the following authors, publishers, and agents for permission to use the material indicated.

Chapter 1: 9: Table 1.1 from G.M. Pion, M.T. Mednick, H.S. Astin, C.C. Hall, M.B. Kenkel, G.P. Keita, J.L. Kohout, and J.C. Kelleher, *American Psychologist,* 51, 1996, p. 513. Copyright © 1996 American Psychological Association. Reprinted by permission.

Chapter 2. 41: Figure 2.1 from J.D. Friesen, *Structural-strategic Marriage and Family Therapy,* 1985, p. 46. Copyright © 1985 Garner Press. Reprinted by permission.

Chapter 3: 62: Figure 3.3 reprinted by permission of the publishers from *Families and Family Therapy* by Salvador Minuchin, p. 53. Cambridge, Mass.: Harvard University Press, Copyright © 1974 by the President and Fellows of Harvard College. **63:** Figure 3.4 from R. Sherman and N. Fredman, *Handbook of Structured Techniques in Marriage and Family Therapy,* 1986, p. 100. Copyright © 1986 Brunner/Mazel, a member of the Taylor & Francis Publishers group. Reprinted by permission. **69:** Figure 3.5 from "Circumplex Model of Family Systems: Integrating Ethnic Diversity and Other Social Systems" by D.M. Gorall and D.H. Olson. In R.H. Mikesell, D.D. Lusterman, and S.H. McDaniel (Eds.), *Integrating Family Therapy: Handbook of Family Psychology and Sytems Theory,* p. 219. Copyright © 1995 American Psychological Association. Reprinted by permission. **74:** Table 3.1 modified and reproduced by special permission of the Publisher, Consulting Psychologists Press, Inc., Palo Alto, CA 94303 from *Introduction to Type®,* 6th Ed. by Isabel Briggs Myers, p. 10. Copyright © 1998 by Consulting Psychologists Press Inc. All rights reserved. Further reproduction is prohibited without the Publisher's written consent. **77:** Figure 3.6 from "Family models: Comparing and contrasting the Olson circumplex with the Beavers model" by W.R. Beavers and M.N. Voeller, *Family Process,* p. 90, 1983.

Chapter 5. 105: Table 5.1 from J.S. Weltner, "Matchmaking: Therapist, Client, and Therapy," *Topics in Family Psychology and Counseling* I(3), 1992, p.39. Copyright © 1992 Aspen Publishers, Inc. Reprinted by permission. **106:** Table 5.2 fom J.S. Weltner, "Matchmaking: Therapist, Client, and Therapy," *Topics in Family Psychology and Counseling* I(3), 1992, p. 40. Copyright © 1992 Aspen Publishers, Inc. Reprinted by permission.

Chapter 6: 122: Figure 6.1 from L. Saxton, *The Individual, Marriage and the Family,* Ninth Edition, p. 285. Copyright © 1996 Wadsworth Publishing Company. Reprinted by permission. **125:** Table 6.1 from "Treating Divorce in Family Therapy Practice," by C.A. Everett and S.S. Volgy, p. 513. In A.S. Gurmand and D.P. Kniskern (Eds.), *Handbook of Family Therapy,* Vol. III. Copyright © 1991 Brunner/Mazel, a member of the Taylor & Francis Publishers Group. Reprinted by permission of Taylor & Francis, Inc., http://www.routledge-ny.com. **126:** Figure 6.2 from T.P. Gullotta, G.R. Adams, and S.J. Alexander, *Today's Marriages and Families: A Wellness Approach,* 1986, p. 240. Copyright © 1986 by Brooks/Cole.

Chapter 7: 169: Table 7.1 from C.J. Sager, H.S. Brown, H. Crohn, E. Rodstein, and L. Walker, *Treating the Remarried Family,* 1983, p. 65. Copyright © 1983 Brunner/Mazel, a member of the Taylor & Francis Publishers Group. Reprinted by permission of Taylor & Francis, Inc., http://www.routledge-ny.com. **174:** Figure 7.1 from E.B. Visher and J.S. Visher, *Old Loyalties, New Ties: Therapeutic Strategies with Stepfamilies,* 1988, p.13. Copyright © 1988 by Brunner/Mazel, a member of the Taylor & Francis PublishersGroup. Reprinted by permission of Taylor & Francis, Inc., http://www.routledge-ny.com. **184:** Table 7.2 from Betty Carter and Monica McGoldrick, "Overview: The Changing Family Life Cycle: A Framework for Family Therapy." In E.A. Carter and M.McGoldrick (Eds.), *The Changing Family Life Cycle: A Framework for Family Therapy,* 2nd ed., 1989, Table 1-2, p. 22. Copyright © 1989 by Allyn and Bacon. Reprinted by permission. **185:** Table 7.3 from Betty Carter and Monica McGoldrick, "Overview: The Changing Family Life Cycle: A Framework for Family Therapy." In E.A. Carter and M.McGoldrick (Eds.), *The Changing Family Life Cycle: A Framework for Family Therapy,* 2nd ed., 1989, Table 1-3, p. 24. Copyright © 1989 by Allyn and Bacon. Reprinted by permission. **190:** Table 7.4 from C.J. Sager, H.S. Brown, H. Crohn, E. Rodstein, and L. Walker, *Treating the Remarried Family,* 1983, pp. 51–53. Copyright © 1983 Brunner/Mazel, a member of the Taylor & Francis Publishers Group. Reprinted by permission of Taylor & Francis, Inc., http://www.routledge-ny.com. **193:** Table 7.5 from E.B. Visher and J.S. Visher, *Old Loyalties, New Ties: Therapeutic Strategies with Stepfamilies,* 1988, p. 237. Copyright © 1988 Brunner/Mazel, a member of the Taylor & Francis Publishers Group. Reprinted by permission of Taylor & Francis, Inc., http://www.routledge-ny.com. **203:** Box 7.2 from E.B. Visher and J.S. Visher, *Stepfamily Workbook Manual,* 1986, pp. 235–236. Copyright © 1986 by Stepfamily Association of America. Reprinted by permission.

Chapter 8: 233: Figure 8.1 from "Circumplex Model of Family Systems: Integrating Ethnic Diversity and Other Social Systems" by D.M. Gorall and D.H. Olson. In R.H. Mikesell, D.D. Lusterman, and S.H. McDaniel (Eds.), *Integrating Family Therapy: Handbook of Family Psychology and Sytems Theory,* p. 219. Copyright © 1995 American Psychological Association. Reprinted by permission.

Chapter 9: 243: Excerpt from B. Berzon, *Positively Gay,* p. 88. Copyright © 1979 by Mediamix Press. Reprinted by permission. **250:** Box 9.1 from N. Gartrell, "Gay Patients in the Medical Setting" in C.C. Nadelson and D.B. Marcotte (Eds.), *Interventions in Human Sexuality,* p. 396. Copyright © 1983 Plenum Publishing Group. Reprinted by permission.